MASTERING MULTIPLE CHOICE *FOR*
FEDERAL CIVIL PROCEDURE

MBE BAR PREP *AND* 1L EXAM PREP

Third Edition

WILLIAM M. JANSSEN
Professor of Law,
Charleston School of Law

STEVEN F. BAICKER-McKEE
Associate Dean of Teaching Excellence and Strategic Initiatives
Associate Professor of Law,
Duquesne University School of Law

WEST
ACADEMIC
PUBLISHING

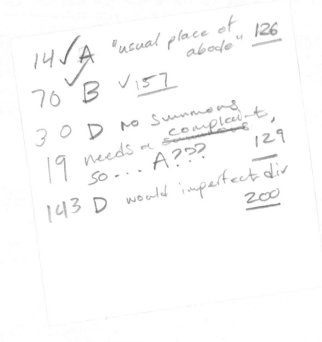

© 2015, 2016 LEG, Inc. d/b/a West Academic
© 2018 LEG, Inc. d/b/a West Academic
    444 Cedar Street, Suite 700
    St. Paul, MN 55101
    1-877-888-1330

West, West Academic Publishing, and West Academic are trademarks of West Publishing Corporation, used under license.

Printed in the United States of America

ISBN: 978-1-64242-420-1

Preface to the Third Edition

Civil Procedure was first added as a testing topic to the multistate bar examination's multiple choice test ("MBE") in February 2015. It has been included in each administration of the MBE since then.

Civil Procedure remains a topic area that both 1L students and bar exam studiers find often dense and unsettling. This book is intended to help both— those trying to learn the nuances of Civil Procedure for the first time and those trying to remember those nuances as their bar examination approaches.

The 200 questions, answers, and explanations contained here have been created by two law professors who teach Civil Procedure in their classrooms, but who also practiced civil litigation for many years in federal and State courts. The questions encompass every one of the topics and subtopics that the National Conference of Bar Examiners identified in its Subject Matter Outline as within the scope of coverage for the MBE portion of national bar examinations. This Third Edition has expanded the total question volume by 28% with all new multiple choice questions, answers, and explanations. It also incorporates the December 1, 2018 amendments to the Federal Rules of Civil Procedure.

Two Important Notes to Users of this Book:

1. **INTRODUCTION:** Don't skip over the *Introduction* (Part 1). It contains helpful advice and strategies on attacking multiple choice questions.

2. **TABLES for DECODING TOPICS:** In the back of this book, Part 4 and Part 5 decode each question by topic and subtopic, to help you target your practice.

Please let the Authors know if you have suggestions or critiques for improving this book. We enthusiastically welcome your comments.

William M. Janssen
wjanssen@charlestonlaw.edu

Steven F. Baicker-McKee
baickermckees@duq.edu

August 2018

Acknowledgments

This is a book by two colleagues, who began a friendship as law clerks that has continued and enriched our lives for nearly thirty years.

Professor Janssen thanks his co-author for their tremendous adventure through federal civil procedure, as well as Jeffrey M. Domanico, Caitlin M. Plocica, and Christopher T. Lewis for their editing assistance in polishing this edition's manuscript. He dedicates his work on the book to the love of his life, Mary Kay Schwemmer.

Professor Baicker-McKee also thanks his co-author, without whose friendship and encouragement he might not have made the rewarding shift to legal education. He thanks Parke Junker, Ashley Puchalski, and Nicoline van de Haterd for their assistance and dedication in preparing this edition's manuscript. He dedicates this book to his wife Carol and his children, Kyle, Eric, and Sara, and pays homage to the squash gods—may they smile down on him.

About the Authors

William M. Janssen is a professor of law at the Charleston School of Law in Charleston, South Carolina, where he teaches civil procedure, products liability, mass torts, and constitutional law. He has been honored six times by the Charleston students as their "Professor of the Year." He is also the author of *Federal Civil Procedure Logic Maps*, a graphical mapping resource for learning civil practice, and various journal articles and book chapters on federal civil procedure. Along with Professor Baicker-McKee, he also annually authors *A Student's Guide to the Federal Rules of Civil Procedure*, a civil procedure study resource for law students. Additionally, he, Professor Baicker-McKee, and a third author write the *Federal Civil Rules Handbook*, a comprehensive coverage of the federal civil rules for practitioners, and Volume 12B of the national treatise *Wright & Miller's Federal Practice and Procedure*. He also is an annual contributing author of *Attorney-Client Privilege in the United States*. Prior to joining the Charleston faculty, Professor Janssen was a longtime civil litigator in Philadelphia.

Steven Baicker-McKee is the Associate Dean of Teaching Excellence and Strategic Initiatives and an associate professor of law at Duquesne University School of Law in Pittsburgh, Pennsylvania, where he teaches civil procedure, advanced pretrial litigation techniques, and energy law and has been honored by the Duquesne students as their "Professor of the Year." He is a co-author of *Learning Civil Procedure*, a casebook for civil procedure students, the *Federal Litigator*, a monthly publication capturing federal procedural developments, and numerous other articles and resources in civil practice. As noted above, he is also a co-author of *Federal Civil Procedure Handbook*, *A Student's Guide to the Federal Rules of Civil Procedure*, and Volume 12B of *Wright & Miller's Federal Practice and Procedure*. Prior to joining the Duquesne faculty, Professor Baicker-McKee was a longtime civil litigator in Pittsburgh. He has been recognized as one of the Outstanding Lawyers of America and elected to the Academy of Trial Lawyers.

Summary of Contents

Table of Contents

MASTERING MULTIPLE CHOICE *FOR*

FEDERAL CIVIL PROCEDURE

MBE BAR PREP *AND* 1L EXAM PREP

Third Edition

PART 1
Introduction to Mastering Multiple Choice *for* Federal Civil Procedure

A. DON'T SKIP THIS INTRODUCTION!

This Introduction is different. It is not about why we chose to write this book or how wonderful we think we are. It does not provide idle historical background for the academically curious or contrast esoteric philosophies about the nature and value of testing theory.

Instead, this Introduction is entirely substantive content. Here, we will try to impart concrete, easily adaptable, practical tips on how you can prepare for—and succeed with—multiple choice Civil Procedure questions.

B. WHO THIS BOOK CAN HELP

This book has two audience targets—(1) law school graduates who are preparing to sit for their State's Bar Examination and (2) law school students who are preparing for course examinations in Civil Procedure.

We will presume that both audiences are already familiar with the substance of the law of federal Civil Procedure. Consequently, this book's objective is not to *introduce* concepts in Civil Procedure to readers as new knowledge. Wonderful study aids are already widely available to fill that need. Instead, the goal here is to challenge and press that level of learned knowledge to a point that simulates how it will be examined in these two multiple choice testing environments.

This book, then, is *practice*. It is created to give users a rigorous exposure to the examination-context experience of demonstrating a mastery of Civil Procedure. Through this practice, it is our hope that working through this book brings our two audiences closer to their shared goals: performing well on the MBE's group of Civil Procedure questions and performing well on law school Civil Procedure examinations.

C. WHAT THIS BOOK OFFERS

Mindful of our twin audiences, this book has been designed with three objectives:

1. **To SIMULATE the experience** of an actual multiple choice testing environment for Civil Procedure knowledge;

2. **To CHECK YOUR UNDERSTANDING** of the topics covered in Civil Procedure courses and encompassed on the MBE; and

3. **To EXPLAIN, clearly and concisely,** all tested concepts, so that you'll gain a better understanding of those principles of Civil Procedure you might not have fully understood before.

The book contains 200 multiple choice questions on all the topics and subtopics included in the National Conference of Bar Examiners' (NCBE) subject matter outline for Civil Procedure (which we have reprinted below). The volume of this book's questions on each topic correlates to the percentages that the NCBE has stated it is now using in the Civil Procedure segment of the MBE. The questions are also posed to you in a manner that simulates the format used on the MBE (which is also the format often used in law school exams).

Like the questions you will encounter on the MBE or in a law school exam, the order of questions in this book is intentionally randomized; this gives you practice in identifying the topics and subtopics being tested, much as you will need to do on the MBE and in your law school exams. (Note, however, that the end of this book contains two **Tables** to help you zero in on particular testing topics and subtopics, if that is your wish.)

This book also contains something that the MBE and your Civil Procedure examinations will not—answers. Following the 200 multiple choice questions are the corresponding answers, with explanations, to each multiple choice question. Those answers and explanations will tell you which choice was right and why, and why the other choices were wrong.

D. OVERVIEW OF CIVIL PROCEDURE TOPICS COVERED

The NCBE included Civil Procedure as a tested topic in the MBE for the first time on the February 2015 administration of the national multiple choice bar examination. Previously, the topic of Civil Procedure had been tested on bar examinations principally through the use of essay questions.

The MBE tests national, federal civil practice only. Many States continue to test their State-specific Civil Procedures by essay or other means, but will relegate most (or all) of their testing on national Civil Procedure to multiple choice questions such as those sampled in this book. It is not this book's function to impart any State-specific Civil Procedure test practice assistance; for obvious reasons, that type of practice needs to be keyed to the enacted and decisional law of each particular State.

As of 2018, the NCBE employs a subject matter outline for its Civil Procedure MBE purposes, and it contains 7 main topics, with a total of 26 subtopics, as follows:

I.   **Jurisdiction and venue**

  A.   Federal subject-matter jurisdiction (federal question, diversity, supplemental, and removal)
  B.   Personal jurisdiction
  C.   Service of process and notice
  D.   Venue, forum non conveniens, and transfer

II.   **Law applied by federal courts**

  A.   State law in federal court
  B.   Federal common law

III. **Pretrial procedures**

  A.   Preliminary injunctions and temporary restraining orders
  B.   Pleadings and amended and supplemental pleadings
  C.   Rule 11
  D.   Joinder of parties and claims (including class actions)
  E.   Discovery (including e-discovery), disclosure, and sanctions
  F.   Adjudication without a trial
  G.   Pretrial conference and order

IV.   **Jury trials**

  A.   Right to jury trial
  B.   Selection and composition of juries
  C.   Requests for and objections to jury instructions

V.   **Motions**

  A.   Pretrial motions, including motions addressed to face of pleadings, motions to dismiss, and summary judgment motions
  B.   Motions for judgments as a matter of law (directed verdicts and judgments notwithstanding the verdict)
  C.   Post-trial motions, including motions for relief from judgment and for new trial

VI.   **Verdicts and judgments**

  A.   Defaults and dismissals
  B.   Jury verdicts—types and challenges
  C.   Judicial findings and conclusions
  D.   Effect; claim and issue preclusion

VII. **Appealability and review**

  A.   Availability of interlocutory review
  B.   Final judgment rule
  C.   Scope of review for judge and jury

This same grouping of topics and subtopics mirrors the traditional organizing structure of many law schools' 1L Civil Procedure survey courses. Consequently, that same organizing structure provides a prudent studying platform for law students preparing for their Civil Procedure examinations.

E. BAR EXAM STUDYING: WHAT YOU NEED TO KNOW ABOUT CIVIL PROCEDURE QUESTIONS

1. ADDITION OF CIVIL PROCEDURE TO THE MBE

The overall length and structure of the MBE has not changed since the inclusion of Civil Procedure as a tested topic. The test remains a 200-question format: 100 questions in a 3-hour morning session, and 100 questions in a 3-hour afternoon session. But not all 200 questions are scored. Instead, only 175 questions are scored, leaving the remaining 25 as experimental questions under development for future MBE exams. Examinees will not be able to tell which MBE questions are scored and which are experimental; they will all look alike.

The *seven* areas now covered on the MBE are as follows:

- ***Civil Procedure***
- Constitutional Law
- Contracts
- Criminal Law and Procedure
- Evidence
- Real Property
- Torts

Each of these seven areas will contain 25 scored questions (along with some unspecified number of unscored, experimental questions), making Civil Procedure, like the other six doctrinal areas, worth a little more than 14% *of the raw score* that a MBE examinee will earn.[1]

2. ALIGNMENT OF THE MBE WITH THE MULTISTATE ESSAY EXAMINATION

Beginning in February 2015, the subject matter outline for Federal Civil Procedure on the Multistate Essay Examination (MEE) was modified to conform to the subject matter outline for Civil Procedure on the MBE; thus, there is now one unified set of specifications for Civil Procedure on both

---

[1] **Scaled scores** on the MBE—that is, the score you will receive from the NCBE and the type of score used by States to determine pass rates, etc.—are determined by re-computing your raw score to adjust for the difficulty level of each particular exam administration. Therefore, you cannot tell precisely what raw score you will need either from a particular topic area or from an overall perspective in order to earn a passing MBE grade.

The scaled score needed to pass the bar exam has varied from year to year, and by administration time (February or July exam). Historically, the passing scaled score has hovered around 140. With the NCBE's increase in the number of unscored, experimental questions from 10 to 25, along with the arrival of the Uniform Bar Examination (UBE) and its adoption by an increasing number of States, reliably predicting how well you need to perform on the MBE to pass your bar exam has become a bit less certain. Experts in the field continue to subscribe to the view that a scaled MBE score of 140 remains a strong predictor for bar exam success.

examinations. This should make it easier for you to prepare for both those parts of the examination.

3. WHAT IS COVERED ON THE MBE, AND HOW?

Federal Civil Procedure is a constantly changing discipline. Aside from the annual waves of new case law construing and applying the rules and principles of civil practice, the Federal Rules of Civil Procedure and the U.S. Judiciary Code undergo frequent adjustment. For example, the Rules were amended in December 2015, December 2016, December 2017, and December 2018. The NCBE has generally considered new amendments eligible for inclusion in the MBE a short while after their adoption. This pattern is likely to repeat itself. You should assume, then, that changes to federal practice that occur by the close of one calendar year are likely eligible to be tested in the following summer's bar examination.

Accordingly, in preparing to take the Civil Procedure question group on the MBE, you should assume the application of:

a.   the most current amendments to the Federal Rules of Civil Procedure; *and*

b.   the sections of the federal Judiciary Code, Title 28 to the U.S. Code, pertaining to jurisdiction, venue, and transfer, also as most currently amended; *and*

c.   the comprehensive body of nationally significant case law interpreting and applying civil procedure principles.

The seven main topics listed earlier under "Overview of Topics Covered" will all be tested on the MBE (*i.e.*, jurisdiction and venue, law applied by the federal courts, pretrial procedures, jury trials, motions, verdicts and judgments, and appealability and review). Given the 25-scored question limit allocated to Civil Procedure, the 26 subtopics comprising these main topics cannot each be tested on each MBE administration, nor can each individual knowledge category within each subtopic be tested on each MBE. Because you will not know what subtopics and knowledge categories will or will not be tested during any particular administration of the MBE, you will need to be prepared to answer questions on all subtopics and all knowledge categories.

Take careful note, however, that there are some areas where you will want to concentrate your preparation. Approximately *two-thirds* of the Civil Procedure questions (*i.e.*, about 16 or 17 of the 25 scored questions) on the MBE will be based on these three categories:

-     I.   Jurisdiction and venue;

-     III.   Pretrial procedures; and

-     V.   Motions.

Approximately one-third (*i.e.*, about 8 or 9 of the 25 scored questions) will be based on the remaining four categories:

-     II.   Law applied by the federal courts;

- IV. Jury trials;
- VI. Verdicts and judgments; and
- VII. Appealability and review.

4. OTHER IMPORTANT INFORMATION

You should bear a few other nuggets of information in mind as you begin to prepare for the Civil Procedure group of MBE questions:

- **Question Types Are Not Flagged:** The MBE will not identify for you a question's doctrinal type. While taking the MBE, you will have to discern whether the question is testing Civil Procedure, torts, contracts, evidence, etc. You will need to learn to scan for words, phrases, and contexts related to each discipline, as well as appropriate fact patterns, to discern questions in each area. Identifying the area being tested will likely improve your chances of success on a particular question.

- **Questions Are Randomized:** The MBE also does not test in order. So, your first question might test Civil Procedure, and the next one torts, followed by two evidence questions, then four contracts questions, then another Civil Procedure question, etc.

- **Questions Test Knowledge *In Application*:** The MBE requires you to demonstrate your mastery of rules and principles by showing that you know how to apply those concepts in a fact pattern you will be seeing for the first time. Rarely (if ever) will the MBE ask you to merely define a legal principle abstractly, outside of an applied setting.

- **There Is No Guessing Penalty:** You should answer *every single question*. When possible, try to eliminate one or more wrong answers before answering; this (obviously) improves your odds. But answer every question. Choosing an incorrect answer does not detract from your score (it simply will not add to it).

- **Timing:** You have a total of 3 hours to answer the morning set of 100 questions, and then 3 hours to answer the afternoon set of 100 questions. This works out to an average of 1.8 minutes (or 1 minute 48 seconds) per question. The questions will not be uniform in difficulty. You should expect some of them to take more time and thought than average, and others to need less. But be vigilant in ***pacing yourself*** across each 100-question set. Taking more time with any one question means there will be less time available for later questions.

F. LAW SCHOOL EXAM STUDYING: WHAT YOU NEED TO KNOW ABOUT CIVIL PROCEDURE QUESTIONS

1. CIVIL PROCEDURE IS A CLASS-SPECIFIC COURSE

Different schools and different professors teach Civil Procedure differently. There was a time when Civil Procedure was taught—fairly uniformly—as a two-semester 3-credit doctrinal course. Typically, the Fall semester half of this traditional course was devoted to issues of judicial power (jurisdiction, venue, notice) and pleadings, with the Spring semester half devoted to joinder, discovery, pretrial procedures, *Erie*, post-trial/appellate procedures, and preclusion. Many law schools continue to follow this traditional approach to Civil Procedure, but not all do. Some schools have even reduced the 1L credit load for Civil Procedure, inviting students who wish to learn more on the topic to enroll in 2L/3L elective courses.

Because of these curricular variations among law schools, the material you need to study for your own test will depend on your course's specific coverage. Traditional model students will be learning (and, therefore, being tested on) traditional Fall semester topics during the Fall semester exam, and traditional Spring semester topics during the Spring semester exam. In schools following a different model, students will likely be learning a selection of material from both the traditional Fall and the traditional Spring topic groups, with some traditional topics removed entirely from their 1L course coverage. Consequently, to effectively study for your Civil Procedure exam, you need to know which questions are testing which information.

2. YOUR "DECODER-RING" FOR THIS BOOK

Because this book presents all 200 questions in a topically randomized order (to simulate the randomized presentation that will appear in most testing environments), law students preparing for Civil Procedure examinations are likely to come across some questions that test topics that they have not yet learned. To ensure that you are able to focus your efforts on only those questions relevant to your particular exam, consult **Table 5** at the end of this book. That Table identifies questions by broad topic, subtopic, and knowledge category, so that your use of this book can be tailored to how you have learned Civil Procedure in your law school.

3. OTHER IMPORTANT INFORMATION

You should bear a few other nuggets of information in mind as you begin to prepare for your Civil Procedure law school examination:

- **The Forest *and* the Trees:** Acquiring a broad, generalized familiarity with the topics and subtopics of Civil Procedure is not enough. Professional schools (law schools, medical schools, MBA schools, etc.) focus on major principles and technical nuances.

You need to master the big picture, for sure; but you cannot neglect the details. Law school tests will require you to display a mastery of both.

- **Questions Test Knowledge *In Application*:** As with the bar exam, your professor is likely to require you to demonstrate your mastery of rules and principles by showing that you know how to apply those concepts in a fact pattern you will be seeing for the first time. Consequently, your professor is unlikely to pose a multiple choice question that asks you to merely define a legal principle abstractly, outside of an applied setting.

- **Pace Yourself:** Most professors will use a variety of testing formats for their law school examinations, blending multiple choice questions with large essays, short answers, and, perhaps, other sorts of exercises to comprehensively test students' mastery of the material. Embracing the time-triage process that good students employ at the beginning of a law school examination, you should review your exam completely, identify how it is separated and the grading weights for each part, and then allocate your time to comfortably complete each part of the examination.

- **National and Local:** Law schools (and individual professors) differ on whether, and to what degree, to test local State law. This book (and most all national study guides) will not aid you in preparing for State-specific questioning.

- **Timing:** A good rule-of-thumb for multiple choice questions is that you should move through them at a *less-than-2-minutes-per-question* clip. That is the pace expected for the MBE when you graduate law school and sit for the bar examination, and that pace will ordinarily afford you a comfortable time margin for completing the other, non-multiple choice portions of your course's examination.

G. WHY IS MULTIPLE CHOICE SO TOUGH?

It's a common refrain: "I am a disaster when it comes to multiple choice tests." But why is that? Even students who excel in law school, and who graduate with high honors, can often fall prey to multiple choice questions. Nonetheless, multiple choice questions have been with us in the profession for a long time, and they are likely to remain with us for a long time to come. Rather than resigning yourself to a future of disappointment with this testing environment, let's try to understand it a bit better. Why is multiple choice so difficult a testing regime, even for highly successful law students?

1. ATTRIBUTE ONE: THEY GIVE YOU THE ANSWER

Multiple choice questions show the test-taker the correct answer. It's right there, staring back at you. It's obscured, to be sure; the correct answer may be worded deceptively and it's camouflaged by three other enticing (but wrong) answer choices. In truth, it is even more stark than that. In designing an ideal, valid question, test drafters search to ensure that all true ambiguities in the question have been dispelled; a really good multiple choice question offers the test-taker four answer choices, of which one is absolutely, incontestably correct, surrounded by three that are unequivocally, indisputably wrong.

2. ATTRIBUTE TWO: THERE'S NO WIGGLE ROOM

Essay questions permit the possibility of "close" and "partial-credit" answers, where the test-taker can talk around a concept or legal principle and, perhaps, earn some credit for verifying his or her command of the topic in general. Not so with multiple choice questions. Multiple choice forces test-takers into a black-and-white box: test-takers are either correct (in which case they get *all* the available points for that question) or they are incorrect (in which case they get none). Ergo, that unmistakable feeling that you're living on the knife's-edge when you take multiple choice tests . . .

3. ATTRIBUTE THREE: SLIPS ARE UNFORGIVING

Because there is no chance for "partial-credit," an oversight in reading the fact-pattern, or a misunderstanding of what the question asks of you, or a slip in comprehension when perusing the available answer choices, is often disastrous. What's more, the test-developers likely injected language, facts, or context designed to deliberately coax an inattentive or careless reader into a wrong choice. Consequently, reading accurately, completely, and with genuine comprehension is rarely more critical than it is with multiple choice tests.

4. ATTRIBUTE FOUR: "BEST," NOT "PERFECT"

Multiple choice answers rarely offer the test-taker the *perfect* choice. There's a good reason for this: the *perfect* choice is usually an obvious one. But the test-developer is endeavoring to validate whether you possess a true mastery of the legal principles, not just a 50,000-foot level of vague awareness.

So, often, the *perfect* choice is intentionally left out, and the four available choices may each suffer from an incompleteness or an over-generalization or an under-inclusion. For the test-taker who has truly mastered the principle tested, the "best" selection among the available choices will still stand out.

5. ATTRIBUTE FIVE: SECOND-GUESSING IS ENTICING

Because the correct answer is present, and because the incorrect answers look so inviting, another unnerving dynamic is created by multiple choice questions: an urge to second-guess. Test-takers who find themselves disappointed that the *perfect* choice is not available can tend to over-think the question or imagine a nuance that is not fairly present or a theoretical ambiguity that the fact pattern doesn't really possess. Test-takers often select the correct answer, and then talk themselves out of it to an incorrect choice as they second-guess themselves.

6. ATTRIBUTE SIX: TIME PRESSURE

Multiple choice questions are usually designed to be completed in a very brief time-span (on the bar exam, that period is less than 2 minutes per question). That is a very tight window to read through the question and answer choices, identify the area being tested, become topically re-oriented to that area, conduct a considered analysis, and make a thoughtful selection. With essay questions, the performance expectations of the test-taker are more elaborate: you have to write out a correct, sophisticated, and structurally appropriate prose answer. But there's a bit of time built into the essay question for meandering; a test-taker could, perhaps, misread an essay question, start writing, come to an epiphany during the drafting that the question is actually asking something else, and pivot the essay response into a position that still earns some (or most) of the available essay points. That's just not the case with multiple choice questions. The time is so short that meandering or misreading generally means error (and, worse yet, over-spending time on one question, leaving insufficient time for later questions).

7. ATTRIBUTE SEVEN: BREADTH AND DEPTH

While a multiple choice exam will not cover 100% of the subtopics listed above, it will cover a great deal of them. That reality, coupled with the time pressure, means test-takers need to have mastered a wide breadth of material—and often in more depth than they might expect. Professors and bar examiners both design most of their questions to require the test-taker to **apply** legal knowledge to unfamiliar fact patterns. You cannot perform well if you rely solely on simple rote memorization of rules and concepts. In addition, you will need to have enough comfort with all the topics and subtopics to apply your knowledge quickly and efficiently. In many cases, you will be tasked with discovering subtle distinctions between the correct and incorrect answers. These require high level thinking skills and overlearning of the material being tested.

8. ATTRIBUTE EIGHT: TRICKY, TRICKY, TRICKY

Excellent multiple choice question drafting has a very particular objective: to distinguish those test-takers who have merely a vague, generalized understanding of the material from those who have truly mastered it. Savvy question-drafters have perfected a laundry list of techniques to accomplish this objective, and all of those techniques involve attempting to coax that test-taker who has an incomplete command of the material *away* from the correct answer. Remember, multiple choice question drafters start at one significant disadvantage: they have to include the correct answer among the four available answer choices. So, the "art" of effective multiple choice question drafting is nudging, inducing, enticing the test-taker into error.

Understanding how question-drafters accomplish this is the first step in immunizing yourself from the effects of these tricky techniques:

a. The Sneaky "Call-of-the-Question"

Disorientation is an often-used question-drafting technique. One form of this is to pose an *unexpected* call-of-the-question. The question might ask the *opposite* of what the test-taker was expecting (*e.g.*, "Why should the court not grant the relief requested?"), or ask you to assume a perspective the test-taker was not anticipating (*e.g.*, "What fact would be most useful in opposing such a motion?"). This is sneaky because, in a quick read, test-takers might *think* they understand what the question is asking, when it actually is asking something else. *Antidote:* You must accurately absorb the call-of-the-question.

b. The Sinister Misdirection

A similar technique is to misdirect the test-taker by ladling on detail after detail that implies a certain inquiry or analysis, when most (or all) of those details have no bearing on the legal principle being tested. Consider an example: a fact-pattern supplies elaborate detail about the citizenship of each of the parties, and how the amount in dispute in the litigation exceeds $75,000 exclusive of interests and costs. Naturally, skillful test-takers will be anticipating a diversity jurisdiction question, yet the call-of-the-question actually raises a service of process issue. All those citizenship details were red herrings, included to entice careless readers away from the correct analysis. *Antidote:* You must bear the call-of-the-question in mind when reading the facts.

c. The Tricky Inducement

Another nasty technique is the "distractor" scenario. Here, the question-drafter includes as an answer-choice a substantively-correct statement that roughly touches on the broad topic being tested. The problem is that this correct statement of law does not answer the question posed. For example, the question may be plainly testing personal jurisdiction concepts, and one answer choice includes the phrases "minimum contacts" and "traditional notions of fair play and substantial justice." Eureka! You remember that refrain from Civil

Procedure class! Unfortunately, the question was asking about the timing for filing a motion to dismiss on this basis, not for a summary of the legal standard that will govern resolving that motion. *Antidote:* Your answer selection must not only correctly state the law, it must correctly answer the question.

d. The Only-*Partially* Right Answer

Another common drafting approach is to include two sets of similar answers. For example, "Yes, the court will grant the motion because. . ."; "Yes, the court will grant the motion because. . ."; "No, the court will deny the motion because. . ."; and "No, the court will deny the motion because. . .". The challenge here, obviously, is that both components of the answer must be correct. The binary "Yes"/"No" choice needs to be right, but the explanation that accompanies that binary choice needs to be right also. A correct binary choice coupled with an incorrect explanation is still wrong. *Antidote:* You must recognize the dual-layered nature of this format, and ensure that both are correct.

e. The All-Wrong Answers

Another drafting convention offers the test-taker four answer choices that all seem wrong. Take, for example, a question on federal pleading that asks whether a certain complaint is properly prepared. From the fact pattern, the test-taker is certain the answer is "yes". However, each of the four answer choices begins with the word "no," followed by an explanation. This technique can be disorienting to even the most accomplished test-taker. Often, the correct answer will be one that *adds* new facts that change the perceived analysis ("No, if the pleading is not signed by counsel in compliance with Rule 11."). That new information converts what would seemingly be a "yes" answer into a "no" one. *Antidote:* You need to be mindful of new information supplied in an answer choice that changes the answer selection approach.

f. The Phantom Absolutes

MBE questions often pose sensible summaries of the law that become wrong because of an "absolute" added to the fact pattern or answer choice. "Always" and "never" and "every" are classic examples. An answer choice that is often true, but not "always" so, is likely wrong. In a service of process question, an answer choice that states that service at a defendant's home is "always" proper feels instinctively correct, until you consider how variables could prove that "always" to be false (for example, if the person who accepts service is not a resident in the home, not a person of suitable age and discretion, or not an authorized agent). *Antidote:* Circle any "absolute" terms you encounter as a reminder to be on guard against them.

g. The "You-Gotta-Be-Kidding-Me" Choice

On occasion, the correct answer may be so obscure, so impossibly nuanced and inaccessible that you can hardly imagine that any 35-year federal litigator could have answered it correctly. This, too, is a test-development technique.

While it is possible that your Civil Procedure professor or the MBE drafters asked a truly unfair question, it is far more likely that the question framer *never* expected you to know the correct answer to be correct. What you were expected to know was that the other three choices were unquestionably wrong. With this type of question, the student who has mastered Civil Procedure should know that three of the choices were plainly wrong, and that the fourth choice—introducing a knowledge element that may well seem foreign—had to be the correct choice simply by process of elimination. *Antidote:* Don't get flustered if you do not know why the surviving answer is right, if you know for certain that all the other choices are wrong.

h.   The "No-Earthly-Clue" Question

Embrace these. That's why you invested in a practice book like this one. Encountering a question that leaves you scratching your head is an optimal learning moment for you. Make your best-reasoned selection. Then, read with special care the explanations offered for the answers, and commit the new piece of knowledge to your memory and to your topical outline. There you go! You are now more ready for your test than you were before practicing. This experience may also help you identify a broader hole or gap in your knowledge that you hadn't realized you had. Once again, practicing has helped.

H. THE METHOD:
AN APPROACH FOR SUCCESS
WITH MULTIPLE CHOICE QUESTIONS

You can excel with multiple choice questions. It's true. You really can. But to do so requires that you embrace a different mindset than you might when taking an essay test. To master multiple choice, you must: *first*, know the underlying legal principles that are being tested; *second*, follow a reliable method for tackling the questions and answer choices as they come; and *third*, be vigilant about the techniques and tricks that multiple choice question developers use in drafting their exam questions. Here's the method we recommend:

#1. LEARN IT THOROUGHLY

Multiple choice questions test *genuine* command of the content. There is no substitute for knowing the tested information completely. Until you know—truly *know*—the substantive law the exam is testing, you cannot refine the process of effective exam-taking. So, success with multiple choice exams begins with a thorough command of the material.

#2. REMIND YOURSELF: "BEST ANSWER"

Before beginning any multiple choice test, remind yourself that your search among the available answer choices is not necessarily a search for the *perfect* answer, but for the *best* available answer choice. Reminding yourself, at the outset, that the *perfect* answer may not be offered frames your mindset and diminishes the risk of frustration as you work through the questions.

#3. READ THE CALL-OF-THE-QUESTION FIRST

A natural temptation is to attack a question top-to-bottom. That approach is inefficient and, sometimes, counterproductive. Before reading the fact pattern, learn what you are searching for. Read the call-of-the-question first. This will quickly focus your attention on the destination. It may be obvious that the fact pattern is posing a discovery question, but your focus, as the test-taker, materially differs depending on whether the call-of-the-question asks "Should the court compel plaintiff to answer the defendant's interrogatory?" or "If the court refuses to compel plaintiff to answer the defendant's interrogatory, what is most likely to be the court's reason?"

#4. SKIM THROUGH THE ANSWER CHOICES

This "skimming" should be more than a breeze-through read but less than an exhaustive study. You need to get a sense—just a quick sense, for now—of the answer choices available to you. This will aid you when you read the fact pattern. It will also often give you clues to the area of law being tested and even the topic, subtopic, and knowledge category within that area. Identifying these clues will increase your chances of selecting the right answer.

#5. *NOW,* READ THE FACT PATTERN . . . SLOWLY

Armed, now, with the knowledge of what the call-of-the-question is asking of you, and having previewed the available answer choices, you are well primed to read the fact pattern. Read it carefully. Circle words or concepts. Underline stuff. Scribble yourself a note or two. Concentrate as you read. You will find that you are better able to quickly home-in on the details in the fact pattern that matter and those that might be there just to distract you. Students often refer to this step as the "neon-light" step: because you've waited to read the fact pattern, now—because you know what you are looking for—the pivotal facts and elements seem to leap out as though they were lit in neon colors.

#6. WATCH OUT FOR ANY USE OF THE WORD "NOT"

The word "not" is an answer-killer: "What argument would not justify a court's denial of the judgment as a matter of law?" If you miss the "not" in that sentence, you are searching for the exact wrong answer. It is also likely, in a well-drafted multiple choice question, that the drafters included that exact wrong answer among the answer choices, there to trip up the careless reader. Get into the habit of boldly circling any use of the word "not" to prevent yourself from being misled.

#7. SIMILAR WORDS ARE TROUBLE, TOO

The word "not" is just one of many words that redirect the meaning of a multiple choice question. "Least" and "most" are among those redirection terms, too. Asking which pre-answer Rule 12 motion is "least" likely to prevail is, of course, precisely the opposite of asking which pre-answer Rule 12 motion is "most" likely to prevail. Again, highlight any appearance of these words.

#8. BE SUSPICIOUS OF "ALWAYS," "EVERY," "NEVER"

These are words of absolutism. Not a lot in the law is "always" true or "never" possible—the law, as you've now come to learn, is often far more circumstance-dependent than that. Of course, this is not to say that all "always," "every," and "never" answer choices are wrong. But you should be instinctually wary of these terms. A question that asks what a court must "always" do, what an objection to discovery may "never" have, or what "every" pleading must include is a very dangerous question. Be alert.

#9. NOW, RETURN TO THE ANSWER CHOICES

Having read carefully through the fact pattern (with both the call-of-the-question and your skimmed-familiarity of the answer choices in mind), look now at the answer choices again. Do so carefully. Avoid impulse. Remember, one of these choices is absolutely, positively right, and three are absolutely, positively wrong. Run the choices through a mental checklist. Is the choice:

• A flat-out wrong statement of a legal rule or principle?

- An answer that is partly wrong (*e.g.*, it correctly begins with "yes" but the explanation that follows is incorrect)?

- A correct statement of a legal rule or principle, but misapplied to the details of the fact pattern?

- A correct statement of a legal rule or principle, but one that does not squarely answer the question that is posed?

- An answer phrased in absolutist terms ("always" or "never"), when the same result is not "always" or "never" true?

- A correct statement of a legal rule or principle that faithfully, correctly answers the call-of-the-question?

#10. DECIDE

Most often, you will have about 2 minutes to read, think, and decide. (On the bar exam, the per-question time is 1 minute and 48 seconds.) You can't dither. If you have conscientiously, carefully applied this method we have suggested to the question, you are now best positioned to make your selection. Choose the right answer, if you know it. If you don't, eliminate any available choices you know to be wrong, and make a reasoned guess. If you are still uncertain of your answer after choosing, circle that question number so that you can return to it quickly if time remains at the end of the exam.

#11. MOVE ON

Other questions await. You can't over-spend time on any one multiple choice question without short-changing yourself on the time you have for later ones. You do not need every question answered correctly to earn a fine grade (or a passing MBE score). Don't let an uncertain question haunt you. Laboring over a single question well after its allotted time has passed is *always* a poor choice.

#12. WHEN SHOULD YOU SECOND-GUESS?

If there is time left at the end of the exam, should you go back and second-guess your uncertain answers? We think you should, but in only a very constrained manner. Return to your circled questions. Re-read them, and re-apply the method we've suggested to them. Occasionally, something you overlooked before will become apparent and the correct answer will be obvious. Other times, you'll find yourself as stumped as before. But something, instinctively, led you to select the answer you chose on the first go-round. Maybe you are subconsciously reminded of a concept that, in the rough-and-tumble of an exam setting, you cannot consciously conjure up. We recommend that you change an original answer only when you come to the informed conclusion that you were plainly wrong in your original selection and can articulate for yourself why a new, different choice is clearly right. Unless you have that level of personal certainty, stand on your original selection.

I. HOW TO GET THE MOST OUT OF THIS BOOK

1. LEARN THE MATERIAL THOROUGHLY FIRST

Although you can certainly use this book to pre-test your knowledge or give you a sense of what you will be learning, it will generally be more useful for you to go through these questions after you have studied and mastered the topic, subtopic, and knowledge category. This is true whether you are using the book to prepare for law school exams or the MBE. This book enables you to test your ability to translate substantive knowledge into problem-solving contexts. But until your substantive mastery is in place, you cannot optimally practice that exercise.

2. REVIEW THE MATERIAL BEFORE USING THESE PRACTICE QUESTIONS

Test questions like the ones on the MBE, on law school exams, and in this book require you to *apply* knowledge you know well, not merely to recognize issues. Thus you will be more successful (and likely do a better job of calming your nerves) if you have "over-learned" the material before testing yourself.

One good strategy to aid with over-learning the information is making an annotated outline of the topics, subtopics, and knowledge categories. The type of outline that is ideal for you depends on your learning, studying, and knowledge assimilation aptitude and preferences. Some students prepare short, crisp outlines, 6–12 pages in length, which highlight core points about complicated concepts that their own prior study has already committed to their memory. Other students prefer longer outlines (sometimes 50 pages in length, or more) that capture comprehensively all of the information testable for the exam, which they then read and re-read as the exam time approaches. Still other students use a hybrid approach, combining a longer outline with a "skinny"—a very brief, 3–5 page skeletal summary of the topic as a knowledge trigger that is supported by the fuller outline. And still other students use more elaborate learning devices like flow-charts, mind-maps, flash-cards, topic scrolls, and other creative resources.

Whatever strategy you choose, the goal at this stage is always the same— acquiring a comfortable, working knowledge of the numerous trees without ever missing how they fit together into the doctrinal forest. And while it may be tempting just to copy someone else's outline, short-outline, "skinny," mind-map, or flashcard, resist that path at all costs. It is important to your mastery to draft your own study resource. The process of creating it forces you to organize, prioritize, and cement the ideas you need to recall and use. For many people, hand-writing that study resource is more powerful than typing it—the physical process of writing it by hand seems to impress it into memory more effectively.

3. FILLING IN THE HOLES

In the process of mastering Civil Procedure that ought to precede the use of this book (or, for that matter, any other examination study resource), you should constantly be on guard for knowledge "holes" or "gaps." When you encounter a topic, subtopic, or knowledge category that leaves you feeling that your command is incomplete or your confidence with that material is shaky, you've discovered a hole. In neither the MBE nor a law school class on Civil Procedure is the "kinda-get-it" level of mastery a recipe for success. You are being tested on your ability to demonstrate so complete and comprehensive a command of difficult Civil Procedure concepts that you are able to translate that knowledge into an applied context. If your mastery is weak, your capacity at application will almost certainly be as well. Fill in the holes! Go see your professor. Pull out a study guide or a hornbook or your casebook. Do some independent research. Confer with a friend. But get certain. Before you head into any examination, know the law well and master its nuances. Only then will this book's practice offer you its best value.

4. USE ACTIVE LEARNING TECHNIQUES

This book is intended to help you with recalling substantive knowledge of Civil Procedure that you may have forgotten, as well as learning how to apply information you know to new situations. You will therefore get more out of the practice this book facilitates if you make an effort to approach the questions with your brain turned on and "interacting" with the material rather than merely breezily reading over the questions and answers. Here are some "active-learner" techniques that will help optimize the value of this book:

a. Take Your Time

Before you sit for the MBE or your law school examination, you should take several practice tests under the conditions you will encounter during the actual examination.[2] Use this book, though, before you try to get up to actual test pace. Go through the questions in small sets rather than attempting all 200 questions in a single sitting; spaced practice is more effective than massed practice for retaining large amounts of complex information.

But also avoid doing single-question practice sessions. Relaxing with a morning cup of coffee over a single multiple choice Civil Procedure question is not ideal. Doing so conditions your mind to relax through the process, and will not help you build the "mental-muscle-memory" needed to attack a larger group of questions under tight time constraints, as exam settings demand. We think the very fewest number of questions that should be done in any single sitting is 10, and those should be answered in 30 minutes or less.

---

[2] Many testing experts recommend only taking half-tests—100 questions over 3 hours— rather than the full test, so that you conserve your energy for the actual test day, much as most runners train for marathons by running shorter distances in the lead up to race day. The full marathon, whether test or race, depletes your resources beyond your ability to recover in the short term.

Taking a little bit more time reading and answering the questions as you practice is fine (so long as the pace is not leisurely). A more deliberate pace can help you develop good habits for the critical reading and problem-solving skills that these multiple choice questions demand; later you can work on building speed back to your less-than-2-minute-per-question target. This is similar to the best approach for learning complex physical skills, like hitting a baseball or knitting a sweater: break the task into the component sub-skills, perform each piece deliberately and correctly, make corrections, and practice until the actions become second nature—then get up to speed.

b.   Answer the Questions Using the Method Recommended Above

Following this strategy right from the start will help make it comfortable and reflexive when you use it in the actual testing situation.

Obviously, for the questions in this book, you won't have to try to identify the doctrinal area of law because it will always be Civil Procedure. But, as noted earlier, the questions in the book are still intentionally randomized with regard to the topics, subtopics, and knowledge categories that will be covered. You should make an attempt to home in on what exactly each question is testing as you complete each step.

Practice all the other skills you will want to use in the actual test: fixing the specific question asked in your head, underlining key terms and facts, circling "not," "always," "never," "every," "least," and "most," considering each answer option in light of the common reasons it might be wrong. Force yourself to put your reasoning into words rather than just relying on a general sense; this will make it easier to identify and correct your mistakes.

Be sure to select what you believe to be the correct answer *before* looking at the provided answers and explanations. If you are uncertain, try to at least eliminate one or two of the options before checking your work, again making an effort to put your reasoning into words.

c.   Look at the Answers and the Explanations

Answers for each question are provided in the second half of the book, followed by detailed explanations. Each explanation offers a careful summary of the applicable law and the associated reasoning for why that choice was right or wrong. Citations to legal resources are also supplied, so students can read further. To minimize the length of this book, citations in the explanations section to the Federal Rules of Civil Procedure are referred to simply as "Rule 12" or "Rule 52." Citations to other rules, like the Federal Rules of Appellate Procedure, follow their *Bluebook* format (*e.g.*, Fed. R. App. P. 4).

It is probably best to check the explanations frequently. For this stage of review, it is most effective to get prompt feedback on your performance. Read the answer that you have chosen, taking care to also read the explanation— even if you have gotten it right—to check whether you have also reasoned correctly. Be sure to also review the explanations provided for the distracters (the wrong choices), as those may solidify your understanding of the issues.

If you got the answer wrong, don't panic! Remember that even in the MBE—the gauntlet through which most practicing lawyers must pass before they earn their license—you will likely be able to answer about 60 questions wrong without running into problems. And, often, getting a question wrong while you are practicing will help galvanize your knowledge of that material and help you remember the issue for the future.

After completing the questions in the book and carefully reading the explanations you will almost certainly have deepened your understanding of Civil Procedure *and* improved your test-taking skills.

5. RETURN LATER FOR TIMED PRACTICE

You can certainly return to this book to practice Civil Procedure questions under timed conditions later on, as well as use it to retest your knowledge of areas that gave you trouble the first time through. It may be helpful to answer the questions in a different order the next time through; try doing every other question or starting from a different point in the book.

6. A REMINDER FOR LAW STUDENTS

As discussed in *Law School Exam Studying* above, this book includes two charts—Parts 4 and 5 at the end of the text—that correlate each of the 200 questions to the topics they address. Therefore, if your Civil Procedure class has only covered certain topics at the time you are preparing for a law school examination, you can easily select which of the multiple choice questions are applicable to the topics your exam is likely to test.

J. A FINAL PIECE OF ADVICE
BEFORE GETTING STARTED

We've all been there. Every practicing lawyer was at one time a 1L in law school, struggling to learn about poor Mr. Neff and the unwitting Mr. Pennoyer, the crazy shoe salesmen hawking loafers in Washington State, the free-ride passes awarded to the Mottleys, and the Erie Railroad injury suffered by Mr. Tompkins. Civil Procedure is tough sledding. You've worked hard to gain a command of this difficult material, and are now working still harder to harness that knowledge for an examination setting. Allow this book to help you. Celebrate your correct answers, and learn the patterns of your wrong ones.

As some wise soul once said, good luck always smells of perspiration. Put in the time to solidify your command of this material. We hope our little book helps!

* * *

Now, a quick closing request . . .

Send us your comments! If you have suggestions, a recommendation for an additional helpful nugget of advice, or come upon an error, please let us know. We have been as vigilant as we can be to ensure this book is as reliable as we can make it, but we are certain to benefit from your suggestions.

It is our intention to regularly update the question set in this book, so be on the lookout for a next edition.

PART 2
Multiple Choice Questions

Reminder to Users: This Part 2 contains 200 multiple choice questions, presented in randomized order and type-font to simulate actual examination-taking conditions. Each Question is followed by a reference to the page in Part 3 where its Answer and Explanation can be found.

Decoding the Topics: If you wish to tailor your practice to just certain topics or subtopics, you can do so. At the end of this book are two tables. Part 4 decodes, in order, each question's NCBE group, master category, sub-category, and tested-knowledge area. Part 5 organizes all of this book's questions into groups for you, gathered by NCBE group, master category, sub-category, and tested-knowledge area.

----

1.   Neighbor, a painter, painted the exterior of Homeowner's house. Homeowner believed that Neighbor did an unprofessional job, hired another painter to repaint the house, and sued Neighbor for damages in State court in a State that has adopted the Federal Rules of Civil Procedure as its State procedural rules. Neighbor filed a counterclaim asserting two claims: one seeking the money that Homeowner promised to pay him for the painting job, and one seeking recovery of the riding lawnmower that Homeowner previously borrowed, which is unrelated to the painting fees dispute.

As a matter of procedural propriety only, may Neighbor prosecute each of these counterclaims in this action?

(A)   Neighbor cannot bring either claim.

(B)   Neighbor must bring the claim for the painting fees, but may not bring the lawnmower claim.

(C)   Neighbor must bring the claim for the painting fees, and may bring the lawnmower claim.

(D)   Neighbor must bring both claims or risk waiving them.

See ANSWER on Page 119

2. Customer brought suit in federal court against Baker, contending that Baker's "gluten free" scones contained gluten and made her ill. The trial court entered summary judgment in favor of Baker on all counts. Customer was traveling for her employer in a remote part of China with very limited communications capabilities when the court entered the judgment, and was not due to return to the United States until 40 days after the entry of judgment. Mindful of the 30-day time limit for appealing, counsel for Customer advised counsel for Baker about Customer's whereabouts, and requested a 20-day extension of the deadline for appeal. Counsel for Baker agreed to this request.

    May Customer proceed with the appeal?

    (A) Yes, if the parties reduced the agreement to a written stipulation, filed with the court before the expiration of the 30-day period.

    (B) Yes, if the district court determines, in its discretion, that neither party would be prejudiced by the extension and it is "in the interests of justice" to allow the appeal.

    (C) Yes, if Customer files a motion to extend the time for appeal prior to the expiration of the 30-day period and the district court deems Customer's travel to constitute "good cause" for the extension.

    (D) No, because appellate time limits are considered jurisdictional and cannot be extended by stipulation.

    See ANSWER on Page 120

3. Protestor did not approve of the environmental practices of Big Oil. Protestor came onto Big Oil's property and spray-painted environmental slogans on the façade of Big Oil's new headquarters. Protestor then blogged that he was the one who painted the slogans, and asserted his belief that his actions were protected by the First Amendment to the United States Constitution because his slogans were political speech. Big Oil brought State law trespass and property damage claims against Protester in federal court in the State where the headquarters were located, and where Protestor was domiciled. Big Oil's complaint noted, but vigorously disputed, Protestor's contention that his actions were shielded by the First Amendment.

    Will the federal court have subject-matter jurisdiction over this action?

    (A) No, because there is no diversity of citizenship and because Big Oil's claims do not arise under the Constitution, laws, or treaties of the United States.

    (B) Yes, because Big Oil's claims necessarily depend on an interpretation and application of the First Amendment.

    (C) Yes, because the complaint discloses a constitutional issue, and thus the basis for federal jurisdiction is contained in the "well pleaded complaint."

    (D) Yes, because Big Oil's conduct is governed by federal environmental laws and the United States Environmental Protection Agency, which elevates this action to one of national interest.

    See ANSWER on Page 120

4. Seller refurbished speedboats for resale from his home in Kitty Hawk, North Carolina. One summer, Buyer noticed Seller's roadside advertisement while driving his family to Florida for vacation. On his way back from vacation, Buyer purchased a refurbished speedboat from Seller, agreeing to make three yearly payments for the purchase. The next year, Seller relocated to Pawley's Island, South Carolina. Buyer paid the first of his three installments, but failed to pay the second or third installments. Several months later, Seller saw Buyer having lunch with a business client at a restaurant in Pawley's Island.

   If Seller is able to have Buyer served with a complaint and summons before Buyer finishes his lunch, would it satisfy constitutional due process if the South Carolina courts exercised jurisdiction over Buyer?

   (A) Yes, but only because Seller is now a citizen of South Carolina.

   (B) Yes, but only if Buyer was lunching in South Carolina voluntarily.

   (C) No, unless Buyer has sufficient other minimum contacts with South Carolina.

   (D) No, unless Buyer is a citizen of South Carolina.

   See ANSWER on Page 121

5. While training for competition, Gymnast fell when his pommel horse cracked and split. He suffered various cuts, bruises to his upper body, and a broken ankle. Gymnast brought suit against the balance beam's Manufacturer in federal court, demanding compensation for his broken ankle, medical bills, and lost wages.

   Without the court's intervention, what type of examination can Manufacturer have Gymnast undergo?

   (A) An extraction of his blood, if Gymnast consents, for the purpose of verifying his blood group.

   (B) A physical examination to test for injuries to his arms and torso.

   (C) A mental examination to explore the presence and extent of any emotional distress.

   (D) A physical examination of his injured ankle to confirm extent of injury, speed of healing, and degree of impairment.

   See ANSWER on Page 121

6.   Stockholder sued Corporation in federal court in California, asserting a claim under the
      federal Racketeering Influenced and Corrupt Organization Act (RICO) and an assortment
      of State law claims, contending that Corporation's officers had mismanaged Corporation,
      leading to lower stock prices. After the federal judge suggested that she was going to
      transfer the case to a federal court in Illinois, Stockholder filed a notice of dismissal.
      Stockholder then filed a new complaint in California State court asserting the same claims.
      Corporation removed the case. In a strategy to avoid federal court, Shareholder voluntarily
      dismissed the RICO claim, and moved for remand back to State court. Instead, the
      California federal judge transferred the case to Illinois federal court, after which Corporation
      filed its answer. Stuck in federal court, Stockholder filed a motion to amend the complaint
      to add back the RICO claim.

      How will the court likely rule on this motion to amend?

      (A)   The court will deny the motion, deeming Stockholder's dismissal of the RICO claim
            as a dismissal with prejudice.

      (B)   The court will deny the motion, based on Stockholder's obvious attempts to
            manipulate jurisdiction.

      (C)   The court will deny the motion, because Stockholder's right to amend ended when
            Corporation filed its answer.

      (D)   The court will grant the motion, if Stockholder can demonstrate that Corporation will
            not be prejudiced by the amendment.

                                                              See ANSWER on Page 122

7.   Internet Company marketed and sold a line of residential air filters. Consumer purchased
      one of the filters, installed it, and then developed a debilitating lung illness traced to
      contaminated recirculating air. Consumer sued Internet Company for a defective product,
      and won a large judgment in State court. Internet Company sought to have the large
      judgment reviewed in the State appellate courts, but discovered the State had no
      intermediate court of appeals, and that all review by the State supreme court was
      discretionary by writ of certiorari. The State supreme court subsequently denied Internet
      Company's petition to review the judgment for error.

      If Internet Company challenges this State's appellate judicial structure under the U.S.
      Constitution as a denial of its federal due process rights, what is likely to happen?

      (A)   Internet Company will lose because the federal Due Process Clause does not
            guarantee any right of appeal in the State courts.

      (B)   Internet Company will lose because, although the federal Due Process Clause
            guarantees appellate access in the State courts, that guarantee is satisfied by the
            possibility of discretionary appellate review in the supreme court, even if, as here,
            that access is denied on petition.

      (C)   Internet Company will win because the federal Due Process Clause guarantees every
            civil litigant access to at least one appellate review.

      (D)   Internet Company will win because the federal Due Process Clause guarantees every
            civil litigant access to an appellate court of error, even if access to the State's court
            of last resort is discretionary.

                                                              See ANSWER on Page 122

8. Vendor Supply Company was a partnership that sold napkins, towels, and other paper products. One of its customers was Widgets Corporation, a business that was incorporated under the laws of Delaware with its principal place of business in Houston, Texas. For non-payment on a delinquent invoice, Vendor Supplies Company sued Widget Corporation in Iowa federal court, alleging common law breach of contract. During trial, a witness testified for the first time that one of the general partners in Vendor Supply Company was a retired accountant who was domiciled in Dallas, Texas.

    Can Widget Corporation now have the lawsuit dismissed from federal court for lack of proper diversity?

    (A) No, because lack of jurisdiction is a defense that must be asserted early in the litigation through a pre-answer motion to dismiss.

    (B) No, because once the lawsuit commences, the interests of judicial economy are best served by allowing the case to proceed to judgment in federal court.

    (C) No, if through more probing discovery, Widget Corporation could have uncovered this fact earlier in the litigation.

    (D) Yes.

    See ANSWER on Page 122

9. Purchaser bought a rural farmhouse in Kentucky which sat on 100 acres of farmable land. Purchaser intended to live in the farmhouse and earn a living by growing wheat. Next door to Purchaser's land, however, was a 50-acre tract used by a Kentucky county as a solar array farm to generate municipal electricity. Purchaser complained to the county that the intense brightness generated by the solar farm was adversely impacting the farming of his land. The county refused to close down its solar farm, and advised Purchaser that the prior owner of his land (the party who sold the land to Purchaser) had years earlier litigated a nuisance claim against the county solar farm and lost.

    Is a lawsuit by Purchaser against the county to obtain a removal of the solar array barred by the doctrine of claim preclusion?

    (A) Yes, if the first litigation was resolved by a trial on the merits, but not if it was resolved on a motion for summary judgment.

    (B) No, if the basis for the first litigation was excessive brightness during morning hours, and Purchaser's litigation challenges excessive brightness during afternoon hours.

    (C) No, if the basis for the first litigation was excessive brightness from five-foot wide panels, and Purchaser's litigation challenges excessive brightness from recently installed fifteen-foot panels.

    (D) Yes, but only if Purchaser was personally involved in the first litigation.

    See ANSWER on Page 123

10. Restaurant LLC is a limited liability company that owned and operated an Italian restaurant in San Antonio, Texas. This San Antonio eatery was the LLC's sole asset, and all managers and employees are Texas citizens. The LLC was, in turn, owned jointly by two people (the first who was a citizen of Texas and the second who was a citizen of Louisiana) and a corporation (which was incorporated in Delaware and had its principal place of business in Texas). When business slowed at the Italian restaurant, the LLC had financial difficulties. Several months later, Pasta Co. sued the LLC in federal district court in Texas for $75,000 in unpaid invoices. Pasta Co. was incorporated in California with a principal place of business in Oregon.

Can the federal district court in Texas exercise diversity jurisdiction over Restaurant LLC in this dispute?

(A) Yes, because Restaurant LLC is a citizen of Texas, and Pasta Co. is a citizen of both California and Oregon.

(B) Yes, because Restaurant LLC is a citizen of Texas, Louisiana, and Delaware, and Pasta Co. is a citizen of California and Oregon.

(C) Yes, if Restaurant LLC was organized under the laws of a State other than California and Oregon.

(D) No.

See ANSWER on Page 124

11. Employees worked in a poultry factory, and were represented there by Union, which had negotiated a collective bargaining agreement with Factory. Construing such agreements is a task governed by federal labor laws. The collective bargaining agreement provided that Employees were to be compensated on the basis of "hours worked." Factory paid Employees for hours worked only when the poultry assembly line was running; Union insisted that Employees be paid for all hours when they were at the line ready to work, regardless of whether the assembly line was running or had been shut down. Union brought suit in federal court. Because the language of the collective bargaining agreement was imprecise on the issue, the federal court was tasked to interpret whether the language of agreement favored the Factory's interpretation or the Union's interpretation. The Union argued that the court ought to follow local State contract law in interpreting Factory's wage obligations; Factory contended that the court must create a body of federal common law to resolve this wage dispute.

What law should the federal court apply to resolve the Union's challenge?

(A) Apply federal common law.

(B) Apply State law because there is no such thing as federal common law.

(C) Apply State law because its principles would readily resolve the dispute.

(D) Apply State law because the federal courts may not create common law.

See ANSWER on Page 124

12. Homeowner lived near a chemical manufacturing plant operated by Chemical Co. Chemical Co.'s operations resulted in elevated levels of chemicals in the groundwater. Homeowner sued Chemical Co. in federal court, alleging that he was harmed by exposure to these chemicals, and requested a jury trial. At jury selection, Homeowner's counsel decided that she wanted highly educated jurors if possible. During voir dire, one of the prospective jurors stated that he had not graduated from high school. Homeowner's counsel did not want this person on the jury.

Which of the following is the most accurate statement regarding the selection process?

(A) Homeowner can likely strike the prospective juror for cause.

(B) Homeowner can exercise a peremptory strike of the prospective juror.

(C) Homeowner cannot exercise a peremptory strike of the prospective juror because it is unconstitutional to exercise peremptory strikes in a discriminatory manner.

(D) The court will allow Homeowner to exercise a peremptory strike of the prospective juror if, in the court's discretion, Homeowner articulates a proper basis for exercising the strike.

See ANSWER on Page 125

13. Employees filed a complaint in federal court against Employer, contending that Employer was providing an inhumane workplace, seeking prospective injunctive relief and money damages for their past suffering. Employer filed an answer, denying the claims. At about the same time, Employer announced plans to make improvements in the workplace and working conditions and began implementing some of those improvements. Employees decided they did not want to pursue the claim in light of the planned improvements, but wanted to preserve the right to commence another action asserting the same claims if Employer did not follow through with all of the promised improvements. Employees asked Employer to agree to a dismissal of the lawsuit without prejudice, but Employer responded that it would only agree to dismissal with prejudice.

Which of the following describes Employees' best option?

(A) Employees can voluntarily dismiss the action by filing a notice of dismissal.

(B) Employees can voluntarily dismiss the action by filing a stipulation of dismissal.

(C) Employees can file a motion for voluntary dismissal.

(D) Employees can file a motion for involuntary dismissal.

See ANSWER on Page 125

14. Process Server was hired to serve Ms. Defendant with a summons and complaint. Process Server subsequently learned that Ms. Defendant and her Husband were staying at a nearby hotel for the past 11 months while she was working as a consultant for a local project. The couple maintained their domicile in another State and intended to return there when her assignment concluded. One afternoon, Process Server located their hotel room and knocked on the door. Husband answered the door, and Process Server handed him the summons and complaint.

Has Process Server properly served Ms. Defendant?

(A) Yes, because this constitutes proper service.

(B) No, because the hotel is not Ms. Defendant's permanent residence or place of dwelling.

(C) No, because proper service requires in-hand or personal service on the defendant if possible, and Process Server has not demonstrated that personal service was not possible.

(D) No, because the Constitution requires that service be "reasonably calculated" to provide notice to the defendant.

See ANSWER on Page 126

15. Employee sued Employer for age discrimination, arguing that he was replaced by a younger, less qualified worker. Employee filed a properly supported motion for summary judgment. Employer responded with a brief supported by affidavits indicating that 27% of Employer's employees are over the age of 40, and arguing that the court must draw the inference from that data that Employer does not discriminate on the basis of age.

How will the court likely rule on this motion?

(A) The court will deny the motion because Employer has opposed the motion properly by citing to record evidence creating a genuine dispute of material fact.

(B) The court will deny the motion because the court will draw all inferences from the evidence in favor of the nonmoving party.

(C) The court will grant the motion because Employer has not submitted sufficient evidence to create a genuine dispute of material fact.

(D) The court will grant the motion because allegations in affidavits are not record evidence, and Employer would need documents or deposition testimony to properly oppose the motion.

See ANSWER on Page 126

16. Seaman worked on a barge operated by Shipping Co. After being diagnosed with leukemia, Seaman sued Shipping Co. for negligence in federal court, alleging that Shipping Co. exposed him to asbestos and to other non-asbestos hazardous chemicals which, in combination, caused his leukemia. 120 days after Shipping Co. filed its answer, Seaman filed a motion for leave to file an amended complaint to eliminate all references to asbestos and to identify benzene exposure during the same employment for Shipping Co. as the cause of his leukemia. The date for amending pleadings in the court's case management order had passed. Assume the statute of limitations for Seaman's negligence claims ran 10 days after he filed the original complaint.

Will the court likely grant the motion?

(A) Yes, if Seaman can demonstrate good cause.

(B) Yes, unless Shipping Co. can demonstrate prejudice.

(C) No, because the statute of limitations has passed for the benzene-related negligence claim.

(D) No, because allegations of benzene exposure present an entirely different "case or controversy" from allegations of exposure to asbestos.

See ANSWER on Page 127

17. Vacationer slipped and fell down the main staircase while walking to dinner on a cruise ship. In a subsequent lawsuit against Cruise Line, Vacationer won a large verdict. Cruise Line intends to appeal.

Can Vacationer execute on the money judgment it won against Cruise Line?

(A) Yes, because execution is never stayed pending a civil appeal.

(B) Yes, but not during the first 30 days following entry of the judgment.

(C) No, all execution is stayed automatically throughout the pendency of a civil appeal.

(D) No, because a reversal on appeal would obligate Cruise Line to pursue Vacationer for repayment of the now-vacated judgment.

See ANSWER on Page 128

18. Consumer, who sustained disfiguring facial burns while using cosmetics, brought a products liability claim against the cosmetics' Manufacturer in federal court.

Which of the following will the Federal Rules of Civil Procedure require Manufacturer to supply to Consumer during the pretrial stage of this litigation?

(A) Preliminary drafts of a report by a testifying expert that contain written critiques by Manufacturer's attorney.

(B) Summaries of the expert opinions held by a long-time employee of Manufacturer that are expected to be presented as testimony at trial.

(C) Opinions by a scientist who has been specially retained by Manufacturer to offer consultative guidance on defeating Consumer's lawsuit.

(D) Identity of a Nobel-laureate biologist who, after study, declined Manufacturer's invitation to serve as a testifying expert because he concluded that Consumer's theory of injury was scientifically correct.

See ANSWER on Page 129

19. Parents brought their child to Hospital for medical care, and contended that the care the child received there was negligent. Parents sued Hospital in federal district court. Hospital was a sprawling 500-bed institution, operating in the same location in the same city for more than 100 years. Aware that Hospital was unlikely to attempt to evade service, Parents proposed to Hospital a waiver of formal service of process.

Which of the following is true about using that procedure in federal court?

(A) If Hospital agrees to waive, it will receive an additional 39 days to answer the complaint.

(B) By asking Hospital to waive, Parents ensure that they will avoid the need to serve original process through formal, traditional means.

(C) A waiver by Hospital forecloses its ability to assert any objections it might otherwise have both to the manner of service and to personal jurisdiction.

(D) For the waiver to be effective, it must be delivered to Hospital accompanied by copies of both the complaint and summons.

See ANSWER on Page 129

20. Roofer was balancing on the top rung of a ladder when the ladder collapsed. Roofer sued Ladder Co. in federal court. Ladder Co. submitted a proposed jury instruction to the court asking for a contributory negligence instruction. Prior to closing arguments, the court met on the record with the parties and provided them with a copy of the court's jury instructions, which did not include a contributory negligence instruction. After the jury returned a verdict in favor of Roofer, Ladder Co. moved for a new trial based on the court's failure to give the contributory negligence instruction. The court denied the motion, and Ladder Co. then filed a timely notice of appeal.

Did Ladder Co. properly preserve the right to appeal this issue?

(A) No, because Ladder Co. waived the issue by failing to object to the omission of the instruction before the court read the instructions to the jury and closing arguments.

(B) No, because content of the jury instructions is left to the "sound discretion" of the trial court, and is not normally reviewable on appeal.

(C) Yes, because Ladder Co. submitted a timely written request for the proposed instruction, and the court denied that request when it omitted that instruction from its written instructions.

(D) Yes, because Ladder Co. preserved the issue in its motion for a new trial.

See ANSWER on Page 130

21. Homeowner was injured when he received an electrical shock when using a hedge clipper manufactured by Hedgeclipper, Inc. Homeowner brought a products liability claim against Hedgeclipper, Inc. in federal court, alleging that the clippers were defectively designed. At trial, Homeowner offered evidence regarding the warnings that Hedgeclipper, Inc. included with the clippers, and this evidence was admitted without objection. Homeowner then asked the judge to submit a failure to warn instruction to the jury, and Hedgeclipper, Inc. responded that neither the complaint nor the final pretrial order mentioned failure to warn.

How would the court likely rule?

(A) The court would refuse to give the failure to warn jury instruction because Homeowner failed to seek leave to amend the complaint.

(B) The court would refuse to give the failure to warn jury instruction because the issue was not contained in the final pretrial order.

(C) The court would refuse to give the failure to warn jury instruction if Hedgeclipper, Inc. demonstrated it would be prejudiced by the instruction.

(D) The court would give the failure to warn jury instruction because Hedgeclipper, Inc. failed to object to the evidence.

See ANSWER on Page 130

22. Grandparents owned a vacation home in Malibu, California. When Grandparents died, Son and Daughter fought over ownership of the vacation home. Son was a citizen of Nevada; Daughter was a citizen of Oregon. Son filed an *in rem* lawsuit in federal court in California to have the Malibu home's lawful owner properly determined.

Can the federal district court in California hear the *in rem* lawsuit?

(A) Yes, *in rem* lawsuits are proper in federal court if the property is seized at any time while the lawsuit is pending and brought under the control of the court.

(B) Yes, *in rem* lawsuits are proper in federal court if reasonable efforts to acquire *in personam* jurisdiction have first failed.

(C) No, *in rem* lawsuits are not proper in federal court unless a federal statute authorizes such jurisdiction expressly.

(D) No, *in rem* lawsuits are not proper in federal court unless *in personam* jurisdiction is also proper.

See ANSWER on Page 131

23. Truck Co. owned a fleet of commercial tractor-trailer trucks. One of its trucks weaved into oncoming traffic on the highway, causing a collision with a sightseeing tour bus. Many bus passengers were critically injured. Truck Co. was insured by Reliable Insurer, but for modest policy limits of $200,000. Truck Co. and Reliable Insurer were both citizens of New York. The injured bus passengers were citizens of Pennsylvania, New Jersey, New York, Connecticut, and Maryland.

Can Reliable Insurer force all bus passengers who intend to assert a claim against the $200,000 insurance policy into a single federal lawsuit invoking the court's diversity jurisdiction? Assume Reliable Insurer is prepared to tender the full policy limits without opposition.

(A) A Rule-based joinder of these claims is unlikely, but a statutory-based joinder of the claims is likely.

(B) A Rule-based joinder of these claims is likely, but a statutory-based joinder of the claims is unlikely.

(C) Both a Rule-based and a statutory-based joinder of these claims are likely.

(D) Both a Rule-based and a statutory-based joinder of these claims are unlikely.

See ANSWER on Page 131

24. Outfitters rented personal watercraft to guests staying at local resorts in Hawai'i. Vacationer rented a jet-ski personal watercraft, operated it recklessly, and crashed into an outcropping of coral. He was injured seriously in the accident, and later filed a diversity action in federal court against Outfitters for negligent failure to impart proper operating instructions. During jury selection, Vacationer noticed that all of the prospective jurors were men and, consequently, none of the jurors ultimately empaneled were women.

What is Vacationer's best fact in arguing that this exclusion of women was unlawful?

(A) He has none, because he is not a female.

(B) He was unable to enhance the female representation on his jury through the use of peremptory strikes.

(C) The twelve persons empaneled to serve as his jury contained no women, even though the jury-eligible population of Hawai'i is 52% female.

(D) The four hundred persons summoned for jury duty on the day of his trial contained no women, even though the jury-eligible population of Hawai'i is 52% female.

See ANSWER on Page 132

25. Skier was a citizen of Georgia, and traveled to Resort in Colorado for a skiing vacation. Skier suffered a serious spinal injury when a Resort employee inattentively ran over him in a snowmobile. Skier brought suit in Georgia State court against Resort for personal injuries.

If Resort removes this litigation to federal court, a jury trial will not be convened in which of the following circumstances?

(A) If the pleadings had closed in State court, Resort then removed the case, and Resort served its jury demand 21 days thereafter.

(B) If Skier properly demanded a jury trial in his State court complaint, but neither party filed a later demand for a jury trial in federal court following the removal.

(C) If Skier's complaint contained no jury demand, was removed prior to Resort's answer being filed, and Skier waited until 10 days after Resort's answer was served before serving his jury demand.

(D) If no demand was ever filed in State court because Georgia practice requires no such demand in personal injury lawsuits because they all receive jury trials automatically.

See ANSWER on Page 133

26. Executive commissioned Painter to paint her portrait after seeing his work at an arts festival in Florida. Executive was unhappy with the portrait when she received it, and refused to pay for it. Painter recalled that Executive told him she traveled to Austin, Texas (where Painter lived) to attend a music festival each year. Shortly before the festival, Painter filed a complaint in Texas State court, then hired a process server to locate and serve Executive while she was attending the festival in Austin. Executive was so served. Executive later filed a motion to dismiss on the grounds that the Texas courts did not have personal jurisdiction over her. Assume that the Texas long-arm statute authorized jurisdiction to the full extent allowed by the United States Constitution, and that Executive's only contacts with Texas are her annual vacation trips to Austin.

How will the court likely rule?

(A) The court will likely grant the motion because Painter's claims are unrelated to Executive's contacts with Texas.

(B) The court will likely grant the motion because Executive's annual trips to Texas are not sufficiently regular and systematic.

(C) The court will likely deny the motion because Executive's annual trips to Texas are sufficiently regular and systematic.

(D) The court will likely deny the motion because Executive was served while in Texas.

See ANSWER on Page 134

27. Patient sued Doctor for medical malpractice in federal court under the court's diversity jurisdiction. As part of a statute intended to curtail frivolous medical malpractice actions, the applicable State's law requires that a plaintiff submit a certification of merit from a licensed medical doctor at the time the plaintiff files a medical malpractice action. Assume neither the Federal Rules of Civil Procedure nor any federal statute or federal common law imposes such a precondition.

Will the federal court apply the requirement of a certification of merit?

(A) Yes, because the certification prerequisite is more properly seen as a limitation on the substantive rights of the parties, not the manner and means of pursuing those rights.

(B) Yes, because, in the absence of a federal provision addressing an issue, federal courts always turn to State law to supply the governing law.

(C) Yes, because a federal court hearing a State law claim always applies all applicable State law.

(D) Yes, because a filing requirement is in the nature of procedure, not substantive law.

See ANSWER on Page 135

28. Customer opened a large savings account deposit at Bank several years ago. When Customer later died, the attorney hired to probate Customer's estate withdrew all funds on deposit. Shortly thereafter, Bank notified the attorney that a 10% service charge should have been imposed on the deposited funds, and demanded payment of the new charge. The basis for Bank's charge was a technical misstep made by Customer at the time the account was first opened years earlier. When the attorney refused to pay the charge, Bank brought suit in federal court. Contending that Customer's estate had no defense to liability for the charge, Bank filed for summary judgment. The trial judge denied Bank's motion, and further, upon reviewing the summary judgment record, discovered that Customer's estate was entitled to summary judgment on a statute of limitations defense pleaded in the answer. Although no summary judgment motion had been filed on behalf of Customer's estate, the judge entered summary judgment for the estate.

How is the Court of Appeals likely to rule when Bank appeals the trial court's decision to enter summary judgment in favor of Customer's estate?

(A) Affirm the grant of summary judgment, because the statute of limitations defense qualified as a material fact in the litigation.

(B) Affirm the grant of summary judgment, because the standards for entering summary judgment are relaxed when the motion is raised by the court itself.

(C) Reverse the grant of summary judgment, because Customer's estate never actually filed a motion seeking entry of summary judgment.

(D) Reverse the grant of summary judgment, because the trial judge did not forewarn Bank that an entry of summary judgment for Customer's estate was being considered.

See ANSWER on Page 136

29. Orchestra entered into a contract with Violinist, a famous musician, to play with Orchestra for five seasons. In the middle of the second season, Violinist refused to perform, stating publicly that Orchestra's music director and conductor were "incompetent philistines." Orchestra sued Violinist in federal court for defamation and for specific performance of the contract. Ten days after filing her answer to the complaint, Violinist filed and served a jury trial demand.

Does Violinist have a right to a jury trial?

(A) Yes, as to both claims.

(B) Yes, as to the defamation claim but not as to the contract claim.

(C) Yes, as to the contract claim but not as to the defamation claim.

(D) No, as to both claims.

See ANSWER on Page 136

30. Two business partners operated a field of gas wells, but a disagreement arose over daily pumping practices. Partner A sued Partner B in federal court in Oklahoma. Partner A hired Process Server to accomplish proper service. Process Server obtained a copy of Partner A's complaint, placed that document in a large white envelope, then sealed the envelope shut. Process Server discovered that Partner B owned a farmhouse in rural Oklahoma where he lived with his spouse and three children. On the property was an old barn, which Partner B had since converted into a recreation room with spare bedroom and bath. One day, while Partner B was shooting pool with his children in the barn, Process Server arrived, confirmed Partner B's identity, and then handed him the large white envelope.

Was Partner B served properly in accordance with the Federal Rules of Civil Procedure?

(A) Yes, because he was served by personal delivery.

(B) Yes, because the location of service qualifies as a usual place of abode.

(C) Yes, because service was made upon an adult of suitable age and discretion residing there.

(D) No.

See ANSWER on Page 137

31. Which of the following characteristics are not required of every lawsuit proposed to proceed in federal court as a class action?

(A) The parties who propose to serve as representative litigants will fairly and adequately protect the interests of the class.

(B) The claims or defenses of those representative litigants are typical of the claims or defenses of the class.

(C) Those questions of fact or law that are common to all class members predominate over those questions affecting only individual class members.

(D) The number of class members is so large that conventional joinder of each individual class member would be impracticable.

See ANSWER on Page 137

32. Inmate brought a civil rights action against Prison in federal court under 42 U.S.C. § 1983, claiming he did not receive proper medical care. Prison moved for summary judgment, arguing that Inmate did not have sufficient evidence to establish deliberate indifference, the standard for this type of prisoner civil rights action. The court denied the motion, finding genuine disputes as to material facts. At trial, Prison made a Rule 50 motion at the close of Inmate's case, and the court denied the motion, ruling that Inmate had introduced sufficient evidence to support the claim. Prison renewed the Rule 50 motion at the conclusion of all testimony and evidence, which the court denied. The jury returned a verdict in favor of Inmate, and Prison appealed, contending on appeal that the evidence presented at trial did not satisfy the requirements for deliberate indifference.

Will the appellate court hear the appeal?

(A) Yes, because Prison preserved the issue by filing a Rule 56 motion for summary judgment.

(B) Yes, because Prison preserved the issue by filing a Rule 50 motion after Inmate had been fully heard on the issue.

(C) Yes, because Prison preserved the issue by renewing its Rule 50 motion at the close of the record.

(D) No, because Prison failed to renew the Rule 50 motion again after trial.

See ANSWER on Page 138

33. Which of the following best describes the relationship between a State long-arm statute and the personal jurisdiction analysis under the U.S. Constitution's Due Process Clause when a matter is proceeding in a State court?

(A) They are separate analyses that both affect whether a defendant will be required to come defend a claim in that State.

(B) If the plaintiff can satisfy either the State long-arm statute or the constitutional personal jurisdiction requirements, the defendant will be required to come defend a claim in the State.

(C) Although they are both required, satisfaction of the State long-arm statute will ensure satisfaction of constitutional requirements.

(D) Although they are both required, satisfaction of the constitutional requirements will ensure satisfaction of the State long-arm statute.

See ANSWER on Page 138

34. Power Plant emitted particulate matter that was settling on the property of neighboring homeowners, including Homeowner and Neighbor. Homeowner brought an action in federal court against Power Plant seeking an injunction prohibiting emissions of particulate matter above a specified concentration. Power Plant successfully moved for summary judgment, arguing that Homeowner lacked the expert testimony that was required to support her claims. Homeowner then approached Neighbor, who agreed to file another action in the same court seeking the same relief, this time with a qualified expert. Neighbor engaged the lawyer who had represented Homeowner, and Homeowner consulted with Neighbor and the lawyer as to strategy for the second action. Power Plant moved to dismiss the second action, asserting the doctrine of claim preclusion.

How will the court likely rule on Power Plant's motion?

(A) The court will grant the motion based on the collusion between Homeowner and Neighbor.

(B) The court will grant the motion because the elements of claim preclusion are present.

(C) The court will deny the motion because Neighbor's claim was not litigated in Homeowner's action.

(D) The court will deny the motion because the first action was not decided on the merits, but instead was decided on the lack of expert testimony.

See ANSWER on Page 139

35. Fracking Company drilled a well near Homeowner's property. Homeowner believed her drinking water was contaminated as a result of Fracking Company's hydraulic fracturing activities. She brought a suit in federal court claiming that hydraulic fracturing is an abnormally dangerous activity. Assume no case precedent in the State where she lives addresses whether hydraulic fracturing is an abnormally dangerous activity, but the only three other States to have considered the issue have rejected the claim.

Has Homeowner's attorney violated Rule 11?

(A) No, because Fracking Company did not provide Homeowner with 21-days' notice as required by Rule 11's safe harbor provision.

(B) No, if Homeowner has a nonfrivolous argument for establishing new law.

(C) No, because Homeowner's attorney has a duty to zealously represent her client.

(D) Yes, if there is no legal authority in any State supporting Homeowner's claim.

See ANSWER on Page 139

36. Contractor was constructing a building for Owner. During the project, Owner and Contractor discussed a variety of changes to the design of the building. At the end of the project, Contractor provided Owner with an invoice that included substantial additional charges based on these changes. Owner denied ever having agreed to a change order and refused to pay. Contractor sued Owner in a State that has adopted the Federal Rules of Civil Procedure as its State procedural rules, asserting in Count I a claim for breach of contract relating to the contractual change orders, and in Count II a claim for unjust enrichment. Assume that unjust enrichment claims only exist in the absence of a contract under this State's laws. Owner filed a motion to dismiss, arguing that Contractor cannot pursue two inconsistent claims and must elect one or the other.

How will the court likely rule on this motion?

(A) The court will grant the motion because, under Rule 11, Contractor cannot assert two inconsistent claims in good faith.

(B) The court will grant the motion because, under the doctrine of "election of remedies," Contractor must choose between these claims.

(C) The court will deny the motion because federal courts use "notice pleading."

(D) The court will deny the motion because the two claims are alternative.

See ANSWER on Page 140

37. A deep forest divided the boundaries between State X and State Y, and the center contained a park. The park encompassed land of both States. The park was privately owned by ParkCo. A running path was paved through the park. To ensure the safety of park visitors, ParkCo hired Electric Company to install overhead lights. As Electric Company began its work, it cordoned off the construction site with "Caution—DO NOT ENTER" signs and yellow warning tape. One evening, Jogger ran through the park, encountered the signs and tape, ignored them, and proceeded to run through the active construction site. Jogger was electrocuted upon stepping on several "live" electrical wires. Jogger's estate filed a diversity action in federal court against ParkCo and Electric Company for negligence. Because Jogger proceeded into an area cordoned off from public use, State X's substantive laws would consider Jogger a "limited trespasser," to whom a duty is owed to avoid wanton and willful conduct. Conversely, State Y's substantive laws would consider Jogger a "full trespasser," to whom a duty is owed to avoid wanton and willful conduct. It was uncertain whether Jogger was injured in the portion of the park lying within State X or within State Y.

Which substantive law will the federal court apply to adjudicate the claim of Jogger's estate?

(A) The court will not resolve the conflict between the laws of State X and State Y.

(B) The court will resolve the conflict between the laws of State X and State Y by choosing the law it considers the most fair.

(C) The court will resolve the conflict between the laws of State X and State Y by applying the law of the State that was the actual situs of injury.

(D) The court will resolve the conflict between the laws of State X and State Y by applying the law of the State with the most significant relationship.

See ANSWER on Page 140

38. Vacationer was staying at a spa owned by Resort Co. Vacationer developed food poisoning during her stay, and published an article stating that Resort Co. did not properly refrigerate and clean its food. Resort Co. sued Vacationer for defamation in federal court, contending that the article had caused Resort Co. to lose more than $100,000 in revenue. The federal court properly exercised diversity jurisdiction over the action. Vacationer filed a counterclaim with two claims: one for negligence in connection with the food poisoning seeking $5,000, and one for breach of contract seeking a refund of the $100 fee she paid for a hot mud bath at an earlier visit to a different Resort Co. property because the mud was neither hot nor therapeutic.

    Can Vacationer maintain her counterclaim related to the hot mud bath?

    (A) Yes, because federal procedure allows joinder of the claim, even if it does not arise out of the same transaction or occurrence or series of transactions or occurrences.

    (B) No, because federal procedure does not allow joinder of the claim because it does not arise out of the same transaction or occurrence or series of transactions or occurrences.

    (C) Yes, because the court can exercise supplemental jurisdiction over the hot mud bath claim.

    (D) No, because the court cannot exercise supplemental or diversity jurisdiction over the hot mud bath claim.

    See ANSWER on Page 141

39. Patient took aspirin for a headache, and subsequently suffered from aspirin-induced stomach ulcers. Patient sued Drug Company in federal court for failure to warn of the ulcer-related risks of taking aspirin. Drug Company moved for summary judgment, arguing that Patient lacked any evidence that could show that the particular aspirin he ingested was manufactured by Drug Company (rather than some other drug supplier).

    In resolving Drug Company's motion, how should the district court rule?

    (A) Grant the motion, if Patient responds by citing to those portions of the complaint where Patient alleges Drug Company's liability.

    (B) Deny the motion, if the substance of Patient's response leaves the court with the opinion that Patient is likely to lose at trial.

    (C) Grant the motion, if Patient offers only one witness to support the complaint's allegations, and Drug Company offers eight witnesses opposing those allegations.

    (D) Deny the motion, unless Drug Company first supports its motion papers with evidence that Patient was injured by some other manufacturer's aspirin.

    See ANSWER on Page 141

40. Anyone who wanted to operate a restaurant bearing the Restaurant Chain name had to enter into a form franchise agreement with Restaurant Chain. The franchisees formed an association to increase their bargaining power. Concerned that Restaurant Chain was retaliating against members of the association, some of the franchisees filed suits against Restaurant Chain alleging breach of the cooperation clause of the form franchise agreement. The first two such actions ended in summary judgments against the franchisees, but the third resulted in a summary judgment against Restaurant Chain, finding as a matter of law that Restaurant Chain's conduct violated the form franchise agreement. Franchisee Four, who had already filed her own action against Restaurant Chain, then moved for summary judgment asserting issue preclusion against Restaurant Chain.

Will the trial court preclude Restaurant Chain from contesting whether its conduct violated the cooperation clause of the form franchise agreement?

(A) Yes, because the elements of issue preclusion are satisfied.

(B) Yes, if the court, in its discretion, decides to apply issue preclusion.

(C) No, if either party had filed a jury trial demand.

(D) No, because offensive issue preclusion is prohibited.

See ANSWER on Page 142

41. Homeowners' Association filed a federal lawsuit against Insurance Company for bad faith failure to pay a claim made against a policy it issued to Homeowners' Association. As a litigation strategy, the attorney for Insurance Company chose to file a motion for judgment on the pleadings, instead of an answer to the Homeowners' Association complaint.

Does the attorney's strategy conform to the Federal Rules of Civil Procedure?

(A) Yes, because the legal standard for testing a complaint against a pre-answer motion to dismiss would likely be the same as a pre-answer motion for judgment on the pleadings.

(B) Yes, because an early testing of the pleadings could result in a dismissal of the lawsuit in its entirety.

(C) No, because the answer must be filed before any motion for judgment on the pleadings could be proper.

(D) No, because no motion for judgment on the pleadings is proper until discovery has first been completed.

See ANSWER on Page 142

42. Contractor was the general contractor for a housing development. Subcontractor provided all of the concrete for the foundations and driveways. The job fell behind schedule, and after it was completed, Developer sued Contractor in federal court for damages caused by the delay. Developer was a citizen of Vermont, Contractor was a citizen of New Hampshire, and the dispute involved $750,000. Contractor then filed a third-party complaint against Subcontractor, a citizen of Maine, asserting that Subcontractor had padded its invoices and owed Contractor $250,000.

Is Contractor's claim against Subcontractor properly before the court?

(A) Yes, because Contractor's claim against Subcontractor arises out of the same transaction or occurrence or series of transactions or occurrences as Developer's claim against Contractor.

(B) Yes, because the court has original jurisdiction over Contractor's claim against subcontractor.

(C) No, because Subcontractor's alleged liability is not derivative of Contractor's alleged liability to Developer.

(D) No, because Contractor should have filed a crossclaim against Subcontractor.

See ANSWER on Page 143

43. A tourist from Minnesota spent a week vacationing in Savannah, Georgia. While there, she contracted food poisoning from eating shellfish at a local Savannah restaurant. Upon returning home, the tourist filed a personal injury lawsuit against the Savannah restaurant in Minnesota federal court. The tourist hired a Georgia process server, who delivered the summons and complaint to a busy waiter at the restaurant.

Which of the following is not a proper method for challenging the validity of this service of process?

(A) Filing a pre-answer motion in Minnesota federal court to dismiss the lawsuit for insufficient service of process.

(B) Filing a pre-answer motion in Minnesota federal court to quash the attempted service of process as insufficient.

(C) Filing a pre-answer motion in Minnesota federal court on other grounds, and later filing an answer asserting insufficient service of process as a defense.

(D) Filing no pre-answer motion in Minnesota federal court at all, and instead pleading insufficient service of process as a defense in the answer.

See ANSWER on Page 143

44. TourCo operated a sightseeing bus for tourists in Europe. It is a corporation organized under the laws of Great Britain with its principal and sole place of business in London. TourCo purchased limited advertising space in the *New York Times* Sunday newspaper. Passengers were all retired citizens of Montreal, Canada on an excursion through Europe. They approached TourCo's offices in London, negotiated a group bus rate, and then contracted for TourCo to provide them with two days of sightseeing services. While speeding out to a visit at the Houses of Parliament in London, the TourCo bus crashed over a bridge railing and plummeted twenty feet to an underpass roadway below. The negligent operation of the bus and the plunge off the bridge were witnessed by scores of London bystanders. Passengers were all injured in the accident. Passengers filed a lawsuit against TourCo in federal court in Buffalo, New York. TourCo filed a motion opposing venue in Buffalo.

How is the federal court most likely to rule on TourCo's venue motion?

(A) It may dismiss the case in Buffalo.

(B) It can transfer the case to the London courts because that is where the bus accident occurred.

(C) It must not change the venue if British negligence law is less friendly to the bus passengers than New York negligence law.

(D) It may not grant the motion because the bus passenger plaintiffs all chose to litigate in Buffalo federal court.

See ANSWER on Page 144

45. Engineer brought an infringement claim under federal patent laws in federal court in Kentucky. Assume that under Kentucky law, treble damages are available for any willful and wanton theft of intellectual property. Assume that the federal patent statute contains a list of categories of damages that neither includes, nor expressly excludes, treble damages.

Will the federal court allow Engineer to pursue a claim for treble damages?

(A) Yes, because the federal statute does not exclude treble damages as a recoverable category of damages, which then requires the court to import the damages limitations from State law.

(B) Yes, because the availability of an item of damages is a matter of substantive law.

(C) No, because the federal statute does not include treble damages as a recoverable category of damages.

(D) No, because damages are a procedural issue, not a substantive issue.

See ANSWER on Page 144

46. Italian Glass Blowers created a line of artistic glassware available for purchase through an Internet site. Purchaser discovered the Internet site one day while browsing for glass bowls from his home in Kentucky. While on the site, he ordered a distinctive bowl from Italian Glass Blowers, and then paid via direct withdrawal from his bank account. When the bowl arrived damaged, Purchaser demanded a refund. Italian Glass Blowers refused. Purchaser sued Italian Glass Blowers in Kentucky federal court, invoking national-contacts personal jurisdiction under Federal Rule of Civil Procedure 4(k)(2).

Which of the following facts would defeat Purchaser's attempt to have the Kentucky federal court exercise national-contacts personal jurisdiction over Italian Glass Blowers?

(A) Italian Glass Blowers is being sued for violating a federal law setting minimum standards for any glassware sold in the United States.

(B) Italian Glass Blowers has no sales or marketing personnel stationed permanently in Kentucky.

(C) Italian Glass Blowers does not have sufficient contacts with Kentucky to allow its courts to exercise specific personal jurisdiction there.

(D) Italian Glass Blowers has sufficient minimum contacts with Montana to allow for the exercise of personal jurisdiction there.

See ANSWER on Page 145

47. Employee brought an employment age discrimination claim against Employer in federal court. At trial, Employer sought to introduce into evidence an email that Employee had written to a competitor offering to sell Employer's trade secrets. Employee objected that Employer had not disclosed the email during discovery, despite the fact that it was plainly responsive to a properly served request to inspect. Employer responded that it had only located the email after the close of discovery.

How would the court likely rule on Employee's objection?

(A) The court would exclude the email only if it concludes that the email's prejudicial value outweighs its probative value.

(B) The court would exclude the email because exclusion is the automatic sanction for failure to disclose evidence unless the failure was substantially justified or harmless.

(C) The court would admit the email because Employee failed to file a motion to compel or a motion for sanctions prior to trial.

(D) The court would admit the email because Employee should not be heard to complain about unfair surprise in connection with her own email.

See ANSWER on Page 146

48. Citizen sued the Mayor in federal court. Mayor filed a motion to dismiss for failure to state a claim under Rule 12(b)(6), attaching as an exhibit an affidavit setting forth facts that would establish immunity for Mayor.

    In addressing Mayor's Rule 12(b)(6) motion, may the court consider the affidavit as support for a dispositive ruling in favor of Mayor?

    (A) No, because a motion to dismiss under Rule 12 is limited to the face of the complaint.

    (B) No, unless Citizen admits that the allegations in the affidavit are true.

    (C) Yes, because the court can take judicial notice of the allegations in the affidavit.

    (D) Yes, if the court converts the motion to one under Rule 56.

    See ANSWER on Page 146

49. A State law negligence claim is pending in federal court in Oregon under the court's diversity jurisdiction. Assume that the Oregon Rules of Civil Procedure mandate that judges must give juries a copy of the jury instructions bound in an official Oregon "Jury Instructions" folder. Assume that the Federal Rules of Civil Procedure do not address the topic, but the federal judge handling the case, as a matter of her own standard chambers practice, typically provides her juries with a copy of the jury instructions fastened with just a staple.

    Must the federal judge, hearing this diversity case, provide a copy of the instructions to the jury bound in an Oregon "Jury Instructions" folder?

    (A) No, because this issue is not "outcome determinative."

    (B) Yes, because the manner of providing the jury instructions could be "outcome determinative."

    (C) No, because the Federal Rules of Civil Procedure do not address the issue.

    (D) Yes, because the Federal Rules of Civil Procedure do not address the issue.

    See ANSWER on Page 147

50. Auto Company hired Shipper to transport newly-manufactured cars to various national and international destinations. In the course of transport, numerous cars were damaged. Shipper resisted Auto Company's demand for reimbursement and the return of all vehicles, and Auto Company sued Shipper in federal district court. In the course of that litigation, the district court ruled against Auto Company on several contested orders.

    Based on these facts only, which of the following orders by the district judge could Auto Company immediately appeal to the federal court of appeals, without waiting until the conclusion of the litigation?

    (A) An order directing the production, in discovery, of a document Auto Company believes to be attorney-client privileged.

    (B) An order denying Auto Company's motion for a preliminary injunction against Shipper's continued possession of the cars.

    (C) An order denying Auto Company's motion for summary judgment against Shipper on all claims.

    (D) An order denying Auto Company's motion to join an additional defendant.

    See ANSWER on Page 147

51. Provided it was pleaded consistently with the obligations imposed by Rule 11, which of the following would constitute a proper response in an answer filed in federal court?

    (A) "Each and every single allegation in the plaintiff's complaint is hereby denied."

    (B) "Because discovery on this issue has not yet begun, no response to this allegation is required at this time."

    (C) "This allegation relates to a written document which speaks for itself."

    (D) "This allegation is neither admitted nor denied, and strict proof is demanded at time of trial."

    See ANSWER on Page 148

52. Photographer believed that Magazine was improperly using photographic images that were Photographer's intellectual property. Photographer filed suit against Magazine in federal court. The court established a 90-day period for discovery. After serving written discovery, and reviewing the documents and responses and taking some depositions, Photographer learned that Layout Editor's testimony was critical to establishing his claim. Photographer sought to subpoena Layout Editor for a deposition approximately 60 days into the discovery period, but learned that she was in Paris at a publishing convention. Shortly thereafter, Magazine filed a motion for summary judgment, contending that Photographer did not have sufficient evidence to establish his claim. Photographer requested that the court defer ruling on the summary judgment motion until he could conduct additional discovery.

    How will the court likely rule on this request?

    (A) The court will grant the request because Magazine filed its summary judgment motion prematurely by filing before the end of the discovery period.

    (B) The court will grant the request if it concludes that Photographer acted diligently.

    (C) The court will deny the motion because Rule 11 requires that Photographer have had full evidentiary support for his claim prior to signing and filing the complaint, and cannot use discovery as a "fishing expedition" to establish a claim.

    (D) The court will deny the motion because Photographer knew that the discovery period was 90 days long, and cannot wait until the end of the discovery period to seek necessary evidence.

    See ANSWER on Page 148

53. Rider, domiciled in North Dakota, was injured on a bicycle trip in Wyoming when his bicycle malfunctioned. The bicycle was manufactured by Bicycle Company. Rider purchased it from Store in South Dakota while on a business trip. Rider sued both Bicycle Company and Store in federal court in the District of North Dakota (the only district in that State). Bicycle Company was a Delaware corporation, with its principal place of business in Michigan; it had no activities or property in North Dakota. Store was a North Dakota corporation with its principal place of business in North Dakota. It was a retail chain, with sister stores in South Dakota.

Is venue proper in the District of North Dakota?

(A) Yes, because Rider resides in North Dakota.

(B) Yes, as to Store, but not as to Bicycle Company.

(C) No, because Bicycle Company is a citizen of Delaware and Michigan, not North Dakota.

(D) No, because Bicycle Company does not reside in North Dakota and the sale and accident occurred outside North Dakota.

See ANSWER on Page 149

54. Inventor created a new line of stuffed animals that became all the rage as the holiday shopping season approached. Toy Store contracted with Inventor to supply ten crates of the stuffed toys by October 1. Inventor, however, later signed a far more lucrative contract with Big Box Store for a hundred trailer loads of the stuffed toys, which pressed Inventor's production capabilities past their limits. Inventor was unable to perform for Toy Store until the following February, well past the optimal time for toy sales. Consequently, Toy Store sued Inventor in State court.

Under which circumstance would the Seventh Amendment to the U.S. Constitution guarantee Toy Store an entitlement to a trial by jury in this lawsuit?

(A) If it sued Inventor for common law breach of contract.

(B) If it sued Inventor for tortious breach of contract, but only if such a claim was recognized at common law in 1791.

(C) If it sued Inventor for money damages only, and not equitable relief.

(D) Never.

See ANSWER on Page 149

55. Child's parents are divorced; both are citizens of Tennessee. While on an extended business trip to Kentucky, Custodial Parent enrolled Child in Day Care Center. During an unsupervised playtime incident, Child fell, suffering a serious eye injury that resulted in permanent right-eye blindness.

To avoid a dismissal, what must Custodial Parent allege in a federal lawsuit against Day Care Center?

(A) Detailed factual allegations.

(B) A claim that, based on the pleaded facts, is at least possible.

(C) A demand for relief.

(D) A claim that the court believes will probably persuade the factfinder.

See ANSWER on Page 150

56. Angry Fireworks Corp. was incorporated in Delaware and, for many years, had its sole factory in Missouri. It sold fireworks to passing motorists along a busy Missouri highway. One summer, as they were traveling past the Angry Fireworks Co. factory, Parents stopped and purchased a set of fireworks to entertain their children. That same summer, Parents set off the fireworks near their home in Oklahoma, causing tragic injuries to their entire family. Parents hoped to sue Angry Fireworks Corp. in an Oklahoma court.

The U.S. Constitution would most likely permit Oklahoma to exercise general personal jurisdiction over Angry Fireworks Corp. if which of the following were true?

(A) A steady flow of fireworks manufactured by Angry Fireworks Corp. make their way into Oklahoma each year.

(B) Angry Fireworks Corp. is now operating, but just temporarily, out of leased warehouse space in Oklahoma while its existing factory is being refurbished.

(C) At regular intervals throughout each year, Angry Fireworks Corp. purchased telephone equipment for its manufacturing factory from Oklahoma vendors.

(D) Angry Fireworks Corp. earns sizable volumes of income each year from fireworks sales to Oklahoma citizens.

See ANSWER on Page 150

57. Toddler swallowed cherry-scented furniture polish, and suffered irreversible brain injuries as a consequence. Toddler's Parents filed a diversity lawsuit against Manufacturer in federal court, alleging a defective warning on the furniture polish label. Manufacturer later filed a motion for summary judgment, noting the bottle's explicit warnings to keep the furniture polish out of the reach of children and that the liquid was life-threatening if swallowed, especially to young children. Parents conceded that the written warnings were adequate, but contended that the law ought to impose upon manufacturers a further duty to supplement all written prose warnings with additional pictorial warning illustrations, when the product at issue posed severe health threats. The substantive law of State X will apply to Parents' lawsuit. Neither the legislature nor the supreme court of State X has yet determined whether a product can be deemed to be defective in its warning if pictorial illustrations are omitted.

How should the federal court rule on Manufacturer's motion?

(A) The court should grant the motion, if it believes that the better policy choice is to reject imposing pictorial warning obligations on product makers.

(B) The court should deny the motion, if, from examining decisions of sister States, it determines that the State X supreme court would impose a pictorial warning obligation on product makers.

(C) The court should grant the motion, if it concludes that the State X supreme court would be wise to reject a pictorial warning obligation rule.

(D) The court should dismiss the lawsuit, and instruct Parents to refile their Toddler's claim in State court.

See ANSWER on Page 151

58. Smart Phone Co. entered into a contract with Supplier to provide sapphire glass for the screens for its phones. Supplier had a union strike at its production plants, and was not able to supply the screens. Smart Phone Co. sued Supplier for breach of contract in federal court. In its answer, Supplier asserted as an affirmative defense that the strike triggered the *force majeure* clause of the contract excusing performance for certain circumstances outside the parties' control. Supplier moved for summary judgment on the basis of the *force majeure* clause, submitting the contract and an affidavit from the company representative who negotiated the contract stating that Supplier intended for the *force majeure* clause to include labor disruptions. Smart Phone Co. responded by submitting an affidavit swearing that Smart Phone Co. did not intend for the *force majeure* clause to include labor disruptions.

How will the court likely rule on the motion?

(A) The court will deny the motion because the conflicting affidavits form the classic genuine dispute of material fact.

(B) The court will deny the motion if it determines that the *force majeure* clause could reasonably be construed to include or not include labor disruptions.

(C) The court will grant the motion if it determines that the *force majeure* clause could not reasonably be construed to include labor disruptions.

(D) The court will grant the motion because affidavits cannot be used to contradict a written contract.

See ANSWER on Page 151

59. Arizona enacted a statute that provided that anyone driving on the State's roads shall be deemed to have consented to personal jurisdiction for any accidents occurring on those roads, and shall be deemed, further, to have consented to notice by publication in a newspaper of general circulation in the county where the accident occurred. Driver, domiciled in Ohio, was in an accident with Bicyclist in Tucson, Arizona. Bicyclist sued Driver in federal court in Arizona. Bicyclist published notice of the suit in accordance with the statute. Driver did not see the notices, and default judgment was entered against Driver. At the time of the accident, Driver was just passing through Arizona on his way to California for a work conference, and never had any contacts of any sort with Arizona other than this one incident. When Bicyclist tried to collect on the judgment, Driver challenged notice and personal jurisdiction.

How will the court likely rule?

(A) It will rule that Driver did not receive adequate notice and that the Arizona courts do not have personal jurisdiction over Driver.

(B) It will rule that Driver did not receive adequate notice and that the Arizona courts do have personal jurisdiction over Driver.

(C) It will rule that Driver did receive adequate notice and that the Arizona courts do not have personal jurisdiction over Driver.

(D) It will rule that Driver did receive adequate notice and that the Arizona courts do have personal jurisdiction over Driver.

See ANSWER on Page 152

60. Feaux Fur made artsy fake fur accessories. Feaux Fur obtained a booth at an arts festival to display and sell its products. Protestor, who thought that even fake fur products "sent the wrong message," brought paint from his booth and flung the paint on Feaux Fur's products. Feaux Fur sued Protestor in federal court, seeking compensatory damages for the products that were ruined by the paint, punitive damages, and an injunction prohibiting Protestor from further destructive conduct.

Which issue(s) would the court submit to the jury, which issue(s) would the court retain for itself and resolve by making factual findings, and in what order should it sequence these determinations?

(A) The jury would decide the compensatory and punitive damages issues, and then the court would decide the injunction issue.

(B) The jury would decide the compensatory damages issue, and then the judge would decide the punitive damages and injunction issues.

(C) The judge would decide the punitive damages and injunction issues, and then the jury would decide the injunction issue.

(D) The judge would decide the compensatory damages issue, and then the jury would decide the punitive damages and injunction issues.

See ANSWER on Page 152

61. Traveler was on vacation in Hawai'i and was hit and injured by Surfer. Traveler was a South Carolina domiciliary and Surfer was a Hawai'i domiciliary who frequently vacations in South Carolina. Traveler filed an action against Surfer in federal court in South Carolina. Surfer filed a timely motion to dismiss for lack of venue.

Which response best describes the court's options?

(A) The court may not dismiss the action because venue is proper in South Carolina.

(B) The court must dismiss the action because venue is improper in South Carolina.

(C) The court must either dismiss the action or transfer the case.

(D) The court may dismiss the action but may not transfer the case.

See ANSWER on Page 153

62. In considering a motion to dismiss for failure to state a claim upon which relief can be granted, what will a federal trial court not do?

(A) Presume that all of the contested pleading's allegations of fact are true.

(B) Accept all the contested pleading's legal conclusions as true.

(C) Refrain from dismissing claims that seem unlikely to be believed.

(D) Examine not just the allegations in the complaint itself, but also documents that the complaint incorporates by reference.

See ANSWER on Page 153

63. Three Partners co-owned a hardware store in Little Rock, Arkansas. Two of the Partners conspired to force the third Partner out of the business. That owner, Partner 3, brought a lawsuit against the two conspiring owners (Partner 1 and Partner 2) in Arkansas federal court. Partner 1 and Partner 2 filed a counterclaim against Partner 3.

Which of the following Partners has filed an untimely answer in that federal lawsuit?

(A) Partner 1, who filed an answer 58 days after being sent a waiver of service request, which he had timely returned with his waiver consent.

(B) Partner 2, who filed an answer 21 days after being served by personal delivery with original process.

(C) Partner 3, who filed an answer 20 days after receiving notice that his motion to dismiss Partner 1's counterclaim had been denied by the court.

(D) Partner 1, who filed an answer to Partner 2's crossclaim 18 days after being served with the pleading that contained it.

See ANSWER on Page 154

64. Which of the following is not a proper basis for seeking a new trial following a jury's verdict in federal court?

(A) A motion that the court grant a new trial unless the victorious party is prepared to accept a reduction in the amount of the jury's verdict.

(B) A motion that the court grant a new trial unless the defeated party is prepared to accept an increase in the amount of the jury's verdict.

(C) A motion that the court grant a new trial because the jury's verdict was contrary to the great weight of the trial evidence.

(D) A motion that the court grant a new trial because an attorney made improper remarks to the jury during closing arguments.

See ANSWER on Page 154

65. Student entered Photocopy Store to have her research report printed and bound with a glossy cover. She was refused service by Photocopy Store's President and told to leave the premises immediately. Contending that this maltreatment was due to her race, Student brought a federal discrimination lawsuit against Photocopy Store. During discovery, the videotaped deposition of President was conducted. In the upcoming trial of the discrimination lawsuit against Photocopy Store, testimony from President will be a central piece of evidence in Student's case. Assume President's testimony would be admissible under the Federal Rules of Evidence.

Under what circumstances can Student's attorney play President's video deposition for the jury, rather than calling President to the stand to testify live before the jury?

(A) Only if the trial's courthouse is more than 100 miles from President.

(B) Only if Photocopy Store had notice of or attended the deposition.

(C) Only if President has since died.

(D) Only if an illness or other infirmity now afflicts President.

See ANSWER on Page 155

66. Which of the following statements most accurately describes the procedures at the conclusion of a nonjury bench trial?

    (A) The judge acts as the fact finder and may issue a general verdict or findings of fact and conclusions of law.

    (B) The judge may make oral findings of fact and conclusions of law on the record, followed by a written judgment.

    (C) The judge must make written findings of fact and conclusions of law, followed by a written judgment.

    (D) The judge may make findings of fact and conclusions of law or enter a written judgment.

See ANSWER on Page 155

67. Builder sued Timber Co. in federal court for delivery of non-conforming lumber. The applicable statute of limitations required Builder to file its claim within two years of any alleged non-conforming delivery. Timber Co. contended that this limitations period has now passed.

    Is Timber Co. able to prevail on a pre-answer Rule 12(b)(6) motion seeking dismissal of Builder's lawsuit on the basis of the running of the applicable statute of limitations?

    (A) Yes, if the complaint recited on its face that the delivery of the alleged non-conforming lumber had occurred more than two years prior to the date the lawsuit was filed.

    (B) Yes, if the answer filed by Timber Co. recited on its face that the delivery of the alleged non-conforming lumber had occurred more than two years prior to the date the lawsuit was filed.

    (C) No, because the defending party likely bears the burden of proving them, affirmative defenses may never be tested on a Rule 12(b)(6) motion.

    (D) No, because it would be improper for the court to take judicial notice of the date the Builder's lawsuit had been filed.

See ANSWER on Page 156

68. Orange Inc. is a corporation that produces orange juice for consumers. It is incorporated under the laws of the State of New York. All oranges used in the manufacturing process are grown and harvested in Florida. The orange juice manufacturing plant, where 100% of all of the orange juice is prepared, is located in Georgia. The company's sole business office, where all its executives work, is located in New York. The company has one distribution center, where all the bottled juices are stored, prior to transport to supermarkets; that distribution center is in South Carolina. Sales are made throughout the southeast, but the substantial majority of all sales occur in Florida.

    For purposes of federal diversity jurisdiction, of which of the following is Orange Inc. a citizen?

    (A) New York but not South Carolina.

    (B) Florida, Georgia, and New York.

    (C) Georgia but not Florida.

    (D) South Carolina and New York.

See ANSWER on Page 156

69.   Firm bought and sold securities for its customers. Broker was a longstanding Firm employee
      and one of its most talented securities traders. A messy dispute with a wealthy customer
      over a trade that had been negligently executed by Broker caused Firm to lose several
      million dollars. Firm fired Broker. Broker then filed a lawsuit invoking the court's diversity
      jurisdiction against Firm, asserting breach of several terms of the employment contract. In
      discovery, Broker's attorney issued a broad request to inspect all electronically stored
      information in Firm's possession relating to Broker or any of Broker's clients.

      Which, among the following, would be Firm's best argument in resisting Broker's discovery
      demand?

      (A)   Information that is electronically stored is not discoverable in federal court.

      (B)   Broker failed to designate the form for the production of the electronically stored
            information.

      (C)   Broker's demand exceeds the numerical maximum set in the Federal Rules of Civil
            Procedure for allowable requests for inspection.

      (D)   The requested electronically stored information is not reasonably accessible.

                                                      See ANSWER on Page 157

70.   Promoter engaged Rock Star to perform a concert at Promoter's outdoor stage. Shortly
      before the concert was scheduled to occur, Rock Star decided that he was tired of being
      on the road, and canceled all the events on his tour. Promoter filed a complaint against
      Rock Star in federal court, then personally brought the complaint and summons to Rock
      Star's house. When Rock Star opened the door, Promoter attempted to hand the documents
      to Rock Star. However, Rock Star knocked the papers out of Promoter's extended hand
      and slammed the door.

      Has Promoter properly served Rock Star?

      (A)   No, because personal service requires in-hand delivery.

      (B)   No, because Promoter is a party to the lawsuit.

      (C)   Yes, because abode service is an allowable alternative to personal service.

      (D)   Yes, because a process server may leave process in the "vicinity" of an evasive
            defendant.

                                                      See ANSWER on Page 157

71. Pet Hospital was a corporation organized under the laws of Delaware with its principal place of business in Nevada. It had two veterinarians on staff. The primary pet doctor, Veterinarian #1, was a citizen of California. The assisting pet doctor, Veterinarian #2, was a citizen of Nevada. After a rash of poor veterinary care, Pet Hospital had to close due to loss of business. It sued Veterinarian #1 for $500,000, alleging persistently poor pet care delivered to the facility's customers. Veterinarian #1 joined Veterinarian #2 to the lawsuit, asserting against him a $150,000 claim for persistent failure to follow the medical care instructions dictated by Veterinarian #1 which, the claim alleged, ultimately contributed to the loss of customers. This diversity lawsuit was pending in Nevada federal court.

Which of the following additional claims could now be properly added to this lawsuit?

(A) A $90,000 claim by Pet Hospital against Veterinarian #2 for poor pet care contributing to the loss of the company's business.

(B) A $25,000 claim by Veterinarian #2 against Pet Hospital for defamation relating to its accusations of poor pet care.

(C) A $60,000 claim by Pet Hospital against Veterinarian #2 for breach of terms of a service contract.

(D) A $100,000 claim by Veterinarian #2 against Pet Hospital for damage to his Mercedes automobile while it was parked in the office parking lot.

See ANSWER on Page 158

72. Movie Star had a disagreement with Agent. Agent sued Movie Star in federal court, asserting one count for breach of contract asking for $57,000 and one count for defamation seeking $200,000. Assume that there is complete diversity of citizenship.

Will the federal court be able to exercise diversity jurisdiction over either or both claims?

(A) The court can exercise diversity jurisdiction over the defamation claim but not the breach of contract claim.

(B) The court can exercise diversity jurisdiction over the defamation claim, and also over the breach of contract claim, but only if it arises out of the same transaction or occurrence as the defamation claim.

(C) The court can exercise diversity jurisdiction over the defamation claim, and also over the breach of contract claim, but only if Agent is asserting joint and several liability against Movie Star.

(D) The court can exercise diversity jurisdiction over both the defamation claim and the breach of contract claim.

See ANSWER on Page 159

73. Church has been home to a continuously operating faith community in Williamsburg, Virginia for hundreds of years. It was built near the time of the American Revolution, and remained a treasured remnant of preserved colonial architecture. Zoning Commission approved the construction of a high-rise Hotel immediately next to Church. Historic Preservationists filed a lawsuit in federal court to stop the construction of Hotel, contending that the proximity of the new structure so near Church violated the State of Virginia's historic structures law. Historic Preservationists promptly moved for entry of a preliminary injunction to suspend construction during the pendency of the lawsuit.

Which argument is least likely to help Historic Preservationists obtain the preliminary injunction they seek?

(A) Granting the injunction would preserve the status quo while the merits of the historic structures law claim are considered thoughtfully by the court.

(B) Granting the injunction would prevent an injury to Church that could possibly prove to be irreparable.

(C) Granting the injunction would serve the public interest expressed by the State's legislature in preserving historic structures.

(D) Granting the injunction would be proper because the merits of the litigants' historic structures law claim have a high likelihood of success.

See ANSWER on Page 159

74. Venture Capitalists entered into a contract to buy Founder's company. The contract contained a clause warranting that the company's working capital would be $10 million at the time of the sale, and obligated Founder to make up any working capital shortfall. After the parties executed the contract, they agreed to modified language intended to clarify the working capital provision, and memorialized that agreement in a side letter. After the sale, Venture Capitalists calculated the company's working capital at $9 million, and made a $1 million demand to Founder. When he refused to make the payment, Venture Capitalists sued in federal court. Founder believed that the side letter provided a complete defense, but it was not referenced in or attached to the complaint.

Can Founder present this defense by motion?

(A) Yes, Founder can file a motion to dismiss for failure to state a claim under Rule 12(b)(6) because the terms of the contract are a matter of law to be determined by the court.

(B) Yes, Founder can file a motion for judgment on the pleadings under Rule 12(c) by attaching the side letter to his answer, unless Venture Capitalists deny the validity of the side letter.

(C) Yes, Founder can file a motion for involuntary dismissal under Rule 41(b) because Venture Capitalists violated federal procedure by failing to attach the side letter to the complaint.

(D) Yes, Founder can file a summary judgment motion under Rule 56, but must wait until the close of discovery.

See ANSWER on Page 160

75. Landowner, a citizen of Nashville, Tennessee, was sued in federal court by Neighbor in a diversity case, seeking an order to force the creation of a right-of-way from Neighbor's tract, over Landowner's adjoining property, and out onto an adjacent public highway. Landowner attempted to defend against the lawsuit without counsel. The court ruled in Neighbor's favor, and entered judgment accordingly. Two years later, Landowner's child graduated from law school and desired to reopen the right-of-way litigation.

Which argument would give Landowner's child the best chance for seeking relief from the court's earlier judgment?

(A) Neighbor offered fraudulent testimony during the trial against Landowner.

(B) Landowner was precluded from offering certain documentary evidence because of a mistaken reading of the court's scheduling deadlines.

(C) Although Neighbor often resided in San Francisco, California, Landowner's child has just discovered that Neighbor always retained her Memphis, Tennessee citizenship.

(D) Landowner received from a friend a previously unknown deed signed by Neighbor's predecessor in interest, covenanting that Neighbor's property would never seek a right-of-way over Landowner's property.

See ANSWER on Page 160

76. Saw Company made table saws with automatic braking systems designed to stop the saw blade immediately upon contact with any substance containing moisture (such as a finger). Cabinet Maker was injured when the saw failed to perform as designed. During discovery, Cabinet Maker moved to compel Saw Company to produce a memorandum regarding the injury that was prepared by Engineer, and sent to General Counsel, President, and Vice-President. Saw Company opposed the motion, contending that the memorandum was protected as trial preparation materials and as an attorney-client privileged communication. The court ruled against Saw Company, and ordered it to produce the memorandum.

Can Saw Company appeal the court's order?

(A) Yes, because the ruling is the court's final order regarding the privilege issue.

(B) Yes, because if Saw Company produces the memorandum, the privilege will be lost because the other side will have then seen confidential communications between client and counsel.

(C) No, because the court's order satisfies the requirements of the "collateral order doctrine."

(D) No, because the ruling is not a final order.

See ANSWER on Page 161

77. Shareholder believed that Corporation, through its President, had made false and misleading statements, leading Shareholder to invest in Corporation and subsequently to lose a substantial portion of his investment. Shareholder sued Corporation and President in federal court, contending that the court had diversity jurisdiction over the matter. President filed a motion to dismiss under Rule 12(b)(1) for lack of subject-matter jurisdiction because President was a citizen of the same State as Shareholder. The court granted the motion and dismissed the action. Shareholder filed a second action in federal court against Corporation only. Corporation filed a motion to dismiss this action under Rule 12(b)(2), arguing that the court did not have personal jurisdiction over it.

May Shareholder voluntarily dismiss this action and refile in a State where Corporation is subject to personal jurisdiction?

(A) No, because the third action would be precluded by the "two dismissal rule."

(B) No, because the third action would be precluded by the doctrine of claim preclusion.

(C) Yes, because voluntary dismissals are without prejudice unless the stipulation or notice provides otherwise.

(D) Yes, because the third action would not be precluded by the "two dismissal rule."

See ANSWER on Page 161

78. Which of the following will qualify as a final judgment, from which an appeal may be filed in a federal civil case?

(A) An order disqualifying counsel from further participation.

(B) An order imposing criminal sanctions for violating court orders.

(C) An order refusing to disqualify counsel from further participation.

(D) An order resolving merits liability without addressing appropriate relief.

See ANSWER on Page 162

79. Condominium was built near a scenic patch of the Florida Everglades, with an attached fishing pier that extended far out into the water. When Condominium noticed that certain of the pier's pilings had deteriorated, it hired workers to reset the pilings. Federal environmental officials ordered the repairs stopped, insisting that the replacement pilings violated recently enacted federal wetlands laws. Condominium hired Attorney to resist the federal stop-work order, but Attorney lost the case and the entire fishing pier had to be dismantled. Condominium later sued Attorney for legal malpractice (a State law claim), faulting the Attorney for failing to argue in the earlier wetlands litigation that federal law should have entitled Condominium to a "grandfathering" exemption from all newly enacted pier laws. Condominium brought its lawsuit in Florida federal court. Condominium invoked the court's federal question jurisdiction authority.

Upon testing its jurisdiction over the Condominium's legal malpractice claim against Attorney, what is the court most likely to do?

(A) Dismiss the case for lack of jurisdiction, because State law, not federal law, creates the legal malpractice cause of action.

(B) Dismiss the case for lack of jurisdiction, because the federal issue implicated by the lawsuit is not substantial.

(C) Not dismiss the case for lack of jurisdiction, because the court's resolution of a federal issue is necessary.

(D) Not dismiss the case for lack of jurisdiction, because State law claims containing imbedded federal issues may always be litigated in federal court.

See ANSWER on Page 163

80. Truck Driver side-swiped a taxicab owned and operated by Cabbie. Cabbie sued Truck Driver in State court in a State that has adopted the Federal Rules of Civil Procedure, asserting one count for negligence. Truck Driver filed a timely motion for summary judgment. With respect to the issue of damages, Truck Driver did not submit any record evidence in support of her motion, and instead argued that Cabbie did not have any evidence of damages caused by the incident. In his opposition, Cabbie attached an invoice from a repair shop. In her reply brief, Truck Driver responded that the invoice was not admissible evidence without a sponsoring witness, and therefore could not be admitted to the record for the summary judgment analysis.

How will the court likely rule as to the damages element on the summary judgment motion?

(A) The court will deny the motion on the grounds that there is a genuine dispute of material fact despite the fact that the invoice was inadmissible.

(B) The court will determine the admissibility of the invoice before ruling on the motion.

(C) The court will deny Truck Driver's motion because Truck Driver did not submit any record evidence on the damages issue in support of her motion.

(D) The court will rule that Cabbie failed to create a genuine dispute of material fact and grant the motion as to the damages element.

See ANSWER on Page 164

81. Employee worked as a teller for a neighborhood bank. Two years after his fiftieth birthday, the bank terminated his employment. Employee filed a federal lawsuit against the bank alleging age-based discrimination in violation of federal law. Bank responded by filing a motion to dismiss, contending that employee's lawsuit failed to state a claim upon which relief can be granted.

    What is the most likely reason for the district judge's decision to grant the motion?

    (A) Having examined the allegations the employee asserts, the judge believes it unlikely that a jury would rule in his favor.

    (B) Having examined the admissible witness testimony evidence the employee has mustered, the judge believes it unlikely that a jury would rule in his favor.

    (C) Having examined the complaint, the judge considers that the allegations lack sufficient factual content to permit the reasonable inference that the defendant is liable for unlawful conduct.

    (D) Having examined the pleadings, the judge determines that the defense of failure to state a claim has been waived because it had not yet been asserted in an answer to the complaint.

    See ANSWER on Page 165

82. Guest was injured seriously at Amusement Park in Ohio when the safety bar of the rollercoaster car in which he was riding released, causing him to fall unexpectedly from the ride. He sued in Ohio State court in a single-count complaint, naming as defendants Amusement Park, Ride Manager, and Ride Operator. Guest was a citizen of Indiana; all defendants were citizens of Ohio. Guest's Attorney arranged to serve original process on Amusement Park on September 1. Identifying and then locating service addresses for Ride Manager and Ride Operator, however, proved to be more time consuming. Both Ride Manager and Ride Operator were served on November 1. On November 15, Ride Operator filed a notice of removal to federal court.

    Is the notice of removal proper?

    (A) Yes, because Ride Operator timely filed his notice, the case against him will proceed in federal court, regardless of the preferences of the other defendants.

    (B) Yes, because Ride Operator timely filed his notice, the case against all defendants will proceed in federal court.

    (C) No, because the time for removal expired on October 2, Ride Operator's notice was untimely; the case will remain in State court.

    (D) No, because Amusement Park and Ride Manager have not joined or otherwise consented to the removal, the case will remain in State court.

    See ANSWER on Page 165

83. Owner entered into contracts with Engineering Firm and Builder to construct a new office building in California. Both Engineering Firm and Builder were Massachusetts corporations with their principal places of business in Boston, Massachusetts, but both performed the work for Owner exclusively out of their offices in California. The project did not go smoothly, and Owner eventually fired Engineering Firm and Builder, and then signed contracts with other entities to complete the project at substantial additional cost. For tactical reasons, Owner filed suit against Engineering Firm and Builder in federal court in Massachusetts, which has only one district. Engineering Firm and Builder filed a timely joint motion to dismiss for lack of venue or, in the alternative, to transfer venue to California.

How will the court likely rule on this motion?

(A) The court will grant the motion to dismiss and deny the motion to transfer because Massachusetts has no connection to this action and it is not a proper venue.

(B) The court must deny the motion to dismiss and deny the motion to transfer because venue is proper in Massachusetts and the plaintiff is entitled to pick the forum.

(C) The court may deny the motion to dismiss and grant the motion to transfer because venue is proper in Massachusetts but the location of the witnesses and building in California likely makes California a more convenient forum.

(D) The court will deny the motion to dismiss and deny the motion to transfer because venue is proper in Massachusetts and the defendants should have filed a motion asserting the doctrine of forum non conveniens.

See ANSWER on Page 166

84. Police Department promoted several male police officers to the rank of sergeant. Several female officers then brought an equal protection action against Police Department in federal court, arguing that they had performed better on the promotion testing criteria than the male officers, and had therefore been discriminated against on the basis of gender. The female officers argued that they, not the male officers, should have received the available rank promotions.

May the male officers intervene in the female officers' equal protection lawsuit against Police Department?

(A) The male officers may intervene as of right because their interests implicate questions of fact or law shared by the female officers' claims.

(B) The male officers may not intervene as of right because they lack any interest in the female officers' demands for promotion.

(C) The male officers may intervene as of right because their interests may be impaired by the disposition of the female officers' claims.

(D) The male officers may not intervene as of right because Police Department will adequately represent their interests.

See ANSWER on Page 167

85. For an upcoming winter play season, Manager of a community theater proposed to produce a controversial off-Broadway play that contained scenes which mocked organized religions and depicted simulated sexually explicit behavior involving religious clergy. Owner of the community theater rejected Manager's proposal and forbade the show. In defiance of Owner's instructions, Manager began to proceed with production of the play anyway. Owner fired Manager. Manager brought suit in federal court against Owner for wrongful termination.

    During jury selection, may Manager's attorney use a peremptory challenge to strike a potential juror who is an African-American female?

    (A) Yes, because women are more likely to be offended by the play's scenes.

    (B) Yes, because she is a part-time religious education teacher at a local school.

    (C) No, because such a strike would be an unconstitutional proxy for bias.

    (D) No, because it would eliminate the last potential female juror.

    See ANSWER on Page 168

86. Worker contracted a serious illness while working at Shipyard. Worker filed a federal lawsuit against Shipyard, contending that Shipyard's use of Paint X caused the illness. Worker moved for summary judgment, alleging that discovery in the case had confirmed Shipyard's liability. Shipyard responded to the motion for summary judgment by disputing one issue— that Paint X was capable of causing the illness. Shipyard supported its response with the report of a highly credentialed expert in the field who, through scholarly study, ruled out the possibility that Paint X was a triggering agent for the illness. Worker replied to Shipyard's response by pointing out that Shipyard never contested that Worker contracted the illness, that the illness was serious, or that Worker had sustained numerous economic and non-economic losses as a result of the illness.

    What may the district court do in ruling on Worker's motion?

    (A) Grant the motion; Shipyard was required to offer some actual proof of a genuine dispute as to all material facts, and has failed to do so.

    (B) Deny the motion; Worker may not seek summary judgment until discovery has closed.

    (C) Treat the facts of Worker's illness, its seriousness, and the economic and non-economic losses as established for the case.

    (D) Dismiss the motion; plaintiffs may not seek offensive summary judgment.

    See ANSWER on Page 169

87. Rule 11 of the Federal Rules of Civil Procedure would not authorize which of the following sanctions?

    (A) A monetary sanction imposed by the court *sua sponte*.

    (B) A monetary sanction for an abusive discovery request.

    (C) A monetary sanction against a law firm for a violation by that firm's associate.

    (D) A monetary sanction imposed against an unrepresented party.

    See ANSWER on Page 169

88. For many years, attorneys practicing in State Z have complained that the State's jury pools have produced persistently disinterested and lethargic prospective jurors. Those attorneys have claimed that this juror problem has degraded the quality of justice dispensed in civil cases throughout State Z. To remedy this problem, and at the recommendation of the State's trial attorneys, State Z enacted a statute to increase the number of peremptory challenges available in all civil cases to 6 per side. By federal statute, Congress has continued to set the number of peremptory challenges in federal court at the lower total of 3 per side.

In federal diversity cases in State Z, how many peremptory challenges will a State Z federal judge permit each side to have?

(A) 3, but only if Congress's limit would not influence the outcome of civil verdicts.

(B) 6, if applying Congress's limit would result in the inequitable administration of justice.

(C) 3, but only if Congress's peremptory challenge statute is constitutional.

(D) 6, if applying Congress's limit would incentivize forum-shopping.

See ANSWER on Page 170

89. Buyer and Seller enter into a contract that contained a forum selection clause, reading: "The parties to this contract agree that any action under this contract shall be brought in the federal district court for the Western District of Pennsylvania. The parties hereby consent to, and waive any objections to, personal jurisdiction, subject-matter jurisdiction, and venue in that forum." Buyer filed a complaint in federal court in Pennsylvania, and the Seller filed a motion challenging personal jurisdiction and subject-matter jurisdiction.

Which of the following best describes the effect of this contract clause?

(A) Seller's consent will be effective to establish both personal jurisdiction and subject-matter jurisdiction.

(B) Seller's consent will be effective to establish personal jurisdiction but not subject-matter jurisdiction.

(C) Seller's consent will be effective to establish subject-matter jurisdiction but not personal jurisdiction.

(D) Seller's consent will not be effective to establish either subject-matter jurisdiction or personal jurisdiction.

See ANSWER on Page 170

90. In federal court, which of the following jury verdicts is always improper?

(A) A verdict returned by a jury of 5 members.

(B) A verdict returned by a jury that is not unanimous.

(C) A verdict returned by a jury which included one juror who was not excused but who refused to participate in the verdict.

(D) A verdict returned by a jury that began with 12 members, but lost two members during trial due to illness.

See ANSWER on Page 171

91. Homeowner purchased a backyard trampoline from Manufacturer, and was injured seriously after falling off the trampoline bed while bouncing. Homeowner filed a products liability claim against Manufacturer in federal court, contending that the trampoline was designed defectively because it lacked protective netting to prevent falls. At trial, Homeowner proposed to call three witnesses, each of whom would testify as to certain different dangers posed by a trampoline lacking netting and each of whom would opine that an unnetted trampoline is defective. After the first of Homeowner's witnesses testified, Manufacturer moved for a judgment as a matter of law.

How should the district court rule on that motion?

(A) The motion should be denied, because the final two Homeowner witnesses had not yet testified.

(B) The motion should be denied, because it was made orally and not in writing.

(C) The motion should be denied, because it was not made at the close of all the evidence.

(D) The motion should be granted.

See ANSWER on Page 171

92. Pet Owner kenneled her dog at DogCare, Inc. while she was away for an extended business trip. Upon her return, Pet Owner learned that her dog had died from malnutrition. Pet Owner sued DogCare, Inc. in federal court on a diversity claim but, due to a questionable jury charge, lost the lawsuit. The jury's verdict was returned on October 1. The court entered judgment in favor of DogCare, Inc. on October 5. Pet Owner filed a motion for new trial on October 20 to challenge the court's jury charge, but that motion was denied on November 20 by order entered that same day. Pet Owner filed a notice of appeal on December 1, which DogCare, Inc. challenged as untimely.

How should the federal court of appeals rule on DogCare, Inc.'s motion to dismiss the pending appeal?

(A) The motion will be granted, because the appeal was filed more than 30 days after the jury's verdict.

(B) The motion will be granted, because the appeal was filed more than 30 days after entry of judgment.

(C) The motion will be denied, because the filing of the motion for new trial suspended the running of the appeal period for 30 days.

(D) The motion will be denied, because the appeal was filed before December 21.

See ANSWER on Page 172

93. Shopper was apprehended by Store's security officers, and then detained on suspicion of theft of sweaters. Shopper later sued Store in federal court for common law false imprisonment. Store filed a motion for summary judgment, supporting its motion with a video recorded from internal security cameras showing Shopper, while standing in the sweater aisle, stuffing two sweaters into her handbag.

Which of the following responses by Shopper is least likely to defeat the Store's motion?

(A) Submitting the deposition transcript of one of the Store's security officers who testified that, upon searching Shopper's handbag during her detention, he found no sweaters.

(B) Submitting an affidavit from Shopper's companion that day attesting that Shopper never stuffed sweaters into her handbag.

(C) Submitting an affidavit from a videography expert opining that an inspection of the video reveals evidence of its alteration.

(D) Submitting Shopper's own sworn responses to Store's written interrogatories, attesting that she never left Store with any unpurchased merchandise.

See ANSWER on Page 172

94. Skateboard Company manufactured and sold skateboards in San Francisco, California. For several years, it had placed weekly advertisements in College's Student Newspaper in nearby Reno, Nevada. College Student, a Nevada resident, saw those advertisements and was intrigued by Skateboard Company's product. While visiting a friend in San Francisco, College Student went into the local Skateboard Company store there and purchased a skateboard. College Student returned to Nevada and was subsequently injured when one of his new skateboard's wheels broke. College Student sued Skateboard Company in federal court in Nevada. Skateboard Company does not have any employees or property in Nevada. Skateboard Company filed a motion to dismiss for lack of personal jurisdiction.

How should the court rule?

(A) Grant the motion because College Student lives and was injured in Nevada, and therefore has sufficient minimum contacts with Nevada.

(B) Grant the motion because Skateboard Company does not have sufficient minimum contacts with Nevada.

(C) Deny the motion because Skateboard Company's advertisement in College's Student Newspaper permits Nevada to exercise personal jurisdiction.

(D) Deny the motion because skateboards are portable, and it is "foreseeable" that a customer could take a Skateboard Company skateboard to another State.

See ANSWER on Page 173

95. Borrower and Guarantor, two individuals domiciled in Rhode Island, sued Bank, a Delaware corporation with its principal place of business in New York, in federal court, asserting only State law claims. Borrower's claim against Bank was for $100,000, and Guarantor's claim against Bank was for $25,000. Both claims arose out of the same loan transaction.

Which of the following best describes the status of the federal court's subject-matter jurisdiction over these claims?

(A) The court has diversity jurisdiction over both claims because the claim amounts can be aggregated to reach the jurisdictional limit.

(B) The court has diversity jurisdiction over the claim by Borrower, but must sever out and dismiss the claim by Guarantor.

(C) The court may exercise supplemental jurisdiction over the claims by both Borrower and Guarantor.

(D) The court can exercise diversity jurisdiction over the claim by Borrower, and supplemental jurisdiction over the claim by Guarantor.

See ANSWER on Page 174

96. Oscar, Candace, Jorge, and Miranda were employees at a supermarket in Michigan. They each contributed money to a pool from which the group purchased tickets from Big Lottery. One of those tickets won the monthly drawing and a grand prize of $4 million. Oscar, Jorge, and Miranda were each Michigan citizens. Candace had been a Michigan citizen, but the day before the drawing she relocated to Illinois. Big Lottery was an Illinois citizen. It asked the winners how the prize was to be distributed. Oscar, Jorge, and Miranda instructed that the prize should be divided into four equal shares. Candace insisted that, because she was the one who organized the pool, she should receive one-half of the prize and her co-winners should split the remaining one-half. Big Lottery refused to distribute the winnings absent a unanimous distribution instruction from the four winners. Oscar, Jorge, and Miranda then commenced a diversity lawsuit against Big Lottery in Michigan federal court, demanding that they each receive ¼ shares of the prize money.

What is Big Lottery's best argument to have the Michigan lawsuit dismissed?

(A) In Candace's absence, the court cannot award complete relief to Oscar, Jorge, and Miranda.

(B) The court would be unable to decide Candace's claim for ½ the prize money absent her participation in the lawsuit.

(C) Big Lottery has learned that the Wisconsin State courts would have proper jurisdiction over Oscar, Candace, Jorge, Miranda, and Big Lottery.

(D) Oscar, Jorge, and Miranda could be prejudiced were the lawsuit to proceed in Candace's absence.

See ANSWER on Page 175

97. Turf Co. installed a new artificial playing surface at High School, located in Seattle, Washington. High School refused to pay Turf Co., contending that the surface was too slippery and its star running back kept losing his footing. Turf Co. sued High School in State court in Indiana, where Turf Co. was located. High School filed a motion to dismiss that lawsuit based on lack of personal jurisdiction. The State court granted High School's motion. Turf Co. then filed suit in federal court in Indiana. High School again filed a motion to dismiss for lack of personal jurisdiction under Rule 12(b)(2), asserting that Turf Co. was barred by the doctrine of issue preclusion from contending that the Indiana courts have personal jurisdiction over High School.

How will the court likely rule on High School's motion?

(A) The court will deny the motion because the doctrine of issue preclusion applies to decisions on the merits, and personal jurisdiction is not a merits decision.

(B) The court will deny the motion because this is improper "offensive issue preclusion."

(C) The court will grant the motion if it determines, in its discretion, that application of the doctrine of issue preclusion is equitable under the circumstances.

(D) The court will grant the motion because all of the elements of issue preclusion are satisfied.

See ANSWER on Page 176

98. Which of the following circumstances would not be sufficient to create federal diversity jurisdiction in a lawsuit filed as a federal class action by a class of plaintiffs if the amount in controversy exceeded $5 million, exclusive of interests and costs?

(A) Any plaintiff is a citizen of another country and any defendant is a citizen of a U.S. State.

(B) Any plaintiff is a citizen of a U.S. State and any defendant is foreign nation.

(C) Any plaintiff is a citizen of a different U.S. State than any defendant.

(D) Any plaintiff is a citizen of a different U.S. State than any other plaintiff.

See ANSWER on Page 176

99. Following a nonjury trial of a breach of contract claim in federal court, the judge issued findings of fact and conclusions of law, and then entered final judgment. The appellant filed a timely appeal, challenging aspects of certain of those findings of fact and conclusions of law.

What standard of review will the appellate court use?

(A) The court will review the findings of fact under the "clearly erroneous" standard and the conclusions of law under the "abuse of discretion" standard.

(B) The court will review the findings of fact under the "abuse of discretion" standard and the conclusions of law under the "*de novo*" (or "plenary") review standard.

(C) The court will review the findings of fact under the "clearly erroneous" standard and the conclusions of law under the "*de novo*" (or "plenary") review standard.

(D) The court will review the findings of fact under the "abuse of discretion" standard and the conclusions of law under the "clearly erroneous" standard.

See ANSWER on Page 177

100. Patient sued Hospital in federal court for medical malpractice. During discovery, Patient served a deposition notice on Hospital scheduling the deposition of Nurse, who cared for Patient. Nurse failed to show up for his deposition. Without meeting or conferring, Patient filed a motion for sanctions against Hospital.

How will the court likely rule on the motion?

(A) The court will deny the motion because Patient should have also served a subpoena on Nurse.

(B) The court will deny the motion because Patient failed to meet and confer with Hospital before filing the motion.

(C) The court will deny the motion because Patient first needed to file a motion to compel before filing a motion for sanctions.

(D) The court will grant the motion because the Rules do not require a party to meet and confer or file a motion to compel before filing a motion for sanctions related to failure to appear for a deposition.

See ANSWER on Page 177

101. Passenger brought a federal lawsuit against Airline for loss of checked luggage containing property worth more than $100,000. Counsel for Airline contacted Passenger and discussed a possible settlement of Passenger's claim, but no resolution was reached. Those discussions continued. The time for responding to Passenger's complaint passed, however, without any responsive pleading or pre-answer motion from Airline. Passenger then moved for a default judgment hearing, which the court scheduled for the next day.

At the hearing, may the court grant Passenger's motion for entry of a default judgment?

(A) Yes, because Airline is not a military defendant.

(B) Yes, because, having missed the required response date, Airline is not entitled to defend against entry of a default judgment.

(C) No, because the actual value of the lost luggage is not a sum certain.

(D) No, because Airline has appeared in the litigation.

See ANSWER on Page 178

102. Prisoner brought a civil rights action in federal court, contending that he did not receive proper medical care, and, as a result, his vision was significantly impaired. Prisoner filed a motion *in limine* asking the court to preclude any mention of his underlying crimes or his life sentence. The court granted the motion as to Prisoner's crimes but denied the motion as to his life sentence, ruling that evidence was relevant to damages. At the end of the jury trial, the jury entered a verdict in favor of Prisoner, awarding him $10,000. After entry of judgment, Prisoner took a timely appeal, contending that the court erroneously denied a portion of his motion *in limine*.

May Prisoner appeal the court's order denying in part his motion *in limine*?

(A) Yes.

(B) No, because the order in question was not a final order.

(C) No, because the court's ruling on evidentiary issue would be considered "harmless error" in light of the jury's ruling.

(D) No, because Prisoner won the case, and only the losing party may appeal.

See ANSWER on Page 178

103. Renter lived in a floor-level condominium unit, outside of which she installed a small rock garden with an electric waterfall. To power the waterfall, she purchased an indoor/outdoor extension cord from Retailer, which she then plugged into an exterior outlet near the door to her condominium unit. The cord proved to be defective, and caught fire. Renter was injured and suffered fire and smoke damage to most of her possessions. She filed a diversity-based products liability action in federal court against Retailer. Once served, Retailer impleaded the cord's manufacturer as a third-party defendant.

This lawsuit will proceed as a bench trial, rather than a jury trial, in which of the following circumstances?

(A) If Renter—as plaintiff—failed to timely demand a jury trial, even though Retailer filed a proper demand for one.

(B) If the cord manufacturer demanded a jury trial on the day it was joined into the lawsuit, but that filing was more than 14 days after the complaint was served on Retailer.

(C) If Renter expressed her demand for a jury trial by checking the box marked "jury trial" on the civil cover sheet handed to her when she filed her complaint with the clerk of court.

(D) If Renter demanded a jury trial, but on the eve of trial filed a notice to withdraw the demand in which Retailer joined.

See ANSWER on Page 179

104. A woman was injured while driving her ten-year-old car. She sued the automobile manufacturer in federal court, claiming that the brakes were defectively manufactured. The woman served discovery requests seeking emails regarding the manufacture of the brakes. The automobile manufacturer timely objected to the request to the extent that it applied to emails more than seven years old, asserting that those emails were now only accessible on backup tapes from an obsolete email system that would be very expensive to restore. The woman filed a motion to compel production of all responsive emails from the previous fifteen years.

If the court grants the motion to compel, what is the most likely explanation?

(A) The broad scope of discovery in federal court warrants production of the emails regardless of the burden or expense.

(B) The automobile manufacturer failed to file a motion for a protective order, and thus waived its objections.

(C) The automobile manufacturer failed to demonstrate good cause for withholding the emails.

(D) The automobile manufacturer failed to demonstrate that the discovery was not proportional to the needs of the case.

See ANSWER on Page 179

105. A group of Parents sued School District and each of its Board Members for the failure to provide their elementary school children with minimally nutritious lunches. The lawsuit was filed in federal district court in Idaho. Attorney for Parents served School District at its headquarters and each of the Board Members by mail, in a manner authorized by Idaho State law, sent to their last known addresses. One Board Member challenged this service as improper.

How will the district court resolve that challenge?

(A) Service will be quashed, because service by mail is not permitted in federal court.

(B) Service will not be quashed, if the service by mail satisfied Idaho State law for serving individuals.

(C) Service will be quashed, if the challenging Board Member failed to receive actual notice of the lawsuit.

(D) Service will not be quashed, if the challenging Board Member received actual notice of the lawsuit.

See ANSWER on Page 180

106. Lawyer received an email from Nigerian Prince, informing Lawyer that Nigerian Prince had substantial assets in the United States, and would pay Lawyer a percentage in exchange for assistance in transferring the assets. Lawyer agreed, deposited a check from Nigerian Prince into Lawyer's bank account, then after it cleared, wired money to Nigerian Prince. The check eventually was returned as fraudulent, and Lawyer lost the money he wired to Nigerian Prince. Lawyer filed suit against Nigerian Prince in federal court, knowing that was not really his name, but not yet knowing his actual name. Lawyer was able to learn Nigerian Prince's real identity quickly, and filed a motion to amend his complaint to name the proper party 45 days after filing the original complaint, which the court granted. Lawyer then promptly and properly served the proper defendant.

Will the amended complaint relate back to the date of the original complaint?

(A) Yes, because when the court grants the motion to amend, the amended pleading then replaces the original pleading.

(B) Yes, because Lawyer moved diligently and quickly to determine the true identity of the defendant, then timely served him.

(C) No, because the amended complaint does not arise out of the same case or controversy as the original complaint, in that it involves a different defendant.

(D) No, because Lawyer was not mistaken about the identity of Nigerian Prince.

See ANSWER on Page 180

107. Shopper was injured when he tripped on loose carpeting in Department Store in New Mexico. Shopper sued Department Store, asserting a State law negligence claim. The claim was filed in federal court in Arizona, where Shopper is domiciled, invoking the court's diversity jurisdiction. Assume Arizona's choice of law statute calls for application of the law of the State where the allegedly negligent acts occurred. Department Store filed a motion to dismiss for failure to state a claim. Assume no federal preemption applies.

What law will the court apply in ruling on Department Store's motion?

(A) Arizona pleading standards and federal substantive common law.

(B) New Mexico pleading standards and federal substantive common law.

(C) Federal pleading standards and Arizona substantive common law.

(D) Federal pleading standards and New Mexico substantive common law.

See ANSWER on Page 181

108. Goaltender plays on State University's traveling soccer team. During a soccer match held at a college in a neighboring State, Goaltender was injured severely when the opposing team started a brutal fist-fight. Goaltender brought a personal injury diversity lawsuit in federal court.

In such a lawsuit, which of the following would not ensure that the federal court had personal jurisdiction over Midfielder, a student playing for that opposing team?

(A) If Midfielder were subject to personal jurisdiction of the courts of the State where the federal court is located, and was served properly with process.

(B) If Midfielder were joined to the lawsuit as a required party and was served with process in the United States within 100 miles of the place where the summons was issued.

(C) If Midfielder were agreeable to waiving formal service of process.

(D) If Midfielder were subject to personal jurisdiction in accordance with the terms of a federal statute, and served with process as the statute required.

See ANSWER on Page 181

109. In the event that the court gives a jury both a general verdict and written questions, and the jury returns a general verdict that is inconsistent with its answer to the written questions, the court has multiple options.

Which of these is not one of the court's options?

(A) The court may order the jury to deliberate further to try to reconcile the general verdict with the written question answers.

(B) The court may ignore the general verdict and enter judgment consistent with the answers to the written questions.

(C) The court may ignore the answers to the written questions and enter judgment consistent with the general verdict.

(D) The court may order a new trial.

See ANSWER on Page 181

110. Three of the following are requirements for obtaining a Temporary Restraining Order in federal court.

Which one is not?

(A) No adequate remedy at law.

(B) A reasonable likelihood of success on the merits.

(C) Notice to all other parties.

(D) Posting of security.

See ANSWER on Page 182

111. Attorney tried a civil litigation in federal court in Virginia. The jury returned its verdict on September 1. On September 4, judgment was entered in the case on the basis of the jury's verdict. On September 16, Attorney filed a motion for new trial. Attorney's adversary opposed the motion, contending that the motion was untimely and must be dismissed.

How should the trial court rule on the timeliness objection?

(A) The motion was untimely filed because such motions must be filed within 10 days, and that period expired on September 11.

(B) The motion was untimely filed because such motions must be filed within 10 days, and that period expired on September 15.

(C) The motion was timely filed because post-trial motions seek to remedy an injustice tolerated by a federal trial judge, and therefore may be filed at any time.

(D) The motion was timely filed because it was filed during the month of September.

See ANSWER on Page 182

112. Driver and Passenger were involved in an automobile accident caused by Driver's inattentive texting while driving. Passenger was injured seriously, and accumulated more than $100,000 in medical bills alone. At the time of the accident, both Driver and Passenger were citizens of Colorado. Passenger's parent was later stricken by a serious, lingering illness, and Passenger relocated indefinitely to her parent's home in Arizona to become the principal caregiver. Passenger's parent later died, and Passenger relocated back to Colorado.

Can Passenger bring a diversity action against Driver in Colorado federal court?

(A) Yes, if Passenger was a citizen of Arizona at the time the lawsuit was filed.

(B) Yes, if Passenger was a citizen of Colorado at the time the lawsuit was filed, so long as she had lawfully changed her citizenship to Arizona while the case was pending.

(C) No, if Passenger was a citizen of Arizona at the time the lawsuit was filed, but later lawfully changed to her citizenship back to Colorado while the case was pending.

(D) No, because Passenger and Driver both were citizens of Colorado at the time the cause of action arose.

See ANSWER on Page 182

113. Carpenter was injured while hammering a defective nail. Carpenter brought a diversity action in Oklahoma federal court against the nail's Manufacturer. The case was filed on the eve before Oklahoma's statute of limitations for personal injuries would have expired. Oklahoma's limitations statute, however, provided that, to be timely filed, personal injury plaintiffs must file their lawsuits within the limitations period and then either (a) complete service of process on the defendant within that limitations period as well or, alternatively, (b) complete service within 60 days after filing. Carpenter filed the complaint within the limitations period, but failed to complete service on Manufacturer within 60 days thereafter. Federal Rule of Civil Procedure 3 provides that a federal civil action is commenced simply by filing a complaint with the court. Manufacturer moved to dismiss Carpenter's lawsuit as time-barred; Carpenter responded that under Rule 3, the lawsuit was properly and timely commenced.

How must the federal court rule on the motion to dismiss?

(A) Grant the motion, because State rules must be applied in preference to federal rules if to do otherwise would prove outcome determinative.

(B) Grant the motion, because timely service was not completed as Oklahoma law required.

(C) Deny the motion, because Rule 3 is a Federal Rule of Civil Procedure that is both valid and on-point.

(D) Deny the motion, because federal law always supplants inconsistent State law.

See ANSWER on Page 183

114. Software Co. filed suit against Programmer, a former employee, contending that Programmer stole company trade secrets in violation of his employment agreement. At trial, Programmer testified that he developed the programming technique in question independently, without any reference to or use of Software Co.'s trade secrets, and provided documentation of his independent development. Following a nonjury trial, the judge entered judgment in favor of Programmer. Six months later, Software Co. obtained documentary evidence that Programmer had fabricated the documentation he presented to the court.

What is Software Co.'s best avenue for seeking a change to the court's ruling?

(A) A motion for relief from judgment under Rule 60.

(B) A motion for a new trial under Rule 59.

(C) A motion for judgment as a matter of law under Rule 50.

(D) A motion for sanctions under Rule 11.

See ANSWER on Page 183

115. Pagoda Co. manufactured pagodas and sold them to the public through a distributor over the Internet. Homeowner, who was a citizen of New York, ordered a pagoda for her vacation home in Florida for $80,000, and wired payment to Pagoda Co. Pagoda Co. failed to deliver the Pagoda, and Homeowner sued Pagoda Co. in federal court in New York. Pagoda Co. filed a motion under Rule 12(b)(2) challenging personal jurisdiction. The court denied that motion. Pagoda Co. then answered. Following some preliminary discovery, Pagoda Co. filed a new Rule 12 motion, arguing that discovery revealed that Homeowner failed to join the distributor, who was required to be joined by Rule 19. Pagoda Co. also argued that, pursuant to a recently issued case, Homeowner's complaint failed to state a claim.

Will the court likely allow Pagoda Co. to pursue the defenses asserted in its new motion?

(A) No, the court will not allow Pagoda Co. to pursue either as it waived them by not including them in the original Rule 12 motion.

(B) Yes, the court will allow Pagoda Co to pursue the motion regarding the failure to join the distributor, but Pagoda Co. waived the motion asserting failure to state a claim by not including it in the original Rule 12 motion.

(C) Yes, the court will allow Pagoda Co to pursue the motion asserting failure to state a claim, but Pagoda Co. waived the motion regarding the failure to join the distributor by not including it in the original Rule 12 motion.

(D) Yes, the court will allow Pagoda Co. to pursue both motions.

See ANSWER on Page 184

116. Financial Officer lives and works in Connecticut, but had an important business meeting to attend in Phoenix, Arizona. Financial Officer booked a flight on Airline for the trip. The trip had a connection with one stop: Connecticut to Chicago, then Chicago to Phoenix. After landing at the Chicago airport, Financial Officer became belligerent with Airline Employee over seat assignments on his connecting flight to Phoenix. The confrontation caused Employee to leave the flight counter in distress. Co-Employee witnessed the entire incident, and schemed a retaliation. By altering Financial Officer's reservation record, Co-Employee caused Financial Officer to miss his connecting flight to Phoenix and, as a consequence, to be fired from his employment back in Connecticut.

If Financial Officer files a lawsuit in Connecticut, which fact would be most helpful to establish that State's personal jurisdiction over Co-Employee?

(A) In a negligent infliction of emotional distress claim, that Co-Employee was aware that Financial Officer's trip to Phoenix was related to his employment back in Connecticut.

(B) In an emotional battery claim, that Co-Employee's alteration of Financial Officer's airline reservation record was an intentional tort.

(C) In an intentional infliction of emotional distress claim, that Co-Employee's actions had a deleterious effect on Financial Officer that was felt in Connecticut.

(D) In a libel claim, that Co-Employee knew Financial Officer lived and worked in Connecticut, and posted a notice to Airline's office there describing him as evil.

See ANSWER on Page 184

117. In the 1972, the United States Congress passed the Clean Water Act. After the Act's passage, the United States government initiated proceedings in federal court against Polluter seeking monetary civil penalties for each day that Polluter was out of compliance with the Act. In its answer, Polluter included a demand for a jury trial. The United States promptly moved to strike the jury demand.

Will the court likely order a jury trial?

(A) No, because the concept of civil penalties did not exist at common law when the Seventh Amendment was ratified.

(B) No, because a government enforcement action is more like an equitable action than an action at law.

(C) Yes, because an action for monetary penalties is more like an action at law than an equitable action.

(D) Yes, because the United States is seeking money, and actions seeking money always trigger the right to a jury trial.

See ANSWER on Page 185

118. Mining Co. took out business interruption insurance from Insurer. Mining Co. experienced mechanical problems in an overseas operation, resulting in a business interruption loss. Insurer refused to cover Mining Co.'s claim. Mining Co. sued Insurer in federal court. Insurer believed that it was not subject to personal jurisdiction in the State in which Mining Co. filed its action.

Which of the following is the most accurate description of Insurer's options?

(A) Insurer must file a motion to dismiss for lack of personal jurisdiction under Rule 12(b)(2) or it will waive the defense.

(B) Insurer may file a motion to dismiss for lack of personal jurisdiction under Rule 12(b)(2), but must do so pursuant to a "special appearance."

(C) Insurer may allow default to be taken against it, and then collaterally attack the default.

(D) Insurer may preserve lack of personal jurisdiction as a defense in its answer, then raise the issue at trial.

See ANSWER on Page 185

119. Artist operates a popular art instruction studio in Connecticut, where he has been a life-long resident. He purchased a year's supply of paints online from Internet Vendor headquartered in Illinois. When his order arrived, Artist noticed that the paints were all dried out and unusable. Artist emailed Internet Vendor, demanding a refund, but the vendor never responded. Artist then filed a breach of contract action against Internet Vendor in Connecticut federal court. Internet Vendor was then properly served. When Internet Vendor failed to answer the complaint, the court entered a default in Artist's favor and against Internet Vendor.

Upon receiving notice of the entry of default, what may Artist now do?

(A) Execute upon the default by seizing any assets Internet Vendor may have in Connecticut.

(B) Execute upon the default by invoking the U.S. Constitution's Full Faith and Credit Clause to seize assets Internet Vendor has in Illinois.

(C) Execute upon the default by moving the federal court in Connecticut to issue a writ of execution against Internet Vendor.

(D) None of the above.

See ANSWER on Page 186

120. Homeowner, domiciled in New Jersey, was badly injured while using a lawnmower made by Manufacturer, a California corporation with its principal place of business in California, and sold by Store, a Delaware Corporation with its principal place of business in New York. Homeowner filed suit in State court in New York asserting a State law negligence claim. Manufacturer and Store jointly filed a timely notice of removal. Homeowner then filed a motion to remand.

How is the federal court most likely to rule on the Homeowner's remand motion?

(A) The court will deny the motion because the defendants both joined in the notice of removal and filed it timely.

(B) The court will deny the motion because there is complete diversity of citizenship among the parties and the amount in controversy likely exceeds $75,000 exclusive of interests and costs.

(C) The court will grant the motion because Store is a citizen of New York.

(D) The court will grant the motion because the plaintiff's choice of forum is entitled to considerable deference.

See ANSWER on Page 186

121. Minivan Driver and Taxi Driver had an accident at an intersection. Minivan Driver sued Taxi Driver in federal court. The party's dispute hinged on the color of the traffic light at the intersection at the moment before the accident. At the jury trial, Minivan Driver, Taxi Driver, and four eyewitnesses testified about the color of the traffic light, with Minivan Driver providing the only testimony that the light favored him. The jury entered a verdict in favor of Minivan Driver. Taxi Driver filed a Rule 50 motion challenging the sufficiency of the evidence at the close of Minivan Driver's case, and renewed the motion after the trial. Taxi Driver then took a timely appeal, arguing that the verdict was not supported by the weight of the evidence and that the jury was prejudiced against him based on his nationality.

Which of the following statements regarding the appeal is most accurate?

(A) The court of appeals will likely affirm the verdict because an appellate court may not count witnesses and cannot "second guess" the jury which heard the testimony and evaluated witness credibility.

(B) The court of appeals will likely affirm the verdict despite the imbalance of evidence unless the court finds that no reasonable jury could have reached a verdict against Taxi Driver.

(C) The court of appeals will likely vacate the verdict because other than the biased testimony of the parties, all of the unbiased witnesses favored Taxi Driver.

(D) The court of appeals will likely vacate the verdict because, when considered in light of Taxi Driver's nationality, the verdict's inconsistency with the testimony of all of the unbiased witnesses provides a compelling indication that the jury was biased or prejudiced.

See ANSWER on Page 187

122. Retailer brought an action for breach of contract in federal court based on diversity jurisdiction against Supplier seeking lost profits. In the complaint, Retailer included a demand for a jury trial. The State legislature had passed a statute that established a panel of independent "special masters," to whom the State courts delegate the calculation of lost profits for all lawsuits filed in the State courts, stating that the measure was intended to advance the important public policy of ensuring uniform standards for lost profit claims. Assume that the Seventh Amendment of the U.S. Constitution establishes a right to a jury trial in a contractual claim for lost profits. Supplier filed a motion asking the court to submit the lost profits determination to a special master instead of the jury, citing the State statute.

Which of the following best describes the court's analysis?

(A) The court will refer the lost profits determination to a special master because the claim is a State law claim, not a federal law claim.

(B) The court will refer the lost profits determination to a special master because the State's special master program was intended to advance a substantive policy, not a procedural matter.

(C) The court will allow the jury to make the lost profits determination because the Seventh Amendment right to a jury trial is a fundamental right which cannot be abridged in either State or federal courts.

(D) The court will allow the jury to make the lost profits determination because the right to a jury trial in this case is directed by Rule 38 and by the Seventh Amendment.

See ANSWER on Page 187

123. Investor owned a condominium unit at the beach on the seashore, but was delinquent in paying property taxes. After three years of nonpayment, the seashore taxing authority bought an action against Investor in the seashore's federal court. A default judgment was entered against Investor when no answer to the complaint was filed.

Under what circumstances may Investor have the default judgment lifted?

(A) Any request by Investor to lift the default judgment will be granted, because defaults are disfavored at federal law as contrary to the preference for adjudications on the merits.

(B) A request by Investor showing good cause for mistakenly failing to file an answer will compel the lifting of the default judgment.

(C) A request by Investor to lift the default judgment on the basis of mistake or inadvertence will prompt the court to consider whether the default was willful, whether a meritorious defense exists, and whether the claimant will be prejudiced.

(D) No request by Investor to lift the default judgment will be granted, because public policy dictates that there be an end to litigation, and that once matters are resolved they are to be considered forever settled between the parties.

See ANSWER on Page 188

124. Subcontractor sued General Contractor in federal court for unpaid invoices. Shortly after filing the complaint, Subcontractor began having financial difficulties. General Contractor tried to schedule the Rule 26(f) conference, but Subcontractor did not cooperate. The court scheduled a Rule 16 conference, and Subcontractor failed to appear. General Contractor then served extensive written discovery requests on Subcontractor, and Subcontractor failed to respond.

What is General Contractor's best course of action?

(A) File a motion to dismiss under Rule 12 for failure to comply with the Federal Rules of Civil Procedure.

(B) File a motion for sanctions under Rule 37 seeking dismissal as a sanction.

(C) File a motion for involuntary dismissal under Rule 41.

(D) All of the above.

See ANSWER on Page 188

125. A mining company sued an electricity supplier for breach of the master services agreement. Neither party filed a jury demand, but the court decided to empanel an advisory jury and neither party objected. At the conclusion of the trial, the advisory jury reached a verdict in favor of the mining company. The judge entered a judgment adopting the advisory jury's verdict, and the electricity supplier appealed, contending that the judge improperly adopted the advisory jury's verdict.

How will the court of appeals likely rule?

(A) The court of appeals will likely affirm the district court, because district courts have broad discretion to empanel advisory juries.

(B) The court of appeals will likely affirm the district court, because district courts have broad discretion to accept or reject the verdict reached by advisory juries.

(C) The court of appeals will likely reverse the district court if it finds that the advisory jury's verdict was not supported by the weight of the evidence.

(D) The court of appeals will likely reverse the district court, because the district court failed to make findings of fact and conclusions of law.

See ANSWER on Page 189

126. Buyer purchased a new automobile from Dealer. Two weeks later, Buyer returned the automobile and demanded a full refund, insisting that the brakes sometimes failed to work. Dealer carefully inspected the vehicle and uncovered no braking malfunction. Buyer sued Dealer in federal court for violation of federally-mandated automobile warranties, which covered all brake failures. At the jury trial, Buyer offered only his own testimony that, occasionally (once or twice during the time he possessed the car), the brakes failed to engage. Dealer introduced evidence from its senior mechanic, its director of service, and two expert witnesses that, after many hours of testing and inspection, the braking system on the automobile proved to be working perfectly. Dealer also introduced the manager of a local accounting firm, who testified that, during the time Buyer possessed the automobile, he was laid off by that accounting firm and had later expressed worry about his ability to pay his monthly bills. Dealer timely moved the trial judge for a judgment in its favor as a matter of law.

How should the trial judge rule on Dealer's motion?

(A) Grant the motion because any verdict in Buyer's favor would be against the weight of the evidence.

(B) Deny the motion because Buyer offered his own testimony that his claim has merit.

(C) Grant the motion because, in face of Dealer's evidence, a jury would be unlikely to find Buyer's story credible.

(D) Deny the motion because Buyer has a constitutionally guaranteed right to a trial by jury.

See ANSWER on Page 189

127. At the trial of a tort action, the federal judge accidentally omitted the word "gross" when reading a jury instruction proposed by the defendant that instructed the jury as to the law if it found gross negligence on the part of the defendant. As a result, the jury instruction as read attributed those consequences to ordinary negligence. Counsel for the defendant did not notice the omission, and did not object. After the jury reached a general verdict in favor of the plaintiff, the defendant noticed the omission in reviewing the trial transcript.

May the defendant raise the erroneous jury instruction on appeal?

(A) No, because failure to object to jury instructions before the jury is discharged is an absolute waiver of the objection.

(B) No, because inattentiveness of a party's lawyer is not an adequate excuse for failure to object to jury instructions before the jury is discharged.

(C) Yes, if the court finds that the judge's omission was a plain error that affected the defendant's substantial rights.

(D) Yes, if the instruction was not an accurate statement of the law, a party may always challenge it on appeal.

See ANSWER on Page 190

128. Parent purchased a toy drone for Minor Child from a local toy shop near their home in Salt Lake City, Utah. They both read carefully all operating instructions. One weekend day, while flying the drone in a vacant parking lot in Salt Lake City, the drone's software malfunctioned, causing the drone to crash into Minor Child who sustained serious injury. Parent filed a lawsuit in the local State court in Salt Lake City against both Drone Co. (the manufacturer) and Design Co. (the software designer). Both corporate defendants are subject to personal jurisdiction in Boise, Idaho, the same location where the drone's software was negligently designed.

If the defendants successfully remove the lawsuit to federal court, where will its venue lie at the moment that removal takes effect?

(A) In the federal court embracing the city of Salt Lake City, Utah because that is where Parent and Minor Child reside.

(B) In the federal court embracing the city of Salt Lake City, Utah because the State claim had been pending there at the time of removal.

(C) In the federal court embracing the city of Boise, Idaho because that is where both defendants reside.

(D) In the federal court embracing the city of Boise, Idaho because that is where a substantial part of the events or omissions giving rise to the case occurred.

See ANSWER on Page 190

129. Passenger brought a federal lawsuit against Cruise Line, alleging that one evening during a transatlantic ocean crossing, while Passenger was enjoying her lobster-with-crab-meat dinner, the negligently-piloted ship collided with an iceberg and sank. Passenger made it safely to a lifeboat, but she suffered traumatic stress, various incidental injuries, and a complete loss of her belongings. Passenger sought damages to compensate her for these injuries and losses. At the same time that she filed her complaint, Passenger also filed a motion for summary judgment, seeking prompt entry of judgment in her favor, supporting each element of her claim with competent proof. Cruise Line opposed the motion with credible, sworn affidavits which averred simply that, on the night in question, the ship's restaurant did not serve a lobster-with-crab-meat dinner.

How should the court rule on the pending motion for summary judgment?

(A) The court should grant the motion, because the motion record reveals no factual dispute.

(B) The court should grant the motion, because the motion record reveals no material facts in dispute.

(C) The court should deny the motion, because only defendants may file summary judgment motions.

(D) The court should deny the motion, because summary judgment motions cannot be made prior to the filing of the defendant's answer.

See ANSWER on Page 191

130. A Chinese company manufactured hoverboards. It entered into a contract with an American distribution company to sell the hoverboards in State A, which had many colleges with students that the manufacturer thought would be receptive to hoverboards. A college student, attending college in State A, bought a hoverboard manufactured by the Chinese company after seeing advertisements in the college's newspaper placed by the distributor. The student then transferred to another college in State B. While the student was at college in State B, the hoverboard subsequently caught on fire in the student's dormitory room, injuring the student and destroying some of his personal property. The student filed suit in federal court in State B, naming the Chinese manufacturer and the U.S. distributor as defendants. Both the manufacturer and the distributor filed motions challenging personal jurisdiction, submitting affidavits asserting that neither defendant had any employees or property in State B, neither had placed advertising in State B, and neither had made sales in State B. The student responded that specific jurisdiction was appropriate because the harm had occurred in State B.

Will the defendants likely succeed in their challenge to personal jurisdiction?

(A) Neither defendant will likely succeed.

(B) The manufacturer will likely succeed but the distributor will likely not succeed.

(C) The distributor will likely succeed but the manufacturer will likely not succeed.

(D) Both defendants will likely succeed.

See ANSWER on Page 191

131. MediCo manufactured a gel to be injected into the human body to detect the presence of a certain bacteria, X2R7. The gel MediCo produced was solely diagnostic; it simply assisted physicians in identifying the presence of this X2R7 bacteria and had no medicinal effect on the body whatsoever. Physicians suspected that Patient had contracted the X2R7 bacteria, and injected Patient with the MediCo gel to check. Patient developed a severe adverse reaction to the gel. Patient filed a diversity lawsuit against MediCo in federal court seeking compensation for the resulting injury. It was undisputed that the merits of Patient's claim were to be governed by the substantive law of State X, but that law was uncertain. State X required special warnings for persons prescribed a "medicine," but far fewer warnings for persons receiving a "device." If the MediCo gel was found to be a "medicine," Patient's case was strong. Conversely, if the gel was merely a "device," Patient's case was weak. Finding no controlling precedent from State X to answer this question, the federal trial court predicted that State X would consider the gel to be a "medicine" and then awarded Patient substantial damages. No post-trial motions or appeals were filed. Two years later, in a different lawsuit filed by a different individual, the State X Supreme Court held that the MediCo gel was a "device" that required no special warnings.

What is the likely consequence of the later, definitive holding by the State X Supreme Court on the federal court's mistaken prediction in Patient's lawsuit of the substantive law of State X?

(A) The result in Patient's lawsuit will not be disturbed.

(B) The result in Patient's lawsuit will be vacated because the federal court mistakenly predicted State X's substantive law.

(C) The result in Patient's lawsuit will be vacated, but only if a federal appeals panel decides that the trial judge conducted a methodologically flawed *Erie* analysis.

(D) The result in Patient's lawsuit will be vacated, but only if the federal trial judge first determines that the equities favor a retrial.

See ANSWER on Page 192

132. In an assault and battery case, the federal judge carefully—and correctly—instructed the jury for an hour on the controlling law and the parties' respective burdens. The judge reminded the jury of the elements of the torts plaintiff had to prove, that plaintiff bore the burden of proof as to each element, and that plaintiff had to carry that burden by a preponderance of the evidence. In the final sentence delivered to the jury prior to their deliberations, however, the judge inadvertently misspoke: "And so, ladies and gentlemen of the jury, unless you find that the *defendant* has carried each of these burdens, you must return a verdict in defendant's favor." Assume a proper objection to the error was made, but the judge (misremembering the sentence) believed no error had actually occurred. The jury returned a verdict for the plaintiff.

Is this misspoken jury instruction sufficient to overturn the verdict and grant defendant a new trial?

(A) Yes, because the statement assigning the defendant the burden was legally incorrect.

(B) No, because the instructions have to be considered in their entirety.

(C) Yes, because the error certainly misled the jury.

(D) No, because errors in jury instructions are considered harmless error.

See ANSWER on Page 192

133. Soccer Fan One attended the World Cup in a country outside the United States. Soccer Fan One met two other United States citizens while at the event, Soccer Fan Two and Soccer Fan Three, and they struck up a friendship. Between World Cup matches, Soccer Fan Two and Soccer Fan Three told Soccer Fan One that they knew a local bar where there was good music and the food and beverages were inexpensive. Soccer Fan One (who had never before traveled outside the United States) asked whether the bar was in a safe part of the city, and Soccer Fan Two and Soccer Fan Three assured him it would be safe. Soccer Fan One went to the bar and had a nice evening, but when he left the bar, he was robbed and beaten, suffering significant injuries. Subsequent investigation revealed that the bar was in a notoriously dangerous neighborhood. Soccer Fan One was a domicile of State A. Soccer Fan Two was a domicile of State B. Soccer Fan Three was a domicile of State C. After returning to the United States, Soccer Fan One brought a State law claim in federal court in State B, invoking the court's diversity jurisdiction. Soccer Fan Three brought a motion challenging venue.

How will the judge likely rule on the venue motion?

(A) The judge will likely grant the motion if it finds that Soccer Fan Three is not subject to personal jurisdiction in State B with respect to Soccer Fan One's claim.

(B) The judge will likely grant the motion if it finds that a substantial part of the events or omissions giving rise to Soccer Fan One's claim did not occur in State B.

(C) The judge will likely deny the motion if Soccer Fan Two did not join in the motion.

(D) The judge will likely deny the motion if it finds that Soccer Fan Two is subject to personal jurisdiction in State B with respect to Soccer Fan One's claim.

See ANSWER on Page 193

134. Farmer purchased a special, organic insecticide from ChemCo to help resolve an infestation that was destroying a cornfield. After applying the insecticide, Farmer noticed no change in the level of infestation. When attempts seeking an amicable refund failed, Farmer sued ChemCo in federal court. The lawsuit was filed on March 1. Because ChemCo was a small enterprise, Farmer's process server was unable to complete service on ChemCo until June 15.

Is Farmer's service of process vulnerable to a pre-answer dismissal motion?

(A) Yes, because it was untimely.

(B) No, provided the service occurred within the applicable statute of limitations expired on Farmer's claim, service is always considered timely.

(C) No, because the service was made within the 120-day window following filing.

(D) No, unless ChemCo can show that the service delay until June 15 prejudiced its substantial rights in the litigation.

See ANSWER on Page 194

135. Patient sued Doctor in federal court for medical malpractice. Shortly after Doctor filed an answer to Patient's complaint, the presiding federal judge issued a scheduling order to govern the future progress of this litigation.

The judge's scheduling order would be improper under the Federal Rules of Civil Procedure if it did which of the following?

(A) Issued after the judge consulted with the parties only through mailed correspondence.

(B) Established a time deadline by which all amendments to the pleadings must be completed.

(C) Changed the deadline set by the Rules for the parties to make their initial disclosures.

(D) Ordered the parties to request a conference with the court before filing any discovery motion.

See ANSWER on Page 194

136. Student was a foreign national—a citizen of Country X—who was admitted into the United States for the purposes of obtaining a post-graduate degree in environmental engineering at College. Prior to the start of the autumn semester, College refused to allow Student to participate in a federal loan program. Student filed a federal question lawsuit against College contesting the denial of federal loan eligibility. To the same lawsuit, Student added a second claim, under State law, faulting College for refusing to allow Student to enroll in extracurricular activities using only a passport as photo identification. The State in which College was located forbade any student from participating in State-funded extracurricular activities unless the student first presented a State-issued driver's license. A treaty between the United States and Country X permitted citizens of Country X to use their passports as acceptable photo identification for "all purposes" within the United States.

How is the federal court most likely to resolve the merits of Student's second claim?

(A) If the second claim is based on alienage diversity jurisdiction, the federal court will rule that State law governs because, under the *Erie* doctrine, it is outcome determinative.

(B) If the second claim is based on alienage diversity jurisdiction, the federal court will rule that federal law governs because, under the *Erie* doctrine, there is no countervailing federal issue.

(C) If the second claim is based on supplemental jurisdiction, the federal court will rule that State law governs because the *Erie* doctrine does not apply in any supplemental jurisdiction case.

(D) If the second claim is based on supplemental jurisdiction, the federal court will rule that federal law governs because it is supreme.

See ANSWER on Page 195

137. A group of consumers brought a class action in federal court against telecommunications companies asserting a variety of federal and state law causes of action relating to the prices for text messaging. The defendants moved to dismiss only the cause of action asserting violations of federal antitrust laws, arguing that the complaint did not satisfy the pleading requirements set forth in *Bell Atlantic Corp. v. Twombly*, 550 U.S. 544 (2007), as to the antitrust violations. The court granted the motion.

May the consumers take an immediate appeal from this ruling?

(A) Yes, if both the trial court and the court of appeals exercise their discretion to allow an immediate appeal.

(B) Yes, because the ruling constitutes an appealable final order as it is a final determination of the antitrust claim.

(C) Yes, if the defendants consent to an immediate appeal.

(D) No, because the presence of other claims that were not dismissed renders the ruling interlocutory.

See ANSWER on Page 196

138. Department Store was served with a complaint and summons drafted by Customer who was representing himself. The complaint was inartfully drafted, leaving Department Store uncertain as to the precise claims that Customer was asserting. Department Store filed an answer that included failure to state a claim as a defense. Department Store simultaneously filed a motion for a more definite statement, arguing that the complaint was so vague and ambiguous that it did not state a proper claim.

How will the trial judge most likely rule on Department Store's motion?

(A) Deny the motion because Customer was representing himself *pro se*, and courts relieve *pro se* plaintiffs of the obligation to meet pleading requirements.

(B) Deny the motion because Department Store also filed an answer.

(C) Grant the motion if the motion was Department Store's first motion under Rule 12 and the court agrees that the complaint was impermissibly vague and ambiguous.

(D) Grant the motion because failure to state a claim may be raised as late as trial.

See ANSWER on Page 197

139. An investor deposited a portion of her assets in a money market account operated by a bank. Someone hacked her account and transferred those funds through a series of untraceable transactions. The investor filed suit in federal court, asserting a claim for restitution of her funds, and seeking a judgment in the proper, unhacked amount of her account balance plus interest. Her complaint contained the phrase, "jury trial demanded." She did not file any separate documents containing a jury trial demand. The bank filed a motion to strike the jury trial demand at the same time it filed its answer, 25 days after the investor filed her complaint.

Does the investor have a right to a jury trial?

(A) No, because her claim is one for restitution.

(B) No, because she did not file a proper jury trial demand.

(C) Yes, because she is seeking money damages, the traditional legal remedy, and the demand may be part of the complaint.

(D) Yes, because the bank waived its objection to the jury trial demand by not filing its motion to strike within 21 days.

See ANSWER on Page 197

140. A citizen filed a complaint against a police officer in federal court asserting a State law claim contending that the police officer had negligently harmed the citizen. The police officer filed a motion to dismiss for failure to state a claim, arguing that the police officer was immune from negligence claims under an applicable State statute. Upon reading this motion, the citizen decided to file an amended complaint asserting reckless conduct by the police officer, which would fall outside the scope of the State immunity statute.

Does the citizen need the court's permission to amend the complaint?

(A) Yes, unless the police officer stipulates in writing to the amendment.

(B) Yes, unless the citizen files the amendment within 30 days of service of the police officer's motion to dismiss.

(C) No, if the citizen has not previously amended the complaint and files the amended complaint timely.

(D) No, as long as the claims in the amended complaint arise out of the same conduct, transaction, or occurrence set out—or attempted to be set out—in the original complaint.

See ANSWER on Page 198

141. A manufacturer entered into a contract to obtain parts from a supplier. One shipment contained parts that the manufacturer believed to be defective. It filed suit in federal court against the supplier for breach of contract. Three months after the supplier filed its answer, the manufacturer received another shipment that it believed also contained defective parts.

What is the manufacturer's best procedural option for adding a claim relating to the second shipment?

(A) The manufacturer may, without the opponent's consent or leave of court, file an amended complaint, assuming that the manufacturer had not already amended its complaint previously.

(B) The manufacturer must file a motion to amend the complaint.

(C) The manufacturer may, without opponent's consent or leave of court, file a supplement to the complaint, assuming that the manufacturer had not already supplemented its complaint previously.

(D) The manufacturer must file a motion to supplement the complaint.

See ANSWER on Page 198

142. At the conclusion of a bench trial in federal court, the district court judge entered a judgment that stated in its entirety, "Having reviewed the evidence presented at trial and having assessed the credibility of the witnesses, this Court finds as a matter of fact and law that the plaintiff failed to carry its burden of proving negligence on the part of the defendant. Accordingly, the Court enters judgment in favor of the defendant and against the plaintiff."

Does this filing comply with the rules regarding trials by the court?

(A) No, because the Federal Rules of Civil Procedure require that the court first issue a report and recommendation and allow the parties an opportunity to object.

(B) No, because the Federal Rules of Civil Procedure require that the court state its findings of fact and conclusions of law on the record in sufficient detail to permit meaningful appellate review.

(C) Yes, if the plaintiff did not request detailed findings.

(D) Yes, because hearing the evidence and assessing the credibility of witnesses lies within the sound discretion of the judge.

See ANSWER on Page 199

143. Power Company operated an electrical power plant in San Diego, California. With the success of its off-shore wind power installation, Power Company decommissioned its electrical plant and agreed to sell the plant's antiquated transformers to a municipality in Georgia. Power Company is only amenable to personal jurisdiction in California. Power Company hired CalFreight to coordinate the shipping. CalFreight's sole place of business is in Los Angeles, California. CalFreight engaged Railroad to transport the transformers to Georgia. As a result of a moment of careless inattention, Railroad's train derailed in Texas, which caused the destruction of Power Company's transformers. Power Company sued CalFreight and Railroad in Texas federal court to recover for the loss. Railroad is a Missouri corporation, amenable to personal jurisdiction in several States, but not in California. Thereafter, Power Company filed a motion for a transfer of venue to California federal court, citing the convenience of the parties and witnesses and the interests of justice.

If CalFreight and Railroad both agreed to the motion, how should the court rule?

(A) The motion will be granted; venue is properly laid in California because both Power Company and CalFreight reside there.

(B) The motion will be granted, even though California would have been an improper venue at the time the lawsuit was originally filed.

(C) The motion will be denied; venue in California is improper because defendants do not all reside there and no substantial part of the events or omissions giving rise to the claim occurred there.

(D) The motion will be denied, because the improper California venue cannot be excused by consent.

See ANSWER on Page 200

144. A man domiciled in State A traveled to State C for a skiing vacation. While skiing, he hit a loose piece of equipment, lost control, and struck a woman who was also on a skiing vacation at the time of the incident. The woman was domiciled in State B. The woman filed suit in federal court against the man in State A, which has only one federal district. The man filed a motion to transfer venue to State C, arguing that the witnesses and evidence were all located in State C. The court granted the motion. Following the transfer, the man moved for dismissal for failure to state a claim, arguing that the woman's claim was barred by the statute of limitations. Under the statute of limitations in State A, the woman's claim would be timely, but under the statute of limitations in State C, her claims would be barred.

Will the court be likely to grant the motion?

(A) Yes, if State A's choice-of-law provisions would apply the substantive laws of State C.

(B) Yes, because, when hearing a State law claim, a federal court applies the substantive law of the forum state and federal procedural law, and statutes of limitation are generally held to be substantive.

(C) No, because, when hearing a State law claim, a federal court applies the substantive law of the forum state and federal procedural law, and statutes of limitation are generally held to be procedural.

(D) No, if State C's choice-of-law provisions would apply the laws of State A.

See ANSWER on Page 201

145. Homeowner acquired an investment property in a planned residential community in Florida, governed by a detailed set of covenants and property restrictions. One such covenant obligated Homeowner to make monthly payments to the Community Association for neighborhood upkeep. For years, Homeowner failed to make the required monthly payments, and the delinquent debt eventually rose to $85,000. At that point, the Community Association sued Homeowner (a citizen of Ohio) in federal court, demanding payment of the past-due sum. After a day-long bench trial, the judge announced her intention to rule in favor of the Community Association. Hearing the judge's decision, Homeowner immediately filed a notice of appeal. However, before she could formally enter judgment in the Community Association's favor, the judge was stricken with a serious illness, causing her to remain absent from court for four months. Eventually, the judge recovered, resumed her service on the court, and then entered final judgment in favor of the Community Association in the lawsuit.

Has Homeowner filed a proper appeal?

(A) Homeowner's notice of appeal was prematurely filed, but the appeal was nonetheless proper.

(B) Homeowner's notice of appeal was timely, because it was filed within 30 days of the judge's announcement of a decision adverse to the appealing party.

(C) Homeowner's notice of appeal was improperly filed, but the error will be overlooked given the post-announcement disruption caused by the judge's poor health.

(D) Homeowner's notice of appeal was a nullity, because it was filed before the judge had entered an appealable final order in the litigation.

See ANSWER on Page 201

146. A taxpayer believed that his accountant had given him poor tax advice, and engaged an attorney to prepare a complaint to file in federal court. The attorney hired a process server. The accountant lived alone, and the process server repeatedly attempted unsuccessfully to serve the accountant at his residence. Believing that the accountant was deliberately attempting to evade service, the process server delivered the summons and complaint to the receptionist at the accountant's office, who promised to deliver it to the accountant.

Did the process server properly effect service on the accountant?

(A) No, because service at the accountant's regular place of business was not reasonably calculated to apprise the accountant of the action.

(B) No, because the Federal Rules of Civil Procedure never authorize service at the defendant's regular place of business.

(C) Yes, but only if the State law of the State where the taxpayer filed the complaint authorizes service at the defendant's regular place of business.

(D) Yes, but only if the court finds the process server was sufficiently diligent in attempting to effectuate abode service before resorting to service at the accountant's regular place of business.

See ANSWER on Page 202

147. A man sued a national magazine in state court in State A, contending that its editorial policies unfairly portrayed male behaviors. The magazine filed a motion to dismiss the complaint for failure to state a claim, and the man then voluntarily dismissed the complaint without prejudice. The man then filed another complaint in federal court in State A that asserted the same claim. Again, the magazine filed a motion to dismiss for failure to state a claim. The man filed a notice of dismissal, again specifying that the dismissal was without prejudice.

If the man makes substantive changes to the complaint to address the issues that the magazine raised in its motions to dismiss, may the man file and pursue a third action in federal court in State B asserting the same claim?

(A) Yes, if the substantive law of State B is different from the substantive law of State A.

(B) Yes, if the court determines that the man was operating in good faith and was not harassing the magazine.

(C) Yes, if the man reimburses the magazine for its attorney's fees in defending the first two actions.

(D) No.

See ANSWER on Page 203

148. Movie Star was accused by Tabloid of arranging for the poisoning death of a former spouse who had died mysteriously. Movie Star sued Tabloid in State court for defamation. Because the applicable State law forbade it, the complaint filed on Movie Star's behalf did not assign a value to the claimed reputational injury nor did it demand a particular sum as compensation.

If the parties have citizenships that are diverse, can Tabloid remove the lawsuit to federal court under diversity jurisdiction?

(A) Yes, where a State court complaint seeks monetary relief but fails to assign a value, a qualifying amount in controversy is presumed.

(B) No, where a State court complaint seeks monetary relief but fails to assign a value, the case has lost its capacity to invoke a qualifying amount in controversy.

(C) Yes, so long as the factfinder is certain to conclude that the claimed reputational injury exceeds the jurisdictional minimum, the case is removable.

(D) No, unless Tabloid alleges a proper qualifying amount in controversy in its notice of removal, which the federal court properly finds exceeds the jurisdictional minimum.

See ANSWER on Page 203

149. Family General Store had been operating in the valley for more than one hundred years. The U.S. Government exercised its eminent domain authority and condemned the land on which Family General Store was located in order to construct a hydroelectric plant. The U.S. Government tendered payment to Family General Store for the condemnation, but Family General Store believed the tendered sum was insufficient. Family General Store then filed a lawsuit in federal court against the U.S. Government, seeking greater compensation. As a result of a calendaring oversight, the attorneys for the U.S. Government never filed an answer to Family General Store's complaint.

Can Family General Store default the U.S. Government?

(A) Yes, both default and default judgments against the U.S. Government proceed in the same manner as they would with any other defendant.

(B) No, a default cannot be entered against the U.S. Government.

(C) No, a judgment by default cannot be entered against the U.S. Government.

(D) No, unless Family General Store first satisfies the judge that the Store's claim is meritorious.

See ANSWER on Page 204

150. A pedestrian slipped and fell on some ice outside a railroad terminal. The pedestrian sued the railroad in federal court, alleging that the ice remained from a previous snowstorm, and that the railroad terminal operator was negligent for failing to remove the ice or warn the pedestrian. At trial, the pedestrian testified to the above facts. The railroad terminal operator presented records from the United States Weather Bureau, arguing that the records irrefutably proved that the ice could not have come from the previous storm. After introducing this evidence, the railroad terminal operator moved for judgment as a matter of law. Assume the applicable State law would require the pedestrian to prove that the ice was formed during the previous snowstorm.

How should the trial judge rule on the railroad terminal operator's motion?

(A) Grant the motion if the court concludes that the United States Weather Bureau data conclusively demonstrates that the ice was not formed in the previous snowstorm.

(B) Deny the motion because the court may not assess the pedestrian's credibility in ruling on a motion for judgment as a matter of law.

(C) Grant the motion because documentary evidence is always considered more credible than witness testimony.

(D) Deny the motion because, in the context of a motion for judgment as a matter of law, documentary evidence is treated the same as witness testimony.

See ANSWER on Page 204

151. Novelist contracted with Publishing House to publish a new work of fiction, for which Novelist would be paid royalties on each sale. Novelist later believed Publishing House was wrongfully concealing the true volume of book sales in a scheme to deprive Novelist of earned royalties. Novelist's attorney brought suit in federal court against Publishing House. Although the attorney had Publishing House's proper postal mailing address, the attorney chose to serve original process on Publishing House by email, relying on a local procedure permitting service by email in State court. The email address Novelist's attorney used was the one Publishing House supplied to Novelist for all business correspondence and which had proven highly reliable in the past. This time, however, Novelist's attorney received an immediate, automated, bounce-back email reply which read: "This Email Recipient's mailbox is full. Delivery will not be re-attempted. Try again later." The attorney made no further attempt at service.

What best describes the status of the attorney's attempted service of process by email?

(A) The email service was invalid because email service is never permitted in federal court.

(B) The email service was valid because it was, at the time of transmission, reasonably calculated under the circumstances to afford Publishing House constitutionally proper notice.

(C) The email service was invalid because it deprived Publishing House of its due process rights.

(D) The email service was valid if the service comported with the State procedures for service of original process by email.

See ANSWER on Page 205

152. Dentist A and Dentist B were long-time business partners who had a damaging professional disagreement. Dentist A subsequently sued Dentist B in federal court for attempting to privately solicit common patients, and Dentist B counterclaimed against Dentist A for breach of their contract for distributing profits. After a lengthy trial, the jury found against Dentist A on the wrongful solicitation claim, and against Dentist B on the wrongful profits distribution claim. Neither Dentist received any recovery. Both decided to appeal the outcome.

What best describes the proper time for filing an appeal?

(A) Within 30 days of the date the jury returned its verdict.

(B) Within 30 days of the date the trial judge signed the judgment.

(C) Within 30 days after an assistant clerk of court typed the judgment onto the docket.

(D) Within 30 days after the litigant receives service of the judgment.

See ANSWER on Page 205

153. A client came to a lawyer seeking to bring a claim against a defendant. The lawyer was familiar with the area of law implicated by the client's situation and, without conducting any new research, filed a diversity complaint in federal court on behalf of the client. Unbeknownst to the lawyer, the relevant State supreme court had recently issued an opinion changing the law, undermining the claim set forth in the complaint. The federal district court issued an order to show cause why it should not impose sanctions pursuant to Rule 11, and the lawyer candidly admitted to having failed to look for or find the recent State supreme court case.

Which of the following sanctions would not be authorized under Rule 11?

(A) An order requiring the lawyer to attend continuing legal education courses relating to Rule 11.

(B) An order requiring the client to pay a monetary penalty into the court.

(C) An order requiring the lawyer to pay a monetary penalty into the court.

(D) An order dismissing the complaint.

See ANSWER on Page 206

154. A construction worker was struck by a backhoe being operated by a different contractor at a job site. The construction worker sued the contractor in federal court, asserting a claim for negligence. At trial, the construction worker presented expert testimony that he was disabled as a result of injuries to his back sustained when the backhoe struck him. The contractor presented contrary expert testimony that the construction worker had a preexisting back condition from an incident that occurred a year before the backhoe accident that caused his disability and pain and suffering. The jury returned a verdict in favor of the contractor. Twenty-three months after the judge entered the final judgment, the construction worker received a letter from his primary doctor stating that the doctor had found an x-ray taken a few weeks before the backhoe accident that proved that the construction worker did not have a preexisting back injury. During discovery, the construction worker had asked his primary doctor for any records that might help demonstrate that he did not have a preexisting condition, but the doctor had not been able to locate the x-ray at that time. Upon receiving the x-ray, the construction worker promptly moved for relief from the judgment.

How should the trial judge rule on the construction worker's motion?

(A) Grant the motion because the construction worker filed it less than two years after entry of the judgment.

(B) Grant the motion because the construction worker could not have, with reasonable diligence, discovered the new evidence in time to move for a new trial.

(C) Deny the motion because the construction worker discovered the new evidence too late.

(D) Deny the motion because the failure to locate the evidence was in no way the fault of the contractor.

See ANSWER on Page 206

155. Harbor Worker retired from the shipyards several years ago, and has since learned that several of his former co-workers have contracted life-endangering illnesses from many years of asbestos exposure. Harbor Worker sought a physician's advice who, after a comprehensive exam, pronounced him presently free of asbestos-related injuries. But the physician also cautioned that such illnesses can develop over time and that Harbor Worker should be vigilant in having his health checked. Harbor Worker later sought legal counsel, who filed a federal lawsuit on Harbor Worker's behalf against Employer for Harbor Worker's "fear of" contracting a future asbestos injury. Employer filed a pre-answer motion to dismiss, arguing that the applicable law did not recognize "fear of" claims, and that Harbor Worker's claim was therefore unripe and must be dismissed.

If Harbor Worker's legal counsel fails to respond to Employer's motion, how will the court rule on that motion?

(A) The court will grant the motion, because the failure to oppose the motion rendered it uncontested.

(B) The court will deny the motion, unless the court first determines that Employer's contention is correct as a matter of applicable law.

(C) The court will grant the motion, because unripe claims fail to raise a case or controversy sufficient to trigger the subject-matter jurisdiction of the federal courts.

(D) The court will deny the motion, because Employer's argument cannot be resolved on a pre-answer motion to dismiss.

See ANSWER on Page 207

156. Consumer applied to CreditCo for a credit card. CreditCo denied Consumer's application. Consumer thereafter filed a complaint in federal court against CreditCo, alleging that the denial of Consumer's credit card application violated certain federal anti-discrimination laws.

CreditCo may not choose which of the following options if it wishes to properly respond to this lawsuit?

(A) File a one-paragraph answer, reading: "All allegations in the complaint are denied."

(B) Deny a paragraph in the complaint because it is mostly false, even if it is also partially true.

(C) Respond to certain paragraphs in the complaint by stating that it cannot either admit or deny those allegations because the information and knowledge it has is insufficient to allow it to do so.

(D) Move for a dismissal of the lawsuit without ever first having filed an answer to the paragraphed allegations.

See ANSWER on Page 207

157. Molecular Biologist, a citizen and resident of Sweden, collaborated with University, located in Colorado, to investigate whether a certain protein could be artificially modified to provide a new cancer treatment. All of the scientific work Molecular Biologist performed occurred in laboratories in Arizona, California, and Sweden. Neither he nor University conducted any experiments in Colorado. After the investigation proved successful, Molecular Biologist filed to have himself named as sole owner of the intellectual property rights for the new treatment. University responded by filing a lawsuit against Molecular Biologist in Colorado federal court, alleging breach of the terms of a contract under which Molecular Biologist and University had agreed to share equally any intellectual property rights from this work.

If Molecular Biologist files a motion with the court to dismiss University's lawsuit for improper venue, how is the court most likely to rule?

(A) It will deny the motion.

(B) It will grant the motion, because no substantial part of the events or omissions giving rise to University's claim occurred in Colorado.

(C) It will grant the motion, because Molecular Biologist does not reside in Colorado.

(D) It will grant the motion, unless the University's contract contains a forum selection clause choosing Colorado as the site for any litigation.

See ANSWER on Page 208

158. Assume Plaintiff sued Defendant in a federal court. The lawsuit has ended, and judgment has been entered. Now pending before the court is a motion to alter or amend the judgment.

In which of the following circumstances might the trial court properly grant the motion to alter or amend?

(A) Plaintiff lost on summary judgment, without having contested choice of law. Plaintiff now argues that the judgment must be revisited because the court applied the wrong State's substantive law in making its ruling.

(B) Defendant lost on summary judgment, having been unable to prove her title to artwork. Defendant now argues that the judgment must be revisited because the art thief was just apprehended with evidence confirming her title.

(C) Defendant lost on summary judgment, without having raised a certain defense. Defendant now argues that the judgment must be revisited because each of the elements of that defense is satisfied.

(D) Plaintiff lost on summary judgment, unable to prove his entitlement to a certain number of stock options. Plaintiff now argues that the judgment must be revisited because under another theory he is clearly entitled to a different number of stock options.

See ANSWER on Page 209

159. Customer often visited Shopping Mall. While there, Customer was frustrated by certain physical barriers in place at two of Shopping Mall's tenants—Food Store and Pet Store—that impeded her wheelchair use. Food Store designed its check-out lanes so narrowly that Customer's wheelchair could not pass through easily. Pet Store designed its entryway with two large aquariums that impeded Customer's ability to even enter the store. Customer repeatedly requested each store to adjust its physical barriers to avoid impeding her wheelchair access, but neither has done so. Customer contended that both stores, along with Shopping Mall as their landlord (who, pursuant to the leases, had to separately approve each tenant's store design), were violating her rights as a disabled person to access places of public accommodation.

May Customer file a single federal lawsuit against Shopping Mall, Food Store, and Pet Store for disability discrimination?

(A)   Customer may sue Shopping Mall, Food Store, and Pet Store in a single lawsuit.

(B)   Customer may sue Food Store and Pet Store in a single lawsuit, but cannot sue all three in a single lawsuit.

(C)   Customer may sue Shopping Mall and Food Store in a single lawsuit, or sue Shopping Mall and Pet Store in a single lawsuit, but cannot sue all three in a single lawsuit.

(D)   Customer may sue Shopping Mall, Food Store, and Pet Store, but may only do so in three separate lawsuits.

See ANSWER on Page 210

160. Retailer sued Manufacturer in federal court for breach of a supply contract. The dispute arose out of Manufacturer's failure to supply the products that Retailer had ordered, following a fire in Manufacturer's facility. During trial, the contract was admitted into evidence, and each party offered testimony about its understanding of the contract's force majeure clause, without objection from the other party. In the context of the parties' dispute, if the force majeure clause were triggered, Retailer should lose, otherwise Retailer should win. Following a bench trial, the judge made findings of fact and conclusions of law, then entered judgment in favor of Retailer. Manufacturer timely appealed, arguing that the judge erroneously found that the facility fire was not covered by the contract's force majeure clause.

Which of these most accurately describes the standard of review that the court of appeals will use when considering the trial court's conclusion of law regarding the meaning of the contract's force majeure clause?

(A)   The court of appeals will review for plain error, based on the lack of any objections to the relevant testimony during the trial.

(B)   The court of appeals will use the clearly erroneous standard, whether or not the contract language is found to be ambiguous.

(C)   The court of appeals will review for abuse of discretion, because in a bench trial, the judge has broad discretion over the proceedings.

(D)   The court of appeals will review de novo, if the contract language is unambiguous.

See ANSWER on Page 211

161. Franchisor developed a patented method for flavoring soft-serve ice cream. Franchisor licensed to local operators the right to use this patented method, provided those local operators paid a monthly franchise fee and faithfully obeyed all of Franchisor's operating conditions. Town Ice Co. acquired the right to use Franchisor's patented ice cream method, but then adjusted certain ingredients in producing the ice cream. Franchisor sought a preliminary injunction from the local federal court. The federal judge issued the following one-sentence court order: "Town Ice Co. is hereby ordered to cease violating Franchisor's rights."

Which of the following arguments is least likely to help Town Ice Co. in vacating the court's order?

(A) The terms of the order failed to describe the acts that were forbidden.

(B) Town Ice Co. was never given an explanation for why the order was entered.

(C) The terms of the order were not specific.

(D) Town Ice Co. received a copy of the order only from Franchisor's attorney, but no copy from the court itself ever arrived.

See ANSWER on Page 211

162. Zookeeper cares for lions and tigers at the municipal zoo. While cleaning part of an exhibit, Zookeeper was badly mauled by two tigers who broke through a protective fence designed to safeguard him from harm. Zookeeper sued the manufacturer of the protective fence in federal court for negligent fence design and for negligent fence installation. Zookeeper sought damages for the severe injuries he suffered. In the final paragraph of his complaint, Zookeeper requested that the fence manufacturer's "negligence in installing the fence be determined by a jury." No other mention of "jury" or "jury trial" appeared elsewhere in the complaint. The fence manufacturer did not separately request a jury trial.

Should Zookeeper be permitted to try his case to a jury?

(A) A jury should resolve all of Zookeeper's claims against the manufacturer.

(B) A jury should resolve only Zookeeper's contention that the manufacturer's installation of the fence was negligent.

(C) A jury should resolve both Zookeeper's contention that the manufacturer's installation of the fence was negligent and the amount of any damages.

(D) A jury should resolve none of Zookeeper's claims against the manufacturer.

See ANSWER on Page 212

163. Spectator took her young son and daughter to Arena to watch a hockey game. Midway through the second period, a flying hockey puck sailed near or through a gap in the protective plexiglass panels and struck Spectator in the face, injuring her seriously. She filed a negligence action against Arena, invoking the federal court's diversity jurisdiction. During trial, Arena introduced into evidence six nearly identical photographic images of the plexiglass panels in question. The jury returned a verdict in favor of Arena. Spectator's attorney believed the trial court erroneously permitted the jury to view all six photographic images (rather than just three or four, which Spectator's attorney believed would have been plenty), and is now convinced that viewing them all led the jury to a mistaken verdict. Spectator's attorney has filed a motion for new trial.

Which of the following would not be a proper basis for the trial court to deny this motion?

(A) Spectator's attorney failed to object to the image during the trial.

(B) Spectator's attorney failed to file an earlier, pre-verdict motion.

(C) Spectator's attorney failed to file the motion within 28 days of the judgment.

(D) Spectator's attorney failed to contest the admission of all of the other images.

See ANSWER on Page 212

164. Grandson has possession of a priceless manuscript written by his recently deceased grandmother, a renowned but reclusive novelist. Aware that several of his siblings and cousins intend to claim ownership to the manuscript, Grandson filed an interpleader action in federal court naming eleven family members. The court issued an order directing Grandson to deliver the manuscript on Monday, September 1, into the possession of the clerk of court, whom the court ordered to retain it safely until the time of trial. Assume the court issued its order at 9:00 a.m. on Friday, August 22.

How will the Federal Rules of Civil Procedure compute Grandson's time for compliance with the court's order?

(A) The time period will begin to run on August 23 because triggering days are not counted in computing time.

(B) The time period will begin to run on Monday, August 25 because intervening Saturdays, Sundays, and official holidays are excluded while counting.

(C) The time period will be extended, if September 1 is an official holiday, to the next day that is not a weekend day or a holiday.

(D) The Rules' time computation procedures will not apply in computing this time period.

See ANSWER on Page 213

165. Renter hired Pesticide LP to spray her Arkansas apartment for spiders. Renter subsequently developed a degenerative nerve condition, and filed suit against Pesticide LP in federal court in the Northern District of Texas. Pesticide LP was a Louisiana partnership with its headquarters in Baton Rouge, Louisiana.

Is venue proper in the Northern District of Texas?

(A) No, unless Pesticide LP is subject to personal jurisdiction in the Northern District of Texas.

(B) No, unless the court concludes that, for the convenience of the parties and witnesses, in the interest of justice, the case should proceed in the Northern District of Texas.

(C) Yes, if Renter is a resident of the Northern District of Texas.

(D) Yes, if at least one of the partners of Pesticide LP is a resident of the Northern District of Texas.

See ANSWER on Page 213

166. Camper went mountain hiking several States away from his home. After brushing against a poisonous plant, Camper developed a rash, left the campsite, and sought assistance from a local doctor. The doctor prescribed an ointment, and Camper had the prescription filled at a local pharmacy. Unbeknownst to Camper, the ointment was incompatible with another medicine he was already taking for his high cholesterol. Camper suffered a stroke. In a federal diversity lawsuit, Camper sued the doctor, pharmacy, and ointment manufacturer for failing to alert him to this drug interaction danger. The pharmacy filed a motion to dismiss, arguing that it should have no legal obligation to investigate what other medicines a new customer is taking when it fills a prescription. The district court agreed, and dismissed the pharmacy from the lawsuit. Camper's lawsuit against the doctor and the ointment manufacturer has just begun discovery and, likely, still more than a year away from trial.

Can Patient appeal the dismissal of the pharmacy now, in the hope of obtaining a reversal in time for a single jury to hear his claims against all three defendants?

(A) Yes, the dismissal constitutes a final judgment as to the pharmacy.

(B) Maybe, if the district court permits such an appeal.

(C) Maybe, if the district court and appeals court both permit such an appeal.

(D) No, the lawsuit is not yet final as to all parties.

See ANSWER on Page 214

167. Appliance Store ordered 2,500 refrigerators from Refrigerator Supply. When the refrigerators arrived, they were of poor quality and not saleable. Appliance Store returned the refrigerators and ordered different refrigerators from another supplier, all at considerable expense, and sued Refrigerator Supply in federal court. Following trial, the jury returned a verdict of $2,510,000. When the judge subsequently entered judgment, however, the judgment mistakenly wrote "$2,150,000" (transposing the second and third digits of the award). The judge had not issued any orders or opinions indicating an intent to reduce the jury's verdict, and Appliance Store did not notice the discrepancy until, 61 days after the entry of judgment, it initiated proceedings to execute on the judgment.

What, if anything, can Appliance Store attempt to do to address this mistake?

(A) Appliance Store can move for a new trial.

(B) Appliance Store can move for relief from the judgment.

(C) Appliance Store can appeal the judgment.

(D) Because Appliance Store failed to take action within 60 days, it now has no recourse.

See ANSWER on Page 214

168. Dancer gave an interview alleging that, several years earlier, she had been assaulted by Celebrity in a hotel room in Florida. Celebrity sent a letter to Newspaper, located in New York, contesting the allegations and contending that Dancer had lied. Newspaper published the letter in its next morning's edition, which was distributed to and sold in every American State. Dancer sued Celebrity for defamation in federal court in Massachusetts (where her mother lived), alleging that she had been libeled nationwide. The conflicts of law rules adopted in Massachusetts require, in defamation cases, that the substantive law of the State with the most significant relationship to the occurrence and the parties be applied. Both at the time of publication and at the time the lawsuit was filed, Dancer was a domicile of Wisconsin and Celebrity was a domicile of California.

Which State's substantive defamation laws will the federal court must likely apply?

(A) Wisconsin.

(B) California.

(C) New York.

(D) Massachusetts.

See ANSWER on Page 215

169. Owner filed a lawsuit against Car Corp. for selling her a car that suddenly and unexpectedly accelerates, thus exposing her and her family to obvious dangers. The lawsuit was filed in a court in State X. In State X, service of process by U.S. Mail is considered proper, so long as the mail is correctly addressed to the defendant and proper postage is affixed. Owner mailed the service papers to Car Corp., correctly addressing the envelope to Car Corp.'s last known address. However, because Car Corp. had just recently relocated its place of business, the mail was returned to Owner marked "undelivered—bad address." Car Corp. maintains an official company website, on which its new business address now appears.

Does Owner have to arrange to serve Car Corp. again, this time at its new address?

(A) Yes, but only if the lawsuit was filed in federal court.

(B) Yes, regardless of whether the lawsuit was filed in federal or State court.

(C) No, because State X permits the manner of service Owner used.

(D) No, because Owner addressed the mail to Car Corp.'s last known address.

See ANSWER on Page 215

170. Environmentalist learned that Chemical Company was planning to start discharging liquid wastes into the nearby river without an environmental discharge permit. Environmentalist filed a complaint in federal court, along with a motion seeking a preliminary injunction. The court granted the motion and issued a preliminary injunction prohibiting Chemical Company from discharging liquid wastes into the nearby river.

Which of these methods of appeal is Chemical Company's best option?

(A) An immediate interlocutory appeal, but only if the district court first authorizes such an appeal.

(B) An immediate interlocutory appeal, but only if the district court and the court of appeals authorize such an appeal.

(C) An immediate appeal as of right.

(D) Disobey the injunction, then appeal any contempt sanctions the district court imposes.

See ANSWER on Page 216

171. Rider was in a motorcycle accident and filed a claim with Insurance Company. Insurance Company responded that its policy did not cover Rider's accident. Rider countered that the broker who sold Rider the policy, Brokerage, Inc., had misrepresented the nature of the policy. Insurance Company filed a declaratory judgment action in federal court against Rider, seeking a declaration that its policy did not cover Rider's accident. Insurance Company did not include Brokerage, Inc. as a party. Rider moved to dismiss under Rule 12(b)(7), contending that Brokerage, Inc. was a required party to the lawsuit. In its opposition to the motion, Insurance Company submitted a pleading from another action that, it contended, supported its position that Brokerage, Inc. was not a required party.

May the court consider this pleading when ruling on the Rule 12(b)(7) motion?

(A) Yes, but only if the court first converts the Rule 12 motion to a motion for summary judgment under Rule 56.

(B) Yes, because a court may take "judicial notice" of pleadings from another case.

(C) No, because Rule 12 motions test the adequacy of the complaint, and extrinsic materials are not properly considered in ruling on a Rule 12 motion.

(D) No, unless Insurance Company first obtains Rider's consent to do so.

See ANSWER on Page 216

172. Consumer believed that Candy Manufacturer was deceptively packaging its candy in boxes that contained excessive empty space or "slack fill." To remedy this deception on behalf of all customers of Candy Manufacturer's products, Consumer filed a class action complaint against Candy Manufacturer in federal court seeking an injunction requiring Candy Manufacturer to change the packaging for its candy. Consumer timely moved for class certification. The court conducted a class certification hearing, then prepared to rule.

Which of the following most likely describes how the court will rule?

(A) The court will not certify the class if it concludes that Consumer's claim shares no common questions of fact or law with each member of the class.

(B) The court will not certify the class if it deems each of the class members' claims too trivial to be pursued on its own.

(C) The court will not certify the class unless it concludes that Consumer is likely to succeed on the merits.

(D) The court will not certify the class unless it concludes that Consumer has a unique claim distinguished from those of the class in general.

See ANSWER on Page 217

173. Employee filed a complaint in federal court against his Supervisor and the company President (to whom Supervisor reported), alleging that the Supervisor and President were liable to him for negligent infliction of emotional distress. In the complaint, Employee alleged that Supervisor was emotionally abusive, and that President was aware of the abusive atmosphere and did nothing to curb the abuse. The complaint stated that Supervisor and President were domiciled in Pennsylvania, that Employee was a domiciliary of West Virginia, and that Employee was seeking $80,000 in damages for his emotional distress. President filed a motion to dismiss under Rule 12(b)(1), contending that the court lacked subject-matter jurisdiction over the claim asserted against her.

Will the court grant President's motion?

(A) Yes, because the complaint does not assert a claim against President exceeding $75,000 exclusive of interests and costs.

(B) Yes, if President convinces the court that her share of the liability is unlikely to exceed $75,000 exclusive of interest and costs.

(C) No, because the claims against Supervisor and President involve common questions of law and fact.

(D) No, if the court concludes that Supervisor and President would be jointly liable under the applicable substantive law.

See ANSWER on Page 217

174. Athlete plays professional basketball. During one game held at an opposing team's stadium, Athlete was verbally taunted by Fan who was sitting near the basketball court. The abuse was loud and relentless, prompting game officials to twice caution Fan to behave. Late in the game, as Fan loudly mocked Athlete after a missed shot, Athlete lost his temper, turned, and slapped Fan. Athlete was ejected from the game, and Fan were escorted out of the stadium. Fan later sued Athlete in federal court for battery. At trial, Fan offered only his own testimony, then rested his case. Athlete's counsel then called Athlete and several other players to testify, and played a video recording showing Fan's relentless taunting. Counsel then rested Athlete's defense. After brief deliberations, the jury returned a verdict in favor of Fan, awarding him $150,000 in damages from Athlete.

If Athlete's counsel now files a motion for judgment as a matter of law, how is the court most likely to rule?

(A) Grant the motion, if the court concludes that the jury's verdict was against the weight of the admitted evidence.

(B) Grant the motion, if the court concludes that the jury had no reasonable evidentiary basis for their verdict.

(C) Deny the motion, because, under the circumstances, Athlete's counsel had no right to seek a judgment as a matter of law following the jury's verdict.

(D) Deny the motion, if Athlete's counsel filed the motion more than 10 days of the jury's verdict.

See ANSWER on Page 218

175. Guest was a paid visitor to Amusement Park. During his visit, Guest decided to ride "SuperCoaster," the premiere, signature roller coaster operated at Amusement Park. Guest sat in row 7, seat 2. Amusement Park equipped each SuperCoaster seat with a lap-bar as a safety restraint. Guest's lap-bar, however, would not lock properly in place. As he rode the ride, Guest tore his sneakers as he tried to restrain himself inside the coaster. When Amusement Park refused to reimburse him for his ruined sneakers, Guest sued the park for negligent failure to maintain the lap-bar, and won $103.72 in damages from the jury. On the very same day that Guest ruined his sneakers, NextGuest also rode SuperCoaster. She also sat in row 7, seat 2, encountered the same non-locking lap-bar, and was tossed around during her ride. NextGuest exited the ride feeling a bit sore, but otherwise seemed fine. Six months later, NextGuest discovered that she had suffered a life-endangering abdominal injury linked to her SuperCoaster ride. After a few more months, she sued Amusement Park in federal court for negligent failure to maintain the lap-bar in row 7, seat 2.

If the court refuses NextGuest's request to apply issue preclusion to foreclose Amusement Park from contesting negligence, what most likely is the reason?

(A) The parties to the two lawsuits are not identical.

(B) The issue raised in the two lawsuits is not identical.

(C) Applying issue preclusion in the second lawsuit would not be fair.

(D) The finding of negligence in the first lawsuit was not essential to its outcome.

See ANSWER on Page 219

176. Sculptor owns a blown-glass art studio in Providence, Rhode Island. To accommodate her growing business, Sculptor drove 60 miles to Boston, Massachusetts to purchase a special glass-baking stove from Stove Corp. In creating the product, Stove Corp. had purchased that particular stove's heating component from Electric Corp., a vendor having its sole place of business 70 miles from Sculptor's art studio in Hartford, Connecticut. Sculptor sued Stove Corp. in Rhode Island federal court (located just across the street from Sculptor's studio) for damages when her stove caught fire and destroyed her art studio. Electric Corp. has no contacts with Rhode Island that would support personal jurisdiction over it in the lawsuit Sculptor has filed in that State against Stove Corp.

Under which of the following circumstances would the Rhode Island federal court have authority to exercise personal jurisdiction over Electric Corp.?

(A) If Electric Corp. was permissively joined by Sculptor as a new defendant.

(B) If Electric Corp. was joined by Stove Corp. as a third-party defendant

(C) If Electric Corp. agreed to waive formal service of process.

(D) The court could not exercise personal jurisdiction over Electric Corp.

See ANSWER on Page 220

177. Flag Designer brought an action against Patriotic Products, contending that Patriotic Products had infringed Flag Designer's trademarks. During discovery, Patriotic Products served interrogatories and production requests asking for information and documents related to when Flag Designer first became aware of the alleged infringement. Because laches—delay in defending a trademark—can be a defense, this date was important. Counsel for Flag Designer prepared and signed discovery responses providing a date that Flag Designer first became aware of the alleged infringement. Later, after substantial litigation activities and time, Patriotic Products learned that Flag Designer had purchased one of the allegedly infringing products—and thus was aware of the alleged infringement— well before the date that Flag Designer's counsel had identified in the discovery responses.

If Patriotic Products wants to seek sanctions against Counsel for Flag Designer, what is the best procedure for seeking such sanctions?

(A) File a motion for sanctions under Rule 11 for violation of the signature certification, after providing Flag Designer with the 21-day safe harbor.

(B) File a motion for sanctions under Rule 26(g) for violation of Counsel's signature certification.

(C) File a motion for sanctions under Rule 37(d) for failure to respond to the interrogatories and production requests, after meeting and conferring.

(D) Patriotic Products cannot obtain sanctions because the information became available to it later during discovery.

See ANSWER on Page 220

178. In litigation concerning an alleged theft of intellectual property, Software Company was concerned about obtaining access to certain computer source code for software developed by Competitor during discovery.

Which of these options presents the earliest opportunity for Software Company to present this issue to the court?

(A) Software Company could raise the issue in the Rule 26(f) report of the parties' discovery planning conference.

(B) Software Company could raise the issue at the initial Rule 16 conference.

(C) Software Company could raise the issue in an early Rule 34 request.

(D) Software Company could raise the issue in an early Rule 37(e) motion.

See ANSWER on Page 221

179. Producer brought a lawsuit against Downloaders, contending that Downloaders illegally downloaded and shared copies of Producer's movies. After discovery concluded, Producer filed a motion for summary judgment. Downloaders filed a brief in opposition to that motion and a request for an evidentiary hearing followed by oral argument. The court denied this request, and instead issued summary judgment in favor of Producer based solely on the parties' briefs and the documentary evidence attached to those briefs. Downloaders appealed, contending that the district court deprived them of their Due Process right to an opportunity to be heard.

How will the court of appeals likely rule?

(A) The court of appeals will deny the motion because the district court afforded Downloaders an adequate opportunity to be heard for this particular situation.

(B) The court of appeals will deny the motion because the Due Process Clause guarantee of an opportunity to be heard never entitles parties to litigation the right to evidentiary hearings and oral arguments.

(C) The court of appeals will grant the motion because the district court did not afford Downloaders an adequate opportunity to be heard in this particular situation.

(D) The court of appeals will grant the motion because the Due Process Clause guarantee of an opportunity to be heard always entitles parties to litigation to evidentiary hearings and oral arguments.

See ANSWER on Page 221

180. In a federal litigation related to surgery that went poorly, the plaintiff, Patient, and the defendant, Hospital, agreed to settle the lawsuit.

How should Patient and Hospital end the litigation in light of the settlement?

(A) Patient and Hospital should enter into a settlement agreement, which operates to end the litigation.

(B) Hospital should seek dismissal under Rule 12(b).

(C) Patient should seek dismissal under Rule 41(a).

(D) Hospital should seek summary judgment under Rule 56(a).

See ANSWER on Page 222

181. Prisoner brought a civil rights claim in federal court against Prison contending he was subjected to cruel and unusual punishment in violation of the Eighth Amendment to the U.S. Constitution based on his prolonged assignment to solitary confinement. Following discovery, Prison filed a motion for summary judgment. The court granted Prison's motion without oral argument and without issuing findings of fact and conclusions of law. Prisoner appealed, contending that the court failed to make findings of fact or conclusions of law.

How will the appeals court likely rule on Prisoner's argument?

(A) The court will likely rule in favor of Prisoner because parties have the right to an opportunity to be heard and the trial court failed to conduct an oral hearing.

(B) The court will likely rule in favor of Prisoner because the Federal Rules of Civil Procedure require the court to make separate findings of fact and conclusions of law before entering summary judgment.

(C) The court will likely rule in favor of Prison because the Federal Rules of Civil Procedure do not require the court to make separate findings of fact and conclusions of law before entering summary judgment.

(D) The court will likely rule in favor of Prison if Prisoner failed to request that the court state findings of fact and conclusions of law.

See ANSWER on Page 222

182. After Programmer was told her services were no longer needed, Programmer sued Tech Company for employment discrimination under a federal statute addressing discrimination against employees. Tech Company defended the action on two separate grounds. First, Tech Company argued that Programmer was an independent contractor, not an employee, and thus not covered by the statute. Second, Tech Company argued that Programmer was fired for failure to follow company rules, not because of her gender. The jury returned a general verdict for Tech Company. Subsequently, Programmer learned that Tech Company was using an algorithm that Programmer had developed. Programmer sued Tech Company in federal court under a statute that accorded certain intellectual property rights to employees, and Tech Company sought to invoke the doctrine of issue preclusion to bar Programmer from contending that she was an employee of Tech Company.

How will the court likely rule on Tech Company's issue preclusion argument?

(A) The court will likely rule in favor of Programmer because Programmer's employment status was not necessarily decided in the first action.

(B) The court will likely rule in favor of Programmer because offensive issue preclusion is discretionary, and application here would prejudice Programmer.

(C) The court will likely rule in favor of Tech Company if Programmer did not appeal the jury verdict from the first action.

(D) The court will likely rule in favor of Tech Company because all the elements of issue preclusion are satisfied.

See ANSWER on Page 223

183. Scientist injured herself when a beaker in which she was mixing chemicals fractured. In federal court, Scientist sued Lab Shop, the retail company from which she had purchased the beaker, to recover for the serious personal injuries the fractured beaker caused her. Lab Shop, in turn, impleaded Glass Corp. into the lawsuit, contending that Glass Corp. was the one that actually manufactured the fractured beaker. Scientist endorsed her complaint with a demand for a jury trial. The week before the trial, Scientist reconsidered her request for a jury trial and notified the court that she was withdrawing her request and consenting to a bench trial instead.

Must the court nonetheless convene a jury trial for Scientist's lawsuit?

(A) No, as the litigant who demanded a jury trial, Scientist was entitled to withdraw that demand.

(B) No, so long as the judge first determines that the withdrawal was made in good faith.

(C) No, if the original defendant—Lab Shop—agreed to the bench trial by stipulation.

(D) Yes.

See ANSWER on Page 223

184. Customer purchased a motor scooter from Dealer to help save gasoline costs and to protect the environment. While scootering to work one morning, Customer was hit by a tractor-trailer truck that had failed to notice Customer on the roadway. After a lengthy trial in federal court, the jury returned a verdict in favor of the tractor-trailer truck and denied Customer any recovery. Convinced that the jury had no reasonable evidentiary basis to deny recovery, Customer's attorney intended to request a post-trial judgment as a matter of law. But the attorney was also worried. There were a scattered, few pieces of evidence at trial that might be seen as supporting the tractor-trailer truck, and the judge might, on that basis, deny judgment as a matter of law. Customer's attorney wondered whether a motion for new trial might be safer.

Is there a way for Customer's attorney to pursue both motions, one as a primary argument and one as an alternative, fallback one?

(A) Yes, Customer's attorney can file both motions simultaneously.

(B) Yes, Customer's attorney can file for judgment as a matter of law first and, if that motion is denied, then file a later, second motion for a new trial.

(C) Yes, Customer's attorney may file for both post-trial remedies, but only after seeking and receiving the court's permission to do so.

(D) No, Customer's attorney cannot pursue both post-trial motions; the attorney will have to choose which one is strategically best.

See ANSWER on Page 224

185. Client sued Law Firm in federal court for malpractice after Law Firm lawyers failed to file a complaint before the statute of limitations expired. In the complaint, Client alleged that, at the time of the filing of the complaint, Client was a resident of New Jersey, Law Firm was a partnership with its principal place of business in New York, and all of the partners in Law Firm were New York residents. Client also alleged that she had lost a claim valued in excess of $1 million as a result of Law Firm's malpractice. The complaint did not mention diversity jurisdiction or cite the diversity jurisdiction statute.

Has Client properly alleged a basis for diversity jurisdiction?

(A) No, because there is not enough information in the complaint to determine whether there is complete diversity of citizenship.

(B) No, because the complaint fails to cite the diversity jurisdiction statute, in violation of the pleading standard.

(C) Yes, if complaint also references the evidence supporting these allegations.

(D) Yes, the complaint is sufficient as described.

See ANSWER on Page 224

186. Taxi Driver struck Pedestrian while she was crossing a road in California. Pedestrian, a New Jersey domiciliary temporarily residing in Delaware, sued Taxi Inc., Taxi Driver's employer, for negligence in federal district court in Delaware under the court's diversity jurisdiction. Taxi Inc., a Delaware corporation with its headquarters in California, moved to transfer venue to California, arguing that the witnesses and other evidence were all located in California. Pedestrian argued that her medical records were all in Delaware and that she endured most of her suffering in Delaware. Nonetheless, the court granted Taxi Inc.'s motion and transferred the case to federal district court in California.

Which body of substantive law will the California federal court apply?

(A) The federal district court in California will apply federal common law.

(B) The federal district court in California has discretion to apply the substantive law of the State that the court deems most appropriate, considering all of the circumstances.

(C) The federal district court in California will apply the common law selected by California's choice of law provisions.

(D) The federal district court in California will apply the common law selected by Delaware's choice of law provisions.

See ANSWER on Page 225

187. Philanthropist, a citizen of Connecticut, was in Museum, a citizen of New York, and noticed a painting hanging on the wall that had been previously stolen from Philanthropist's house. When Museum refused to return the painting to her, Philanthropist filed suit in federal court invoking the court's diversity jurisdiction. Philanthropist sought from the court a declaration that she was the lawful owner of the painting and an order compelling Museum to surrender the painting to her. Museum moved to dismiss under Rule 12(b)(7), contending that Art Collector, who had loaned the painting to Museum and who was a citizen of Connecticut, was a required party to Philanthropist's lawsuit. Philanthropist argued in opposition that Art Collector would destroy diversity jurisdiction.

How would a court likely rule on Museum's motion?

(A) The court should deny the motion because diversity of citizenship is evaluated at the time the complaint is filed, and Art Collector was not a party at that time.

(B) The court should deny the motion because subject-matter jurisdiction is a constitutional prerequisite to proceeding in federal court that is not subject to judicial discretion or waiver.

(C) The court should grant the motion unless it concludes, in its discretion, that proceeding without Art Collector is preferable to dismissal.

(D) The court should grant the motion if it concludes that Philanthropist was forum shopping by deliberately omitting Art Collector from the complaint.

See ANSWER on Page 226

188. For a jury trial in federal court that the judge and parties anticipated to be lengthy, the judge impaneled seven jurors. During the trial, one juror got sick and was excused by the judge. The judge subsequently excused a second juror who complained that the stress of the trial was affecting him adversely. The judge did not ask the parties to consent to the excusing of either juror. At the end of the trial, the five-member jury returned a verdict in favor of the plaintiff, and the defendant appealed.

How will the appellate court likely rule?

(A) The appellate court will affirm if the parties had stipulated to a jury of less than 6 members.

(B) The appellate court will affirm unless the excusing of the two jurors led to a jury panel that was unrepresentative in terms of race or gender.

(C) The appellate court will reverse because the trial court failed to obtain the consent of the parties to the excusing of the jurors.

(D) The appellate court will reverse because a jury in federal court must always comprise at least six and not more than twelve members.

See ANSWER on Page 226

189. While skiing at a mountain resort, Skier 1's skis struck a powercord that a resort employee had negligently left on one of the ski slopes. Skier 1 sustained serious personal injuries from his resulting fall, and sued the resort for negligence in its placement of the powercord. The jury returned a substantial verdict in his favor. Later, the same day that Skier 1 was injured, a different skier—Skier 2—hit the very same powercord while skiing down the same slope at the resort and was also injured seriously.

If Skier 2 later brings a lawsuit against the resort for personal injuries caused when she struck the powercord, what type of preclusion might the court apply?

(A) Claim preclusion, but only because the negligent cause of both skiers' injuries was identical.

(B) Claim preclusion, but only if the court follows a "single wrongful act" approach to defining "claim."

(C) Issue preclusion, but only because there is actual identity between the plaintiffs in both lawsuits.

(D) Issue preclusion, but only if the jury's finding that the resort was negligent was essential to their verdict in Skier 1's lawsuit.

See ANSWER on Page 227

190. Teacher had worked at Private School for six years until he resigned from his position citing a hostile work environment. Teacher then sued his former employer in federal court, alleging violations of federal law designed to ensure a non-discriminatory workplace. In his complaint, Teacher described Private School as a "concentration camp" where he and other employees were "mentally tortured" by the "sadist" senior management, led by a Principal who was "always too busy cheating on her spouse."

How is the court most likely to rule if Private School files a motion to strike these allegations from the complaint?

(A) It will grant the motion if the court finds that the allegations are discourteous and offensive to Private School.

(B) It will grant the motion if the court concludes that a reasonable jury is unlikely to find the allegations fair to Private School.

(C) It will deny the motion unless Private School can show that the allegations prejudicially cast it in an unfairly derogatory light.

(D) It will deny the motion because allegations in a pleading can be later disproved at trial with competent evidence.

See ANSWER on Page 228

191. Professor was terminated by College for persistent failure to teach his assigned classes. Following the termination, College arranged to have Professor's personal belongings from his campus office boxed up and placed in storage. Professor later sued College, alleging that he had been suffering from a medical condition that forced his absence from class. He argued that his termination violated a federal statute barring employers from terminating employees due to certain disabilities. To this same lawsuit, Professor added a second, State law claim for $10,000 in personal property damage, contending that College subsequently lost his stored personal belongings. Professor filed his lawsuit 30 days before the statutes of limitation applicable to both these two claims expired. The district court, 60 days later, dismissed Professor's federal law claim for failure to state a claim and declined to exercise supplemental jurisdiction over his surviving State law personal property damage claim. Assume the applicable State law has no special timing rules concerning such dismissals.

May Professor re-file his State law $10,000 property damage claim in State court?

(A) Yes, but only if he does so within 60 days after the dismissal.

(B) Yes, but only if he does so within 120 days after the dismissal.

(C) Yes, but only if he does so within 30 days after the dismissal.

(D) No, because that claim is now time-barred.

See ANSWER on Page 229

192. Racket Company entered into an endorsement contract with Squashplayer. Pursuant to the contract, Squashplayer was to play exclusively with Racket Company brand rackets in all public events. Squashplayer subsequently found that she performed better with ProSquash rackets and switched to that brand. Racket Company brought suit against Squashplayer in federal court, seeking specific performance and lost profits. Ten days after serving her answer, Squashplayer filed and served a jury trial demand.

Does Squashplayer have a right to a jury trial?

(A) Yes, as to both claims.

(B) Yes, as to the specific performance claim but not as to the lost profits claim.

(C) Yes, as to the lost profits claim but not as to the specific performance claim.

(D) No, as to both claims.

See ANSWER on Page 230

193. Property Purchaser sued Seller of commercial property for breach of warranty, contending that an electric car charging station located on that property was not working. In its answer, Seller contended that the warranty only covered "fixtures," and did not cover the charging station. During discovery, Seller served a request for an admission that the charging station could be physically removed and returned to the manufacturer for repairs. Purchaser admitted the request. At trial, Purchaser sought to introduce testimony that the charging station was a "fixture" that was permanently attached to the property. Seller objected to this testimony.

Should the court allow Purchaser to introduce the testimony?

(A) Yes, but only if the court concludes that Purchaser would be prejudiced if not allowed to offer the testimony.

(B) Yes, but only if the court concludes that Purchaser had made a good faith error in making the admission.

(C) No, unless the court allows Purchaser to amend or withdraw its admission, because matters admitted pursuant to a request for admission are conclusively established.

(D) No, if Seller filed a motion for sanctions under Rule 37 seeking exclusion of the testimony.

See ANSWER on Page 230

194. Homeowner, who lived in Kansas City, Kansas, was injured when Gardner's lawnmower struck a rock and a piece of the blade flew off and struck Homeowner in the leg while he was lounging on the deck at his home. At the time of the incident, Gardner was operating the lawnmower, which was manufactured by Lawnmowers, Inc. Homeowner filed a complaint in federal court in the Eastern District of Missouri, asserting a claim against Gardner for negligence in Count I and a claim against Lawnmowers, Inc. for products liability in Count II. At the time Homeowner filed the complaint, Gardner was domiciled in the Eastern District of Missouri and Lawnmowers, Inc. was incorporated in Kansas with its principal place of business in Kansas City, Missouri.

Is venue proper in the Eastern District of Missouri?

(A) Yes, as to the claim against Gardner, but no as to the claim against Lawnmowers, Inc.

(B) Yes, as to the claim against Lawnmowers, Inc., but no as to the claim against Gardner.

(C) Yes, as to both claims.

(D) No, as to both claims.

See ANSWER on Page 231

195. Government filed a civil action in federal court against Manufacturer for violating the federal anti-racketeering laws. In its complaint, Government accused Manufacturer of committing at least 100 separate acts of wire fraud and mail fraud. In discovery, Manufacturer served an interrogatory on Government requesting that Government identify any additional acts of alleged racketeering that it intended to try to prove against Manufacturer at trial. Government answered this interrogatory by identifying 30 new acts. Manufacturer served no further discovery requests on Government, and Government served no further discovery responses on Manufacturer. Two years later, as trial approached, Government announced to the court its intention to rely, at trial, on 650 additional, new acts of racketeering that it had discovered eight months earlier.

How should the court rule if Manufacturer files a motion to bar Government from relying on the 650 additional acts of racketeering at trial?

(A) Grant the motion because Government must always disclose relevant information to a defendant pursuant to *Brady v. Maryland*.

(B) Grant the motion because Government's failure to disclose the additional acts violated its obligations under the discovery rules.

(C) Deny the motion because Government's response to Manufacturer's interrogatory was actually accurate and complete at the time it was served.

(D) Deny the motion because Manufacturer failed to request Government to supplement its earlier interrogatory answers.

See ANSWER on Page 231

196. Driver races cars professionally for a living. She is sponsored by Famous Motor Oil Co., which pays her a large fee for advertising its logo on the doors of her race car. The day before an important race, Driver accidently dropped a heavy box against one of her race car's doors, causing the painted Famous Motor Oil Co. logo to be badly scratched. Realizing that her sponsor fee depended on a perfect logo image, Driver hired Painter A and Painter B to perform an emergency overnight paint repair job on her car door. The morning of the race, Driver arrived to discover that the repair paint work on the scratched logo had not yet even begun. Driver later sued both Painter A and Painter B in federal court for the sponsor fee that she lost. Subsequently, Driver learned that Painter A and Painter B had spent that entire night drinking at Happy's Bar & Grill, where they completely forgot about the emergency paint repair job.

Driver can insist that Happy's Bar & Grill answer interrogatories in discovery about the whereabouts of Painter A and Painter B on the night in question only if which of the following is true?

(A) Driver's interrogatories seek information she "may use" in proving her case.

(B) Driver has not already asked twenty-five interrogatories in her lawsuit.

(C) Driver's interrogatories are neither privileged nor otherwise objectionable.

(D) Driver sues Happy's Bar and Grill.

See ANSWER on Page 232

197. Surfer brought an action *pro se* against Internet Corporation, contending that Internet Corporation was invading his privacy and stealing his personal data. When Internet Corporation invited Surfer to meet for the parties' Rule 26(f) discovery conference, Surfer refused, stating that he believed the meeting was a ploy to steal his identity. Internet Corporation submitted a unilateral Rule 26(f) discovery plan that included a description of the parties' exchange. The judge issued an order instructing Surfer to participate in a telephonic meeting with Internet Corporation, and Surfer again refused. The judge then issued an order scheduling a Rule 16 conference. Surfer failed to appear at the time the Rule 16 conference was scheduled.

What is Internet Corporation's best procedural option for seeking dismissal of the action on the basis of Surfer's recalcitrant behavior?

   (A)   Internet Corporation should file a motion to dismiss under the court's inherent authority over cases on its docket.

   (B)   Internet Corporation should file a motion to dismiss under Rule 12(b).

   (C)   Internet Corporation should file a motion to dismiss under Rule 37.

   (D)   Internet Corporation should file a motion to dismiss under Rule 41.

See ANSWER on Page 232

198. Original Author wrote a series of popular books about three high school students who aid local police as amateur detectives. Recently, New Author wrote what seems to be the first in a series of books that also feature young amateur detectives helping police solve crime. Original Author believed that New Author's work infringed on his copyright, and filed a federal lawsuit against New Author for federal copyright infringement. Original Author hired a process-server to deliver service of process. The process-server arrived at New Author's home—123 Maple Street—and handed the service papers to Alice.

This effort at service of process is improper if which of the following is true?

   (A)   If New Author is only 18 years old.

   (B)   If Alice is not related to New Author.

   (C)   If Alice does not also reside at 123 Maple Street.

   (D)   If New Author was physically present at 123 Maple Street at the time.

See ANSWER on Page 233

199. Prisoner filed a civil rights action in federal court, representing himself *pro se*. Prison filed a motion to dismiss Count I, which had asserted a claim based on Prison's failure to provide Prisoner with access to streaming video services. In his signed brief in opposition, Prisoner made arguments that had been squarely rejected in earlier, settled precedent from the court of appeals covering the district court where the case was pending.

May the district court impose Rule 11 sanctions on Prisoner?

(A) Yes, unless Prisoner had a good faith belief that the court of appeals had erroneously decided the issue.

(B) Yes, if the Prison served a motion for sanctions on Prisoner, filed it with the court, and Prisoner did not file an amended brief taking out the referenced argument.

(C) Yes, if the Prison served a motion for sanctions on Prisoner, waited twenty-one days during which time Prisoner did not file an amended brief taking out the referenced argument, then filed the motion with the court.

(D) Yes, unless the Prison served a motion for sanctions on Prisoner, waited twenty-one days during which time Prisoner did not file an amended brief taking out the referenced argument, then filed the motion with the court, and Prisoner failed to receive, from the court, a show-cause hearing to allow him to demonstrate why the court should not enter sanctions.

See ANSWER on Page 233

200. Wedding Planner hired City Yacht Club as a venue for two separate clients' weddings— one in April and another in October. Wedding Planner later discovered that she was overcharged on both occasions due to fake vendor invoices that City Yacht Club had fabricated. The amount of the April wedding overcharge was $84,000. The amount of the October wedding overcharge was $16,500. Wedding Planner is a citizen of New York; the City Yacht Club is a privately-held corporation incorporated in Delaware with its principal place of business in Connecticut.

If Wedding Planner sued City Yacht Club in a federal diversity action for the April overcharges, could she add into that same lawsuit her claim for the October overcharges?

(A) Yes, supplemental jurisdiction is not necessary to provide the court with authority to consider these two overcharge claims in the same lawsuit.

(B) Yes, supplemental jurisdiction can rescue the absence of original subject-matter jurisdiction because both overcharge claims arise from a common nucleus of operative facts.

(C) No, supplemental jurisdiction is unavailable since the two overcharge claims involve unrelated wedding clients who had separate weddings that occurred on different dates.

(D) No, supplemental jurisdiction is unavailable to a plaintiff who proposes to use it to acquire jurisdiction over a claim that otherwise fails Section 1332.

See ANSWER on Page 234

PART 3
Multiple Choice Answers
(with Explanations and Citations)

Reminder to Users: This Part 3 contains the Answers (with explanations and citations) to all 200 multiple choice questions of Part 2. Remember to read Part 1 (Introduction) on how best to maximize your review of this material. And remember also that Parts 4 and 5 contain tables to enable users to decode the NCBE topic, subtopic, and tested-knowledge-area for each Question.

---

1. **Answer (A) is wrong:** As Answer (C) explains, Rule 13 permits Neighbor to bring either claim.

    Answer (B) is wrong: As Rule 13(b) provides, a defendant may, but is not required to, bring an entirely unrelated claim against the plaintiff as a permissive counterclaim. Thus, the unrelated painting fees claim may be included, but need not be.

    Answer (C) is the best choice: Rule 13(a) provides that a defendant must bring, as a compulsory counterclaim, any claim the defendant has at the time of service of the counterclaim that arises out of the transaction or occurrence that is the subject of the plaintiff's claim (so long as it does not require adding another party over whom the court cannot assert jurisdiction, is not already pending elsewhere, or if only *in rem* personal jurisdiction is asserted over a defendant who is not otherwise counterclaiming). The painting fees claim falls into this category because both it and the plaintiff's claim arise out of the house painting, and the claim does not fall within any of the three exceptions noted above. Rule 13(b) also permits, but does not require, a defendant to bring any other type of counterclaim—a permissive counterclaim—against the plaintiff. The lawnmower claim falls into this category; it is not related to the house painting, and the question specifies that it is not related to the painting fee dispute.

    Answer (D) is wrong: Parties waive a compulsory counterclaim, as described in Answer (C), if they fail to assert it, but do not waive a permissive counterclaim, and instead may file it in the pending lawsuit or wait until later to litigate it. Therefore, Neighbor would waive the painting fees claim if Neighbor fails to assert it as a counterclaim, but Neighbor can assert the lawnmower claim in a separate action at a later date.

2.   **Answer (A) is wrong:** Generally, the time for appeal cannot be extended by agreement among the parties, as explained in Answer (D).

Answer (B) is wrong: Generally, the time for appeal cannot be extended by agreement among the parties even if the court deems the agreement appropriate, unless the party seeking an extension files a motion seeking the extension, as explained in Answers (C) and (D).

Answer (C) is the best choice: Upon showing of excusable neglect or good cause, the district court may briefly extend the time for appeal. *See* Fed. R. App. P. 4(a)(5). The extension motion must be made within the original 30-day appeal period, and the court may only extend the period until 30 days after the original deadline or 14 days after the court's order granting the motion, whichever is later. *See* Fed. R. App. P. 4(a)(5)(C). Good cause generally exists where there is no fault, and the extension is necessitated by circumstances outside the movant's control. *See Bishop v. Corsentino*, 371 F.3d 1203, 1206 (10th Cir. 2004).

Answer (D) is wrong: Generally, the time for taking an appeal is considered mandatory and cannot be extended by agreement or stipulation. *See Bowles v. Russell*, 551 U.S. 205, 209 (2007). However, the period may be extended by timely motion, as explained in Answer (C).

3.   **Answer (A) is the best choice:** Both Protestor and Big Oil are citizens of the same State, so the court cannot exercise diversity jurisdiction. With respect to federal question jurisdiction, the U.S. Supreme Court has held that it is the plaintiff's complaint, and not the defendant's anticipated defense, that must arise under the Constitution, laws, or treaties of the United States. *See Louisville & Nashville R.R. Co. v. Mottley,* 211 U.S. 149, 152 (1908). Here, the only federal question is the anticipated First Amendment issue that Protestor may raise as a defense, so the court does not have federal question jurisdiction.

Answer (B) is wrong: Sometimes, a federal court may exercise federal question jurisdiction over a plaintiff's State law claims if resolution of those claims necessarily depends on a substantial question of federal law. *See Merrell Dow Pharms., Inc. v. Thompson*, 478 U.S. 804, 807 (1986). However, as explained in Answer (A), federal question jurisdiction cannot be premised on a federal question implicated by a defense.

Answer (C) is wrong: As explained in Answer (A), the "well pleaded complaint" rule requires that the claims arise under federal law, not a defense (even if set forth in the complaint).

Answer (D) is wrong: While Big Oil's conduct may be governed by federal law, the question specifies that its claims against Protestor are not (*see* Answer (A)).

4.   **Answer (A) is wrong:** In assessing whether personal jurisdiction satisfies the U.S. Constitution's Due Process Clause, the contacts of the plaintiff with the forum are not dispositive. The proper inquiry focuses on the defendant's contacts with the State, not the plaintiff's contacts. *See Keeton v. Hustler Magazine, Inc.*, 465 U.S. 770, 779 (1984).

   Answer (B) is the best choice: The U.S. Supreme Court has confirmed that transient (or "tag") jurisdiction satisfies the Due Process Clause, at least so long as it is exercised over someone who is voluntarily and knowingly within the forum. *See Burnham v. Superior Ct. of Cal.*, 495 U.S. 604, 616–622 (1990) (plurality); *id.* at 639–40 (Brennan, J., concurring).

   Answer (C) is wrong: Were Buyer to have minimum contacts with South Carolina, that, too, might be a basis for the South Carolina courts' exercise of personal jurisdiction. But, as explained in Answer (B), such minimum contacts are not essential if transient personal jurisdiction exists.

   Answer (D) is wrong: Like in Answer (C), Buyer's citizenship in South Carolina could support domicile-based personal jurisdiction. But, again as noted in Answer (B), Buyer's domicile is not essential to South Carolina's assertion of personal jurisdiction over Buyer if transient jurisdiction exists.

5.   **Answer (A) is the best choice:** Compelling a party to submit to a physical or mental examination is one of the rare discovery tools that may not be demanded independently of the court. To the contrary, absent consent of the examined party, these sorts of examinations require a court order. *See* Rule 35(a). But examinations are often liberally granted, upon a showing that the examinee's physical condition, mental condition, or blood group is "in controversy," *see* Rule 35(a)(1), and that "good cause" exists for the exam, *see* Rule 35(a)(2)(A). However, no court order is necessary where, as here, the opposing party agrees voluntarily to submit to the examination. Indeed, such examinations by consent are the usual way in which physical, mental, and blood group examinations are conducted. *See Herrera v. Lufkin Indus., Inc.*, 474 F.3d 675, 688–89 (10th Cir. 2007). Without the court's intervention, an examination upon the examinee's consent is proper.

   Answer (B) is wrong: Physical examinations are permitted under Rule 35, but only upon court order or consent of the examinee. *See* Rule 35(a)(1).

   Answer (C) is wrong: Mental examinations are permitted under Rule 35, but only upon court order or consent of the examinee. *See* Rule 35(a)(1).

   Answer (D) is wrong: As noted in Answer (B), physical examinations are permitted only upon court order or consent of the examinee. *See* Rule 35(a)(1).

6.   **Answer (A) is the best choice:** Under the "two dismissal rule," the second dismissal of a claim acts as a dismissal with prejudice. *See* Rule 41(a)(1)(B). Note that this Rule applies to individual claims as well as entire actions. *See Anderson v. Aon Corp.,* 614 F.3d 361, 364–65 (7th Cir. 2010). Therefore, because Shareholder dismissed the entire claim the first time, and then dismissed the RICO count the second time, Shareholder is precluded from bringing that claim a third time.

Answer (B) is wrong: Although Shareholder obviously tried to manipulate jurisdiction and the forum, that conduct is unlikely to affect the permissive amendment analysis, which focuses on prejudice to the nonmoving party. Furthermore, as explained in Answer (D), the court would be likely to deny the motion to amend.

Answer (C) is wrong: Although it is true that Shareholder's right to amend ended when Corporation filed its answer, as provided by Rule 15(a)(1), Shareholder retained the ability to seek leave to amend by motion under Rule 15(a)(2). However, as explained in Answer (D), the court would be unlikely to grant Shareholder's motion.

Answer (D) is wrong: Prejudice to the nonmoving party is the focus of the court's analysis of a motion to amend under Rule 15(a)(2). *See Equal Rights Ctr. v. Niles Bolton Assocs.,* 602 F.3d 597, 604, n.3 (4th Cir. 2010). However, because Shareholder's RICO claim is barred by the "two dismissal" rule, as explained in Answer (A), the court would likely deny the motion to amend under the doctrine of futility. *See Tripodi v. North Coventry Tp.,* 2013 WL 4034372, *9 (E.D.Pa. 2013).

7.   **Answer (A) is the best choice:** Surprising though it may seem, the U.S. Supreme Court has confirmed that the federal Due Process Clause does not mandate that civil litigants in State courts be given a right of appeal. *See Dohany v. Rogers,* 281 U.S. 362, 369 (1930) ("The due process clause does not guarantee to the citizen of a state any particular form or method of state procedure. Under it he may neither claim a right to trial by jury nor a right of appeal.").

Answer (B), (C), and (D) are wrong: There is no federal due process right to an appeal in State courts. *See* Answer (A).

8.   **Answer (A) is wrong:** A lack of subject-matter jurisdiction may be asserted by a pre-answer motion to dismiss. *See* Rule 12(b)(1). But a failure to raise the defense in this way does not bar its assertion later. *See* Rule 12(h)(3) ("If the court determines at any time that it lacks subject-matter jurisdiction, the court must dismiss the action.").

Answer (B) is wrong: If the federal court lacks subject-matter jurisdiction, it has no alternative but to dismiss the case. *See Firestone Tire & Rubber Co. v. Risjord,* 449 U.S. 368, 379 (1981) ("A court lacks discretion to consider the merits of a case over which it is without jurisdiction."); *In re Brand Name Prescription Drugs Antitrust Litig.,* 248 F.3d 668, 670 (7th Cir. 2001) ("Napoleon at his coronation took the imperial crown out of the hands of the Pope and crowned himself. Federal judges do not have a similar prerogative. A court that does not have jurisdiction cannot assume it, however worthy the cause.").

Answer (C) is wrong: Even a jurisdictional defect that is belatedly discovered cannot be overlooked, but must trigger a dismissal. *See In re Brand Name Prescription Drugs Antitrust Litig.,* 248 F.3d 668, 670 (7th Cir. 2001) (holding that, while perhaps "reprehensible" and even sanctionable as a delaying tactic to postpone raising a jurisdictional defect, "assuming federal jurisdiction where none exists is not a permissible sanction for anything").

Answer (D) is the best choice: A lack of subject-matter jurisdiction will always be cause to dismiss a federal lawsuit. *See* Rule 12(h)(3) ("If the court determines at any time that it lacks subject-matter jurisdiction, the court must dismiss the action.").

9.   **Answer (A) is wrong:** Claim preclusion generally is triggered only by a final judgment on the merits, but an entry of summary judgment that terminates a litigation qualifies as just such a merits judgment. *See Harris v. County of Orange,* 682 F.3d 1126, 1132 (9th Cir. 2012).

     Answer (B) is wrong: Although afternoon brightness was not challenged in the first litigation, there is no indication in the problem why it could not have been. Claim preclusion bars not only the relitigation of those claims that were actually raised during a prior litigation, but also those that could have been raised there as well. *See Rivet v. Regions Bank,* 522 U.S. 470, 476 (1998).

     Answer (C) is the best choice: Unlike Answer (B), newly installed alterations to the county's solar array materially changed the panel sizes and, thus, likely presents a factual situation that is sufficiently different from the first litigation to escape claim preclusion. Claim preclusion applies only where there is identity of claims between the original and later litigations. *See Matrix IV, Inc. v. American Nat'l Bank & Trust Co.,* 649 F.3d 539, 547 (7th Cir. 2011) ("whether an 'identity of the cause of action' exists . . . depends on whether the claims arise out of the same set of operative facts or the same transaction. . . . Even if the two claims are based on different legal theories, the 'two claims are one for purposes of res judicata [claim preclusion] if they are based on the same, or nearly the same, factual allegations.' ") (citations omitted).

     Answer (D) is wrong: Although claim preclusion requires identity of parties in the original and subsequent litigations, this requirement can be satisfied by privity of property interest. *See Meza v. General Battery Corp.,* 908 F.2d 1262, 1266 (5th Cir. 1990) (holding that privity exists "where the non-party is the successor in interest to a party's interest in property"); *see generally* 18A CHARLES A. WRIGHT & ARTHUR R. MILLER, FEDERAL PRACTICE AND PROCEDURE § 4462, at 659 (2002) (noting that cases hold that claim preclusion binds "a nonparty who takes property by transfer from a vanquished party after judgment."). Here, even if Purchaser was personally uninvolved in the first litigation, he would stand in privity with his predecessor in interest to the farm and, therefore, may be bound under the doctrine of claim preclusion.

10. **Answer (A) is wrong:** For purposes of the federal diversity statute, limited liability companies (LLCs)—like all unincorporated associations—are considered to be citizens of every State in which any of its members is a citizen. *See Belleville Catering Co. v. Champaign Mkt. Place, L.L.C.,* 350 F.3d 691, 692 (7th Cir. 2003). Thus, Restaurant LLC is not just a citizen of Texas, but also of Louisiana and Delaware as well.

Answer (B) is wrong: This answer notes correctly the citizenship of all parties, but there are two separate requirements for diversity jurisdiction—complete diversity among the parties and a qualifying amount in controversy. *See* 28 U.S.C. § 1332(a). As explained in Answer (D), this second requirement is not satisfied here.

Answer (C) is wrong: As explained in Answer (A), unincorporated associations are tested for citizenship diversity by examining the citizenship of each of their members. The State where an LLC was organized is not one of its places of citizenship, unless of course one of the LLC's members is a citizen there. *See OnePoint Solutions, LLC v. Borchert,* 486 F.3d 342, 347 n.4 (8th Cir. 2007).

Answer (D) is the best choice: Although the parties to this dispute have citizenships that are completely diverse, the amount in controversy requirement has not been satisfied. Diversity jurisdiction requires that the claim exceed $75,000, exclusive of interest and costs. *See* 28 U.S.C. § 1332(a). Here, the claim is for precisely $75,000, which fails to satisfy the jurisdictional minimum for diversity. *See State Farm Mut. Auto. Ins. Co. v. Powell,* 87 F.3d 93, 96–99 (3d Cir. 1996) (agreeing that a claim equal to the exact amount stated in Section 1332 is "a penny shy" of the amount required for diversity jurisdiction).

11. **Answer (A) is the best choice:** A body of federal common law exists in areas of special federal concern, such as, like here, contracts between employers and unions. Where it exists, that federal common law is applied in those circumstances. *See Barton v. House of Raeford Farms, Inc.,* 745 F.3d 95, 106–07 (4th Cir. 2014).

Answer (B) is wrong: The U.S. Supreme Court in *Erie Railroad* memorably pronounced that there is "no federal general common law." *See Erie R.R. Co. v. Tompkins,* 304 U.S. 64, 78 (1938). Though no "general" federal common law exists, context-specific federal common law persists widely today in areas of special federal concern. *See American Elec. Power Co. v. Connecticut,* 564 U.S. 410, 420–21 (2011).

Answer (C) is wrong: Even if State law is developed in a related area (such as, in this question, wage contracts and employer obligations), federal common law must be applied to areas of special federal concern. *See Barton v. House of Raeford Farms, Inc.,* 745 F.3d 95, 107 (4th Cir. 2014).

Answer (D) is wrong: Developing and apply federal common law for special federal concern are tasks within the proper province of the federal judiciary. *See American Elec. Power Co. v. Connecticut,* 564 U.S. 410, 420–21 (2011).

12. **Answer (A) is wrong:** Rule 47(c) of the Federal Rules of Civil Procedure authorizes the court—but not a party—to strike a prospective juror for cause. *See also* 28 U.S.C.A. § 1870. In any event, Homeowner's preference for highly educated jurors would not likely constitute good cause for striking a juror under Rule 47(c).

Answer (B) is the best choice: Rule 47(b) requires the court to allow parties to exercise the number of peremptory strikes provided by 28 U.S.C. § 1870 (generally 3 challenges). Striking the juror in question would be a proper peremptory strike.

Answer (C) is wrong: Rule 47(b) and the interpretive case law do not permit a party to exercise peremptory strikes on the basis of race or gender. *See Edmonson v. Leesville Concrete Co., Inc.,* 500 U.S. 614 (1991). The courts have not extended that principle to peremptory strikes on the basis of educational background.

Answer (D) is wrong: Except in situations potentially implicating improper discrimination, such as on the basis of race or gender, a party does not need to provide any explanation for its peremptory strikes under Rule 47(b).

13. **Answer (A) is wrong:** Under Rule 41(a)(1) of the Federal Rules of Civil Procedure, a plaintiff may voluntarily dismiss an action by filing a notice of dismissal before the opposing party files an answer or motion for summary judgment. Here, because Employer filed an answer, Employees can no longer voluntarily dismiss the action by filing a notice of dismissal.

Answer (B) is wrong: Under Rule 41(a)(1), a plaintiff may voluntarily dismiss an action by filing a stipulation of dismissal that is signed by all parties who have appeared. Here, because Employer refused to enter into a stipulation of dismissal without prejudice, Employees cannot, by stipulation, obtain the type of voluntary dismissal desired—namely, one that is without prejudice.

Answer (C) is the best choice: If a plaintiff cannot voluntarily dismiss an action by notice or stipulation under Rule 41(a)(1), the plaintiff must either abandon the action (and risk an involuntary dismissal), proceed with the action as it is presently positioned, or seek the involvement of the court by filing a motion for voluntary dismissal under Rule 41(a)(2). Dismissals pursuant to Rule 41(a)(2) motions are deemed to be without prejudice unless the order states otherwise.

Answer (D) is wrong: Involuntary dismissal is a vehicle for a defendant when a plaintiff fails to prosecute a case or fails to comply with the Federal Rules of Civil Procedure or a court order. Rule 41(b). Thus, it is not an option for Employees as plaintiffs.

14. **Answer (A) is the best choice:** Rule 4(e)(2)(B) of the Federal Rules of Civil Procedure authorizes service by "leaving a copy at the individual's dwelling or usual place of abode with someone of suitable age and discretion who resides there." A hotel is usually not considered an abode, but will be if it has been the defendant's dwelling place for a long, continuous period of time. *See Howard Johnson Int'l, Inc. v. Wang,* 7 F. Supp. 2d 336, 340 (S.D.N.Y. 1998), *aff'd,* 181 F.3d 82 (2d Cir. 1999). Because Husband is residing with Ms. Defendant in the same hotel room, and qualifies as someone of suitable age and discretion, the service would be proper.

Answer (B) is wrong: For the reasons set forth in Answer (A), a hotel can be considered an abode if the defendant is staying there for a long, continuous period of time.

Answer (C) is wrong: Although personal service is authorized by Rule 4(e)(2)(A) of the Federal Rules of Civil Procedure, the Rules do not require personal service or elevate it above abode service. *See Rosa v. Cantrell,* 705 F.2d 1208, 1214 (10th Cir. 1982).

Answer (D) is wrong: Although the U.S. Supreme Court has held that the Constitution requires "notice reasonably calculated, under all the circumstances, to apprise interested parties of the pendency of the action," *see Mullane v. Central Hanover Bank & Trust,* 339 U.S. 306 (1950), proper abode service meets this constitutional requirement. *See Rosa v. Cantrell,* 705 F.2d 1208, 1214 (10th Cir. 1982).

15. **Answer (A) is wrong:** Rule 56(c) does require a party opposing a motion for summary judgment on the grounds that there are genuine disputes of material fact to do so by citing to materials "in the record." However, as explained in Answer (C), the record evidence that Employer submitted is not sufficient to create a "genuine" dispute of material fact.

Answer (B) is wrong: It is true that the court will draw all reasonable inferences in favor of the nonmoving party. *See Crawford v. Metropolitan Gov't of Nashville & Davidson Cnty.,* 555 U.S. 271, 274, n.1 (2009). However, as explained in Answer (C), even the inferences from Employer's data do not create a "genuine" dispute of material fact.

Answer (C) is the best choice: Rule 56(a) precludes summary judgment when there is a "genuine" dispute of material fact. A genuine dispute is not created by "a mere scintilla" of favorable evidence. *See Anderson v. Liberty Lobby, Inc.,* 477 U.S. 242, 252 (1986). Here, the fact that 27% of Employer's employees are over the age of 40, without more, probably does not demonstrate that Employer did not discriminate against Employee. For example, those employees might be top-level executives, whereas Employee might be a mid-level or lower level employee, and Employer might only discriminate against older employees like Employee. *See Simpson v. Midland-Ross Corp.,* 823 F.2d 937, 944 (6th Cir. 1987) (summary judgment was appropriate despite statistical evidence regarding employment of protected class because statistics do not establish that age was the more likely reason for the employee's discharge, rather than merely a speculative possibility).

Answer (D) is wrong: Rule 56(c)(1)(A) explicitly allows parties to use affidavits to support their factual positions in connection with a motion for summary judgment. Although affidavits are normally not admissible at trial, Rule 56(c)(2) only authorizes an objection to evidence that cannot be presented in a form that would be admissible. Statements in an affidavit normally would be admissible if made by a competent witness live at trial.

16. **Answer (A) is the best choice:** The normal standard for amending pleadings is established in Rule 15 and the case law construing that rule. However, once the date for amending pleadings set in the case management order has expired, the standard shifts to the standard for amending a pretrial order, which is set by Rule 16. *See, e.g., Kassner v. 2nd Avenue Delicatessen Inc.,* 496 F.3d 229, 243 (2d Cir. 2007). Under that standard, the moving party must show "good cause" for amending the order. *See O'Connell v. Hyatt Hotels of Puerto Rico,* 357 F.3d 152, 154 (1st Cir. 2004).

Answer (B) is wrong: Although amendment is liberally allowed under Rule 15 in the absence of prejudice to the opposing party, once the date for amendment established in the case management order has passed, the "good cause" standard under Rule 16 applies, as explained in Answer (A).

Answer (C) is wrong: Generally, the question of whether the statute of limitations has passed is part of the "relation back" analysis, not the threshold issue of whether to permit amendment (although if the statute of limitations defense is apparent on the face of the complaint, the doctrine of futility might lead a court to deny a motion to amend). Moreover, here, Seaman is not seeking to add a new party and Seaman's original complaint alleged exposure to "asbestos and other non-asbestos hazardous chemicals" from the same work. Accordingly, the original claim and the new benzene-related claim appear to arise out of the same case or controversy. The amended complaint would likely relate back to the original complaint and would therefore be timely. *See* Rule 15(c)(1)(B); *Miller v. American Heavy Lift Shipping,* 231 F.3d 242, 248–49 (6th Cir. 2000).

Answer (D) is wrong: Rule 15(c)(1)(B) provides that a claim relates back if, among other things, it asserts a claim that "arose out of the same conduct, transaction, or occurrence set out—or attempted to be set out—in the original pleading." The "case or controversy" phrase, although similar, pertains more to subject-matter jurisdiction. *See* 28 U.S.C. § 1367(a). Here, the question states that both the original claim and the benzene-related claim arose out of the same employment for Shipping Co., and therefore would likely be considered as arising out of the same conduct, transaction, or occurrence, or as part of the same case or controversy, as explained in Answer (C).

17. **Answer (A) is wrong:** Execution on a civil judgment is often stayed on appeal by the filing of a supersedeas bond approved by the court. *See* Rule 62(d).

Answer (B) is the best choice: Money judgments are stayed automatically for 30 days after entry. *See* Rule 62(a). (Note, this period of automatic stay was enlarged, effective December 2018, from its former 14-day length.) The purpose of this 30-day "quiet" period is to allow the defeated party unmolested time to decide how to proceed, whether by post-trial motion, appeal, negotiated resolution, or otherwise. *See* 11 CHARLES A. WRIGHT, ARTHUR R. MILLER, & MARY KAY KANE, FEDERAL PRACTICE AND PROCEDURE § 2902, at 666 (2012). This is a good example of a question where, even if you weren't sure of the correctness of this answer, you should be able to eliminate all the other choices.

Answer (C) is wrong: To the contrary, execution on a money judgment is only automatically stayed for 30 days, as discussed in Answer (B). Although a further stay during pendency of an appeal is possible through the posting of a supersedeas bond or other security, *see* Answer (D), once the initial 30 days expire, there is no longer any automatic stay of execution in civil money judgments. *See Acevedo-Garcia v. Vera-Monroig,* 368 F.3d 49, 58 (1st Cir. 2004) ("The federal rules contemplate that, absent a stay, a victorious plaintiff may execute on the judgment even while an appeal of that judgment is pending.").

Answer (D) is wrong: While "re-claiming" an already dispensed judgment after it is reversed on appeal is clearly problematic, a postponement in executing on a judgment while an appeal is pending places the collectability of the judgment in question (because the defeated party's ability to pay may be unexpectedly compromised by circumstances, or that party may intentionally (or fraudulently) fritter away assets that are necessary to collectability). To balance these competing concerns, the execution of civil money judgments can be stayed in federal court, but only upon the posting of a supersedeas bond or other security approved by and filed with the court. *See* Rule 62(d). Such a bond functions as security for the payment of the judgment, yet avoids passing the contested judgment monies along to the opponent while the appeal is still pending. The bond is normally set in an amount equal to the full judgment plus interest, costs, and delay damages. *See* 11 CHARLES A. WRIGHT, ARTHUR R. MILLER, & MARY KAY KANE, FEDERAL PRACTICE AND PROCEDURE § 2905, at 716 (2012).

18. **Answer (A) is wrong:** Most communications between attorneys and their testifying expert witnesses are generally shielded from discovery under the work product protection. *See* Rule 26(b)(4)(C) (noting exceptions to this protection for compensation, attorney-provided facts or data, and attorney-provided assumptions). This protection specifically includes drafts of expert reports. *See* Rule 26(b)(4)(B).

Answer (B) is the best choice: Whenever a witness is proposing to offer expert opinions at trial, that witness's identity must be disclosed, *see* Rule 26(a)(2)(A), as well as that witness's testimonial opinions, *see* Rule 26(a)(2)(B)(i) & Rule 26(a)(2)(C)(ii). For expert witnesses who are retained, who are specially-employed, or whose duties as a party's employee regularly involve giving expert testimony, the disclosure obligation is broad. *See* Rule 26(a)(B)(i) ("a complete statement of all opinions the witness will express and the basis and reasons for them"). For all other testifying expert witnesses, disclosure is still compelled, though the scope of the disclosure is narrower. *See* Rule 26(a)(C)(ii) ("a summary of the facts and opinions to which the witness is expected to testify"). The long-time employee in this Answer (B) could, depending on further facts, fall into either category; but in either event, there will be disclosure of that employee's opinions.

Answer (C) is wrong: Unless that expert is expected to testify at trial, the opinions held by a party's consulting expert—even one retained or specially employed as an expert—are generally protected from discovery. *See* Rule 26(b)(4)(D). Neither of the two recognized exceptions to this protection apply to these facts. *See* Rule 26(b)(4)(D)(i)–(ii) (protection does not apply to medical examinations or when exceptional circumstances are shown to exist).

Answer (D) is wrong: The identity of an expert consulted but not hired generally need not be disclosed to an opponent. *See* Rule 26(a)(2)(A) (directing that only the identity of testifying experts need be disclosed). *See also Ager v. Jane C. Stormont Hosp. & Training Sch. for Nurses,* 622 F.2d 496, 501 (10th Cir. 1980) (identity of experts consulted informally but not retained need not be disclosed).

19. **Answer (A) is the best choice:** Ordinarily, defendants in federal court must serve an answer within 21 days after service of original process. *See* Rule 12(a)(1)(A)(i). Defendants who timely waive service of process under the Rules, however, receive 60 days (or 39 days more) to file their answer. *See* Rule 12(a)(1)(A)(ii).

Answer (B) is wrong: Although encouraged to do so (and at risk of cost-shifting if they refuse), the Rules do not mandate that defendants agree to waive service. To the contrary, if the defendants refuse to waive, the plaintiffs are then obligated to complete formal service through traditional means. *See Cambridge Holdings Group, Inc. v. Federal Ins. Co.,* 489 F.3d 1356, 1362 (D.C. Cir. 2007).

Answer (C) is wrong: Agreeing to the waiver will excuse the need to complete formal service and, consequently, there can be no occasion to complain about a formal service that will never be performed. *See* Rule 4(d)(4). However, agreeing to the waiver does not waive any objections to personal jurisdiction or venue that a defendant might have. *See* Rule 4(d)(5).

Answer (D) is wrong: A proper waiver form must be accompanied by a copy of the complaint, *see* Rule 4(d)(1)(C), but no summons need be included. *See* Rule 4(d) advisory committee's note to 1993 amendment.

20. **Answer (A) is the best choice:** A party who intends to object to the court's failure to give an instruction must do so on the record, and that if the party was aware that the court was not going to give the objection, the party must object at the time the court provides the instructions and gives the parties an opportunity to object. *See* Rule 51(c). Here, Ladder Co. failed to make any objection at the proper time. Rule 51(d) provides that a party may not base an appeal unless the party properly objected, as explained in Answer (C).

   Answer (B) is wrong: Rule 51(d) expressly authorizes appeals of properly preserved objections to the jury instructions.

   Answer (C) is wrong: Rule 51(d)(1)(B) relieves a party from the obligation to put an objection on the record if the court has made a definitive ruling that it will not give a requested objection. This relieves the parties of the awkward position of putting a formal objection on the record to the action the court has just taken. Here, however, the court did not make any definitive determination, it simply provided a set of instructions without the requested one. In such circumstances, the party must object to preserve the issue. *See* Rule 51(d)(1)(B).

   Answer (D) is wrong: As explained in Answer (A), a party must raise issues concerning the jury instructions before the jury is charged, not after-the-fact in a motion for a new trial.

21. **Answer (A) is wrong:** The pleadings are typically treated as amended "to conform to the evidence" under Rule 15(b)(2) when the evidence is admitted without objection at trial, as explained in Answer (D).

   Answer (B) is wrong: In general, the final pretrial order supersedes the pleadings and controls the issues to be determined at trial. *See, e.g., Friedman & Friedman, Ltd. v. Tim McCandless, Inc.,* 650 F.3d 494 (8th Cir. 2010). However, as explained in Answer (D), failure to object to the evidence is deemed implied consent. *See Clark v. Martinez,* 295 F.3d 809, 814 (8th Cir. 2002).

   Answer (C) is wrong: Prejudice is one of the court's considerations when a party objects to evidence as outside the issues raised in the pleadings, as provided by Rule 15(b)(1). In contrast, Rule 15(b)(2) provides that when an issue is tried by the parties' implied consent—such as when evidence is admitted without objection—the issue is treated as if it were part of the pleadings without regard to claims of prejudice.

   Answer (D) is the best choice: Rule 15(b)(2) of the Federal Rules of Civil Procedure provides that, "When an issue not raised by the pleadings is tried by the parties' express or implied consent, it must be treated in all respects as if raised in the pleadings." Courts typically treat failure to object as "implied consent." *See, e.g., Eich v. Board of Regents for Cent. Missouri St. Univ.,* 350 F.3d 752 (8th Cir. 2003).

22. **Answer (A) is wrong:** *In rem* is jurisdiction over property; *in personam* is jurisdiction over persons. The U.S. Supreme Court long ago confirmed that seizure of property will only authorize *in rem* jurisdiction if that seizure occurs prior to the entry of the judgment (so that the defendant can be placed on notice of the obligation to defend). *See Pennoyer v. Neff,* 95 U.S. 714, 727 (1878) ("The law assumes that property is always in the possession of its owner, in person or by agent, and it proceeds upon the theory that its seizure will inform him not only that it is taken into the custody of the court, but that he must look to any proceedings authorized by law upon such seizure for its condemnation and sale.").

    Answer (B) is the best choice: Federal courts are authorized to hear *in rem* actions when it is shown that *in personam* jurisdiction cannot be obtained in the district by reasonable efforts to properly serve the summons. *See* Rule 4(n)(2).

    Answer (C) is wrong: Federal statutes may authorize *in rem* jurisdiction. *See* Rule 4(n)(1). But, as noted in Answer (B), that is not the only instance in which in rem lawsuits would be proper.

    Answer (D) is wrong: Jurisdiction *in rem* and *in personam* are separate paths to personal jurisdiction. Either can be proper independent of the other. Indeed, unless a federal statute authorizes *in rem*, it is actually unavailable if personal jurisdiction could be obtained *in personam*. *See* Answer (B).

23. **Answer (A) is the best choice:** The joining of parties who have competing claims against a defendant is available through interpleader. The federal courts permit two styles of interpleader—one authorized by Rule 22 and one authorized by statute (*see* 28 U.S.C. § 1335). Rule 22 interpleader requires the presence of a claim that may expose the defendant to double or multiple liability. *See* Rule 22(a). Statutory interpleader requires the presence of competing claims challenging rights to money, property, notes, bonds, certificates, insurance policies, or other instruments having a value of $500 or more. *See* 28 U.S.C. § 1335(a). Here, the contested asset is $200,000, well above the $500 threshold set by the statute, and, notwithstanding the $200,000 policy limit, even a theoretical exposure to multiple liability—no matter how remote or unlikely—satisfies the dictates of Rule 22. *See Pan Am. Fire & Cas. Co. v. Revere*, 188 F. Supp. 474, 480 (E.D. La. 1960). But compliance with the procedural obligations for interpleader does not answer the further question of whether the federal court would have subject-matter jurisdiction over the interpleader. *See* Rule 82. Like joinder under any of the other Federal Rules of Civil Procedure, Rule 22 interpleader would require complete diversity among the parties. *See Lee v. West Coast Life Ins. Co.*, 688 F.3d 1004, 1007 n.1 (9th Cir. 2012). Thus, the stakeholder (here, Reliable Insurer) must be diverse from every claimant. Because Reliable Insurer is a citizen of New York, a citizenship it shares with some of the injured bus passenger claimants, there would be no subject-matter jurisdiction over a Rule 22 interpleader. But statutory interpleader requires only "minimal" diversity—that is, at least one claimant must be diverse from another claimant. *See id. See also* 28 U.S.C. § 1335(a)(1). Here, the bus claimants include citizens of Pennsylvania, New Jersey, New York, Connecticut, and Maryland. Consequently, statutory interpleader is likely to enjoy subject-matter jurisdiction here.

    Answer (B) is wrong: As explained in Answer (A), Rule 22 interpleader cannot be used here due to lack of subject-matter jurisdiction, though statutory interpleader can be invoked.

    Answer (C) is wrong: As explained in Answer (A), it is likely that statutory interpleader can be used here, though Rule interpleader cannot.

    Answer (D) is wrong: As explained in Answer (A), it is unlikely that Rule interpleader can be used, though statutory interpleader can.

24. **Answer (A) is wrong:** For criminal cases, the U.S. Supreme Court has ruled that the U.S. Constitution requires that juries be drawn from a fair cross-section of the community. *See Taylor v. Louisiana*, 419 U.S. 522, 530 (1975). There is authority that this constitutional fair cross-section standard applies in civil cases as well as criminal, *see Thiel v. Southern Pacific Co.,* 328 U.S. 217, 220 (1946), but other courts are less certain of that conclusion, *Fleming v. Chicago Transit Auth.,* 397 Fed. Appx. 249, 249 (7th Cir. 2010). In any event, whether of constitutional dimension or not, the U.S. Congress has enacted a statutory mandate that directs that all federal juries be drawn from a fair cross-section of the community. *See* 28 U.S.C. §§ 1861–74. Vacationer has a right to see this fair cross-section mandate enforced, regardless of his own gender. *See id.* at § 1867(c). *See also Taylor v. Louisiana,* 419 U.S. 522, 526 (1975).

Answer (B) is wrong: The requirement of a fair cross-section does not command that any particular jury mirror the demographic profile of the community, only that no distinctive group within the community be excluded from jury eligibility. *See Taylor v. Louisiana*, 419 U.S. 522, 538 (1975). Consequently, the requirement does not ensure that there be a fulsome gender division during jury selection that would allow for the strategic use of peremptory strikes to enhance gender representations. In fact, such a strategic use of peremptory strikes to eliminate male and increase female jury representation may well implicate constitutional concerns against gender-based discrimination in jury selection. *See J.E.B. v. Alabama*, 511 U.S. 127, 141–42 (1994).

Answer (C) is wrong: As explained in Answer (B), the fact that an individual jury panel does not contain women is unlikely to offend the fair cross-section requirement, so long as there is no systematic exclusion of women from jury eligibility. *See Taylor v. Louisiana*, 419 U.S. 522, 538 (1975).

Answer (D) is the best choice: As explained in Answer (B), a violation of the fair cross-section requirement occurs when the jury gathering process results in the disparate exclusion from jury eligibility of a distinctive group within the community. *See Taylor v. Louisiana*, 419 U.S. 522, 538 (1975). Here, the Hawai'i jury gathering process collected no women from a summons that yielded 400 persons. That complete lack of female representation in a jury-eligible community comprised of 52% women is strong evidence of a fair cross-section flaw.

25. **Answer (A) is the best choice:** Special procedures have been adopted for jury demands in removal cases. Where, as this Answer proposes, the pleadings were completed and closed in State court prior to the removal, a party may make a timely jury demand by serving it within 14 days after filing (or receiving from another party) a notice of removal. *See* Rule 81(c)(3)(B). By waiting until 21 days after its removal to seek a jury trial, Resort's demand was untimely. In the absence of a proper demand, the case is tried to the court, not before a jury. *See* Rule 39(b).

Answer (B) is wrong: A demand for a jury made properly in State court need not be repeated or renewed following removal. *See* Rule 81(c)(3)(A). Here, the timely-made State court demand by Skier will afford him a trial by jury.

Answer (C) is wrong: When the pleadings have not closed in State court, the traditional procedures applicable in federal court apply. Here, a jury demand served by either party within 14 days after service of the last pleading directed to the issue in question (namely, personal injuries due to snowmobiling negligence) constitutes an effective demand. *See* Rule 38(b).

Answer (D) is wrong: If the applicable State's law does not require parties to formally demand a jury trial because one is provided as a matter of course, no formal demand will ordinarily be required in federal court following removal (unless the federal judge instructs otherwise). *See* Rule 81(c)(3)(A).

26. **Answer (A) is wrong:** The personal jurisdiction analysis required by the U.S. Constitution's Due Process Clause demands a lower threshold amount of contacts with the State when the cause of action arises from or relates to those contacts. Thus, if a defendant has only one contact with a State, but that one contact was the defendant's commission of tort within the State, the State's courts would likely have personal jurisdiction in a lawsuit arising from or relating to that same tort (but likely not in a lawsuit unrelated to that tort). *See International Shoe Co. v. Washington*, 326 U.S. 310 (1945). Jurisdiction when the claim arises from or relates to in-forum contacts is often referred to as "specific jurisdiction" or "case-linked jurisdiction." *See Burger King Corp. v. Rudzewicz,* 471 U.S. 462, 463 (1985). Here, Painter's claim does not relate to Executive's contacts with Texas, so the Texas court could not exercise specific jurisdiction over Executive. However, as explained in Answer (D), the court can exercise jurisdiction over Executive because she was served in Texas.

Answer (B) is wrong: In contrast to "specific jurisdiction," a court may exercise "general jurisdiction" (also known as "all-purpose jurisdiction") over a defendant even when the lawsuit does not arise from or relate to the defendant's contacts with the State. *See Goodyear Dunlop Tires Ops., S.A. v. Brown*, 564 U.S. 915, 919 (2011). But the required level of contacts to support general jurisdiction is far more demanding. General jurisdiction exists only when a defendant has such substantial, systematic, and continuous contacts with the forum State that the defendant is considered to be "essentially at home" there. *See Brown*, 564 U.S. at 919. Executive's regular vacation trips to Texas would not meet this test for general jurisdiction. *Cf. BNSF Ry. Co. v. Tyrrell*, 137 S. Ct. 1549, 1559 (2017) (defendant not amenable to general jurisdiction even though it maintained "over 2,000 miles of railroad track and more than 2,000 employees in" forum State); *Brown*, 564 U.S. at 929 (defendants' "attenuated connections" to the forum State (tens of thousands of tires delivered there) "fall far short" of the contacts needed to support general jurisdiction); *Helicopteros Nacionales de Colombia, S.A. v. Hall*, 466 U.S. 408, 418 (1984) (regular contacts with forum State for purchases and training activities not sufficient to support general jurisdiction). However, as explained in Answer (D), the court can exercise jurisdiction over Executive because she was served in Texas.

Answer (C) is wrong: As explained in Answer (B), Executive's regular vacation trips to Texas would not support general jurisdiction.

Answer (D) is the best choice: A court can exercise personal jurisdiction over a defendant who is served while voluntarily in the State, even the defendant was only temporarily within the State for reasons unrelated to the matter before the court. *See Burnham v. Superior Court of Cal.*, 495 U.S. 604, 610–11 (1990). Because Executive was served in Texas, the Texas court can properly exercise personal jurisdiction over her.

27. **Answer (A) is the best choice:** At base, the *Erie* Doctrine provides that a federal court hearing a case under its diversity jurisdiction applies federal procedural law and the substantive law of the State whose laws govern the claim. *See Gasperini v. Center for Humanities, Inc.,* 518 U.S. 415, 427 (1996). When the Federal Rules of Civil Procedure (or other federally enacted law) do not address an issue, the court will evaluate whether the issue governs "the manner and means" by which the litigants' rights are enforced—which suggests it is procedural—or whether it alters "the rules of decision by which the court will adjudicate those rights,"—which suggests it is substantive law. *See Shady Grove Orthopedic Assocs., P.A. v. Allstate Ins. Co.,* 599 U.S. 393, 407 (2010). The court will also consider whether the issue implicates the *Erie* doctrine's "twin aims"—namely, the discouraging of forum-shopping and the avoiding of an inequitable administration of the laws. *See Hanna v. Plumer,* 380 U.S. 460, 468 (1965). Here, requiring a certificate of merit does not conflict or clash with a Federal Rule of Civil Procedure. On close inspection, the certification requirement would likely be seen as a limitation on the substantive right to bring a medical malpractice claim; after all, the purpose of imposing the requirement was substantive (namely, reining in frivolous medical malpractice actions). Additionally, if the requirement were present in State court but not in federal court, that would encourage forum shopping. *See Chamberlain v. Giampapa,* 210 F.3d 154, 161 (3d Cir. 2000) (finding that New Jersey's certificate of merit requirement does not clash with the Federal Rules, was substantive and, thus, was properly applied under *Erie* principles). Finally, as explained below, all of the other answers are plainly wrong, allowing you to confirm that Answer (A) is correct even if you were not sure how a court would view a certificate of merit.

Answers (B) and (C) are wrong: As explained in Answer (A), federal courts do not "always" turn to State law if the Federal Rules are silent.

Answer (D) is wrong: As explained in Answer (A), federal courts sitting in diversity apply federal procedural law and State substantive law. Consequently, were this certification requirement a procedural, rather than substantive, law, it would likely not be applied.

28. **Answer (A) is wrong:** To justify an entry of summary judgment, the facts implicated by the motion must be "material." *See Anderson v. Liberty Lobby, Inc.,* 477 U.S. 242, 248 (1986) ("Only disputes over facts that might affect the outcome of the suit under the governing law will properly preclude the entry of summary judgment. Factual disputes that are irrelevant or unnecessary will not be counted."). But those facts must also be "genuinely disputed" as well. *See id.* ("summary judgment will not lie if the dispute about a material fact is 'genuine,' that is, if the evidence is such that a reasonable jury could return a verdict for the nonmoving party."). Here, the fact that the limitations defense is "material" is important, but the trial court was obligated also to determine whether that material fact was genuinely disputed. As explained in Answer (D), the court cannot make that determination without giving all parties notice and an opportunity to respond.

Answer (B) is wrong: In granting summary judgment in favor of a *non-moving* party, the trial judge is required to determine that the "normal standards" for entering summary judgment are satisfied. *See Caswell v. City of Detroit Housing Comm'n,* 418 F.3d 615, 617–18 (6th Cir. 2005). Indeed, because the court must additionally determine that its discretion is properly exercised by initiating a summary judgment consideration, the standards are likely more demanding, not less so, than when the motion is raised by the court itself. *See id.*

Answer (C) is wrong: The fact that Customer's estate never formally asked for summary judgment is not dispositive. The Rules expressly authorize a trial court, on its own initiative, to enter summary judgment in favor of a *non-moving* party and against the moving party. *See* Rule 56(f)(1).

Answer (D) is the best choice: Before a court may enter such a summary judgment against the moving party and in favor of the non-moving party, it must give all parties notice and an opportunity to respond. *See* Rule 56(f). Because the trial court did not do so here, Bank is likely entitled to a reversal.

29. **Answer (A) is wrong:** As explained in Answer (B), Violinist has no right to a jury trial as to the specific performance claim.

Answer (B) is the best choice: Under Rule 38 of the Federal Rules of Civil Procedure and the Seventh Amendment of the U.S. Constitution, parties have the right to jury trial for any claims that were common law claims (generally those seeking money damages) at the time that the Seventh Amendment was ratified in 1791. Defamation is a common law claim, but specific performance is an equitable claim, so Violinist has no right to a jury trial for that claim. *See, e.g., Klein v. Shell Oil Co.,* 386 F.2d 659, 663 (8th Cir. 1967); *Rosenblatt v. Baer,* 383 U.S. 75 (1966). Under Rule 38, a party preserves the right to a jury trial by filing and serving a demand within 14 days of the last pleading addressing the issue (which, typically, is the answer to the complaint).

Answer (C) is wrong: As explained in Answer (B), Violinist has a right to a jury trial for the defamation claim, but no right to a jury trial as to the specific performance claim.

Answer (D) is wrong: As explained in Answer (B), Violinist has a right to a jury trial for the defamation claim.

30. **Answer (A) is wrong:** Service on an individual by personal delivery is permitted by the Federal Rules of Civil Procedure, *see* Rule 4(e)(2)(A), but this service was improper as explained in Answer (D).

    Answer (B) is wrong: Service on individuals by delivery to their usual places of abode is permitted by the Rules, *see* Rule 4(e)(2)(B), but service remains improper as explained in Answer (D).

    Answer (C) is wrong: Service at an individual's usual place of abode is proper if made "with someone of suitable age and discretion who resides there," *see* Rule 4(e)(2)(B), but service is still improper as explained in Answer (D).

    Answer (D) is the best choice: To constitute proper service, both the complaint *and* a properly-issued summons must be served, and they must be served together. *See* Rule 4(c)(1) & 4(e)(2)(A). Here, only the complaint was placed in the sealed, large white envelope that Process Server handed to Partner B. Consequently, the service was improper. *See Bolivar v. Director of FBI,* 846 F. Supp. 163, 166 (D.P.R. 1994), *aff'd,* 45 F.3d 423 (1st Cir. 1995) (Table). This is another question where test-taking strategies should help you. Absent the failure to include the summons, Answers (A), (B), and (C) would all be correct, which suggests none of them is correct.

31. **Answer (A) is wrong:** The Rules prescribe four prerequisites that must be satisfied before any lawsuit can proceed in federal court as a class action. *See* Rule 23(a). One of those four prerequisites is this one, that the class representatives will fairly and adequately protect the class's interests. *See* Rule 23(a)(4).

    Answer (B) is wrong: Another of the four prerequisites required of every federal class action is that the representative parties' claims (or defenses) are typical of those of the rest of the class membership. *See* Rule 23(a)(3).

    Answer (C) is the best choice: Another of the four prerequisites is that there are questions of law or fact common to the class membership. *See* Rule 23(a)(2). But those common questions of law or fact need not "predominate" in every federal class action. Instead, such predomination of common questions is only required of the third of the various types of authorized class actions authorized by Rule 23(b)—namely, where the plaintiffs are able to demonstrate that class treatment will be "superior to other available methods for fairly and efficiently adjudicating the controversy." *See* Rule 23(b)(3). But this is just one of four types of allowable class actions, and predominance of common questions is not mandated for the other three.

    Answer (D) is wrong: Also a required prerequisite for every federal class action is "numerosity," or a class population that is so numerous that joining all of its members under other joinder Rules would prove to be "impracticable." *See* Rule 23(a)(1).

32. **Answer (A) is wrong:** As explained in Answer (D), for issues regarding the sufficiency of the evidence, a party may not appeal the denial of a summary judgment motion without also raising the issue under Rule 50. *See Ortiz v. Jordan*, 562 U.S. 180, 188–89 (2011).

    Answer (B) is wrong: In order to preserve for appeal an issue relating to the sufficiency of evidence, a party must both file a motion for judgment as a matter of law during trial under Rule 50(a), and then renew the motion *after trial* under Rule 50(b). *See Unitherm Food Servs., Inc. v. Swift-Eckrich, Inc.*, 546 U.S. 394, 396 (2006). Here, Prison filed a Rule 50(a) motion twice during trial, but failed to file a Rule 50(b) motion after the verdict.

    Answer (C) is wrong: As explained in Answer (B), Prison failed to file a Rule 50(b) motion after trial, and therefore did not preserve the issue it sought to raise on appeal related to the sufficiency of the evidence.

    Answer (D) is the best choice: As explained in Answer (B), Prison failed to file a Rule 50(b) motion after trial, and therefore did not preserve the issue it sought to raise on appeal related to the sufficiency of the evidence.

33. **Answer (A) is the best choice:** The Due Process Clause of the United States Constitution prohibits a court from requiring a defendant to come to the court and defend itself unless the defendant has sufficient "minimum contacts" with the State where the court is situated such that "traditional notions of fair play and substantial justice" are not offended. *See International Shoe Co. v. Washington*, 326 U.S. 310, 316 (1945). However, a State is not required to make its courts available for every claim that does not violate the Due Process Clause. States define the situations where their courts may hear claims against out-of-State defendants in their "long-arm statutes." In order to pursue a claim against an out-of-State defendant, therefore, a plaintiff must satisfy both the State's long-arm statute and the United States Constitution's due process requirements.

    Answer (B) is wrong: As explained in Answer (A), the plaintiff must satisfy both the State's long-arm statute and the United States Constitution's due process requirements—either one without the other is not sufficient.

    Answer (C) is wrong: Even if a claim satisfies the State's long-arm statute, it may still run afoul of the constitutional due process protections.

    Answer (D) is wrong: The long-arm statutes in some States grant their courts authority to exercise personal jurisdiction over a defendant to the full extent permitted by the U.S. Constitution, but other States frame their long-arm statues more narrowly. Therefore, it is entirely possible that a court's exercise of personal jurisdiction over a defendant would satisfy the U.S. Constitution's due process requirements but not satisfy the State's long-arm statute.

34. **Answer (A) is wrong:** Claim preclusion has three elements: a claim that was previously litigated on the merits; the same claim asserted in a subsequent action, and the same parties, or someone in privity with those parties, present in both actions. *See Community State Bank v. Strong,* 651 F.3d 1241, 1263–64 (11th Cir. 2011). This question implicates the third element. In *Taylor v. Sturgell,* 553 U.S. 880 (2008), the U.S. Supreme Court held that parties were not in privity merely because they knew each other, shared the same objective, and used the same lawyer. Rather, the Court remanded that case for the trial court to determine whether the second plaintiff was acting as the representative or agent of the first plaintiff. Under the facts in the question, the court might need more facts to determine whether Neighbor was acting as the agent for Homeowner. However, the question also implicates the first element—a claim that was previously litigated on the merits. Neighbor's claim related to emissions falling on Neighbor's property was not litigated in the first action, so the doctrine of claim preclusion does not apply.

Answer (B) is wrong: As explained in Answers (A) and (C), the elements of claim preclusion are not present based on the facts in the question.

Answer (C) is the best choice: As explained in Answer (A), one of the elements for claim preclusion is that the claim was previously litigated. While Homeowner's right to an injunction based on emissions deposited on Homeowner's property was litigated, the question does not suggest that Homeowner's action included a claim based on impacts to Neighbor's property. Therefore, a court is unlikely to apply claim preclusion.

Answer (D) is wrong: A summary judgment is normally considered a decision on the merits. *See Mitchell v. Trumbull Memorial Hosp.,* 23 Fed. Appx. 494 (6th Cir. 2001). Indeed, dismissal for failure to state a claim under Rule 12(b)(6) is an adjudication on the merits for purposes of claim preclusion. *See Federated Dep't Stores, Inc. v. Moitie,* 452 U.S. 394, 399 (1981).

35. **Answer (A) is wrong:** Rule 11(a) requires attorneys (or parties, if unrepresented) to sign court papers. Rule 11(b) spells out what the Rule 11(a) signature certifies. If an attorney signs a pleading in violation of the Rule 11(b) certifications, the attorney has violated Rule 11, and the court can sanction the attorney *sua sponte. See* Rule 11(c)(3). If another party wants to file a motion for Rule 11 sanctions, Rule 11(c) requires the moving party to provide notice to the alleged violator and then wait 21 days to give the alleged violator a chance to correct the violation. *See* Rule 11(c)(2). But an attorney violates Rule 11 the moment the attorney signs and files a pleading in violation of the certifications in Rule 11(b).

Answer (B) is the best choice: Rule 11(b)(2) provides that a signature on court papers certifies that "the claims, defenses, and other legal contentions are warranted by existing law or by a nonfrivolous argument for extending, modifying, or reversing existing law or for establishing new law." Here, because Homeowner's State is silent on whether hydraulic fracturing is an abnormally dangerous activity, and despite the fact that three other States have considered the issue and rejected the argument Homeowner is making, if Homeowner offers a nonfrivolous argument for establishing new law then Homeowner will not violate Rule 11. *See Ario v. Underwriting Members of Syndicate 53 at Lloyds for 1998 Year of Account,* 618 F.3d 277, 298 (3d Cir. 2010).

Answer (C) is wrong: The duty to zealously represent a client does not justify violating Rule 11. *See United States v. Int'l Bhd. of Teamsters, Chauffeurs, Warehousemen & Helpers of Am., AFL-CIO,* 948 F.2d 1338, 1344 (2d Cir. 1991) (Rule 11 "draw[s] a line between zealous advocacy and frivolous conduct").

Answer (D) is wrong: As explained in Answer (B), the absence of relevant authority in a State relating to a particular argument does not automatically mean that advancing that argument violates Rule 11.

36. **Answer (A) is wrong:** As explained in Answer (D), a party is allowed to plead in the alternative even if the two claims are inconsistent. Rule 11 would only prohibit Contractor's pleading if Contractor's attorney violated one of the certifications in Rule 11, which the question does not suggest.

    Answer (B) is wrong: As explained in Answer (D), although the doctrine of election of remedies may prevent a party from presenting two inconsistent claims to a jury or judge at trial, *see Homeland Training Ctr., LLC v. Summit Point Auto. Research Ctr.*, 594 F.3d 285, 293 (4th Cir. 2010) ("The basic purpose of the [election of remedies] doctrine is to prevent a plaintiff from obtaining a windfall recovery, either by recovering two forms of relief that are premised on legal or factual theories that contradict one another or by recovering overlapping remedies for the same legal injury."), a party is allowed to plead two inconsistent claims in the alternative.

    Answer (C) is wrong: While the standard for pleading in Rule 8 of the Federal Rules of Civil Procedure is often referred to as "notice pleading," Rule 8(d)(2) authorizes a party to plead two inconsistent claims in the alternative.

    Answer (D) is the best choice: Rule 8(d)(2) of the Federal Rules of Civil Procedure specifically authorizes "A party [to] state as many separate claims or defenses as the party has regardless of consistency." Contractor is entitled to argue that the parties executed contractual change orders or, if discovery or the court determines that the parties did not enter into a contract, Contractor is entitled to recover in the alternative under the doctrine of unjust enrichment. *See Prudential Ins. Co. of Am. v. Clark Consulting, Inc.*, 548 F. Supp. 2d 619, 623–24 (N.D. Ill. 2008) ("The law is clear that Prudential cannot *recover* under both a breach of contract theory and an unjust enrichment theory. . . . Thus, if this Court determines in subsequent proceedings that an enforceable contract exists between the parties, then Prudential's unjust enrichment claim cannot stand.") (citations omitted).

37. **Answer (A) is the best choice:** As the question relates, there is a conflict between State X and State Y—namely, one State would consider Jogger a "limited trespasser" while the other State would consider Jogger a "full trespasser." But as a substantive matter, this conflict is a "false" one because the legal outcome would be the same under either definition (namely, in either State, the defendants' behavior will be tested under a wanton and willful conduct standard). Consequently, the federal court will not need to resolve the conflict between the two States' laws, but will apply their common substantive standard to adjudicating the claim of Jogger's estate. *See In re Chinese Mfd. Drywall Prods. Liab. Litig.*, 742 F.3d 576, 586 (5th Cir. 2014); *Fioretti v. Massachusetts Gen. Life Ins. Co.*, 53 F.3d 1228, 1234 (11th Cir. 1995).

    Answer (B) is wrong: The federal court has no right to ignore a State's conflicts rules. It is dutybound to apply the conflicts rules of the State in which it sits, if there is a conflict in laws that must be resolved. *See Klaxon Co. v. Stentor Elec. Mfg. Co.*, 313 U.S. 487, 497 (1941). Here, however, as explained in Answer (A), there is no actual, substantive conflict in need of resolution.

    Answer (C) is wrong: In following the *Klaxon* standard, the federal court might have borrowed the applicable State's situs-of-injury conflicts rule had a true conflict of laws been presented here (if situs-of-injury was the approach that State's conflicts rule dictated). As discussed in Answer (A), no conflicted exists here.

    Answer (D) is wrong: Similarly, the federal court might have found that the applicable State's conflicts rule would apply the law of the State having the most significant relationship. But here, too, no actual, substantive conflict was presented.

38. **Answer (A) is wrong:** Rule 13 does allow joinder of the hot mud bath claim as a permissive counterclaim. However, as explained in Answer (D), every claim must have not only a procedural basis for its inclusion, but also must properly invoke federal subject-matter jurisdiction, and the hot mud bath claim does not have such a basis.

Answer (B) is wrong: Rule 13 allows joinder of a counterclaim, even if it does not arise out of the same transaction or occurrence or series of transactions or occurrences as the plaintiff's claim. As explained in Answer (D), however, every claim must also have a basis for federal subject-matter jurisdiction, and the hot mud bath claim does not have such a basis.

Answer (C) is wrong: Supplemental jurisdiction may be available when a claim arises out of the same case or controversy as another claim over which the court has original jurisdiction—typically diversity or federal question jurisdiction. *See* 28 U.S.C. § 1367(a). Here, the court has supplemental jurisdiction over the food poisoning claim, but the court would likely hold that the hot mud bath claim, being a different type of claim at a different property at a different time, did not arise out of the same case or controversy.

Answer (D) is the best choice: The court does not have diversity jurisdiction over the hot mud bath claim because it does not meet the amount in controversy requirement of 28 U.S.C. § 1332. Although the amount in controversy could be aggregated with the food poisoning claim, even together they do not exceed $75,000. As explained in Answer (C), the court does not have supplemental jurisdiction either. Therefore, while the joinder rules permit Vacationer to bring her hot mud bath claim, that claim would nevertheless be improper because the court does not have subject-matter jurisdiction over the claim.

39. **Answer (A) is the best choice:** In responding to a proper summary judgment motion, an opponent must go "beyond the pleadings" and by submitting supporting materials (like affidavits, depositions, interrogatory answers, or admissions) "designate specific facts showing that there is a genuine issue for trial." *See Celotex Corp. v. Catrett,* 477 U.S. 317, 324 (1986) (although *Celotex* cites the language of Rule 56 as it existed prior to the 2010 Summary Judgment Amendments, the Rule's Advisory Committee confirms that the post-amended "standard for granting summary judgment remains unchanged," Rule 56 advisory committee's note to 2010 amendment). Thus, a party who opposes a proper summary judgment motion by merely citing to that party's own pleaded allegations has not carried its burden necessary to defeat the motion.

Answer (B) is wrong: In ruling on a motion for summary judgment, it is not the role of the court "to weigh the evidence and determine the truth of the matter," but instead simply "to determine whether there is a genuine issue for trial." *See Anderson v. Liberty Lobby, Inc.,* 477 U.S. 242, 249 (1986).

Answer (C) is wrong: Which sides enjoys the numerical advantage in witnesses or other evidence is not the test for summary judgment. Instead, "[c]redibility determinations, the weighing of the evidence, and the drawing of legitimate inferences from the facts are jury functions, not those of a judge." *See Anderson v. Liberty Lobby, Inc.,* 477 U.S. 242, 255 (1986).

Answer (D) is wrong: A party moving for summary judgment need not negate (or affirmatively disprove) the opponent's allegations. *See Celotex Corp. v. Catrett,* 477 U.S. 317, 323 (1986) ("we find no express or implied requirement in Rule 56 that the moving party support its motion with affidavits or other similar materials *negating* the opponent's claim.") (emphasis in original).

40. **Answer (A) is wrong:** Although the formulation varies, issue preclusion or collateral estoppel generally has the following requirements: the issue in a subsequent case is the same as in a prior case that resulted in a final judgment on the merits; the litigant against whom issue preclusion is sought was a party to the prior case or in privity with a party to the prior case; and the issue was actually litigated and decided. *See Community State Bank v. Strong*, 651 F.3d 1241, 1263–64 (11th Cir. 2011). Here, while the elements of issue preclusion are satisfied, as explained in Answer (B), the court has discretion as to whether to apply offensive issue preclusion.

Answer (B) is the best choice: The U.S. Supreme Court has held that the use of "offensive issue preclusion"—the use of issue preclusion to establish a claim against the defendant—is within the discretion of the trial court. *See Parklane Hosiery Co., Inc. v. Shore*, 439 U.S. 322 (1979).

Answer (C) is wrong: In *Parklane*, the district court held that offensive issue preclusion was not appropriate because it would deny the other party of its right to a jury trial. The U.S. Supreme Court rejected this argument, and held that offensive issue preclusion was appropriate under the circumstances before the court. *See Parklane Hosiery Co., Inc. v. Shore*, 439 U.S. 322, 336–37 (1979).

Answer (D) is wrong: As explained in Answer (B), offensive issue preclusion is neither automatically required nor prohibited, but rather lies within the discretion of the trial court.

41. **Answer (A) is wrong:** Many courts have found that the same pleading standard that guides Rule 12(b)(6) motion to dismiss rulings also guides Rule 12(c) motion for judgment on the pleadings rulings. *See Johnson v. Johnson,* 385 F.3d 503, 529 (5th Cir. 2004) ("The standard for dismissal under Rule 12(c) is the same as that for dismissal for failure to state a claim under Rule 12(b)(6)."). However, motions for judgment on the pleadings are only proper "[a]fter the pleadings are closed." *See* Rule 12(c). Therefore, a pre-answer motion for judgment on the pleadings would not be proper.

Answer (B) is wrong: However desirable the attorney's strategy may be, motions for judgment on the pleadings are only properly filed "[a]fter the pleadings are closed." *See* Rule 12(c). Because the answer has not yet been filed, the pleadings here remain open.

Answer (C) is the best choice: As explained in Answer (A), the pleadings must be closed before a motion for judgment on the pleadings is appropriate.

Answer (D) is wrong: Motions for judgment on the pleadings generally need not await the completion of discovery. *See Carlson v. Reed,* 249 F.3d 876, 878 n.1 (9th Cir. 2001) (rejecting as frivolous an argument that such motions must await the close of discovery).

42. **Answer (A) is wrong:** Even if a defendant's claim against a nonparty arises out of the same transaction or occurrence as the plaintiff's claim, the defendant may not implead the nonparty unless the defendant is asserting derivative liability, as explained in Answer (C).

    Answer (B) is wrong: Although the court does have diversity jurisdiction over Contractor's claim against Subcontractor, Rule 14 does not authorize Contractor to implead Subcontractor without asserting a claim that Subcontractor is or may be liable for some or all of Subcontractor's liability to Developer, as explained in Answer (C).

    Answer (C) is the best choice: Rule 14(a) of the Federal Rules of Civil Procedure permits "impleader"—the addition to the lawsuit—of a nonparty "who is or may be liable to it for all or part of the claim against it" by serving a summons and third-party complaint on the nonparty. This type of liability is sometimes referred to as "derivative liability." *See* 6 CHARLES ALAN WRIGHT, ARTHUR R. MILLER, MARY KAY KANE, RICHARD L. MARCUS, FEDERAL PRACTICE AND PROCEDURE § 1446 ("The secondary or derivative liability notion is central [to a Rule 14(a) impleader]"). Here, Contractor is not contending that Subcontractor is responsible for the delay claims that Developer asserted against Contractor, but instead is asserting an independent, albeit related, claim against Subcontractor, which is not authorized by Rule 14.

    Answer (D) is wrong: Crossclaims are claims between parties of a similar status in the action—typically one defendant against another. *See* Rule 13(g). A nonparty is "impleaded" under Rule 14, as explained in Answer (C), and thus does not share a similar status with the original defendant.

43. **Answer (A) is wrong:** Rule 12(b)(5) permits a defending party to file a pre-answer motion to dismiss on grounds that an attempted service of process was insufficient.

    Answer (B) is wrong: A pre-answer motion made under Rule 12(b)(5) may alternatively seek to have the service of process quashed, rather than the lawsuit dismissed. *See Thermo-Cell Southeast, Inc. v. Technetic Indus., Inc.,* 605 F. Supp. 1122, 1124 (N.D. Ga. 1985) (noting broad discretion vested in the district judge to dismiss the action or quash the improper service).

    Answer (C) is the best choice: A defending party may raise insufficiency of service as a defense in the party's answer, but only if no pre-answer motion was earlier filed (or, if it a pre-answer motion was filed, that the service of process objection was included there). Filing a pre-answer motion that omits the defense of insufficient service of process constitutes a waiver of the service defense. *See* Rule 12(h).

    Answer (D) is wrong: A defending party is not required to file a pre-answer motion to dismiss, and will be deemed to have timely asserted a challenge to service of process if that defense is pleaded in the defending party's answer. *See* Rule 12(b).

44. **Answer (A) is the best choice:** It is unclear from these facts whether personal jurisdiction exists over TourCo, and lack of jurisdiction would provide an independent ground for dismissal. Even were jurisdiction proper, the district court could exercise its discretionary power to decline to exercise its jurisdiction on the basis of the convenience of the witnesses and the interests of justice. This authority, a dismissal for *forum non conveniens*, is the most likely ruling here, given that the eyewitnesses to the accident were Londoners, the accident occurred in London, the negligence of the bus's operation would be judged under British law, and TourCo was a British entity.

Answer (B) is wrong: Although the place of the bus accident will likely weigh on the court's decision on TourCo's motion, the federal court may not *transfer* the case to a London court. The transfer power of the federal court is limited to transfers to other federal courts where the case could have been brought. *See* 28 U.S.C. § 1404(a). Ordinarily, federal courts have no authority to transfer into a foreign nation's judicial system.

Answer (C) is wrong: The U.S. Supreme Court has ruled that use of the *forum non conveniens* power is not disallowed where the new forum's internal law is less favorable that the original forum's internal law. *See Piper Aircraft Co. v. Reyno*, 454 U.S. 235, 247–55 (1981).

Answer (D) is wrong: Plaintiffs' choice of forum is ordinarily weighed heavily in a *forum non conveniens* analysis because plaintiffs, when they sue from home, are presumed to have chosen a convenient forum. This analysis will apply with far lesser force where, as here, the plaintiffs have chosen a foreign forum in which to litigate. *See Piper Aircraft Co. v. Reyno*, 454 U.S. 235, 255–56 (1981). Consequently, these Canadian plaintiffs' choice of an American forum will be given much less deference in the venue analysis, and will likely not offset the convenience factors described in Answer (A).

45. **Answer (A) is wrong:** As explained in Answer (C), State law has no effect on a federal court hearing a claim arising under a federal statute; rather, a federal court applies State law to claims heard under the court's federal question jurisdiction.

Answer (B) is wrong: As explained in Answer (C), the substantive law/procedural law dichotomy has no *Erie* significance for a federal court hearing a claim arising under a federal statute; rather, these *Erie* doctrine concepts apply when a federal court adjudicates a State law claim under its diversity jurisdiction.

Answer (C) is the best choice: The *Erie* doctrine applies to State law claims before the court under diversity jurisdiction. *See Gasperini v. Center for Humanities, Inc.*, 518 U.S. 415, 426–28 (1996). To issues arising under federal law, the *Erie* principles have no role to play. *See Summers v. Texas Dep't of Criminal Justice*, 206 Fed. Appx. 317, 320 (5th Cir. 2006) ("In addressing a federal question, the court applies federal law."); *Wilmer v. Board of County Comm'rs of Leavenworth County*, 844 F. Supp. 1414, 1417 (D. Kan. 1993), *aff'd*, 28 F.3d 114 (10th Cir. 1994) (when court's jurisdiction is based on federal questions rather than diversity, "there was no *Erie* question to address."). Engineer's claim seeks relief for a violation of a federal statute, so both federal procedure and substantive law control.

Answer (D) is wrong: As explained in Answer (C), the substantive law/procedural law dichotomy has no *Erie* significance for a federal court hearing a claim under a federal statute; rather, these *Erie* doctrine concepts apply when a federal court adjudicates a State law claim under its diversity jurisdiction.

46. **Answer (A) is wrong:** National-contacts personal jurisdiction was created to permit federal courts to exercise personal jurisdiction over any nonresident who has sufficient contacts with the United States as a Nation to support such jurisdiction, even though the nonresident lacks sufficient contacts with any particular U.S. State to allow for conventional State-based jurisdiction. To qualify for such national-contacts personal jurisdiction, the claim *must* arise under federal law. *See* Rule 4(k)(2). If the claim arose solely under State law, national-contacts jurisdiction would be unavailable.

Answer (B) is wrong: Because the question asks about national-contacts personal jurisdiction, the lack of contacts with Kentucky (or with any other specific State) does not necessarily defeat jurisdiction. To qualify for national-contacts personal jurisdiction, Italian Glass Blowers also must have sufficient contacts with the Nation of the United States as a whole that exercising such jurisdiction would be "consistent with the United States Constitution and laws." *See* Rule 4(k)(2)(B). Were Italian Glass Blowers to have sales or marketing personnel stationed anywhere in the United States, those contacts might be useful in establishing constitutionally adequate minimum contacts. *See International Shoe Co. v. Washington*, 326 U.S. 310, 321 (1945) (activities of sales personnel in forum State can give rise to minimum contacts). But the U.S. Supreme Court has confirmed that the absence of physical presence does not alone defeat the exercise of personal jurisdiction. *See Burger King Corp. v. Rudzewicz*, 471 U.S. 462, 476 (1985) ("So long as a commercial actor's efforts are 'purposefully directed' toward residents of another State, we have consistently rejected the notion that an absence of physical contacts can defeat personal jurisdiction there.").

Answer (C) is wrong: National-contacts personal jurisdiction is only available where the nonresident lacks sufficient contacts with any particular U.S. State to vest personal jurisdiction there. Thus, to be amenable to national-contacts personal jurisdiction, Italian Glass Blowers must *not* be subject to the jurisdiction of Kentucky's (or any other individual State's) courts of general jurisdiction. *See* Rule 4(k)(2)(A).

Answer (D) is the best choice: As noted in Answer (C), national-contacts personal jurisdiction requires that *no* individual State has constitutionally proper authority to exercise jurisdiction over Italian Glass Blowers. If Italian Glass Blowers has sufficient contacts with Montana (or any other State) to support personal jurisdiction there, national-contacts personal jurisdiction would be unavailable.

47. **Answer (A) is wrong:** The balancing between prejudice and probative value is part of the admissibility analysis under the Federal Rules of Evidence, and particularly Rule 403. Even assuming the email is admissible, however, Rule 37(c) requires that the email be excluded unless the court finds that Employer's failure to disclose it was substantially justified or harmless, as explained in Answer (B).

    Answer (B) is the best choice: Rule 37(c) of the Federal Rules of Civil Procedure provides that, if a party does not disclose information, "the party is not allowed to use that information . . . unless the failure was substantially justified or was harmless." *See R & R Sails, Inc. v. Ins. Co. of Pennsylvania,* 673 F.3d 1240, 1247 (9th Cir. 2012).

    Answer (C) is wrong: Although in some situations, the courts cannot impose sanctions unless the opposing party files a motion to compel under Rule 37(a), failure to disclose a witness or information does not have such a prerequisite. This makes sense, because a party many not know that an opposing party has failed to disclose a document until the opposing party offers the previously undisclosed document into evidence.

    Answer (D) is wrong: Although the document was Employee's own email, the question does not indicate that Employee had a copy or had any indication that Employer intended to use the email at trial. Absent such facts, the court would more likely exclude the email. *See* Rule 26(a)(1)(A)(ii), which requires disclosure of all documents in a party's "possession, custody, or control" that the party may use to support its defenses, without limitation based on who created the document. *See also* Rule 26(e), which does not require supplementation of the disclosures if the opposing party has already received the documents or information.

48. **Answer (A) is wrong:** Although a Rule 12(B)(6) motion to dismiss for failure to state a claim is normally limited to the face of the complaint, Rule 12(d) allows the court to consider extrinsic evidence if it converts the motion to a motion for summary judgment, as explained in Answer (D).

    Answer (B) is wrong: Disposition of the motion does not depend on admission by Citizen of the accuracy of the affidavit, although that might be important. Rather, if the court converts the motion to a summary judgment motion under Rule 56, then the court could consider Mayor's affidavit, and Citizen would have the burden to produce record evidence creating a genuine dispute as to one of the material facts relating to immunity. *See* Rule 56(c)(1)(A). Failure to produce such record evidence may result in the court granting Mayor's motion without an admission by Citizen.

    Answer (C) is wrong: A court may take judicial notice of certain facts, such as facts or documents in the public record. *See Newman v. Krintzman,* 723 F.3d 308, 309 (1st Cir. 2013). The question does not contain any facts suggesting that the affidavit falls into that category, however.

    Answer (D) is the best choice: Rule 12(d) allows the court to consider materials outside the complaint submitted in support of a motion to dismiss for failure to state a claim, if the court converts the motion to a motion for summary judgment under Rule 56 and gives opposing parties an opportunity to submit their own evidence. *See Greater Baltimore Ctr. for Pregnancy Concerns, Inc. v. Mayor & City Council of Baltimore,* 721 F.3d 264, 281 (4th Cir. 2013).

49. **Answer (A) is the best choice:** In *Guaranty Trust Co. of New York v. York*, 326 U.S. 99 (1945), the U.S. Supreme Court identified the determination of whether an issue would affect the outcome of the case as an important part of the *Erie* analysis. *See id.* at 109 ("The nub of the policy that underlies *Erie R. Co. v. Tompkins* is that for the same transaction the accident of a suit by a non-resident litigant in a federal court instead of in a State court a block away, should not lead to a substantially different result."). Although important, determining that a difference in law could trigger a difference in outcome would not, alone, dictate the *Erie* answer. *See Hanna v. Plumer*, 380 U.S. 460 (1965) (explaining that "outcome determinative," while part of the analysis, was not the "talisman" or the end of the analysis). Here, though, a difficult *Erie* analysis is avoided because the manner in which the jury instructions are fastened together is not outcome determinative. Therefore, the federal court need not apply the State rule regarding how the jury instructions are fastened together.

Answer (B) is wrong: As explained in Answer (A), the State rule dictating the manner of fastening the jury instructions is not outcome determinative and thus does not implicate the concerns that *Erie* seeks to protect; therefore, the federal court need not apply it.

Answers (C) and (D) are wrong: An issue that is squarely addressed by the Federal Rules of Civil Procedure will normally be considered procedural. *See Shady Grove Orthopedic Assocs., P.A. v. Allstate Ins. Co.,* 559 U.S. 393, 398 (2010). When an issue is not addressed by the Rules, however, a court must still consider whether it is procedural or substantive and whether, mindful of *Erie*'s admonitions, the issue ought to be governed by federal or State law. *See Gasperini v. Center for Humanities, Inc.*, 518 U.S. 415, 427–28 (1996). Thus, the absence of this issue from the Federal Rules of Civil Procedure is not the end of the analysis.

50. **Answer (A) is wrong:** Generally, litigants may not immediately appeal the various orders entered by the district judge during a litigation but, instead, must wait until the court enters its "final order" in the case, at which time all orders may be appealed collectively at one time. *See* 28 U.S.C. § 1291. Over the years, legislative and judicial exceptions to this procedure have been crafted to permit immediate appeals from certain interlocutory orders. The U.S. Supreme Court, however, has ruled that immediate appeals from discovery orders raising attorney-client privilege issues do not ordinarily qualify for such an exception. *See Mohawk Indus., Inc. v. Carpenter*, 558 U.S. 100, 108–09 (2009).

Answer (B) is the best choice: Congress has established that an order that refuses to grant an injunction will qualify for an exception that allows an immediate appeal. *See* 28 U.S.C. § 1292(a)(1).

Answer (C) is wrong: Denials of summary judgment motions, like discovery orders, are considered interlocutory rulings and not ordinarily subject to immediate appeal. *See Ortiz v. Jordan*, 131 S. Ct. 884, 891 (2011).

Answer (D) is wrong: Joinder orders are likewise considered interlocutory rulings that are usually not immediately appealable. *See Alto v. Black,* 738 F.3d 1111, 1130 (9th Cir. 2013) (holding that even required party joinder errors are not immediately appealable).

51. **Answer (A) is the best choice:** The Federal Rules of Civil Procedure confirm expressly that a general denial is a proper response to a pleading filed in federal court. *See* Rule 8(b)(3) ("A party that intends in good faith to deny all the allegations of a pleading—including the jurisdictional grounds—may do so by a general denial.").

   Answer (B) is wrong: Federal civil litigants are given only three options in counter-pleading to a claim's allegations. They may admit the allegation, they may deny the allegation, or they may state that they lack knowledge or information sufficient to form a belief about the truth of an allegation. *See* Rule 8(b)(1)(B) & (b)(5). There is no other option recognized or permitted by the Rules. Thus, attempting to deflect the obligation to counter-plead merely because discovery is not yet completed will not, alone, be a sufficient response.

   Answer (C) is wrong: Similarly, a response that an allegation concerns a written document which "speaks for itself" is also improper. *See Lane v. Page,* 272 F.R.D. 581, 602–03 (D.N.M. 2011). In an especially memorable passage, Judge Shadur in Illinois made the point quite eloquently: "[I]nstead of providing forthright responses to the specific allegations, [the defendant] asserts that the documents 'speak for themselves.' This Court has been attempting to listen to such written materials for years (in the forlorn hope that one will indeed give voice)—but until some such writing does break its silence, this Court will continue to require pleaders to employ one of the only three alternatives that *are* permitted by Rule 8(b) in response to all allegations, including those regarding the contents of documents." *Chicago Dist. Council of Carpenters Pension Fund v. Balmoral Racing Club, Inc.,* 2000 WL 876921, at *1 (N.D. Ill. June 26, 2000).

   Answer (D) is wrong: These non-responsive "strict-proof" answers, evidently some archaic remnant of a long-passed pleading regime, are likewise not permitted in federal court. *See King Vision Pay Per View, Ltd. v. J.C. Dimitri's Restaurant, Inc.,* 180 F.R.D. 332, 333–34 (N.D. Ill. 1998) (ruling "strict-proof" responses to be improper under the Federal Rules, and ordering each of the thus-unrebutted allegations to be deemed admitted for the remainder of the litigation).

52. **Answer (A) is wrong:** Rule 56(b) sets a default outer limit for filing motions for summary judgment—30 days after the end of discovery unless a different time is set by local rules or court order. The Rule, however, does not prohibit summary judgment motions filed early in the case.

   Answer (B) is the best choice: Rule 56(d) allows a party opposing a motion for summary judgment to demonstrate to the court that the party has not had an adequate opportunity to develop the facts necessary to oppose the motion. The court then has the discretion to defer or deny the motion (or to issue any other appropriate order). Courts generally require the nonmoving party to have been diligent in seeking the missing facts before they will grant relief under Rule 56(d). *See Rivera-Torres v. Rey-Hernandez,* 502 F.3d 7, 11 (1st Cir. 2007).

   Answer (C) is wrong: Rule 11(b)(3) allows a party to make factual allegations when the party believes it can develop evidentiary support "after a reasonable opportunity for further investigation or discovery." *See Rotella v. Wood,* 528 U.S. 549, 560 (2000). Thus, Rule 11 does not require the plaintiff to have "full evidentiary support."

   Answer (D) is wrong: As explained in Answer (B), courts will generally grant relief under Rule 56(d) if the nonmoving party has been diligent in seeking the missing information. Here, the facts suggest that Photographer served written discovery and conducted depositions during the first 60 days of the discovery period, learned of the need to depose Layout Director from the responses, and then sought to depose Layout Director (who was beyond the court's subpoena power) with 30 days remaining in the discovery period. A court would likely consider this diligence and grant Rule 56(d) relief.

53. **Answer (A) is wrong:** 28 U.S.C. § 1391(b)(1) authorizes venue based on the *defendants'* residence if all of the defendants reside in the same State. As explained in Answer (D), none of the venue provisions in 28 U.S.C. § 1391 authorize venue based on the *plaintiff's* residence.

Answer (B) is wrong: For venue purposes, residence for individuals is their place of domicile. *See* 28 U.S.C. § 1391(c)(1). For corporations, residence varies on litigating posture—when plaintiffs, corporations are deemed residents of their principal place of business; when defendants, corporations are deemed residents of any judicial district in which they are subject to personal jurisdiction regarding the dispute. *See* 28 U.S.C. § 1391(c)(2). Because North Dakota has only one district, a corporate defendant will be deemed to reside in North Dakota if its contacts with North Dakota would support personal jurisdiction. *See* 28 U.S.C. § 1391(c)(2). Because Bicycle Company has no contacts with North Dakota, it does not reside there. Accordingly, residence based venue is not proper because *all* defendants do not reside in North Dakota. It is improper to conduct this analysis on a party-by-party basis; residence-based venue requires all defendants to reside in the same State. As discussed further in Answer (D), the second option—where a substantial part of the operative events occurred—will also not permit venue in North Dakota.

Answer (C) is wrong: The defendants' *citizenship*—critical to the diversity jurisdiction analysis—is not relevant to the venue analysis for a corporate defendant. Rather, as discussed in Answer (B), it is the corporate defendants' *residence* (that is, amenability to personal jurisdiction) that can establish venue.

Answer (D) is the best choice: Venue in federal court is governed by 28 U.S.C. § 1391. Absent a special federal law providing otherwise, federal venue is proper: (1) in any judicial district where defendants reside, so long as all defendants are residents of that State, or (2) in a judicial district where a substantial part of the events or omissions giving rise to the claim occurred (or where a substantial part of the property that is the subject of the lawsuit is situated). *See* 28 U.S.C. § 1391(b)(1)–(b)(2). If neither of those formulas would locate a proper venue, then venue will be proper in any judicial district where any defendant would be subject to the court's personal jurisdiction regarding the lawsuit. *See* 28 U.S.C. § 1391(b)(3). As explained in Answer (B), the defendants do not all reside in North Dakota, so residence-based venue is not proper there. Likewise, the accident occurred in Wyoming and the sale occurred in South Dakota. None of the facts suggest any events or omissions in North Dakota, so venue is not proper there under § 1391(b)(2). Therefore, venue is not proper in North Dakota.

54. **Answer (A) is wrong:** The U.S. Constitution's Seventh Amendment guarantee of a trial by jury does not extend to State courts, as explained in Answer (D).

Answer (B) is wrong: For the same reason as explained in Answer (D), there can be no Seventh Amendment guarantee in State court.

Answer (C) is wrong: Again, for the same reason explained in Answer (D), no federal jury trial guarantee applies to the State courts.

Answer (D) is the best choice: The U.S. Supreme Court has affirmed repeatedly that the U.S. Constitution's guarantee to a trial by jury as enshrined in the Seventh Amendment applies only the federal courts, not the State courts. *See Gasperini v. Center for Humanities, Inc.,* 518 U.S. 415, 432 (1996); *Minneapolis & St. L.R. Co. v. Bombolis,* 241 U.S. 211, 217 (1916). Thus, although the Seventh Amendment preserves a citizen's right to a civil jury trial "[i]n Suits at common law," *see* U.S. Const. amend. VII, that guarantee does not extend to State trials. Note, however, that a State court jury right can be granted by State constitutions and State statutes, but such rights (obviously) would not emanate from federal law.

55. **Answer (A) is wrong:** Quite expressly, the U.S. Supreme Court has rejected the notion that a pleader must include detailed factual allegations in order to avoid dismissal. *See Bell Atlantic Corp. v. Twombly,* 550 U.S. 544, 555 (2007).

Answer (B) is wrong: The U.S. Supreme Court has made clear that a claim that, on the basis of the facts alleged, is merely possible will not suffice; to the contrary, the allegations must show that the claim is "plausible." *See Ashcroft v. Iqbal,* 556 U.S. 662, 678 (2009).

Answer (C) is the best choice: Rule 8(a)(3) requires that every pleading must contain "a demand for relief sought." *See* Rule 8(a)(3). Furthermore, as explained in Answer (B), the standard for pleading the claim is plausibility, and the absence of that phrase from the other answers is a clue that this is the correct answer.

Answer (D) is wrong: The U.S. Supreme Court has made plain that a claim need not be "probable" to avoid a dismissal; so long as the pleaded allegations state a "plausible" claim, the federal pleading standards are satisfied. *See Ashcroft v. Iqbal,* 556 U.S. 662, 678 (2009).

56. **Answer (A) is wrong:** "General" personal jurisdiction (also called "all-purpose" personal jurisdiction) exists over defendants who have affiliations with the forum that are so "continuous and systematic" that the defendant is "essentially at home" there. *See Goodyear Dunlop Tires Ops., S.A. v. Brown,* 564 U.S. 915, 919 (2011). Unlike "specific" (or "case-linked") personal jurisdiction, general personal jurisdiction permits a court to decide a case having no relation at all to the conduct that gives rise to the lawsuit. In testing for general personal jurisdiction, a unanimous U.S. Supreme Court ruled that a flow of products into the forum may bolster an argument for "specific" personal jurisdiction, but will "not warrant a determination that, based on those ties, the forum has *general* jurisdiction over a defendant." *Id.* at 927 (emphasis in original).

Answer (B) is the best choice: In its "textbook" case of general personal jurisdiction, the Supreme Court ruled that Ohio could exercise general jurisdiction over a Philippine mining company that had moved its offices and files to Ohio during the Japanese occupation of the Islands during WWII. *See Perkins v. Benguet Consol. Mining Co.,* 342 U.S. 437 (1952). General jurisdiction was proper in that instance, the Court explained later, because "Ohio was the corporation's principal, if temporary, place of business." *Keeton v. Hustler Magazine, Inc.,* 465 U.S. 770, 780 n.11 (1984).

Answer (C) is wrong: The Supreme Court has also held that "mere purchases, even if occurring at regular intervals, are not enough to warrant a State's assertion of *in personam* jurisdiction over a nonresident corporation in a cause of action not related to those purchase transactions." *See Helicopteros Nacionales de Colombia, S. A. v. Hall,* 466 U.S. 408, 418 (1984).

Answer (D) is wrong: The Supreme Court has also held that sizable, continuous, and systematic sales into a forum are likewise insufficient to warrant the exercise of general personal jurisdiction. *See Daimler AG v. Bauman,* 571 U.S. 117, 139 (2014) ("Such exorbitant exercises of all-purpose jurisdiction would scarcely permit out-of-State defendants 'to structure their primary conduct with some minimum assurance as to where that conduct will and will not render them liable to suit.' "). *Cf. BNSF Ry. Co. v. Tyrrell,* 137 S. Ct. 1549, 1559 (2017) (defendant not amenable to general jurisdiction even though it maintained "over 2,000 miles of railroad track and more than 2,000 employees in" forum State); *Brown,* 564 U.S. at 929 (defendants' "attenuated connections" to the forum State (tens of thousands of tires delivered there) "fall far short" of the contacts needed to support general jurisdiction); *Helicopteros Nacionales de Colombia, S.A. v. Hall,* 466 U.S. 408, 418 (1984) (regular contacts with forum State for purchases and training activities not sufficient to support general jurisdiction).

57. **Answer (A) is wrong:** One of the teachings of the U.S. Supreme Court in *Erie R.R. Co. v. Tompkins*, 304 U.S. 64, 78 (1938), is that federal courts have "no power to declare substantive rules of common law applicable in a State," but must instead simply apply the laws of the State as they exist. Where the law of the State is unclear, the task of the federal court is to "predict" how the highest court in the State would rule on the matter in question, not to conjure up the rule that the federal judge thinks is soundest in principle or policy. *See West v. American Tel. & Tel. Co.,* 311 U.S. 223, 236–37 (1940).

Answer (B) is the best choice: In "predicting" how a State's highest court would rule, the federal courts are permitted to consult a wide range of sources, including decisions from intermediate appellate courts, decisions from other jurisdictions, statutes, restatements of law, treatises. *See Pippen v. NBCUniversal Media,* LLC, 734 F.3d 610, 615 (7th Cir. 2013); *Walker v. City of Lakewood,* 272 F.3d 1114, 1125 (9th Cir. 2001). In the end, though, the job of the federal court is to "predict" how the State's highest court would resolve the question at issue.

Answer (C) is wrong: The "predictive" task is not to consider what the wisest rule, in the judgment of the federal tribunal, would be, but instead to assess what the State's highest court would do, were it confronted with the question at issue. *See West v. American Tel. & Tel. Co.,* 311 U.S. 223, 237 (1940) ("State law is to be applied in the federal as well as the state courts and it is the duty of the former in every case to ascertain from all the available data what the state law is and apply it rather than to prescribe a different rule, however superior it may appear from the viewpoint of 'general law' and however much the state rule may have departed from prior decisions of the federal courts.").

Answer (D) is wrong: It is the duty of a federal court, sitting in diversity, to discern and apply State law. Difficulty in ascertaining the substance of that State law is not a proper basis for a federal court to decline to exercise its jurisdiction to decide the case. *See Meredith v. City of Winter Haven,* 320 U.S. 228, 234 (1943).

58. **Answer (A) is wrong:** Normally, conflicting affidavits regarding a material fact would create a genuine dispute regarding that material fact, precluding summary judgment. Interpretation of unambiguous contract language, however, is a matter of law for the court, not a matter of fact. *See, e.g., Royal Ins. Co. of Am. v. Orient Overseas Container Line Ltd.,* 525 F.3d 409, 421 (6th Cir. 2008). Therefore, conflicting affidavits regarding the meaning of contract language would not automatically preclude summary judgment.

Answer (B) is the best choice: Contract language becomes ambiguous, and therefore a matter of fact subject to extrinsic evidence, when it is reasonably susceptible of more than one meaning. *See, e.g., Westport Ins. Corp. v. Tuskegee Newspapers, Inc.,* 402 F.3d 1161, 1167 (11th Cir. 2005). Therefore, if the *force majeure* clause can reasonably be construed to include or not include labor disruptions, extrinsic evidence would be admissible as to the meaning of the clause, and the court will not decide the issue on summary judgment in the face of conflicting extrinsic evidence.

Answer (C) is wrong: Supplier moved for summary judgment, arguing that the *force majeure* clause should be construed to include labor disruptions. Therefore, the court would grant Supplier's motion only if it concluded that the *force majeure* clause could not reasonably be construed to favor the nonmoving party, Smart Phone Co. Smart Phone Co.'s contention is that the *force majeure* clause did *not* include labor disruptions. Thus, if the court agreed with Smart Phone Co.'s interpretation of the *force majeure* clause, as postulated in Answer (C), it would not grant summary judgment against Smart Phone Co.

Answer (D) is wrong: While affidavits cannot be used to contradict unambiguous contract language, they can be used to explain ambiguous contract language, as explained in Answers (A) and (B).

59. **Answer (A) is wrong:** In *Hess v. Pawloski*, 274 U.S. 352 (1927), the U.S. Supreme Court held that a statute that implied consent to personal jurisdiction when a motorist used the State's roads was constitutional. *See also Elkhart Eng'g Corp. v. Dornier Werke*, 343 F.2d 861, 865–66 (5th Cir. 1965). Therefore, the Arizona court likely has personal jurisdiction over Driver.

Answer (B) is the best choice: As explained in Answer (A), the court likely has personal jurisdiction over Driver. In *Mullane v. Central Hanover Bank & Trust Co.*, 339 U.S. 306 (1950), however, the U.S. Supreme Court held that the Constitution does not require actual notice, but it does require notice "reasonably calculated, under all the circumstances, to apprise interested parties of the pendency of the action and afford them an opportunity to present their objections." *Id.* at 314. Simply publishing notice in a local newspaper is not reasonably calculated to put an out-of-State driver on notice of the lawsuit. *See id.* at 315 (holding that the means chosen for notice "must be such as one desirous of actually informing the absentee might reasonably adopt to accomplish it," and finding that notice-by-publication to persons with known addresses is little "more than a feint"). Therefore, while the Arizona court would likely rule that it had personal jurisdiction over Driver, it would also likely rule that Bicyclist failed to give Driver adequate notice. *See also Banks v. Leon,* 975 F. Supp. 815 (W.D. Va. 1997).

Answer (C) is wrong: As explained in Answers (A) and (B), the Arizona court would likely rule that it had personal jurisdiction over Driver, but that Bicyclist failed to give Driver adequate notice.

Answer (D) is wrong: As explained in Answers (A) and (B), the Arizona court would likely rule that it had personal jurisdiction over Driver, but that Bicyclist failed to give Driver adequate notice.

60. **Answer (A) is the best choice:** If a case combines both issues triable to a jury and issues triable only to the judge, the court will ordinarily direct the jury to reach its verdict first, then the court will proceed to resolve the judge-tried issues next. This order tends to avoid the judge's determinations encroaching into those issues reserved to the jury, in violation of the Seventh Amendment. *See Beacon Theaters, Inc. v. Westover,* 359 U.S. 500, 510 (1959). Here, the compensatory and punitive damages issues are jury issues, *see Jones v. United Parcel Serv., Inc.,* 674 F.3d 1187, 1202 (10th Cir. 2012), so the jury would make those determinations first and then the court would rule on the request for an injunction, which is equitable relief.

Answer (B) is wrong: As explained in Answer (A), punitive damages is a jury issue.

Answer (C) is wrong: As explained in Answer (A), the jury makes its determinations first, in order to ensure that the parties' Seventh Amendment rights are preserved.

Answer (D) is wrong: As explained in Answer (A), the jury makes its determinations first, in order to ensure that the parties' Seventh Amendment rights are preserved.

61. **Answer (A) is wrong:** 28 U.S.C. § 1391 authorizes venue on two grounds (plus a fail-safe catch-all third ground which is only available when neither of the other two is available, so does not apply here). One ground allows for venue in a district in which a substantial part of the events or omissions giving rise to the claim occurred. *See* 28 U.S.C. § 1391(b)(2). Here, the accident occurred in Hawai'i, so venue would be proper there on this venue ground, but no part of the events occurred in South Carolina. The second ground for venue arises when all of the defendants reside in the same State. *See* 28 U.S.C. § 1391(b)(1). For venue purposes, an individual resides where that individual is domiciled. *See* 28 U.S.C. § 1391(c)(1). Surfer is domiciled in Hawai'i, so again venue is good there but not in South Carolina. Therefore, venue is not proper in South Carolina, and Answer (A) is incorrect.

Answer (B) is wrong: As explained in Answer (C), 28 U.S.C. § 1406 gives the court the option of dismissing a case lacking venue or transferring it.

Answer (C) is the best choice: 28 U.S.C. § 1406 controls the court's options when a case is filed in a district where venue is improper—and as explained in Answer (A), venue was not proper in South Carolina. Section 1406 authorizes the court to dismiss the action or, if it is in the interest of justice, to transfer it to any district or division in which it could have been brought. Here, the court could transfer the action to Hawai'i, where venue is proper, if it determines that it would be in the interest of justice to do so.

Answer (D) is wrong: As explained in Answers (A) and (C), 28 U.S.C. § 1406 gives the court the option of dismissing a case lacking venue or transferring it.

62. **Answer (A) is wrong:** On a motion to dismiss, courts must assume the truth of the facts alleged in the complaint. *See Leatherman v. Tarrant Cnty. Narcotics Intelligence & Coordination Unit,* 507 U.S. 163, 164 (1993).

Answer (B) is the best choice: The U.S. Supreme Court has expressly reaffirmed that a pleader's legal conclusions need *not* be accepted as true, though the pleaders' factual allegations must be. *See Bell Atlantic Corp. v. Twombly,* 550 U.S. 544, 555 (2007).

Answer (C) is wrong: On a motion to dismiss, judges may not dismiss a claim simply because they disbelieve the allegations. *See Neitzke v. Williams,* 490 U.S. 319, 327 (1989).

Answer (D) is wrong: On a motion to dismiss, courts may properly examine documents that a complaint incorporates by reference. *See Tellabs, Inc. v. Makor Issues & Rights, Ltd.,* 551 U.S. 308, 322 (2007).

63. **Answer (A) is wrong:** Federal civil litigants who agree to waive formal service of process are rewarded under the Rules with a response time of 60 days from the date the request for waiver was sent. *See* Rule 12(a)(1)(A)(ii). Because Partner 1 answered within the required 60 days, that answer was timely.

Answer (B) is wrong: Federal civil litigants who have not waived service, but are instead served traditionally with original process, have 21 days from service to file their answers. *See* Rule 12(a)(1)(A)(i). Because Partner 2 answered within that 21-day period, that answer was timely.

Answer (C) is the best choice: Plaintiffs are required under the Rules to file an answer to counterclaims. *See* Rule 12(a)(1)(B). The time for filing any answer is suspended by the filing of a timely motion to dismiss. *See* Rule 12(a)(4). If the court denies that motion, the moving party then has 14 days from the date of the court's action to file an answer. *See* Rule 12(a)(4)(A). Because Partner 3's answer to the counterclaim was filed outside that 14-day period, it was untimely.

Answer (D) is wrong: Co-defendants are required under the Rules to file an answer to crossclaims. *See* Rule 12(a)(1)(B). The time for filing such an answer is 21 days after service of the pleading that contained the crossclaim. *See* Rule 12(a)(1)(B). Because Partner 1's answer to the crossclaim was filed within this 21-day period, it was timely.

64. **Answer (A) is wrong:** New trials may be granted in federal court "for any reason for which a new trial has heretofore been granted in an action at law in federal court." *See* Rule 59(a)(1)(A). Motions to accept a reduced verdict—or *remittitur*—are properly considered by a federal court. *See Linn v. United Plant Guard Workers of Am., Local 114*, 383 U.S. 53, 65–66 (1966).

Answer (B) is the best choice: Unlike motions for verdict reductions, the United States Supreme Court has ruled that motions seeking a verdict increase—or *additur*—encroach unconstitutionally on the Seventh Amendment right to a trial by jury. *See Dimick v. Schiedt*, 293 U.S. 474, 486–87 (1935).

Answer (C) is wrong: New trial motions can be based on the trial judge's conclusion that the jury's verdict was against the great weight of the evidence. *See Byrd v. Blue Ridge Rural Elec. Co-op., Inc.*, 356 U.S. 525, 540 (1958) ("The trial judge in the federal system has . . . discretion to grant a new trial if the verdict appears to him to be against the weight of the evidence.").

Answer (D) is wrong: New trials may also be granted for improper jury arguments. *See Caudle v. District of Columbia*, 707 F.3d 354, 359 (D.C. Cir. 2013).

65. **Answer (A) is wrong:** The law generally prefers live testimony to recorded testimony. But the law also recognizes that sometimes recorded testimony may be the only alternative available. Thus, the Rules recognize that where a witness is geographically unavailable (defined as more than 100 miles from the courthouse), recorded testimony may be used. *See* Rule 32(a)(4)(B). But this is not the "only" proper circumstances in which a party may use recorded testimony.

    Answer (B) is the best choice: The law's general preference for live testimony is relaxed in the case of testimony from a party to the lawsuit (as opposed to a non-party witness). A party's deposition testimony may be used "for any purpose" (*i.e.,* as substantive evidence or for impeachment), as may the deposition testimony of an organizational party's officers, directors, managing agents, and designees. *See* Rule 32(a)(3). But no deposition testimony may be used against any party who neither attended the deposition nor had reasonable advance notice of the deposition. *See* Rule 32(a)(1)(A). So long as that threshold requirement is satisfied, however, this deposition of an officer of a party may be used at trial in place of live testimony.

    Answer (C) is wrong: If a testifying witness has since died, his or her recorded testimony may be used. *See* Rule 32(a)(4)(A). This, however, is not the "only" proper use of recorded testimony.

    Answer (D) is wrong: Similarly, the recorded testimony of a witness who, due to illness or infirmity, cannot attend the trial may be used. *See* Rule 32(a)(4)(C). But, again, this is not the "only" permitted use of recorded testimony.

66. **Answer (A) is wrong:** Rule 52 mandates that the court make findings of fact and conclusions of law in a nonjury trial, so a general verdict is not an option. *See* Rule 52(a)(1).

    Answer (B) is the best choice: Rule 52 allows the court to make its findings of fact and conclusions of law orally on the record or in a filed memorandum of decision. *See* Rule 52(a)(1). Rule 52 also requires entry of a judgment under Rule 58, which requires that a judgment be set out in a separate document. *Id.*

    Answer (C) is wrong: Rule 52 gives the court the option of making its findings of fact and conclusions of law in a written memorandum of decision or orally on the record. *Id.*

    Answer (D) is wrong: Rule 52 and 58 require that the court both make findings of fact and conclusions of law and enter a separate judgment. *See* Answer (B).

67. **Answer (A) is the best choice:** Where the face of a complaint reveals an obvious affirmative defense—such as running of the statute of limitations—the court may dismiss under Rule 12(b)(6). *See Lutz v. Chesapeake Appalachia, LLC*, 717 F.3d 459, 464 (6th Cir. 2013).

    Answer (B) is wrong: The Rule 12(b)(6) defense of failure to state a claim upon which relief can be granted may be filed before answering the complaint. *See* Rule 12(b) ("A motion asserting any of these defenses must be made before pleading if a responsive pleading is allowed."). If, as the question recounts, an answer has already been filed, a pre-answer Rule 12(b)(6) motion challenging the limitations period would be impossible.

    Answer (C) is wrong: Although generally Rule 12(b)(6) motions are improper vehicles for dismissing on limitations grounds, such a dismissal is nonetheless appropriate where the allegations supporting the dismissal are affirmatively shown on the face of the pleading. *See Lutz v. Chesapeake Appalachia, LLC*, 717 F.3d 459, 464 (6th Cir. 2013).

    Answer (D) is wrong: In considering a motion to dismiss under Rule 12(b)(6), it is not inappropriate for the deciding court to take judicial notice of materials of record in the pending case. *See Dittmer Props., L.P. v. Fed. Deposit Ins. Corp.*, 708 F.3d 1011, 1021 (8th Cir. 2013) ("While courts primarily consider the allegations in the complaint in determining whether to grant a Rule 12(b)(6) motion, courts additionally consider . . . items subject to judicial notice, matters of public record, orders, [and] items appearing in the record of the case . . .").

68. **Answer (A) is the best choice:** For diversity purposes (except for certain insurance actions), a corporation is considered to be a citizen of any State (or foreign nation) where it has been incorporated, as well as the State (or foreign nation) where it has its principal place of business. *See* 28 U.S.C. § 1332(c)(1). For years, the lower federal courts applied various tests for locating a corporation's "principal place of business." In 2010, the U.S. Supreme Court settled the confusion by adopting the "nerve center" test—holding that a corporations' principal place of business is generally that place "where the corporation's high level officers direct, control, and coordinate the corporation's activities." *See Hertz Corp. v. Friend*, 559 U.S. 77, 80–81 (2010). The Court confirmed that this analysis must always settle on one, single location as the principal place of business, not several locations. *Id.* at 93. Under this nerve center test, only New York qualifies as Orange Inc.'s principal place of business. Because that is also Orange Inc.'s place of incorporation, the company is only considered a citizen of New York.

    Answers (B), (C), and (D) are wrong: Although Orange Inc. is a citizen of New York, as two of these answers propose, it is not a citizen of Florida, Georgia, or South Carolina. Formerly, some lower federal courts had examined the locus and nature of the corporation's various business activities in plotting its principal place of business; the Supreme Court overturned those approaches in *Hertz*. As noted in Answer (A), Orange Inc. is a citizen of New York alone.

69. **Answer (A) is wrong:** Early on, litigants had contended that electronically stored information ought not to be subject to discovery at all. It is now expressly clear that electronically stored information is, indeed, discoverable as a category. *See* Rule 34(a)(1)(A).

    Answer (B) is wrong: The Rules permit a requesting party to designate a preferred form for the production of electronically stored information. *See* Rule 34(b)(1)(C). But even if no preferred form of production is expressed, the responding party is under a duty to make electronically stored information available for inspection, and must state the form or forms in which it will make that material available. *See* Rule 34(b)(2)(D).

    Answer (C) is wrong: The Rules install numerical maximums for certain discovery, such as a limit on the number of interrogatories, *see* Rule 33(a)(1), and a limit on the number of depositions, *see* Rule 30(a)(2)(A)(i). But there is no numerical maximum for requests for inspection.

    Answer (D) is the best choice: A party is relieved of its burden to produce electronically stored information from sources that it identifies—appropriately—to be not reasonably accessible because of undue burden or cost. *See* Rule 26(b)(2)(B). Were such an objection asserted, the requesting party may respond by filing with the court a motion to compel the production of the requested discovery, notwithstanding its associated burden and cost. *See id.*

70. **Answer (A) is wrong:** Although personal service is typically accomplished by in-hand delivery, the courts will allow service in the "vicinity" of an evasive defendant. *See Travelers Casualty & Surety Co. of Am. v. Brenneke,* 551 F.3d 1132, 1136 (9th Cir. 2009). However, as explained in Answer (B), a party may not make service.

    Answer (B) is the best choice: Rule 4(c)(2) provides that "[a]ny person who is at least 18 years old and ***not a party*** may serve a summons and complaint." Here, Promoter is a party, and therefore may not make service.

    Answer (C) is wrong: As explained in Answer (B), a party may not make service.

    Answer (D) is wrong: As explained in Answer (A), while service in the vicinity of an evasive defendant may be proper, that service may not be made by a party.

71. **Answer (A) is wrong:** The claim by Veterinarian #1 against Veterinarian #2 is an "impleader"—a claim by a defending party that the third-party is or may be liable for all or part of the defending party's obligations to the plaintiff. *See* Rule 14(a)(1). Once the impleader has been added, the original plaintiff can then assert against the third-party any claim arising out of the transaction or occurrence that is the subject of that plaintiff's claim against the original defendant. *See* Rule 14(a)(3). Here, that relatedness requirement appears satisfied; Pet Hospital's original claim against Veterinarian #1 and this new claim against Veterinarian #2 arise out of the same poor animal care that resulted in the company's loss. But meeting the procedural obligations established by the Rules does not end the inquiry; there must still be a jurisdictional basis for the plaintiff's new claim. *See* Rule 82. Here, the claim by Pet Hospital against Veterinarian #2 lacks a subject-matter jurisdiction foundation. There is no diversity jurisdiction for the claim; both parties are citizens of Nevada. There also is no supplemental jurisdiction for the claim; although the claim may be sufficiently related to pass the case-or-controversy inquiry of 28 U.S.C. § 1367(a), supplemental jurisdiction is foreclosed by 28 U.S.C. § 1367(b). *See* 28 U.S.C. § 1367(b) (instructing that supplemental jurisdiction will not exist in diversity cases over claims by plaintiffs against persons made parties under Rule 14, if, as here, the exercise of jurisdiction would be inconsistent with the requirements of the federal diversity statute). Because Pet Hospital and Veterinarian #2 share the same citizenship, that inconsistency is obvious.

Answer (B) is the best choice: After an impleader is added, the third-party may assert against the original plaintiff any claim arising out of the transaction or occurrence that is the subject matter of the plaintiff's claim against the defendant. *See* Rule 14(a)(2)(D). Here, that relatedness requirement appears satisfied. Again, though, the claim must be tested for subject-matter jurisdiction. As in Answer (A), this claim will lack diversity jurisdiction because of both parties' Nevada citizenships and because the required amount in controversy is not met. But this claim will enjoy supplemental jurisdiction support. Unlike Answer (A), this is not a claim by a plaintiff against a Rule 14-added party, but rather a claim by a Rule 14-added party against a plaintiff. For that situation, 28 U.S.C. § 1367(b) has no exclusion. This claim would be proper.

Answer (C) is wrong: This claim fails for largely the same reasons as the claim in Answer (A) failed. The fact that this claim is also below the jurisdictional limit for original diversity simply adds a further ground for why diversity jurisdiction cannot be invoked.

Answer (D) is wrong: Although this claim is configured in the same manner as Answer (B), this claim will likely have neither Rule 14 nor supplemental jurisdiction support. The damages to Veterinarian #2's costly automobile lack the requisite relatedness to the original claim by Pet Hospital against Veterinarian #1 to satisfy either Rule 14(a)(2)(D) (arising out of the same transaction/occurrence that is the subject matter of the original claim) or Section 1367(a) (so related that the claims form part of the same case or controversy).

72. **Answer (A) is wrong:** As explained in Answer (D), the court has diversity jurisdiction over both claims.

Answer (B) is wrong: As explained in Answer (D), the court has diversity jurisdiction over both claims regardless of whether they arise out of the same case or controversy.

Answer (C) is wrong: As explained in Answer (D), the aggregation rules permit a single plaintiff to aggregate claims against a *single defendant* without limitation. In contrast, in order for a single plaintiff to aggregate claims against *multiple defendants*, the plaintiff must be asserting claims that impose joint and several liability on the defendants.

Answer (D) is the best choice: The defamation claim plainly meets the requirements for diversity jurisdiction under 28 U.S.C. § 1332, as there is complete diversity of citizenship and $200,000 satisfies the amount in controversy requirement. The rules of aggregation allow a single plaintiff to aggregate claims against a single defendant even if the claims are entirely unrelated. *See Werwinski v. Ford Motor Co.,* 286 F.3d 661, 666 (3d Cir. 2002). Therefore, the amount in controversy requirement is also satisfied for the breach of contract count, even though it does not meet the requirement on its own.

73. **Answer (A) is wrong:** One of the objectives of entering a preliminary injunction is to "preserve the relative positions of the parties until a trial on the merits can be held." *See University of Texas v. Camenisch,* 451 U.S. 390, 395 (1981).

Answer (B) is the best choice: The mere possibility of irreparable injury is insufficient to warrant the entry of a preliminary injunction in federal court. Instead, to obtain preliminary injunctive relief, a litigant must show that irreparable injury is likely in the absence of the requested injunction. *See Winter v. Natural Resources Defense Council, Inc.,* 555 U.S. 7, 22 (2008).

Answer (C) is wrong: In weighing whether to grant a preliminary injunction, the federal courts must consider the impact on the public interest. *See Winter v. Natural Resources Defense Council, Inc.,* 555 U.S. 7, 23–24 (2008).

Answer (D) is wrong: To obtain a preliminary injunction, the movants must also show a likelihood of success on the merits of their claim. *See Munaf v. Geren,* 553 U.S. 674, 690–91 (2008).

74. **Answer (A) is wrong:** A Rule 12(b)(6) motion to dismiss for failure to state a claim is limited to the face of the complaint, and cannot be based on facts outside the complaint. *See Smith v. Frye*, 488 F.3d 263, 274 (4th Cir. 2007). Although a court may consider certain documents outside the pleadings, such as matters of public record or those referenced in the complaint, *see Newman v. Krintzman,* 723 F.3d 308, 309 (1st Cir. 2013), the question specifies that the side letter was not referenced in, attached to, or incorporated into the complaint. Therefore, Founder cannot base a Rule 12(b)(6) motion on the side letter.

    Answer (B) is the best choice: When a defendant asserts an affirmative defense that does not involve genuine disputes of material fact, the preferred way to raise the defense is by a motion for judgment on the pleadings under Rule 12(c). *See Yassan v. J.P. Morgan Chase & Co.,* 708 F.3d 963, 975 (7th Cir. 2013). Here, Founder would attach the side letter to his answer, then could move for judgment on the pleadings unless Venture Capitalists deny that they signed the side letter or otherwise dispute its authenticity.

    Answer (C) is wrong: Although Rule 41(b) authorizes involuntary dismissal if the plaintiff fails to comply with the Federal Rules of Civil Procedure, the Rules do not compel Venture Capitalists to attach the side letter to their complaint.

    Answer (D) is wrong: Founder can file a motion for summary judgment, but need not wait until the close of discovery to do so. Rule 56 sets an outer limit for filing summary judgment motions of 30 days after the close of discovery, but does not require that a party wait until after the close of discovery. *See* Rule 56(b). If Founder filed a motion for summary judgment while discovery was pending, however, Venture Capitalists could ask the court to defer ruling on the motion while they conducted necessary discovery. *See* Rule 56(d).

75. **Answer (A) is wrong:** The time for filing a motion for relief from judgment is set in Rule 60(c)(1). Motions based on a party's fraud must be filed "no more than one year after the entry of the judgment." *See* Rule 60(c)(1). Landowner's child will be unable, therefore, to raise fraud two years after the judgment's entry.

    Answer (B) is wrong: Motions based on mistake, inadvertence, surprise, or excusable neglect are, likewise, bound by the same one-year time limit described in Answer (A). *See* Rule 60(c)(1).

    Answer (C) is the best choice: Unlike certain other grounds for relief from judgment, a Rule 60 motion asserting that the underlying judgment is void will not be bound by the one-year period. *See* Rule 60(c)(1). Instead, such motions are timely if they are brought "within a reasonable time," a period the courts tend to construe liberally. *See "R" Best Produce, Inc. v. DiSapio,* 540 F.3d 115, 123–24 (2d Cir. 2008) ("Although Rule 60(b) provides that most motions for relief, including a motion [on voidness grounds], must be made 'within a reasonable time,' this Court has been exceedingly lenient in defining the term 'reasonable time,' with respect to voidness challenges. In fact, it has been oft-stated that, for all intents and purposes, a motion to vacate a default judgment as void 'may be made at any time.' "). A lack of diversity of citizenship would defeat the court's subject-matter jurisdiction, and cause the underlying judgment to be void. Consequently, a fairly quick discovery by Landowner's child of the fact of non-diverse litigants is likely to merit relief from judgment.

    Answer (D) is wrong: A motion for relief based on newly discovered evidence is bound by the one-year time bar, and therefore would be untimely as described in Answer (A). *See* Rule 60(c)(1).

76.   **Answer (A) is wrong:** In order to be reviewable as a "final order," the order normally must dispose of the entire case; it is usually not enough for the order to dispose of one issue "finally," as explained in Answer (D).

Answer (B) is wrong: Denial of a privilege assertion can place a party in a real bind. As explained in Answer (D), such rulings are interlocutory rulings not immediately appealable. A party who is sufficiently confident of its privilege assertion can defy the order, then appeal any resulting contempt order. *See Hickman v. Taylor*, 329 U.S. 495 (1947).

Answer (C) is wrong: The "collateral order doctrine" is a doctrine developed by the U.S. Supreme Court that allows a party to appeal an otherwise interlocutory order when it: 1) is conclusive on the issue sought to be immediately appealed; 2) resolves an important question that is completely separate from the underlying merits; and 3) is effectively unreviewable if the appeal were to await a final order. *See Will v. Hallock*, 564 U.S. 345 (2006). Thus, if the court's order satisfied the requirements of the collateral order doctrine, the order would be appealable at the time it was entered, without waiting for a final judgment.

Answer (D) is the best choice: Generally, litigants may not immediately appeal the various orders entered by the district judge during a litigation but, instead, must wait until the court enters its "final order" in the case, at which time all orders may be appealed collectively at one time. *See* 28 U.S.C. § 1291. Over the years, legislative and judicial exceptions to this procedure have been crafted to permit immediate appeals from certain interlocutory orders. The U.S. Supreme Court, however, has ruled that immediate appeals from discovery orders raising attorney-client privilege issues do not ordinarily qualify for such an exception. *See Mohawk Indus., Inc. v. Carpenter*, 558 U.S. 100, 108–09 (2009).

77.   **Answer (A) is wrong:** As explained in Answer (D), the "two dismissal rule" does not apply when the first dismissal was not voluntary.

Answer (B) is wrong: The doctrine of claim preclusion only applies when the claim was adjudicated on the merits in the prior action. A dismissal for lack of subject-matter jurisdiction or lack of personal jurisdiction is not an adjudication on the merits. *See Wilkins v. Jakeway*, 183 F.3d 528, 533 (6th Cir. 1999).

Answer (C) is wrong: Although Rule 41 provides that a voluntary dismissal is normally without prejudice, it also provides that the second voluntary dismissal is with prejudice. *See* Rule 41(a)(1)(B). Therefore, a voluntary dismissal is not automatically without prejudice and the analysis ultimately turns on the analysis of the "two dismissal rule" as explained in Answer (D).

Answer (D) is the best choice: The "two dismissal rule" is embodied in Rule 41(a)(1)(B), and provides that a voluntary dismissal becomes with prejudice if the plaintiff has previously dismissed an action based on or including the same claim. Here, Shareholder previously brought the same claim, but he did not dismiss it, the court did for lack of subject-matter jurisdiction. The "two dismissal rule" does not apply when the first dismissal was not a voluntary one. *See ASX Inv. Corp. v. Newton*, 183 F.3d 1265, 1267–68 (11th Cir. 1999).

78. **Answer (A) is wrong:** Orders of attorney disqualification are not considered final orders. *See Richardson-Merrell, Inc. v. Koller,* 472 U.S. 424, 426–41 (1985).

Answer (B) is the best choice: Orders imposing sanctions for criminal contempt are considered immediately appealable as final orders because they arise from " 'a separate and independent proceeding . . . to vindicate the authority of the court' " and are " 'not a part of the original cause.' " *See Marrese v. American Academy of Orthopaedic Surgeons,* 470 U.S. 373, 379 (1985).

Answer (C) is wrong: Orders denying attorney disqualification are not considered final orders. *See Firestone Tire & Rubber Co. v. Risjord,* 449 U.S. 368, 373–78 (1981).

Answer (D) is wrong: Orders by a court that resolve liability without addressing the requests for relief are not considered final. *See Riley v. Kennedy,* 553 U.S. 406, 419 (2008).

79. **Answer (A) is wrong:** Federal question jurisdiction allows the federal courts to hear civil actions "arising under the Constitution, laws, or treaties of the United States." *See* 28 U.S.C. § 1331. Civil actions "arise under" federal law in two ways. First, an action arises under federal law when federal law creates the right to sue. *See American Well Works Co. v. Layne & Bowler Co.,* 241 U.S. 257, 260 (1916) ("A suit arises under the law that creates the cause of action."). The "vast bulk" of federal question lawsuits fall into this first category. *See Gunn v. Minton,* 133 S. Ct. 1059, 1064 (2013). This Answer notes correctly that this first "arising-under" jurisdiction cannot apply; as the Question recounts, State law, not federal law, created the right to sue for legal malpractice. However, as explained in Answer (B), a second category of "arising-under" jurisdiction claims is recognized.

Answer (B) is the best choice: An action created by State law can still qualify for "arising-under" jurisdiction if that State law claim necessarily raises a federal issue, which is actually disputed and substantial, and which the federal court can hear "without disturbing any congressionally approved balance of federal and state judicial responsibilities." *See Grable & Sons Metal Prods., Inc. v. Darue Eng'g & Mfg.,* 545 U.S. 308, 314 (2005). This second "arising-under" category is considered to be a "special," "small," and "slim" one. *See Empire Healthchoice Assurance, Inc. v. McVeigh,* 547 U.S. 677, 699 & 701 (2006). This second category cannot apply here. The U.S. Supreme Court has confirmed that legal malpractice claims of this sort are unlikely to implicate a federal issue that is "substantial." *See Gunn v. Minton,* 568 U.S. 251, 260–64 (2013) (because State law legal malpractice cases involve "backward-looking" and "hypothetical" inquiries (namely, how would the federal issue, had it been properly raised by the attorney, have impacted the earlier lawsuit?), the resolution of that federal question "will not change the real-world result of the prior . . . litigation"). Thus, the action must be dismissed, not because the right to sue arises under State law, but because that State law claim fails to implicate a substantial federal issue.

Answer (C) is wrong: A State law claim that requires resolution of a federal issue can justify "arising-under" jurisdiction. *See Grable & Sons Metal Prods., Inc. v. Darue Eng'g & Mfg.,* 545 U.S. 308, 314 (2005). But to do so, that imbedded federal issue must be a "substantial" one. *Id.* Here, the resolution of a federal issue would be "necessary"; Attorney committed legal malpractice only if a federal law would, in fact, have afforded Condominium a "grandfathering" exemption from all newly enacted pier laws. But, as explained in Answer (B), the legal malpractice claim described here fails the further requirement that it be "substantial."

Answer (D) is wrong: State law claims having imbedded federal issues can indeed justify "arising-under" jurisdiction, but, as explained in Answers (B) and (C), this category of jurisdiction is a "slim" one (and certainly not one that is always present). To the contrary, such jurisdiction is only proper where the federal issue is actually disputed, necessary for resolution, substantial, and capable of disposition without disturbing the balance Congress set for judicial responsibilities. *See Grable & Sons Metal Prods., Inc. v. Darue Eng'g & Mfg.,* 545 U.S. 308, 314 (2005).

80. **Answer (A) is the best choice:** Rule 56(c) provides that "A party may object that the material cited to support or dispute a fact cannot be presented in a form that would be admissible in evidence." This procedure does not require that the evidence be submitted in an admissible form, just that it be capable of being presented in an admissible form. Affidavits are the classic example—they are generally inadmissible at trial, but the information can be presented in an admissible form by calling the affiant as a witness at trial. *See Argo v. Blue Cross & Blue Shield of Kansas, Inc.*, 452 F.3d 1193, 1199 (10th Cir. 2006). Therefore, the invoice would be competent evidence at the summary judgment stage.

     Answer (B) is wrong: The court does not need to determine the admissibility of evidence submitted in support of or in opposition to a motion for summary judgment before ruling on the motion. In fact, many admissibility issues cannot be determined in advance of trial, as they depend on the context in which the evidence is offered. *See, e.g.,* Fed. R. Evid. 801(c) (an out-of-court statement is only hearsay if offered for the truth of the matter asserted in the statement). Rather, as explained in Answer (A), evidence will be considered in the context of a summary judgment motion even if inadmissible, so long as it is capable of being presented in an admissible form.

     Answer (C) is wrong: A party may move for summary judgment on an issue as to which the opposing party will have the burden of proof at trial by asserting that the opposing party does not have sufficient evidence to establish each element of the claim. *See* Rule 56(c)(1)(B). Here, however, Cabbie does have appropriate evidence of damages, as explained in Answer (A).

     Answer (D) is wrong: As explained in Answers (A) and (C), Cabbie satisfied his burden of producing record evidence relating to the damages element of his claim by submitting the invoice, thus creating a genuine dispute of fact precluding summary judgment. Although the court could consider granting summary judgment in favor of Cabbie, the nonmoving party, on the damages issue, the court would be required, before doing so, to give Truck Driver notice and an opportunity to submit its evidence or otherwise respond. *See* Rule 56(f).

81. **Answer (A) is wrong:** The United States Supreme Court has confirmed consistently that a federal pleader is not obligated to allege only "probable" claims or those "likely to prevail," and a trial judge's doubts that the allegations will ultimately persuade a factfinder is not alone sufficient cause to dismiss a claim. *See Twombly v. Bell Atlantic Corp.*, 550 U.S. 544 (2007) (noting that "a well-pleaded complaint may proceed even if it strikes a savvy judge that actual proof of those facts is improbable, and 'that a recovery is very remote and unlikely.' ") (citation omitted).

Answer (B) is wrong: In ruling on a motion to dismiss, the court may not consider evidence outside the pleadings. (Although there are several narrow exceptions to this prohibition, such as matters of public record or documents attached to the complaint, witness testimony would not qualify.) If the court nonetheless considers such evidence, the motion may no longer be considered a motion to dismiss, but the court must convert the motion to dismiss into a motion for summary judgment, and proceed to grant or deny the challenge on that basis. *See* Rule 12(d).

Answer (C) is the best choice: This summarizes the current "plausibility" standard adopted by the United States Supreme Court for testing comportment with Rule 12(b)(6). *See Twombly v. Bell Atlantic Corp.*, 550 U.S. 544 (2007) ("While a complaint attacked by a Rule 12(b)(6) motion to dismiss does not need detailed factual allegations, a plaintiff's obligation to provide the "grounds" of his "entitle[ment] to relief" requires more than labels and conclusions, and a formulaic recitation of the elements of a cause of action will not do. Factual allegations must be enough to raise a right to relief above the speculative level, on the assumption that all the allegations in the complaint are true (even if doubtful in fact).") (citations omitted).

Answer (D) is wrong: The defense of failure to state a claim is not waived if it is included in a pre-answer Rule 12(b) motion to dismiss, in a Rule 7(a) pleading, in a Rule 12(c) motion for judgment on the pleadings, or at trial. *See* Rule 12(b)(6), 12(h)(2).

82. **Answer (A) is wrong:** A notice of removal is timely if the defendant files it within 30 days after receiving a copy of the initial pleading through service or otherwise. *See* 28 U.S.C. § 1446(b)(1). But a claim against multiple defendants cannot be removed unless and until all defendants who are then properly joined and served have joined in or consented to the removal. *See* 28 U.S.C. § 1446(b)(2)(A). Here, Ride Operator's notice can only be effective upon such joining or consent. Consequently, the preferences of the other defendants are essential to a proper removal.

Answer (B) is wrong: For the same reasons explained in Answer (A), the claim against the three defendants can only proceed in federal court upon the consent to or joining in the removal of those defendants.

Answer (C) is wrong: The time for Amusement Park to remove expired on October 1 (the day after 30 days had passed since it received service of a copy of the initial pleading). But all defendants are afforded their own 30-day period, following service on them, to remove. *See* 28 U.S.C. § 1446(b)(2)(B). Ride Operator was served on November 1. So, Ride Operator had 30 days from that date to file for removal. As explained in Answers (A) and (D), however, to do so, Ride Operator needed to obtain the other defendants' agreement to remove.

Answer (D) is the best choice: Even though Ride Operator's notice is not untimely (for the reasons explained in Answer (C)), this case will remain in State court. Ride Operator is obliged under federal procedure not only to file a timely notice of removal, but also to obtain the consent of all other then-joined-and-served defendants to the removal. Because neither Amusement Park nor Ride Manager have joined or otherwise consented to the notice, the removal is improper.

83. **Answer (A) is wrong:** The venue statute, 28 U.S.C. § 1391(b)(1), authorizes venue in a district in which any defendant resides if all of the defendants reside in the same State. A corporation is deemed to reside for venue purposes in any district in which it is subject to personal jurisdiction. *See* 28 U.S.C. § 1391(c)(2). Because both defendants' principal places of business are in Massachusetts, they would be subject to general jurisdiction there, and thus would be deemed to reside there for venue purposes. Therefore, venue is proper in Massachusetts, and the motion to dismiss for lack of venue would likely be denied. As explained in Answer (C), however, the court would likely grant the motion to transfer the case to California.

Answer (B) is wrong: As explained in Answer (A), the court will likely deny the motion to dismiss. However, as explained in Answer (C), the court would likely grant the motion to transfer the case to California.

Answer (C) is the best choice: As explained in Answer (A), the court will likely deny the motion to dismiss. A motion to transfer venue when the case was originally filed in a district with proper venue is governed by 28 U.S.C. § 1404, which allows for transfer "for the convenience of the parties and witnesses, in the interest of justice." Here, a court would likely find the location in California of the witnesses and the building that is the subject of the action, and the lack of connection of Massachusetts to the action, as sufficient grounds to warrant transfer to California. *See Gundle Lining Const. Corp. v. Fireman's Fund Ins. Co.*, 844 F. Supp. 1163, 1165–66 (S.D. Tex. 1994).

Answer (D) is wrong: As explained in Answer (A), the court will likely deny the motion to dismiss. The doctrine of forum non conveniens generally applies to situations in which transfer is not possible. *See Quackenbush v. Allstate Ins. Co.,* 517 U.S. 706, 721–22 (1996) (transfer pursuant to Section 1404 is preferred remedy for problems arising from forum non conveniens; and dismissal is appropriate "only in cases where the alternative forum is abroad."). Here, it is possible for one federal court to transfer an action to a federal court in another State, so the analysis would most likely be governed by 28 U.S.C. § 1404, not the doctrine of forum non conveniens.

84. **Answer (A) is wrong:** An individual hoping to intervene permissively must show a question of law or fact in common with the main action. *See* Rule 24(b)(1)(B). This question, however, asks about intervention as of right. As Answers (B), (C), and (D) explain, the requirements for intervention as of right are more rigorous.

Answer (B) is wrong: Intervention as of right requires the intervenor to demonstrate an interest "relating to the property or transaction that is the subject of the action." *See* Rule 24(a)(2). Here, the male officers have such an interest. The female officers are contesting the constitutional validity of the promotions the male police officers received. The possibility that the male officers' promotions could be declared invalid and rescinded provides the type of "interest" Rule 24(a) requires. *See Cotter v. Massachusetts Ass'n of Minority Law Enforcement Officers,* 219 F.3d 31, 34–35 (1st Cir. 2000).

Answer (C) is the best choice: Intervenors as of right must also demonstrate that the interests they claim may, as a practical matter, be impaired or impeded by the disposition of the pending action. *See* Rule 24(a)(2). For the same reasons noted in Answer (B), the possibility that the male officers could lose their promotions should the female officers prevail is sufficient to satisfy this "impairment" requirement. *See Cotter v. Massachusetts Ass'n of Minority Law Enforcement Officers,* 219 F.3d 31, 35 (1st Cir. 2000).

Answer (D) is wrong: Intervention as of right will be denied if existing parties to the litigation will represent adequately the absent party's interests. *See* Rule 24(a)(2). Here, there is at least the possibility of divergent interests between the male officers and Police Department. For example, the male officers might assert two arguments—that they scored as well or better than the female officers on the testing criteria, or if they did not, that the testing criteria used by Police Department was flawed and unlawful. Obviously, Police Department is less likely to make the second of these arguments. *See Cotter v. Massachusetts Ass'n of Minority Law Enforcement Officers,* 219 F.3d 31, 35–36 (1st Cir. 2000).

85. **Answer (A) is wrong:** The U.S. Supreme Court has held that striking potential jurors on the basis of "the assumption that they hold particular views simply because of their gender" is an unconstitutional use of peremptory challenges. *See J.E.B. v. Alabama*, 511 U.S. 127, 137–42 (1994). Earlier, the Court had ruled that race-based assumptions of a prospective juror's views are unconstitutional as well. *See Batson v. Kentucky*, 476 U.S. 79, 97 (1986). Courts have extended this line of cases to apply not just to strikes by government actors, but to those by private actors as well. *See SmithKline Beecham Corp. v. Abbott Labs.*, 740 F.3d 471 (9th Cir. 2014). Accordingly, striking this potential juror based on an assumption that all women are likely to reason a certain way is a probable constitutional violation.

Answer (B) is the best choice: The fact that this potential juror is African-American or female does not mean that she cannot be stuck from the jury. But what the law requires is a "neutral explanation" for the strike, one that is not grounded in an "assumption" or an "intuitive judgment," grounded merely on the prospective juror's race or gender, that the prospective juror was likely—for that reason—to favor one side in the litigation or the other. *See Batson v. Kentucky*, 476 U.S. 79, 97 (1986). *See also J.E.B. v. Alabama*, 511 U.S. 127, 143 (1994) ("Parties still may remove jurors who they feel might be less acceptable than others on the panel; gender [and race] simply may not serve as a proxy for bias."). Here, because this prospective juror has an avocation which makes unpredictable her views on an important issue implicated in this litigation, striking her for this reason is likely to be permissible.

Answer (C) is wrong: As explained in Answers (A) and (B), the problem with striking this prospective juror is not that she is a female or a minority. Instead, what is forbidden is striking based on assumptions and inferences about how members of a certain gender or racial group think.

Answer (D) is wrong: The elimination of the only remaining female among the group of prospective jurors will not always be improper, as this answer suggests. Indeed, the U.S. Supreme Court has reaffirmed that "[d]efendants are not entitled to a jury of any particular composition." *See Taylor v. Louisiana*, 419 U.S. 522, 538 (1975). So long as a last remaining female juror is struck for constitutionally permissible reasons, as explained further in Answers (A) and (B), the strike is likely to be upheld.

86.   **Answer (A) is wrong:** It is true that summary judgment practice requires the non-moving party to come forward with at least one sworn averment of fact essential to that party's claims or defenses. *See Lujan v. National Wildlife Fed'n*, 497 U.S. 871, 888–89 (1990). Nonetheless, a failure by the non-moving party to come forward with evidence to contest certain facts still will not support a grant of summary judgment unless the moving party is entitled to judgment as a matter of law. *See* Rule 56(a). In other words, the nonmoving party does not need to contest *all* material facts; the court will not enter summary judgment on a claim if there is a genuine dispute as to any fact material to that claim. Here, because Shipyard has credibly contested one essential portion of Worker's claim—general causation—summary judgment would not be proper.

   Answer (B) is wrong: Summary judgment motions often do, but need not, await the close of discovery. To the contrary, unless a specific case's order sets a different schedule, such motions may be filed "at any time until 30 days after the close of all discovery." *See* Rule 56(b).

   Answer (C) is the best choice: Where the briefing record does not justify a grant of complete summary judgment, the court is entitled to "enter an order stating any material fact—including an item of damages or other relief—that is not genuinely in dispute and treating the fact as established in the case." *See* Rule 56(g).

   Answer (D) is wrong: Any party—including a claimant—can seek summary judgment, provided the requirements for the motion are otherwise satisfied. *See Alexander v. CareSource,* 576 F.3d 551, 557–58 (6th Cir. 2009) ("Both claimants and parties defending against a claim may move for summary judgment. . . .").

87.   **Answer (A) is wrong:** Sanctions under Rule 11 may be awarded on the court's own initiative and without motion from a party. *See* Rule 11(c)(3).

   Answer (B) is the best choice: Rule 11 sanctions are expressly not available to discovery requests. *See* Rule 11(d). This prohibition exists because sanctions for discovery misconduct are elsewhere authorized in the discovery rules themselves. *See* Rules 26(g) and 37.

   Answer (C) is wrong: Sanctions under Rule 11 are to be imposed against a law firm for violations committed by its associates, absent "exceptional circumstances." *See* Rule 11(c)(1).

   Answer (D) is wrong: Rule 11 sanctions may be imposed against *pro se* litigants. *See* Rule 11(c)(1).

88. **Answer (A) is wrong:** Testing whether the choice between State law or federal law could unfairly affect the outcome of civil litigation is one of the criteria to be evaluated in conducting an *Erie* analysis. *See Gasperini v. Center for Humanities, Inc.*, 518 U.S. 415, 427–28 (1996). However, as explained in Answer (C), when, as here, a Federal Rule or enacted federal law answers the disputed question, and that law is valid, it applies, without the court having ever to "wade into *Erie*'s murky waters." *See Shady Grove Orthopedic Assocs. v. Allstate Ins. Co.*, 559 U.S. 393, 398 (2010).

    Answer (B) is wrong: Similarly, an *Erie* analysis will also dutifully consider that doctrine's "twin aims"—namely, the discouraging of forum-shopping and the avoiding of an inequitable administration of the laws. *See Hanna v. Plumer*, 380 U.S. 460, 468 (1965). But an *Erie* analysis is unnecessary here, as explained in Answer (C), so long as Congress's peremptory challenge statute is valid and on-point.

    Answer (C) is the best choice: Congress has incontestable authority to prescribe rules of procedure for the federal courts, and may do so even when those rules differ from their companion State procedures. *See Hanna v. Plumer*, 380 U.S. 460, 473 (1965). If Congress has enacted a rule or authorized the promulgation of a rule of procedure for the federal courts that conflicts with a companion procedure that would apply in State courts, the federal procedure governs—so long as it is constitutional and, if a promulgated rule, promulgated lawfully under the Rules Enabling Act, 28 U.S.C. § 2072. *See Hanna v. Plumer*, 380 U.S. 460, 471–74 (1965). Congress's 3-peremptory limit is set by statute, and is plainly constitutional as it is intended to regulate practice and procedure in the federal courts. *See Hanna v. Plumer*, 380 U.S. 460, 472 (1965) ("the constitutional provision for a federal court system (augmented by the Necessary and Proper Clause) carries with it congressional power to make rules governing the practice and pleading in those courts, which in turn includes a power to regulate matters which, though falling with the uncertain area between substance and procedure, are rationally capable of classification as either."). Consequently, it will apply, and no *Erie* inquiry is needed.

    Answer (D) is wrong: As explained is Answer (B), this criterion—though a proper component of an *Erie* inquiry—is not implicated here, where an enacted federal law is on-point and valid.

89. **Answer (A) is wrong:** A forum selection clause is a provision included in many contracts where the contracting parties identify the forum where all or part of any contract-related dispute must be litigated. Parties can consent to personal jurisdiction in such a contract clause unless enforcement of the clause would be fundamentally unfair. *See Carnival Cruise Lines, Inc. v. Shute*, 499 U.S. 585, 600–01 (1991). However, subject-matter jurisdiction is a structural constitutional limitation on the type of cases federal courts are authorized to handle, and the parties cannot create subject-matter jurisdiction by waiver, stipulation, or consent. *See Ins. Corp. of Ireland, Ltd. v. Compagnie des Bauxites de Guinee,* 456 U.S. 694, 702 (1982). Therefore, Seller's agreement to the forum selection clause may invest the Pennsylvania court with personal jurisdiction, but it will not affect the court's subject-matter jurisdiction analysis.

    Answer (B) is the best choice: As explained in Answer (A), the court will likely enforce the parties' agreement as to personal jurisdiction, but will conduct its subject-matter jurisdiction analysis without regard to Seller's consent.

    Answer (C) is wrong: As explained in Answer (A), consent is relevant to the personal jurisdiction analysis, but not the subject-matter analysis.

    Answer (D) is wrong: As explained in Answer (A), consent is relevant to the personal jurisdiction analysis, but not the subject-matter analysis.

90. **Answer (A) is wrong:** Federal practice requires that a verdict be returned by a jury of at least 6 members, "[u]nless the parties stipulate otherwise." *See* Rule 48(b). Consequently, a verdict by 5 members would not be always improper. *See Meyers v. Wal-Mart Stores, East, Inc.*, 257 F.3d 625, 633 (6th Cir. 2001).

   Answer (B) is wrong: Like the 6-person jury requirement, the requirement of jury unanimity can also be excused by stipulation of the parties. *See* Rule 48(b).

   Answer (C) is the best choice: Unlike the 6-person jury requirement and the requirement of unanimity, federal practice requires that all non-excused jurors participate in the verdict. *See* Rule 48(a). *See generally* 9B CHARLES A. WRIGHT & ARTHUR R. MILLER, FEDERAL PRACTICE AND PROCEDURE § 2491, at 77 (2008) ("Once the number of jurors in a civil action has been determined and the jury empanelled, Rule 48 requires all of those seated to participate in the verdict unless excused by the court for good cause. . . . After any juror is excused, all the remaining jurors must participate in the verdict.").

   Answer (D) is wrong: Federal practice expressly authorizes the excusing of jurors, so long as a verdict is reached by at least 6 members (absent stipulation otherwise). *See* Rule 48(a)–(b).

91. **Answer (A) is the best choice:** Motions for judgment as a matter of law may be made only after the non-moving party has been "fully heard on an issue" during the jury trial. *See* Rule 50(a)(1). Because Manufacturer had not yet been heard fully on the issue of the trampoline design's defectiveness, the motion must be denied.

   Answer (B) is wrong: Motions for judgment as a matter of law may be made orally, as well as in writing, so long as the motion is made on the record. *See* 9B CHARLES A. WRIGHT & ARTHUR R. MILLER, FEDERAL PRACTICE AND PROCEDURE § 2533, at 507 (2008).

   Answer (C) is wrong: Motions for judgment as a matter of law are not premature if made prior to the close of all of the evidence, so long as they are made after the non-moving party has been fully heard on an issue. *See* Rule 50(a)(2) ("A motion for judgment as a matter of law may be made at any time before the case is submitted to the jury.").

   Answer (D) is wrong: Because the motion was made prior to Homeowner being fully heard on the issue of design defectiveness, *see* Answer (A), the motion could not be granted.

92. **Answer (A) is wrong:** The time for taking an appeal runs not from the date of the jury's verdict, but from the date of entry of judgment upon that verdict. *See* Fed. R. App. P. 4(a)(1)(A) ("In a civil case, except as [otherwise] provided . . . , the notice of appeal . . . must be filed with the district court within 30 days *after entry of the judgment* or order appealed from.") (emphasis added).

    Answer (B) is wrong: Although the appeal period for civil cases is 30 days from entry of judgment (unless, unlike here, the case involved the federal government or federal agency, officer, or employee as a party), *see* Answer (A), Pet Owner's filing of a timely motion for new trial suspended this 30-day appeal period. *See* Answers (C) and (D).

    Answer (C) is wrong: A timely motion for new trial suspends the running of the time for taking an appeal in federal civil cases, *see* Fed. R. App. P. 4(a)(4)(A)(v), and Pet Owner's new trial motion was timely because it was filed within 28 days after entry of the judgment. *See* Rule 59(b). However, the time for taking the appeal is not suspended merely for 30 days, but rather is suspended until the court enters its order resolving the now-pending new trial motion. *See* Fed. R. App. P. 4(a)(4)(A) (after a party files a timely new trial motion, "the time to file an appeal runs for all parties from the entry of the order disposing of" that motion).

    Answer (D) is the best choice: As explained in Answer (C), the time for Pet Owner to file her appeal began to run on November 20 when the district judge denied her motion for new trial and had the denial entered on the court's docket. Thereafter, Pet Owner had the traditional 30 days to file her appeal. That 30-day period would have expired at midnight on December 20. Thus, so long as Pet Owner filed her notice of appeal during her 30-day window (that is, any time before December 21), her appeal would be timely.

93. **Answer (A) is wrong:** A party opposing summary judgment may do so by citing to deposition passages that reveal a genuine dispute of material fact. *See* Rule 56(c)(1)(A). Here, this deposition testimony from an adversary tends to contradict the basis for Store's motion and, thus, would be helpful in defeating that motion.

    Answer (B) is the best choice: The U.S. Supreme Court has held that a genuine dispute of material fact is not created when the non-moving party asserts as true a fact that undisputed video evidence contradicts. *See Scott v. Harris*, 550 U.S. 372, 380 (2007) (trial court should not adopt plaintiff's version of a high-speed auto chase that was "blatantly contradicted" by unchallenged videotape evidence). Because the companion's attestation is "blatantly contradicted" by Store's video evidence, it is unlikely to be helpful to Shopper in defeating Store's motion.

    Answer (C) is wrong: The U.S. Supreme Court in *Scott v. Harris* intimated, however, that its holding could be different if the reliability of the video evidence is appropriately called into question. *See Scott v. Harris*, 550 U.S. 372, 378 (2007) (noting, from that summary judgment record, that there were "no allegations of indications that this videotape was doctored or altered in any way, nor any contention that what it depicts differs from what actually happened"). Creditable evidence—like that from a videographic expert—that the video has been subject to tampering is likely to be helpful in defeating the motion.

    Answer (D) is wrong: Like deposition passages, a genuine dispute as to material fact can also be established by interrogatory answers supplied during discovery. *See* Rule 56(c)(1)(A). Because Shopper's sworn testimony contradicts Store's summary judgment contention, it is likely to be helpful to her in resisting the motion. Unlike in Answer (B), here, the evidence Shopper offers is not blatantly contradicted by Store's video; that video shows only the sweater aisle, and does not record Shopper's behavior as she moved elsewhere throughout Store while shopping. For example, the limited video cannot disprove that Shopper removed the sweaters and left them in a different aisle while shopping.

94. **Answer (A) is wrong:** Personal jurisdiction generally focuses on the *defendant's* contacts with the State in which the action is filed. The *plaintiff's* contacts are generally irrelevant to the personal jurisdiction analysis. *See Walden v. Fiore*, 571 U.S. 277, 284 (2014) ("We have consistently rejected attempts to satisfy the defendant-focused 'minimum contacts' inquiry by demonstrating contacts between the plaintiff (or third parties) and the forum State."); *Calder v. Jones,* 465 U.S. 783, 788 (1984) ("The plaintiff's lack of 'contacts' will not defeat otherwise proper jurisdiction . . .").

Answer (B) is wrong: As discussed in Answer (C), the court will evaluate whether the defendant has sufficient minimum contacts with the forum State. Skateboard Company's lack of employees and property in Nevada are relevant to this inquiry, but are not dispositive. *See Panavision Int'l, L.P. v. Toeppen*, 141 F.3d 1316, 1320 (9th Cir. 1998) ("It is not required that a defendant be physically present or have physical contacts with the forum, so long as his efforts are 'purposefully directed' toward forum residents"). Because Skateboard Company intentionally targeted College's students in Nevada, it would likely be subject to personal jurisdiction over a claim related to skateboards it sold to those Nevada College's students.

Answer (C) is the best choice: The Supreme Court set forth the analysis for personal jurisdiction in a series of cases starting with *International Shoe Co. v. Washington*, 326 U.S. 310 (1945). That analysis requires that a defendant have sufficient "minimum contacts" with the forum State before the U.S. Constitution's Due Process Clause will permit the court to hale the defendant to the State to defend the action. Purposefully targeting customers in the State for the sale of goods is sufficient to create "specific jurisdiction" over a claim related to those goods. *See Rio Props., Inc. v. Rio Int'l Interlink*, 284 F.3d 1007, 1020–21 (9th Cir. 2002). *See also Soares v. Roberts*, 417 F. Supp. 304, 309 (D.R.I. 1976) (Massachusetts doctor subject to personal jurisdiction in Rhode Island when the doctor attracted a Rhode Island patient to the Massachusetts clinic by advertising in a Rhode Island college newspaper).

Answer (D) is wrong: The U.S. Supreme Court has held that mere foreseeability that a manufacturer's goods might end up in the forum State is not a proper basis for exercising personal jurisdiction over that manufacturer. Rather, personal jurisdiction requires only that the manufacturer foresee that its in-State conduct might cause it to be haled into that State to defend litigation. *See World-Wide Volkswagen Corp. v. Woodson*, 444 U.S. 286, 297 (1980) ("But the foreseeability that is critical to due process analysis is not the mere likelihood that a product will find its way into the forum State. Rather, it is that the defendant's conduct and connection with the forum State are such that he should reasonably anticipate being haled into court there").

95. **Answer (A) is wrong:** Diversity jurisdiction over a claim under 28 U.S.C. § 1332 requires two showings: (1) complete diversity of citizenship, such that no plaintiff in the case is a citizen of the same State as any defendant in the case; and (2) the amount in controversy for each claim is greater than $75,000, exclusive of costs and interest. Here, Borrower and Guarantor have joined together as plaintiffs in a single lawsuit, which they may do provided the prerequisites in Rule 20 are met. Borrower's claim against Bank meets the diversity amount in controversy minimum; Guarantor's claim against Bank does not. A longstanding principle in federal subject-matter jurisdiction is that two plaintiffs generally may not aggregate their claims together to reach the diversity amount in controversy threshold, absent an allegation that the multiple plaintiffs have a "joint or common interest or title in the subject matter of the suit." *Snyder v. Harris,* 394 U.S. 332, 337 (1969).

Answer (B) is wrong: The court has diversity jurisdiction over the claim by Borrower. Bank is a citizen of the State under whose laws it was incorporated—Delaware—and the State where it maintains its principal place of business—New York. 28 U.S.C. § 1332(c)(1). Borrower and Guarantor are individuals, and therefore are citizens of the State in which they are domiciled—Rhode Island. *See Yeldell v. Tutt,* 913 F.2d 533, 537 (8th Cir. 1990). Therefore, there is complete diversity of citizenship, in that no plaintiff is a citizen of the same State as any defendant. *See Strawbridge v. Curtiss,* 3 Cranch. (7 U.S.) 267 (1806). The amount in controversy for Borrower's claim against Bank is greater than $75,000 (exclusive of interest and costs), and therefore the court has diversity jurisdiction over that claim. Because Guarantor's claim against Bank is less than $75,000.01, the court many not exercise diversity jurisdiction over that claim. As explained in Answer (D), however, the court may exercise supplemental jurisdiction over that claim.

Answer (C) is wrong: A federal court may not invoke supplemental jurisdiction to supply the subject-matter jurisdiction authority for *every* claim in a lawsuit. Instead, supplemental jurisdiction only permits the court to allow an otherwise non-qualifying State law claim to "piggy-back" off of another claim in the case that enjoys valid subject-matter jurisdiction. *See Exxon Mobil Corp. v. Allapattah Servs., Inc.,* 545 U.S. 546, 558 (2005).

Answer (D) is the best choice: As explained in Answers (A) and (B), the court has diversity jurisdiction over Borrower's claim against Bank, but not Guarantor's claim against Bank. Supplemental jurisdiction, governed by 28 U.S.C. § 1367, allows a court to exercise jurisdiction over one claim if it arises out of the same constitutional "case or controversy" as another claim over which the court has original subject-matter jurisdiction (typically, federal question or diversity jurisdiction). Here, the court has original subject-matter jurisdiction—diversity jurisdiction—over Borrower's claim against Bank. Guarantor's claim against Bank arises out of the same case or controversy, as they both pertain to the same lending transaction. *See United Mine Workers of Am. v. Gibbs,* 383 U.S. 715, 725 (1966) (to evaluate "same case or controversy," courts look to whether the claims involve a "common nucleus of operative fact" and are "such that [the plaintiff] would ordinarily be expected to try them all in one judicial proceeding"). Thus, Guarantor's claim against Bank is *potentially eligible* for supplemental jurisdiction under 28 U.S.C. § 1367(a). Remember, though, that Section 1367(a) is made subject to the "carve-outs" of Section 1367(b). One aspect of the Section 1367(b) carve out turns on the specific Federal Rule under which the party was joined in the action. Claims by plaintiffs joined under Rule 20, as is the case here, are not on the list. Accordingly, the court may exercise supplemental jurisdiction over Guarantor's claim against Bank. *See* 28 U.S.C. § 1367(b). *See also Exxon Mobil Corp. v. Allapattah Servs., Inc.,* 545 U.S. 546, 560 (2005).

96. **Answer (A) is wrong:** Big Lottery can succeed in having the federal court dismiss the Michigan lawsuit if the court is persuaded that Candace is a required party under Rule 19(a), and that, without her, the Michigan lawsuit cannot in equity and good conscience proceed. *See* Rule 19(b). To determine whether Candace is a required party under Rule 19(a), the court must consider, among other things, whether it could award complete relief among the existing three parties to the lawsuit. Here, it could. Each of the three parties is demanding a one-fourth interest the grand prize, and Big Lottery could be ordered to make those payments. Following such an order, Oscar, Jorge, and Miranda would have received the complete relief they filed the lawsuit to obtain.

Answer (B) is wrong: It is certainly true that Candace's lottery claim cannot be resolved in her absence, but that is not the proper inquiry. Rule 19(a) examines whether, in Candace's absence, her claim may be impaired or impeded, or whether Big Lottery may be left exposed to a substantial risk of incurring multiple obligations. *See* Rule 19(a)(1)(B). Here, those inquires tend to confirm that Candace is a Rule 19(a) required party. *See In re Torcise*, 116 F.3d 860, 865 (11th Cir. 1997) ("It is well established under Rule 19 that all claimants to a fund must be joined to determine the disposition of that fund."). That conclusion, however, does not alone end the Rule 19 inquiry. The court must then further decide whether, in equity and good conscience, it should proceed with the lawsuit by Oscar, Jorge, and Miranda in Candace's absence. *See* Rule 19(b). Until that analysis is completed, Candace's mere unavailability is not enough to warrant a Rule 19 dismissal.

Answer (C) is the best choice: One of the central inquiries to determine whether a pending lawsuit should be dismissed under Rule 19(b) is whether an alternative forum exists elsewhere that could resolve the full controversy. *See* Rule 19(b)(4). Here, Wisconsin State court could hear the competing positions of all the lottery winners, and Big Lottery's concerns of multiple liability would be put to rest. *See Estate of Alvarez v. Donaldson Co.*, 213 F.3d 993, 995 (7th Cir. 2000) (dismissal warranted because, among other concerns, the entire dispute could be resolved in State court).

Answer (D) is wrong: In conducting the Rule 19(b) equity and good conscience inquiry, the court is also obliged to consider whether proceeding with the lawsuit in the absence of the allegedly critical party would prejudice those who are currently parties to the litigation. *See* Rule 19(b)(1). Here, as explained in Answer (A), Oscar, Jorge, and Miranda are unlikely to suffer any prejudice were the court to proceed since they could each be awarded the full relief they seek.

97. **Answer (A) is wrong:** As explained in Answer (D), although dismissal based on lack of personal jurisdiction is not an adjudication on the merits of the substantive claims and defenses in the case, it is an adjudication on the merits as to personal jurisdiction.

Answer (B) is wrong: This question implicates an assessment of defensive issue preclusion, not offensive issue preclusion. Defensive issue preclusion pertains to the use of issue preclusion to defeat a claim, as High School seeks to do here. Offensive issue preclusion would apply where a plaintiff seeks to establish a claim using issue preclusion. For offensive issue preclusion, the U.S. Supreme Court has established a discretionary equitable test. *See Parklane Hosiery Co., Inc. v. Shore*, 439 U.S. 322 (1979).

Answer (C) is wrong: As explained in Answer (B), the Supreme Court has established a discretionary equitable test for offensive issue preclusion, but not for defensive issue preclusion. *See Liberty Mut. Ins. Co. v. FAG Bearings Corp.*, 335 F.3d 752, 757 (8th Cir. 2003) (describing *Parklane* as "adopting a test of discretion with respect to nonmutual offensive collateral estoppel only").

Answer (D) is the best choice: Although the formulation varies, issue preclusion or collateral estoppel generally has the following requirements: the issue in a subsequent case is the same as in a prior case that resulted in a final judgment on the merits; the litigant against whom issue preclusion is sought was a party to the prior case or in privity with a party to the prior case; and the issue was actually litigated and decided. *See Community State Bank v. Strong*, 651 F.3d 1241, 1263–64 (11th Cir. 2011). Normally, if an action is dismissed based on lack of personal jurisdiction, the court never reaches the merits of the substantive claims and defenses. However, many courts have held that when the issue in question is existence of personal jurisdiction, a decision on the merits answering that question—personal jurisdiction—will have preclusive effect in subsequent actions testing the same issue. *See, e.g., Quest Sports Surfacing, LLC v. 1st Turf, Inc.*, 2008 WL 3853385 (S.D. Ind. 2008).

98. **Answer (A) is wrong:** The Class Action Fairness Act of 2005 ("CAFA") expanded the reach of federal jurisdiction over certain larger class actions, where the amount in controversy exceeded $5 million, exclusive of interests and costs. Diversity in such cases now exists when any one of the plaintiff class members is a foreign national and any one of the defendants is a citizen of a U.S. State. *See* 28 U.S.C. § 1332(d)(2)(B).

Answer (B) is wrong: Similarly, CAFA now authorizes diversity jurisdiction in such cases if any one of the plaintiff class members is a citizen of a U.S. State and any one of the defendants is a foreign nation. *See* 28 U.S.C. § 1332(d)(2)(C).

Answer (C) is wrong: Likewise, CAFA now permits the exercise of diversity jurisdiction in such cases if any one of the plaintiff class members is a U.S. citizen who has a State citizenship different from the U.S. State citizenship of any one of the defendants. *See* 28 U.S.C. § 1332(d)(2)(A).

Answer (D) is the best choice: Answer (D) describes the sort of "minimal" diversity that statutory interpleader permits. *Compare* 28 U.S.C. § 1335(a)(1). CAFA did not authorize diversity jurisdiction on this basis.

99. **Answer (A) is wrong:** As explained in Answer (C), the trial court's conclusions of law are subject to *de novo* review. The "abuse of discretion" standard applies to the court's discretionary rulings, including the majority of the discovery rulings. *See Black Horse Lane Assoc., L.P. v. Dow Chemical Corp.,* 228 F.3d 275, 282, n.7 (3d Cir. 2000).

Answer (B) is wrong: The appellate court uses the "clearly erroneous" standard for reviewing the trial court's findings of fact, as explained in Answer (C), not the "abuse of discretion" standard, as described in Answer (A).

Answer (C) is the best choice: The appellate courts are extremely deferential to the trial court's findings of fact because the trial court observed witness credibility in a way that the appellate courts cannot. *See Anderson v. City of Bessemer City, N.C.,* 470 U.S. 564, 575 (1985). Application of this standard allows reversal only if the trial court's fact finding is "clearly erroneous." *See* Rule 52(a)(6). In contrast, the appellate courts make a full, plenary review of the trial court's legal determinations. This is referred to as "*de novo*" or "plenary" review. *See McLane Foodservice, Inc. v. Table Rock Restaurants, L.L.C.,* 736 F.3d 375, 377 (5th Cir. 2013).

Answer (D) is wrong: As explained in Answers (A) and (C), the appellate court uses the "clearly erroneous" standard for findings of fact and the "*de novo*" standard for conclusions of law.

100. **Answer (A) is the best choice:** Although a subpoena is not necessary to require a party to attend a deposition, one is required (absent consent) to take the deposition of a party's employee. Thus, the simple deposition notice here is not effective as to an employee of a party who is not an officer or director or in a position of control. *See, e.g., Calderon v. Experian Info. Solutions, Inc.,* 287 F.R.D. 629, 631 (D. Idaho 2012).

Answer (B) is wrong: Rule 37 requires parties to "meet and confer" before seeking certain types of sanctions, in order to encourage parties to resolve disputes without court intervention. *See, e.g.,* Rule 37(a). In contrast, Rule 37(d) does not require a party to meet and confer before filing a motion for sanctions when another party fails to appear for its deposition after properly being noticed. However, as explained in Answer (A), Patient did not properly notice a "party," but rather an employee of a party. Consequently Nurse is not obligated to attend a deposition pursuant to a notice to Hospital.

Answer (C) is wrong: Rule 37(d) of the Federal Rules of Civil Procedure does not require a party to file a motion to compel before filing a motion for sanctions when another party fails to appear for its deposition after properly being noticed. However, as explained in Answer (A), Nurse is not obligated to attend a deposition pursuant to a notice to Hospital.

Answer (D) is wrong: Answer (D) correctly notes that Rule 37(d) of the Federal Rules of Civil Procedure does not require a party to meet and confer or file a motion to compel before filing a motion for sanctions when another party fails to appear for its deposition after properly being noticed. However, as explained in Answer (A), Nurse is not obligated to attend a deposition pursuant to a notice to Hospital.

101. **Answer (A) is wrong:** The Soldiers' and Sailors' Civil Relief Act of 1940 prohibits the entry of a default judgment against military defendants in certain circumstances. *See* 50 U.S.C.A. App. § 501. But the fact that default against Airline is not prohibited under this Act does not excuse the compliance with the other prerequisites for entry of a default judgment (*see* Answer (D)).

  Answer (B) is wrong: Entry of default bars the delinquent party from contesting most of the pleading's allegations—*except* the amount of damages, which is *not* deemed admitted. *See* Rule 8(b)6). *See also City of New York v. Mickalis Pawn Shop, LLC,* 645 F.3d 114, 128 (2d Cir. 2011). At least on that issue—damages—Airline can contest the default judgment.

  Answer (C) is wrong: The fact that the value of Passenger's lost luggage is not reducible to an incontestably fixed amount does not deprive the court of the power to enter the default, it merely requires that a judge (and not the clerk of court) enter the judgment. *See* Rule 55(b).

  Answer (D) is the best choice: A party who has "appeared" in the litigation is required to give 7-days advance notice of the default judgment hearing. Courts have given the term "appearance" a liberal reading, which includes engaging in settlement negotiations under certain circumstances. *See SEC v. Getanswers, Inc.,* 219 F.R.D. 698, 700 (S.D. Fla. 2004). Because it is likely that a court will rule that Airline—by engaging in such settlement discussions with Passenger—has "appeared" in the litigation, Airline was entitled to receive a 7-day notice of the hearing. Because no such advance notice was supplied, entry of a default judgment would be improper.

102. **Answer (A) is the best choice:** A motion *in limine* is a motion by which a party can ask the court for an evidentiary ruling in advance of trial, to prevent the jury from being exposed to inadmissible documents or testimony. *See Palmieri v. Defaria,* 88 F.3d 136, 141 (2d Cir. 1996). Although the court's ruling on the motion *in limine* would be considered interlocutory at the time the court issued it, most interlocutory rulings may be appealed after the court has issued the final order. *See Koch v. City of Del City,* 660 F.3d 1228, 1237 (10th Cir. 2011).

  Answer (B) is wrong: Many interlocutory orders are appealable after the court enters the final order, as explained in Answer (A).

  Answer (C) is wrong: Although evidentiary rulings are sometimes deemed "harmless error" and do not result in a successful appeal, those issues are nonetheless appealable. *See Obrey v. Johnson,* 400 F.3d 691, 701 (9th Cir. 2005).

  Answer (D) is wrong: A prevailing party who obtains all the relief it was seeking generally cannot appeal. *See California v. Rooney,* 483 U.S. 307, 311 (1987). Here, although Prisoner won, he may argue that the court's ruling lowered his recovery and therefore he has the right to appeal. *See Woods v. Ray,* 173 F.2d 781, 784 (7th Cir. 1949) ("A complainant who has received less than the relief demanded, is aggrieved by the judgment, and he may appeal.").

103. **Answer (A) is wrong:** A jury demand may be made by any party, including a defendant and third-party defendant. *See* Rule 38(b). Once one party files a jury demand, no other party need do so—the jury trial right is deemed to have been triggered. *See California Scents v. Surco Prods., Inc.,* 406 F.3d 1102, 1105–06 (9th Cir. 2005). Consequently, whether Renter timely demanded a jury trial or not, Retailer's timely demand will trigger a jury trial nonetheless.

    Answer (B) is wrong: A demand for a jury trial is proper if it is filed and served no later than 14 days after service of the last pleading directed to the issue for which the jury trial is demanded. *See* Rule 38(b)(1). Here, the relevant timing is 14 days from service of the last pertinent pleading, not 14 days from the service of the complaint. Because the cord manufacturer demanded a jury trial on the very day it was served (and, thus, within 14 days of the service of its own answer), the demand would be effective.

    Answer (C) is the best choice: At the time federal plaintiffs file their complaints, they are obligated to complete an administrative form known as the "civil cover sheet." On this document, plaintiffs are asked to mark a box indicating whether their complaint seeks a trial by jury or a bench trial. However, because this sheet is merely an administrative form, and especially because it is not served on opposing counsel, courts have rejected the contention that it qualifies as a proper jury demand under Rule 38(b). *See Wall v. National R.R. Passenger Corp.,* 718 F.2d 906, 909 (9th Cir.1983). Consequently, Renter's box-checking failed to properly demand a jury trial, and the case would proceed as a bench trial.

    Answer (D) is wrong: The parties to a litigation may withdraw a demand for jury trial after it is filed, but only if all the parties to the lawsuit agree. *See* Rule 38(d) & Rule 39(a)(1). Here, Renter and Retailer have agreed, but there is no indication of agreement from the cord manufacturer. Thus, the waiver will be deemed ineffective, and the prior jury demand will remain in place. *See* Rule 39(b).

104. **Answer (A) is wrong:** Although discovery is generally described as broad under the Federal Rules of Civil Procedure, there are limitations as described in Answer (D).

    Answer (B) is wrong: While Rule 26(c) authorizes parties to file motions for protective orders, parties are also allowed to interpose objections to discovery requests, and failure to file a motion for a protective order does not waive those objections. *See* Rule 34(b).

    Answer (C) is wrong: The scope of discovery, as defined in Rule 26(b)(1), does not impose a burden on either party to demonstrate "good cause." That is a heightened burden of proof that the rules impose on occasion, but does not apply here.

    Answer (D) is the best choice: As amended in 2015, Rule 26(b)(1) defines the scope of discovery to include "nonprivileged matter that is relevant to any party's claim or defense *and is proportional to the needs of the case* . . ." (emphasis added). The Rule then lists a series of factors to consider in making the proportionality determination. The automobile manufacturer's objection appears most likely to trigger a court's assessment of those factors in making a proportionality ruling. If the manufacturer loses this motion, it is most likely because the court, upon performing that inspection, was not persuaded that the email request was disproportional to the needs of the litigation.

105. **Answer (A) is wrong:** The Federal Rules of Civil Procedure do not provide a nationally uniform authorization for mailed service on all individuals served in the United States. *See* Rule 4(e). However, the Rules allow service that follows State law in the State where the district court is located. *See* Rule 4(e)(1).

   Answer (B) is the best choice: This case is pending in Idaho federal court. Consequently, if service is proper under Idaho State law procedures, it will be accepted as proper in that federal court. *See* Rule 4(e)(1).

   Answer (C) is wrong: The U.S. Constitution does not require that the challenging Board Member receive actual notice of the pending lawsuit, only that the service attempted be reasonably calculated, under the circumstances, to apprise that Board Member of the lawsuit. *See Dusenbery v. United States*, 534 U.S. 161, 171 (2002) (actual notice has never been an inexorable requirement of due process).

   Answer (D) is wrong: Conversely, the fact that the Board Member received actual notice does not ensure that the service comported with the applicable service requirements. If it did not, the service may still yet be quashed. *See Williams v. GEICO Corp.*, 792 F. Supp. 2d 58, 65 (D.D.C. 2011).

106. **Answer (A) is wrong:** Although an amended pleading, properly filed as of right or as permitted by the court, replaces the original pleading, the relation back/statute of limitations analysis has separate requirements, as explained in Answer (D).

   Answer (B) is wrong: Diligence by the plaintiff is not part of the relation back/statute of limitations analysis, as explained in Answer (D).

   Answer (C) is wrong: One of the requirements of the relation back doctrine is that the claim against the new defendant must arise out of the same conduct, transaction, or occurrence set out—or attempted to be set out—in the original pleading. Here, the new claim does arise out of the same conduct; it is just the identity of the defendant that is different. However, as explained in Answer (D), that is only 1 of the 3 requirements.

   Answer (D) is the best choice: The relation back doctrine—which allows an amended complaint to be deemed to have been filed at the time of the original complaint for statute of limitations purposes—has 3 requirements: 1) the claim against the new defendant must arise out of the same conduct, transaction, or occurrence set out—or attempted to be set out—in the original pleading; 2) within the time for serving the original complaint—typically 90 days—the new defendant must have received notice of the action; and 3) the plaintiff must show that the new defendant knew it would have been named in the original complaint but for a mistake concerning the party's identity. The courts have held that when a plaintiff knew that the complaint named the wrong defendant, the mistake aspect of the third requirement was not satisfied. *See Worthington v. Wilson*, 8 F.3d 1253, 1256–57 (7th Cir. 1993) (holding that naming a John Doe defendant showed the plaintiff simply did not know who the proper defendant was, not that the plaintiff had made a *mistake* as to the identity of the proper defendant).

107. **Answers (A) and (B) are wrong:** Although the *Erie* analysis can be quite complicated, at its fundamental level, the *Erie* doctrine provides that a federal court, sitting in diversity, applies federal procedure and State substantive law. *See Gasperini v. Center for Humanities, Inc.,* 518 U.S. 415, 427 (1996). The Court in *Erie* also renounced the notion that federal courts can craft "federal general common law." *See Erie R.R. Co. v. Tompkins,* 304 U.S. 64, 78 (1938). Here, the lawsuit asserts a State law negligence claim. Therefore, the court would not apply any State's pleading procedures, nor is there a body of federal substantive common law on general negligence to apply.

Answer (C) is wrong: Although the *Erie* doctrine generally provides for the application of State substantive law, Answer (D) explains that selecting which State's law to apply is determined by the forum State's choice of law principles which, when applied here, would not choose Arizona's substantive law.

Answer (D) is the best choice: In general, the choice of which State's substantive law to apply is controlled by the forum State's choice of law provision. *See Klaxon Co. v. Stentor Electric Mfg. Co.,* 313 U.S. 487, 496 (1941). Because Shopper filed the case in Arizona, Arizona's choice of law statute dictates the substantive law the federal court will apply. It designates New Mexico law, so the court will apply federal pleading standards and New Mexico substantive common law.

108. **Answer (A) is wrong:** The territorial reach of the federal courts is established in Rule 4(k). Rule 4(k)(1)(A) provides that personal jurisdiction is proper over a defendant who, when properly served, is subject to the personal jurisdiction of the State where the federal court is located.

Answer (B) is wrong: Rule 4(k)(1)(B) provides that personal jurisdiction is proper over an impleaded party (Rule 14) or a required party (Rule 19), so long as that party is served within a judicial district of the United States and no more than 100 miles from the place where the summons was issued.

Answer (C) is the best choice: A defendant may, and is encouraged to, waive formal service of process, but such a waiver will not ensure that personal jurisdiction is proper. *See* Rule 4(d)(5) ("Waiving service of a summons does not waive any objection to personal jurisdiction or venue."). Thus, Midfielder could waive formal service and then properly (and, potentially, successfully) contest the court's exercise of personal jurisdiction.

Answer (D) is wrong: Rule 4(k)(1)(C) provides that personal jurisdiction is proper when a federal statute authorizes such jurisdiction and the defendant is properly served.

109. **Answer (A) is wrong:** Rule 49(b)(3)(B) authorizes the court to order the jury to deliberate further when the jury returns a general verdict that is inconsistent with its answers to written questions. *See Kerman v. City of New York,* 261 F.3d 229, 244 (2d Cir. 2001).

Answer (B) is wrong: Rule 49(b)(3)(A) authorizes the court to enter a verdict consistent with the answers to the written questions when the jury returns a general verdict that is inconsistent with its answers to written questions. *See Masters v. UHS of Delaware, Inc.,* 631 F.3d 464, 475 (8th Cir. 2011).

Answer (C) is the best choice: Rule 49(b)(3) does not authorize the court to enter a verdict consistent with the general verdict when the jury returns a general verdict that is inconsistent with its answers to written questions.

Answer (D) is wrong: Rule 49(b)(3)(C) authorizes the court to order a new trial when the jury returns a general verdict that is inconsistent with its answers to written questions. *See Campbell v. Ingersoll Mill. Mach. Co.,* 893 F.2d 925, 930 (7th Cir. 1990).

110. **Answer (A) is wrong:** A court is not likely to grant a TRO if the moving party has an adequate remedy at law. *See* Rule 65(b)(1)(A); *In re Arthur Treacher's Franchisee Litig.,* 689 F.2d 1137, 1141 (3d Cir. 1982).

Answer (B) is wrong: A court is not likely to grant a TRO unless the moving party demonstrates a reasonable likelihood of success on the merits. *See, e.g., Miller v. Skumanick,* 605 F. Supp. 2d 634, 643 (M.D. Pa. 2009).

Answer (C) is the best choice: Rule 65(b) authorizes the court to issue a TRO without notice to the opposing party if "the movant's attorney certifies in writing any efforts made to give notice and the reasons why it should not be required." *See Reno Air Racing Ass'n, Inc. v. McCord,* 452 F.3d 1126, 1130–31 (9th Cir. 2006).

Answer (D) is wrong: Rule 65(c) authorizes the court to issue a TRO "only if the movant gives security in an amount the court considers proper . . ."

111. **Answers (A) and (B) are wrong:** Effective December 2009, the time for filing post-trial motions was extended from 10 days to 28 days. *See* Rule 59(b). Consequently, there is no longer a 10-day deadline for such filings.

Answer (C) is wrong: The Rules do not permit new trial motions to be filed at any time. As noted in Answer (A), the moving party is only afforded 28 days to file.

Answer (D) is the best choice: The 28-day filing period begins to run from "entry of judgment." *See* Rule 59(b). Consequently, Attorney's 28-day period was triggered on the judgment entry date (September 4), and ran for 28 days thereafter. Because the period would make any September filing date timely, this is the correct answer.

112. **Answer (A) is the best choice:** For purposes of the federal diversity statute, a litigant's citizenship is tested at the time of filing. *See Dole Food Co. v. Patrickson,* 538 U.S. 468, 478 (2003). So long as diversity is proper at filing, it will remain proper throughout the lawsuit. If, indeed, Passenger has become a citizen of Arizona as of the time of filing, prior or subsequent changes in citizenship would be irrelevant.

Answer (B) is wrong: Post-filing changes to the citizenship of the parties cannot "cure" a complete diversity defect that existed at the time of filing. Such a case must be dismissed, even if the parties later become diverse. *See Grupo Dataflux v. Atlas Global Group, L.P.,* 541 U.S. 567, 575 (2004).

Answer (C) is wrong: Similarly, post-filing changes to the citizenship of the parties cannot "corrupt" a complete diversity that existed at the time of filing. Such a case may proceed, even if the parties have later lost their diversity. *See Bank One, Texas, N.A. v. Montle,* 964 F.2d 48, 49 (1st Cir. 1992).

Answer (D) is wrong: Because citizenship is dated as of the time of filing, pre-filing events—like citizenship at the time the claim arose—will not alter the legally dispositive fact that diversity exists if it does so at time of filing. *See Altimore v. Mount Mercy College,* 420 F.3d 763, 768 (8th Cir. 2005).

113. **Answer (A) is wrong:** In performing an *Erie* analysis, the federal court will consider whether the decision to apply State law rather than federal law could affect a litigation's outcome. But this outcome-determination assessment is not applied "mechanically"; instead, "its application must be guided by 'the twin aims of the *Erie* rule: discouragement of forum-shopping and avoidance of inequitable administration of the laws." *See Gasperini v. Center for Humanities, Inc.*, 518 U.S. 415, 427–28 (1996). Thus, when an *Erie* inquiry is required, outcome-determination is one, but not the only, factor for the court to examine.

Answer (B) is the best choice: Giving a lawsuit a longer life in federal court than it would have in State court is "adding something to the cause of action," and thus offends the animating principles of the *Erie* doctrine. *See Ragan v. Merchants Transfer & Warehouse Co.*, 337 U.S. 530, 533–34 (1949). The existence of Rule 3 of the Federal Rules of Civil Procedure does not change that conclusion. Although Rule 3 dates the moment when a federal lawsuit is "commenced," nothing in that Rule attempts to control the impact of "commencement" on the applicable statutes of limitation. Thus, Rule 3 is not on-point nor does it control the question at issue. *See Walker v. Armco Steel Corp.*, 446 U.S. 740, 748–53 (1980). In other words, Rule 3 was intended merely to fix the moment of commencement, not to answer the further question of whether that commencement was timely. Thus, Oklahoma State law must be applied to test the timeliness of Carpenter's lawsuit.

Answer (C) is wrong: As Answer (B) explained, Rule 3 is not on-point on the timelness question at issue here, and thus does not actually clash with Oklahoma State law.

Answer (D) is wrong: Federal law does not always supplant State law, as the *Erie* decision and its cloudy progeny so readily confirm.

114. **Answer (A) is the best choice:** Rule 60(b)(3) authorizes the court to relieve a party from a final judgment based on fraud by an opposing party. Fabricating evidence would satisfy this requirement. *See Great Coastal Exp., Inc. v. Int'l Bhd. of Teamsters, Chauffeurs, Warehousemen & Helpers of Am.*, 675 F.2d 1349, 1358 (4th Cir. 1982).

Answer (B) is wrong: A motion for a new trial under Rule 59 could not be timely made; such motions must be made within 28 days after the entry of judgment. *See* Rule 59(b).

Answer (C) is wrong: A motion for judgment as a matter of law under Rule 50 would also be tardy; such motions must be made within 28 days after the entry of judgment. *See* Rule 50(b).

Answer (D) is wrong: Rule 11's sanctions pertain to the certification that a party or attorney makes when signing a pleading or other court papers. It does not address fraudulent testimony at trial. *See* Rule 11(a) and (b). Furthermore, Rule 11 allows the court to impose sanctions for violations, but does not authorize amending a judgment. *See* Rule 11(c).

115. **Answer (A) is wrong:** As explained in Answer (D), Rule 12(h)(1) only applies waiver to defenses under Rules 12(b)(2)–(5), which do not include the defenses that Pagoda Co. has raised.

Answer (B) is wrong: As explained in Answer (D), neither of the defenses that Pagoda Co. has raised is waived under Rule 12(h)(1) by failure to include the defenses in a Rule 12 motion.

Answer (C) is wrong: As explained in Answer (D), neither of the defenses that Pagoda Co. has raised is waived under Rule 12(h)(1) by failure to include the defenses in a Rule 12 motion.

Answer (D) is the best choice: Rule 12(h)(1) provides that a party waives a defense under Rules 12(b)(2)–(5) by failing to include it in a Rule 12 motion. Pagoda Co.'s motion asserts failure to state a claim under Rule 12(b)(6) and the failure to join a party under Rule 19, which is a Rule 12(b)(7) motion. Rule 12(h)(2) provides that a party may raise the defenses of failure to state a claim or failure to join a party under Rule 19 in a Rule 12(c) motion. Accordingly, Pagoda Co. can bring both of these defenses even though it already brought a Rule 12 motion.

116. **Answer (A) is wrong:** The U.S. Supreme Court has confirmed that an actor's knowledge of the plaintiff's connections with the forum State is not enough to confer personal jurisdiction over that actor for actions that cause effects felt in that forum State. *See Walden v. Fiore*, 571 U.S. 277, 287-90 (2014).

Answer (B) is wrong: The Court has likewise confirmed that these same principles apply when the dispute involves intentional torts. *See Walden v. Fiore*, 571 U.S. 277, 286 (2014) ("A forum State's exercise of jurisdiction over an out-of-state intentional tortfeasor must be based on intentional conduct by the defendant that creates the necessary contacts with the forum."). Accordingly, even if Co-Employee's behavior constituted an emotional battery, that battery was inflicted in Chicago, not in Connecticut.

Answer (C) is wrong: The fact that Financial Officer actually was caused to suffer an injury felt in the forum State as a consequence of Co-Employee's actions will also be insufficient to establish personal jurisdiction over Co-Employee in the forum. *See Walden v. Fiore*, 571 U.S. 277, 290 (2014) ("mere injury to a forum resident is not a sufficient connection to the forum. Regardless of where a plaintiff lives or works, an injury is jurisdictionally relevant only insofar as it shows that the defendant has formed a contact with the forum State. The proper question is not where the plaintiff experienced a particular injury or effect but whether the defendant's conduct connects him to the forum in a meaningful way.").

Answer (D) is the best choice: To qualify for "effects"-based personal jurisdiction, those effects must be such as to connect the defendant to the forum, and not just to the suing plaintiff. *See Walden v. Fiore*, 571 U.S. 277, 286-89 (2014). By knowingly "aiming" towards Connecticut a notice that might well have defamed Financial Officer, Co-Employee instigated a reputational injury that, if proven, would connect Co-Employee to Connecticut and the Connecticut public who might see the posted defamatory notice. That connection may well suffice to establish personal jurisdiction over Co-Employee. *See Calder v. Jones,* 465 U.S. 783 (1984).

117. **Answer (A) is wrong:** By their very nature, statutes enacted after 1791 that create causes of action implicate claims that were triable neither at law nor in equity prior to the ratification of the Seventh Amendment. Accordingly, the Supreme Court has developed a framework for considering the right to a jury for such claims, as explained in Answer (C).

Answer (B) is wrong: As explained in Answer (C), the Supreme Court held just the opposite.

Answer (C) is the best choice: The analysis for statutes enacted after the ratification of the Seventh Amendment requires courts to consider whether the nature of the action and the relief sought are more closely analogous to actions which would have been tried to a jury in 1791 or to actions that would have been tried in equity. *See Chauffeurs, Teamsters & Helpers Local 391 v. Terry*, 494 U.S. 558, 565 (1990). The Supreme Court has held that an action for penalties is akin to a money damages claim, and therefore is appropriate for a jury. *See Tull v. United States*, 481 U.S. 412, 418–21 (1987).

Answer (D) is wrong: Although monetary relief is typical of common law claims triable to a jury, some claims for money do not trigger the right to a jury trial, such as a claim for restitution or incidental monetary claims associated with injunctions. *See Chauffeurs, Teamsters & Helpers Local 391 v. Terry*, 494 U.S. 558, 571 (1990).

118. **Answer (A) is wrong:** Rule 12 allows a defendant to raise personal jurisdiction in an early Rule 12(b)(2) motion or by asserting it in the answer, as explained in Answer (D). But this is not a defendant's only option. A defendant may also decline to defend the action, and then collaterally attack a default judgment, as explained in Answer (C).

Answer (B) is wrong: The Rules have abandoned the historical concept of "special" appearances. Now, a party may enter its appearance—"generally" and without restriction— without waiving challenges to personal jurisdiction. *See In re Hijazi*, 589 F.3d 401, 413 (7th Cir. 2009).

Answer (C) is the best choice: A defendant who is confident of the merits of its personal jurisdiction defense can simply ignore the action, then if the plaintiff obtains a default judgment, the defendant can collaterally attack that judgment on the grounds that the issuing court had no personal jurisdiction over the defendant. *See Insurance Corp. of Ireland, Ltd. v. Compagnie des Bauxites de Guinee*, 456 U.S. 694, 706 (1982). Of course, this is a risky strategy, because if the defendant is wrong about personal jurisdiction, it will be stuck with the default judgment.

Answer (D) is wrong: Rule 12 allows a defendant to raise lack of personal as a defense in its answer, rather than by pre-answer Rule 12 motion. If the defendant waits too long to pursue the defense with the court, however, the defendant will be deemed to have waived the defense. *See Hamilton v. Atlas Turner, Inc.,* 197 F.3d 58, 60–61 (2d Cir. 1999). Thus, if Insurer pleaded lack of personal jurisdiction as a defense in its answer and then waited until trial to ask the court to make a determination, it would likely have waived the defense.

119. **Answer (A) is wrong:** In federal court, defaulting an adversary is a two-step process. First, the court must enter the adversary's default on the docket, thus formally recognizing the adversary as defaulting on the obligation to respond properly to the pleading against it. Second, the court must then enter a judgment, upon the default, against the adversary. *See* Rule 55(a)–(b). Although the entry of default admits the well-pleaded allegations of the complaint, it is not until the entry of a default judgment that an award enforceable elsewhere is created. *See City of New York v. Mickalis Pawn Shop, LLC,* 645 F.3d 114, 128–29 (2d Cir. 2011). Thus, no assets of the Internet vendor can be seized until this second step, entry of a judgment upon the default, is completed.

Answer (B) is wrong: For the same reasons in Answer (A) that an award enforceable in Connecticut has yet to be created, so, too, no award enforceable in Illinois has been created either.

Answer (C) is wrong: Federal courts enforce money judgments by writ of execution. *See* Rule 69(a)(1). Nonetheless, no judgment can yet be enforced through such a writ because no judgment has yet been entered.

Answer (D) the best choice: As noted above, Answers (A), (B), and (C) are each wrong.

120. **Answer (A) is wrong:** 28 U.S.C. § 1446 sets timing requirements for removal, and requires that all defendants who have been served join in or consent to the notice of removal. The question indicates compliance with each of these requirements. However, as explained in Answer (C), a case cannot be removed based on diversity jurisdiction if any defendant is a citizen of the State in which the case was filed.

Answer (B) is wrong: In order to be removed properly, there must be a basis for original federal court subject-matter jurisdiction—such as diversity jurisdiction or federal question jurisdiction—evident from the allegations in the complaint. *See Jefferson County v. Acker,* 527 U.S. 423, 430 (1999). Because the complaint at issue raises a State law claim and thus does not seem to qualify for federal question jurisdiction, it would only be removable if there was complete diversity of citizenship and a sufficient amount in controversy. Although these diversity requirements appear satisfied here, it is still not enough to render the case removable. As explained in Answer (C), a case cannot be removed based on diversity jurisdiction if any defendant is a citizen of the State in which the case was filed.

Answer (C) is the best choice: 28 U.S.C. § 1441(b)(2) provides that a case removable solely on the basis of diversity jurisdiction under 28 U.S.C. § 1332(a) may not be removed if any defendant who has been joined and served is a citizen of the State in which the action was brought. Here, Store is a citizen of New York, where Homeowner filed the complaint. So, provided Homeowner's motion properly asserts this home-State defendant exception, the action is not removable and the court will grant the motion to remand it.

Answer (D) is wrong: Although the plaintiff's choice of forum is entitled to deference in some contexts, such as motions to change venue, it is not a factor when the issue is whether the court has proper subject-matter jurisdiction. *See In re Resorts Int'l, Inc.,* 372 F.3d 154, 161 (3d Cir. 2003) ("Where a court lacks subject matter jurisdiction over a dispute, the parties cannot create it by agreement").

121. **Answer (A) is wrong:** Although it happens infrequently, the appellate court can overturn a jury verdict if the evidence was so one-sided that no reasonable jury could have reached the verdict, as explained in Answer (B).

     Answer (B) is the best choice: Appellate courts are very reluctant to overturn jury verdicts on the basis of witness credibility determinations, but will do so if the evidence is so one-sided that no reasonable jury could have reached the verdict. *See Lowery v. Circuit City Stores, Inc.,* 206 F.3d 431, 443 (4th Cir. 2000).

     Answer (C) is wrong: Evaluating the evidence is not a matter of counting witnesses, and the jury is free to believe the testimony of one witness over conflicting testimony by many other witnesses. *See Northern Nav. Co. v. Minnesota Atlantic Transit Co.,* 49 F.2d 203, 207 (8th Cir. 1931).

     Answer (D) is wrong: Without more facts demonstrating prejudice by the jury, there is not sufficient evidence that this jury reached its verdict based on prejudice against Taxi Driver, and not based on the testimony. *See Robinson v. Quick,* 875 F.2d 867 (6th Cir. 1989) (Table).

122. **Answer (A) is wrong:** As explained in Answer (D), a court sitting in diversity will generally apply the Federal Rules of Civil Procedure if they directly control the issue in question.

     Answer (B) is wrong: As explained in Answer (D), a court sitting in diversity will generally apply the Federal Rules of Civil Procedure if they directly control the issue in question.

     Answer (C) is wrong: The Seventh Amendment right to a jury trial applies to federal courts, but generally does not apply to proceedings in State courts. *See Minneapolis & St. Louis R.R. v. Bombolis,* 241 U.S. 211, 217 (1916).

     Answer (D) is the best choice: The *Erie* Doctrine essentially provides that a federal court hearing a case under its diversity jurisdiction applies federal procedural law and the substantive law of the State whose laws govern the claim, "except where the Constitution or treaties of the United States or Acts of Congress otherwise require or provide." *See* Rules of Decision Act, 28 U.S.C. § 1652. Where an issue is squarely addressed by the Federal Rules of Civil Procedure, it will be deemed procedural (except in the unlikely event that the court finds that the rule violated the Rules Enabling Act or the U.S. Constitution). Here, the problem tells us to assume that the Seventh Amendment provides a right to a jury trial for the claim at issue. Rule 38 provides that a party is entitled to a jury trial as declared by the Seventh Amendment. Therefore, the court would likely apply Rule 38 rather than the State law providing for a special master instead of a jury. *See Shady Grove Orthopedic Assocs., P.A. v. Allstate Ins. Co.,* 559 U.S. 393, 398 (2010) (if a Rule "answers the question in dispute," then "it governs . . . unless it exceeds statutory authorization or Congress's rulemaking power").

123. **Answer (A) is wrong:** While default judgments are disfavored for precisely these reasons, and are often lifted liberally, they are not lifted automatically. The requirements set in Rule 55(c) must first be satisfied. *See* Rule 55(c).

   Answer (B) is wrong: A showing of "good cause" may prompt the court to set aside the entry of default, but lifting a default judgment requires a showing that the standard for relief from a judgment under Rule 60(b) are met. *See* Rule 55(c).

   Answer (C) is the best choice: Though it is true none of these three criteria are stated in Rule 55(c) itself, courts consider these three factors in lifting a default judgment on the grounds of mistake or inadvertence. *See Brien v. Kullman Indus., Inc.,* 71 F.3d 1073, 1077 (2d Cir. 1995).

   Answer (D) is wrong: Lifting any default judgment competes with the goal of litigation finality, yet the Rules expressly authorize lifting such judgments when the requirements of Rule 55(c) are satisfied.

124. **Answer (A) is wrong:** Rule 12 does not include any basis for dismissal of a complaint based on the plaintiff's failure to comply with the Federal Rules of Civil Procedure.

   Answer (B) is wrong: Rule 37(d) allows the court to sanction a party for failure to respond to written discovery. However, it requires that a party to meet and confer with the opposing party before filing a Rule 37(d) motion for failure to respond to written discovery. A motion for sanctions under Rule 37(b) does not require that the parties meet and confer, but must be based on the opposing party's failure to comply with an order compelling discovery under Rule 37(a). Furthermore, the courts consider dispositive discovery sanctions like dismissal to be remedies of last resort, to be awarded only when lesser sanctions will not work. *See, e.g., Klein-Becker USA, LLC v. Englert,* 711 F.3d 1153 (10th Cir. 2013). A court is unlikely to dismiss the case on the first discovery motion.

   Answer (C) is the best choice: Rule 41(b) allows a party to move for involuntary dismissal for failure to prosecute or for failure to comply with the Federal Rules of Civil Procedure or a court order. Both grounds potentially apply to Subcontractor's conduct, and this would be General Contractor's best option.

   Answer (D) is wrong: As explained in Answers (A) and (B), General Contractor cannot obtain dismissal of the complaint under Rule 12 or Rule 37 based on the facts set forth in the question.

125. **Answer (A) is wrong:** While district courts have broad discretion when deciding whether to empanel an advisory jury—*see Mala v. Crown Bay Marina, Inc.*, 704 F.3d 239, 249 (3d Cir. 2013)—as explained in Answer (D), the judge may not simply adopt the advisory jury's verdict and instead must make his or her own findings of fact and conclusions of law.

Answer (B) is wrong: While district courts have broad discretion to accept or reject an advisory jury's verdict—*see Kinetic Concepts, Inc. v. Smith & Nephew, Inc.*, 688 F.3d 1342, 1357 (Fed. Cir. 2012)—as explained in Answer (D), the judge may not simply adopt the advisory jury's verdict and instead must make his or her own findings of fact and conclusions of law.

Answer (C) is wrong: While an appellate court would likely reverse a jury verdict that was not supported by the weight of the evidence, the ultimate adjudication of a case tried before a judge with an advisory jury should come from the trial judge, not the advisory jury, as explained in Answer (D). Therefore, the proper question would be whether the judge's findings of fact and conclusions of law are supported by the weight of the evidence, not the advisory jury's verdict.

Answer (D) is the best choice: Rule 52(a) of the Federal Rules of Civil Procedure requires that the judge make findings of fact and conclusions of law on the record, "[i]n an action tried on the facts without a jury *or with an advisory jury.*" (emphasis added). It is improper for a judge to simply adopt an advisory jury's verdict. *See OCI Wyoming, L.P. v. PacifiCorp*, 479 F.3d 1199, 1203 (10th Cir. 2007).

126. **Answer (A) is wrong:** To prevail on a JMOL motion, the moving party must demonstrate that, under the controlling law and in light of the evidence presented, there can be only one reasonable conclusion as to the proper verdict. *See Anderson v. Liberty Lobby, Inc.*, 477 U.S. 242, 250 (1986). Where reasonable minds could differ on the significance of the evidence and the outcome of the verdict, the case cannot be taken away from the jury. *Id.* at 250–51. Following the jury's verdict, if the court determines that the result was against the heavy weight of the evidence, the court might order a new trial. *See* Rule 59(a); *Byrd v. Blue Ridge Rural Elec. Co-op., Inc.*, 356 U.S. 525, 540 (1958). But similar reasoning would not justify the entry of a pre-verdict judgment as a matter of law. Only where there is a complete lack of probative evidence to support the nonmovant's position can the court enter a JMOL. *See Lavender v. Kurn*, 327 U.S. 645, 653 (1946).

Answer (B) is the best choice: Buyer was a competent eyewitness to his automobile's operation, and testified that the brakes occasionally failed. Weighing the respective credibility of trial witnesses is the province of the jury, not the trial judge. *See Reeves v. Sanderson Plumbing Prods., Inc.*, 530 U.S. 133, 150 (2000). As explained in Answer (A), the operative JMOL standard is whether there has been a complete absence of probative facts to support the nonmovant's position, and here, given Buyer's own testimony, that is not the case.

Answer (C) is wrong: Weighing the evidence is a task for the jury, not the trial judge, as explained in Answer (B). That the trial judge believes that the jury will likely side with Dealer's view of the facts is an improper ground for the court to enter a JMOL in Dealer's favor.

Answer (D) is wrong: The constitutionality of a pre-verdict JMOL is long and well settled. Although the Seventh Amendment does indeed recognize a right to trial by jury, a properly entered JMOL does not infringe upon this guarantee—it merely deprives the defeated litigant of the ability to urge the jury to return an unreasonable verdict upon legally inadequate evidence. *See Galloway v. United States*, 319 U.S. 372, 389 (1943).

127. **Answer (A) is wrong:** As a general matter, Rule 51(d) of the Federal Rules of Civil Procedure only authorizes a party to assign as an error on appeal an issue related to a jury instruction if the party properly raised the issue by objection at the trial level. However, Rule 51(d)(2) creates a narrow exception for "plain error" in the instruction if the error affects "substantial rights."

     Answer (B) is wrong: While inattentiveness may be an inadequate excuse for failure to make an objection before the jury is discharged, Rule 51(d)(2) creates a narrow exception that allows a party to raise an issue of "plain error" on appeal even if the party failed to raise the issue as an objection at the trial court level.

     Answer (C) is the best choice: Rule 51(d)(2) authorizes a party to raise an issue of "plain error" in the jury instructions on appeal, even if that issue has not been preserved by a proper objection before the trial court, if the error affects a party's "substantial rights."

     Answer (D) is wrong: In general, Rule 51(d)(1) only allows a party to assign error to issues related to the jury instructions that a party raised by proper objection. Rule 51(d)(2) creates a narrow exception to this general rule for issues of "plain error" that affect a party's "substantial rights." Thus, the defendant does not have an automatic right to base an appeal on an erroneous instruction to which the defendant has not objected, and may only do so if the appellate court agrees that the conditions of Rule 51(d)(2) are met.

128. **Answer (A) is wrong:** As explained in Answer (B), because this case had been pending in Salt Lake City State court, it must be removed to the federal court embracing that same place. The place where the plaintiffs reside has no impact on the venue location for the removed case.

     Answer (B) is the best choice: When a State case is removed to federal court, it shifts out of the State court and into the federal district court for that district and division embracing the place where the case had formerly been pending in State court. *See* 28 U.S.C. § 1441(a). Because this case had been pending in Salt Lake City State court, it must be removed to the federal court embracing that same place.

     Answer (C) is wrong: For *non-removed* cases (that is, cases begun originally in the federal courts), venue can ordinarily be proper where any defendant resides (if all defendants are residents of the State in which the district is located). *See* 28 U.S.C. § 1391(b)(1). That provision, however, does *not* apply to removed cases. *See id.* at § 1390(c).

     Answer (D) is wrong: Like in Answer (C), venue can also ordinarily be proper in *non-removed* cases in that district in which a substantial part of the events or omissions giving rise to the claim occurred. *See* 28 U.S.C. § 1391(b)(2). But, also as explained in Answer (C), that provision does *not* apply to removed cases. *See id.* at § 1390(c).

129. **Answer (A) is wrong:** The motion record most certainly reveals a factual dispute—Passenger contends that her meal was lobster-with-crab-meat; Cruise Line disputes that contention. But, while a dispute exists as to this fact, the mere presence of any dispute is not the pertinent inquiry for summary judgment. Rather, to resist summary judgment, the dispute must be shown to be "genuine". A dispute qualifies under this standard when a rational factfinder, considering the evidence in the motion record, could find in favor of the non-moving party. *See Anderson v. Liberty Lobby, Inc.*, 477 U.S. 242, 247–52 (1986). Consequently, while there is a factual dispute here, that is the wrong standard informing the summary judgment inquiry.

Answer (B) is the best choice: Summary judgment may be granted when a moving party shows that there is no genuine dispute as to any material fact, and that judgment is proper as a matter of law. *See* Rule 56(a). A dispute is "material" if it might affect the outcome of the case, informed by the governing substantive law. *See Anderson v. Liberty Lobby, Inc.*, 477 U.S. 242, 248 (1986). Here, while Cruise Line has indeed shown a factual dispute, that dispute relates to a single fact which would not affect the outcome of whether the ship was negligently piloted or whether Passenger suffered a resulting loss.

Answer (C) is wrong: Any party—plaintiff or defendant—can file for summary judgment. *See Alexander v. CareSource*, 576 F.3d 551, 557–58 (6th Cir. 2009).

Answer (D) is wrong: Summary judgment motions can be filed "at any time" until 30 days after the close of all discovery (unless Local Rules or a specific court order directs otherwise). *See* Rule 56(b). Where, as here, very early motions for summary judgment are filed, a responding party can seek the court to postpone the ruling until further discovery, *see* Rule 56(d), but that would not render the filing improper. *See Jernigan v. Crane*, 64 F. Supp. 3d 1260, 1273 (E.D. Ark. 2014).

130. **Answers (A), (B), and (C) are wrong:** As explained in Answer (D), neither defendant took any actions within or directed at State B, and therefore it would offend constitutional due process for the courts of State B to exercise personal jurisdiction over the defendants. The mere fact that a harm was felt in State B is insufficient to supply the constitutionally required minimum contacts. *See Walden v. Fiore*, 571 U.S. 277, 287-90 (2014).

Answer (D) is the best choice: In order for the exercise of personal jurisdiction over a defendant to satisfy Constitutional Due Process, the defendant must have purposely availed itself of the privilege of conducting activities in the forum State, thereby invoking for itself the benefits and protections of that forum State's laws. *See Goodyear Dunlop Tires Ops., S.A. v. Brown*, 564 U.S. 915, 924 (2011). Thus, the defendant must be able to reasonably foresee being haled into court in the forum State—the mere fact that the product can easily be transported to the forum state is not sufficient. *See World-Wide Volkswagen Corp v. Woodson*, 444 U.S. 286 (1980). Here, neither defendant took any actions to target consumers in State B or to avail themselves of the laws of State B, nor could they have readily foreseen being sued in State B. Accordingly, both defendants' motions will likely succeed.

131. **Answer (A) is the best choice:** In diversity cases, federal courts are dutybound to apply State substantive law (unless preempting federal law exists). This ordinarily obligates the federal court to apply legal principles as established by the State's highest court and, if no such rulings exist, to engage in the unenviable task of "predicting" how that highest court would decide the issue. *See Amparan v. Lake Powell Car Rental Cos.*, 882 F.3d 943, 947–48 (10th Cir. 2018) (in making such predictions, federal judges consider decisions by intermediate State appellate courts and, if appropriate, other sources). Any time a federal court is called upon to predict the answer to an unresolved question of State substantive law there is the chance that it could err. A later decision by the highest court of that State may prove that the federal court's prediction was mistaken. Ordinarily, such a ruling does "not impugn the integrity" of the federal court's decision, nor the fairness of its process. *See DeWeerth v. Baldinger*, 38 F.3d 1266, 1273 (2d Cir. 1994). Where, as here, the case is final with no pending post-trial motions or appeals, it is unlikely to be disturbed.

    Answers (B), (C), and (D) are wrong: Because the ruling in Patient's case has become final, with no open and pending post-trial motions or appeals, the holding is unlikely to be revisited simply because the federal court erred in its *Erie* prediction of State substantive law, as explained in Answer (A).

132. **Answer (A) is wrong:** Although the judge's closing comment to the jury was, indeed, legally incorrect, errors in instructing jurors must be disregarded if they do not affect any party's substantial rights. *See* Rule 61; *Richards v. Relentless, Inc.*, 341 F.3d 35, 48 (1st Cir. 2003). Consequently, the mere fact that the statement was legally incorrect does not, without more, supply a proper ground for granting a new trial.

    Answer (B) is the best choice: In testing whether an errant jury instruction warrants a new trial, the instructions are to be examined in their entirety. *See American Family Mutual Ins. Co. v. Hollander*, 705 F.3d 339, 355–56 (8th Cir. 2013). Given the error-free, hour-long exposition that preceded this brief, closing slip, the instructions—viewed in their entirety— likely would not justify empaneling a new trial.

    Answer (C) is wrong: It is probably impossible to conclude that this one errant statement "certainly" caused the jury to be misled. In any event, that an instruction "certainly" misled the jury is not the operative inquiry. Instead, a new trial may be warranted if the jury *may* have based their verdict on an erroneous instruction. *See Ericsson, Inc. v. D-Link Sys., Inc.*, 773 F.3d 1201, 1235 (Fed. Cir. 2014). Accordingly, both the factual conclusion and the legal test noted in this Answer are flawed.

    Answer (D) is wrong: As noted in Answer (A), errors in jury instructions are indeed tested under the harmless error rule, but as noted in Answer (C), not all instructing errors are harmless, and those that are not harmless merit a grant of a new trial.

133. **Answer (A) is wrong:** As explained in Answer (D), because venue is not available in any district under 28 U.S.C. § 1391(b)(1) or § 1391(b)(2), it is available in any district where any defendant is subject to personal jurisdiction. Accordingly, venue will be proper in State B if Soccer Fan Two is subject to personal jurisdiction in State B, regardless of whether Soccer Fan Three is subject to personal jurisdiction there. Of course, the fact that venue is proper there does not mean that Soccer Fan One can acquire personal jurisdiction over Soccer Fan Three there. If Soccer Fan Three is not amenable to jurisdiction in State B, Soccer Fan One may need to choose a different venue, bring a separate action against Soccer Fan Three, or postpone (or abandon) his claim against Soccer Fan Three.

Answer (B) is wrong: As explained in Answer (D), if Soccer Fan Two is subject to personal jurisdiction in State B, then venue is proper under 28 U.S.C. § 1391(b)(3) regardless of the fact that no substantial part of the events or omissions giving rise to the claim occurred in State B.

Answer (C) is wrong: Nothing in 28 U.S.C. § 1391(b) requires all defendants to join in a motion challenging venue.

Answer (D) is the best choice: 28 U.S.C. § 1391(b) provides two primary bases for venue, plus a third catch-all basis that applies when neither of the other two applies. Section 1391(b)(1) authorizes venue based on the parties' residence, and applies only when all defendants are residents of the same State. Section 1391(c) defines residence for an individual as the place of domicile. Accordingly, because the two defendants are individuals who are domiciled in different States, venue cannot be based on the defendants' residence. Section 1391(b)(2) authorizes venue in any district where a substantial part of the events or omissions giving rise to the claim occurred. Here, the events occurred in a foreign country where there are (obviously) no U.S. District Courts, so venue cannot be based on the location of the occurrence. Section 1391(b)(3) addresses venue when the other two provisions are not available, and authorizes venue in such circumstances in any district where any defendant is subject to the court's personal jurisdiction with respect to the action. Accordingly, if Soccer Fan Two is subject to personal jurisdiction in State B—quite likely because it is Soccer Fan Two's State of domicile—then venue is proper under 28 U.S.C. § 1391(b)(3).

134. **Answer (A) is the best choice:** Service of original process must be completed within 90 days after the complaint is filed. (This period was shortened by the 2015 amendments to the Rules from 120 days.) If service is not made within that 90-day period, the court "must" dismiss without prejudice or direct that service be made within a specified time. *See* Rule 4(m). A defendant may raise this failure, and seek a dismissal on that ground, by pretrial motion filed under Rule 12(b)(5). *See Mikesell v. Taco Bell Corp.*, 300 F.R.D. 329, 330 (S.D. Ind. 2014). Because the service here was made 106 days after filing, it is untimely.

   Answer (B) is wrong: Serving within the applicable statute of limitations could be substantively important; some States hold that a lawsuit tolls their limitations statutes only if that lawsuit is both filed and served within the limitations period. *See Torre v. Brickey*, 278 F.3d 917, 919–20 (9th Cir. 2002). That substantive, merits effect is *in addition to* the requirement set by the Rules for timely service. As noted in Answer (A), service is only considered timely if it is completed within 90 days after filing (or within a different time later specified by the court).

   Answer (C) is wrong: As explained in Answer (A), the Rules formerly applied a 120-day deadline for service (under which this service would have been timely). That period, however, was shortened by the 2015 amendments to 90 days.

   Answer (D) is wrong: By its terms, granting relief for an untimely service is not discretionary or contingent upon prejudice under Rule 4(m). As explained in Answer (A), a court "must" either dismiss or extend the service period when the 90-day service window has not been satisfied. Consequently, Farmer's service here is most certainly untimely and, thus, vulnerable to a pre-answer dismissal motion—even if the judge, upon considering it, chooses to impose an extension remedy rather than an outright dismissal.

135. **Answer (A) is the best choice:** The scheduling order rule was amended in 2015 to mandate greater personal involvement by the judge in the progress of civil litigation. One of the innovations encompassed by this mandate was to direct the judge to issue a scheduling order only after convening a scheduling conference by "direct simultaneous communication." *See* Rule 16(b) advisory committee's note to 2015 amendment. This allows the judge to hold the conference in person, by telephone, or through more sophisticated electronic means, but disallows mere consultation by mail. *See* Rule 16(b)(1)(B).

   Answer (B) is wrong: The scheduling order rule not only permits, but requires, that the order limit the time for amending the pleadings. *See* Rule 16(b)(3)(A).

   Answer (C) is wrong: The scheduling order rule allows (but does not require) the order to modify the timing for the parties' initial disclosures. *See* Rule 16(b)(3)(B)(i).

   Answer (D) is wrong: The scheduling order rule also allows (but does not require) the order to obligate parties to seek a conference with the court prior to discovery motion filings. *See* Rule 16(b)(3)(B)(v).

136. **Answers (A) and (B) are wrong:** The complicated, fitful journey set by the *Erie* doctrine for determining whether to apply federal or State law is triggered only when the Rules of Decision Act's exception does not apply. That Act commands that federal courts apply State substantive law "except where the Constitution or treaties of the United States or Acts of Congress otherwise require or provide." *See* 28 U.S.C. § 1652. When a federal constitutional provision, treaty, or statute does, in fact, "otherwise require or provide," the *Erie* analysis will not compel the application of State law where the federal provision is valid and controlling. *See Hanna v. Plumer*, 380 U.S. 460, 472–74 (1965). *See also Stewart Org. Inc. v. Ricoh Corp.*, 487 U.S. 22 (1988). Testing for "outcome determination" and "countervailing federal issues" are components of the proper *Erie* inquiry, but they have no application where Congress has supplanted State substantive law, as it did in this hypothetical as explained in Answer (D).

Answer (C) is wrong: Although the *Erie* doctrine is most frequently implicated when a federal court sits in diversity, it also applies in supplemental jurisdiction cases for the same reason—just like in diversity cases, a federal court exercising its supplemental jurisdiction is providing a federal forum for a non-federal, State-law based dispute. *See D.S. v. E. Porter Cty. Sch. Corp.*, 981 F. Supp. 2d 805, 815 (N.D. Ind. 2013), *aff'd*, 799 F.3d 793 (7th Cir. 2015). Thus, although the *Erie* doctrine does not apply in this fact pattern for the reasons explained in Answer (D), there is no categorical preclusion of *Erie* in supplemental jurisdiction cases.

Answer (D) is the best choice: State substantive law supplies the "rule of decision" in all federal cases, unless "the Constitution or treaties of the United States or Acts of Congress otherwise require or provide." *See* 28 U.S.C. § 1652. Of course, when the federal Constitution, treaties, or statutes "otherwise require or provide," federal law is supreme and supplants contrary State law. *See* U.S. Const. art. VI. The inquiry for determining whether a law is substantive (dealing with "rights and duties recognized by substantive law") or procedural ("the judicial process for enforcing" those rights and duties) can sometimes be elusive. *See Hanna v. Plumer*, 380 U.S. 460, 464 (1965). Here, however, that answer is not unclear. A U.S. treaty granted Student, a citizen of Country X, the substantive right to use a passport for photo identification purposes. The contrary law of the State where College is located is, therefore, supplanted. *See Shady Grove Orthopedic Assocs., P.A. v. Allstate Ins. Co.*, 559 U.S. 393, 406 (2010) ("Congress has undoubted power to supplant state law . . .").

137. **Answer (A) is the best choice:** The Judiciary Code, 28 U.S.C. § 1292(b), establishes a procedure for appeal from interlocutory orders. Pursuant to this procedure, before a party may take an immediate appeal of an otherwise unappealable interlocutory order, two events must occur. First, the district court must determine that the order "involves a controlling question of law as to which there is substantial ground for difference of opinion and that an immediate appeal from the order may materially advance the ultimate termination of the litigation." Second, the court of appeals must then exercise its discretion to allow the immediate appeal. Thus, if both the trial court and the court of appeals exercised their discretion, pursuant to 28 U.S.C. § 1292(b), the consumers could take an immediate appeal. *See In re Text Messaging Antitrust Litigation,* 630 F.3d 622, 624 (7th Cir. 2010).

Answer (B) is wrong: Ordinarily, an order that disposes of less than all claims in a lawsuit is not immediately appealable. *See Acumen Re Management Corp. v. General Sec. Nat. Ins. Co.,* 769 F.3d 135, 143 (2d Cir. 2014). In an appropriate instance, the district court may direct entry of a final judgment as to one or more, but fewer than all, claims or parties, but this is the exception not the rule, and does not occur automatically. *See* Rule 54(b). Absent such a separate determination, there would be no appealable final order until the entire case resolves.

Answer (C) is wrong: As explained in Answer (A), interlocutory appeal is at the discretion of the courts, and 28 U.S.C. § 1292(b) does not authorize interlocutory appeal by consent.

Answer (D) is wrong: As explained in Answer (A), while interlocutory orders are ordinarily not immediately appealable, 28 U.S.C. § 1292(b) establishes a procedure that gives the courts discretion to allow immediate appeal of an interlocutory order under appropriate circumstances.

138. **Answer (A) is wrong:** Although courts test a *pro se* litigant's pleadings with a more relaxed or liberal eye, *see Erickson v. Pardus,* 551 U.S. 89, 94 (2007), *pro se* pleadings must still satisfy the controlling pleading standards, even though they might be "inartfully" phrased. Thus, contrary to this Answer, *pro se* pleaders are not altogether relieved of their obligation to state sufficient facts to support a cognizable legal claim. *See Ahlers v. Rabinowitz,* 684 F.3d 53, 60 (2d Cir. 2012).

     Answer (B) is the best choice: Rule 12(e) governs motions for a more definite statement. It authorizes a motion when a pleading is "so vague and ambiguous that the party cannot reasonably prepare a response." Courts have held that the fact that the defendant has filed an answer undermines the defendant's ability to argue that it "cannot reasonably prepare a response." *See Boswell v. Panera Bread Co.,* 91 F.Supp.3d 1141, 1144 (E.D. Mo. 2015). Accordingly, because Department Store already filed an answer, it cannot satisfy the requirements for a motion for a more definite statement in Rule 12(e).

     Answer (C) is wrong: Rule 12(g)(2) provides that a party must join all its Rule 12 motions in a single motion, except as provided in Rule 12(h) governing failure to state a claim, failure to join a party under Rule 19, or lack of subject-matter jurisdiction. Accordingly, Department Store's motion for a more definite statement would be barred if it had already filed another Rule 12 motion. However, as explained in Answer (B) above, not only must the complaint be vague and ambiguous, it must be so vague and ambiguous that Department Store could not reasonably answer it. Department Store's answer belies any such contention.

     Answer (D) is wrong: Although Rule 12(h)(2) allows a party to assert failure to state a claim as late as trial, Department Store did not file a *motion* for failure to state a claim under Rule 12(b)(6) (though it did preserve that *defense* in its answer). Rather, it filed a motion for a more definite statement under Rule 12(e). As explained in Answer (B), Department Store's demonstrated ability to file an answer undermined its ability to meet Rule 12(e)'s requirement that the pleading be so vague and ambiguous that the opposing party could not reasonably prepare its response.

139. **Answer (A) is the best choice:** The right to a jury trial under the Seventh Amendment of the U.S. Constitution is generally preserved only for "Suits at common law." Ordinarily, and absent a specially-created entitlement otherwise, jury trials are therefore permitted in claims seeking legal remedies—money damages—and not to equitable actions seeking relief like injunctions. Although the investor here is seeking money, it is in the form of restitution—return of her money, not money damages. Restitution is an equitable remedy that does not trigger the right to a jury trial. *See, e.g., First Nat. Bank of Waukesha v. Warren,* 796 F.2d 999, 1000 (7th Cir. 1986).

     Answer (B) is wrong: Rule 38(b)(1) of the Federal Rules of Civil Procedure expressly allows a jury trial demand to be included in a pleading.

     Answer (C) is wrong: As explained in Answer (A), restitution is an equitable remedy, to which the right to a jury trial ordinarily does not attach.

     Answer (D) is wrong: The Federal Rules of Civil Procedure do not set a time period for filing a motion to strike a jury trial demand. *See Jones-Hailey v. Corporation of Tennessee Valley Authority,* 660 F.Supp. 551, 553 (E.D. Tenn. 1987).

140. **Answer (A) is wrong:** Although a party may amend a pleading by written stipulation, that is not the only way to amend a pleading without court permission. Rule 15(a)(1) of the Federal Rules of Civil Procedure allows amendment once as a matter of course without a stipulation from opposing parties if the other conditions are met.

Answer (B) is wrong: The period for amending a pleading as a matter of course under Rule 15(a)(1) is 21 days, not 30 days.

Answer (C) is the best choice: Rule 15(a)(1) allows a party to amend any pleading one time as a matter of course if the party files the amended pleading within 21 days of serving the pleading or within 21 days of service by an opposing party of a responsive pleading or a motion under Rule 12(b), (e), or (f), whichever is earlier.

Answer (D) is wrong: The Rule 15 language requiring claims in an amended pleading to arise out of the same conduct, transaction, or occurrence set out—or attempted to be set out—in the original pleading only applies to the relation back doctrine as set forth in Rule 15(c), which affects the statute of limitations analysis. No such relatedness requirement is necessary for the general right of amendment under Rule 15(a).

141. **Answer (A) is wrong:** As explained in Answer (D), a Rule 15(d) supplemental pleading (not a Rule 15(a) "amendment") is the proper way to address events that occur after the filing of the initial complaint. Even if an amendment had been the proper course (which it is not), a plaintiff may not amend a pleading as a matter of course more than 21 days after the defendant files its answer under Rule 15(a)(1)(B) of the Federal Rules of Civil Procedure.

Answer (B) is wrong: As explained in Answer (D), a Rule 15(d) supplemental pleading (not a Rule 15(a) "amendment") is the proper way to address events that occur after the filing of the initial complaint.

Answer (C) is wrong: Unlike with amendments, there is no right to file a supplemental pleading as a matter of course. *See Zenith Radio Corp. v. Hazeltine Research, Inc.,* 401 U.S. 321 (1971). Rather, leave of court is always required to file a supplemental pleading.

Answer (D) is the best choice: Rule 15(d) authorizes parties, on motion and with reasonable notice, to file supplemental pleadings "setting out any transaction, occurrence, or event that happened after the date of the pleading to be supplemented." A supplemental pleading does not supplant the original pleading. Accordingly, the original complaint and answer will remain in effect following the filing of a supplement to the complaint.

142. **Answer (A) is wrong:** A report and recommendation is required in certain circumstances, such as under Rules 52 and 72 of the Federal Rules of Civil Procedure for special masters and magistrate judges, but not for a district court judge following a bench trial, as explained in Answer (B).

Answer (B) is the best choice: Rule 52 requires at the conclusion of a bench trial that the district court make findings of fact and conclusions of law on the record. Although the findings of fact and conclusions of law need not address all of the evidence presented at trial, they must contain sufficient detail to permit meaningful appellate review. *See, e.g., Valsamis v. Gonzalez-Romero,* 748 F.3d 61, 63 (1st Cir. 2014). The findings and conclusions here do not contain any detail.

Answer (C) is wrong: The court's obligation to make findings of fact and conclusions of law is automatic and mandatory; the parties do not need to request them. *See In re Frescati Shipping Co. Ltd.,* 718 F.3d 184, 196 (3d Cir. 2013).

Answer (D) is wrong: Although the court hears the evidence and has broad discretion in assessing the credibility of witnesses, those functions are in addition to the court's obligation under Rule 52 to make findings of fact and conclusions of law.

143. **Answer (A) is wrong:** The original laying of venue and the transferring of venue once laid are two different legal propositions. Merely showing that venue would be proper somewhere else is not the dispositive inquiry in transfer motions. Instead, transferring *away* from the venue the plaintiff has chosen is appropriate when that original venue was defective, *see* 28 U.S.C. § 1406(a); or when a different venue would better serve the convenience of the parties and witnesses in the interests of justice, *id.* at § 1404(a). Moreover, in addition to conducting the wrong inquiry, this Answer performed that wrong inquiry incorrectly. This Answer posits that original venue would have been proper in California because both Power Company and CalFreight reside there. But proper original venue examines the residence of the defendants, not the plaintiffs; therefore, the residence of Power Company (the plaintiff) is inapplicable to the laying of proper venue. *See* 28 U.S.C. § 1391(b)(1). Instead, venue is generally proper in any judicial district which any defendant resides, so long as all defendants are residents of that same State. *See id.* Business entities that can sue or be sued in their common names—like the two defendants here—are considered residents of any judicial district where they are subject to the court's personal jurisdiction in the pending action. *See id.* at § 1391(e)(2). Here, there are two defendants: CalFreight, which is deemed to reside in California; and Railroad, which is not. Thus, the reasoning of Answer (A) is flawed not simply for applying the incorrect test, but for applying that incorrect test improperly.

Answer (B) is the best choice: It is true that venue would not have been proper in California at the time of the original filing. As noted in Answer (A), venue based on residency would have failed in California. The remaining venue option—namely, where a substantial part of the events or omissions giving rise to the claim occurred—would also have failed in California, since the sole act of negligence here (momentary, careless inattention) occurred on the tracks in Texas. *See* 28 U.S.C. § 1391(b)(2). However, when a transfer of venue is sought for convenience of the parties or witnesses or in the interest of justice, venue need not be originally proper in the new destination, provided *all* parties consent to the new location. *See id.* at § 1404(a). Here, both defendants have agreed to the sole plaintiff's proposed new venue. Ordinarily, that will be sufficient to grant the transfer.

Answer (C) is wrong: For the reasons noted in Answer (B), although venue in California would have *originally* been improper, a convenience transfer to a consented-to district is authorized by statute. This motion would not be denied.

Answer (D) is wrong: Congress has expressly authorized a convenience transfer of venue to any district or division to which all parties have consented. *See* 28 U.S.C. § 1404(a). Because, as explained in Answer (B), such consent exists here, the motion would have been granted, not denied.

144. **Answer (A) is the best choice:** A federal court typically applies the choice-of-law rules of the State where the federal court is located. *See Klaxon Co. v. Stentor Elec. Mfg. Co.,* 313 U.S. 487, 496 (1941). However, when a case is transferred from a proper venue to another proper venue, the choice-of-law provisions from the first venue follow the case. *See Van Dusen v. Barrack,* 376 U.S. 612, 615 (1964). Congress authorizes in 28 U.S.C. § 1391(b)(1) venue in any district where any defendant resides, as long as all defendants reside in the State where the district is located. Additionally, 28 U.S.C. § 1391(c)(1) defines an individual's residence for venue purposes as the individual's place of domicile. Because the man was a domicile, and therefore resident, of State A and there are no other defendants, venue was proper in State A. If State A's choice-of-law provisions dictate applying the law of State C, under which the woman's claim was untimely, the transfer will not change that outcome and the court will likely grant the motion to dismiss.

Answer (B) is wrong: The *Erie* doctrine governs what is sometimes known as "vertical" choice-of-law—the choice between federal and State law. Here, because the question implicates substantive law, the federal court will indeed apply State law. But that does not complete the inquiry. Rather, the federal court must next decide *which* State's law to apply. This is the "horizontal" choice-of-law inquiry—the choice between the law of the various States—and is typically determined by reference to the forum state's choice-of-law statute. Answer (A) explains which choice-of-law provisions a federal court will apply following transfer of venue.

Answer (C) is wrong: As explained in Answer (B), the *Erie* doctrine governs the choice between federal and State law, and State choice-of-law provisions govern the choice between the law of the various States. Answer (A) explains which choice-of-law provisions a federal court will apply following transfer of venue.

Answer (D) is wrong: As explained in Answer (A), following transfer from a proper venue, the transferee court will apply the law dictated by the choice-of-law provisions in the transferor State.

145. **Answer (A) is the best choice:** To be proper, an appeal in a federal civil case must be filed within 30 days after entry of the judgment appealed from. *See* Fed. R. App. P. 4(a)(1)(A). Because Homeowner's notice of appeal preceded the entry of final judgment, it was premature. However, a prematurely filed notice of appeal is treated, under the federal appeals rules, as filed on the date that the judgment is later entered. *See* Fed. R. App. P. 4(a)(2). Consequently, Homeowner's premature notice was deemed to have remained dormant until the recuperated judge entered the final judgment, at which time the notice immediately took effect.

Answer (B) is wrong: As explained in Answer (A), the 30-day period for filing a notice of appeal runs from entry of the final judgment, not from the oral announcement of a judge's intent to do so.

Answer (C) is wrong: As explained in Answer (A), Homeowner's appeal was prematurely— but not *improperly*—filed, and sufficed to perfect a proper appeal once the judge entered the final judgment.

Answer (D) is wrong: As explained in Answer (A), Homeowner's appeal did precede the filing of an appealable final order in the litigation, but that did not render the notice of appeal a "nullity"; to the contrary, under the federal appeals rules, the notice simply laid dormant until the appealable final order was entered.

146. **Answer (A) is wrong:** In *Mullane v. Central Hanover Bank & Trust Co.*, 339 U.S. 306 (1950), the Supreme Court held that the Constitution requires that service be reasonably calculated to apprise the accountant of the action. Service at the accountant's office by handing it to a company employee who promised to deliver it to the accountant might well satisfy this constitutional minimum. However, that is not the only requirement for proper service. Rather, service must also satisfy the requirements imposed by the Federal Rules of Civil Procedure. Rule 4 governs service of original process, and Rule 4(e) governs service on an individual within the United States. It authorizes personal service, abode service, agent service, service authorized by a specific federal law, and as explained in Answer (C), service by a method authorized for use in the courts of general jurisdiction in the State where the federal court is located. Because service at the defendant's regular place of business is not authorized by Rule 4(e), service on the accountant was only proper if authorized by State law.

Answer (B) is wrong: As explained in Answers (A) and (C), in addition to authorizing specific methods of service, such as personal, abode, or agent service, Rule 4(e) also authorizes service by a method authorized for use in the courts of general jurisdiction in the State where the federal court is located. Thus, the analysis must consider the rules for service in both the Federal Rules of Civil Procedure and the law of the State where the federal court is located.

Answer (C) is the best choice: Rule 4(e)(1) of the Federal Rules of Civil Procedure authorizes service of the complaint and summons by a method allowed in the courts of general jurisdiction in the State where the district court is located. Although, as explained in Answer (B), Rule 4(e) does not include service at the defendant's regular place of business in its list of permitted service means, many States do authorize such service. *See Golub v. U.S.*, 593 Fed. Appx. 546, 549 (7th Cir. 2014).

Answer (D) is wrong: Rule 4(e) does not require a plaintiff to attempt the methods of service expressly described in Rule 4(e) before using a method allowed in the courts of general jurisdiction in the State where the district court is located.

147. **Answer (A) is wrong:** As Answer (D) explains, the second dismissal of an action asserting or including the same claim as a previously dismissed action is deemed to be an adjudication on the merits, or with prejudice, under Rule 41(a)(1)(B) of the Federal Rules of Civil Procedure. This two-dismissal rule does not depend on whether there are substantive differences between the applicable law in the different jurisdictions, as long as the various actions include the same "claim." Rule 41(a)(1)(B).

Answer (B) is wrong: As Answer (D) explains, the second dismissal of an action asserting or including the same claim as a previously dismissed action is deemed to be an adjudication on the merits, or with prejudice, under Rule 41(a)(1)(B). The two-dismissal rule does not depend on whether the plaintiff was acting in good faith or was harassing the defendant. Rule 41(a)(1)(B).

Answer (C) is wrong: Rule 41(a)(2) allows the court to impose conditions on the dismissal of an action by court order, including an award of attorney's fees. *See, e.g., Steinert v. Winn Group, Inc.*, 440 F.3d 1214, 1222 (10th Cir. 2006). That provision, however, is entirely separate from the two-dismissal rule in Rule 41(a)(1)(B). Furthermore, the problem does not state that the court imposed such a condition.

Answer (D) is the best choice: Rule 41(a)(1)(B) sets out the "two-dismissal" rule, which provides that, "if the plaintiff previously dismissed any federal- or state-court action based on or including the same claim, a notice of dismissal operates as an adjudication on the merits." Thus, even though the man stated that his second dismissal was without prejudice, by operation of Rule 41, it functioned as a dismissal on the merits and therefore precludes a third action.

148. **Answer (A) is wrong:** As courts of limited jurisdiction, the right to litigate in federal court is never presumed. To the contrary, federal subject-matter jurisdiction is presumed *not* to exist until the party invoking it establishes otherwise. *See Kokkonen v. Guardian Life Ins. Co. of Am.*, 511 U.S. 375, 377 (1994). *See also* Rule 8(a)(1).

Answer (B) is wrong: As explained in Answer (D) below, a missing amount in controversy allegation can be addressed in the defendant's notice of removal, and thus, such a case might still qualify for diversity jurisdiction.

Answer (C) is wrong: To properly invoke the federal diversity jurisdiction, the plaintiffs must not share a common citizenship with any of the defendants, and the amount in controversy must exceed $75,000, exclusive of interests and costs. *See* 28 U.S.C. § 1332(a). The standard for satisfying this amount of controversy requirement is often a forgiving one, and never compels the invoking party to prove a qualifying amount to a legal certainty. *See Dart Cherokee Basin Operating Co., LLC v. Owens*, 135 S. Ct. 547, 553–54 (2014). Indeed, the claim may result in a recovery below the jurisdictional threshold or may lose outright, all without divesting the federal court of jurisdiction. *See St. Paul Mercury Indem. Co. v. Red Cab Co.*, 303 U.S. 283, 289 (1938).

Answer (D) is the best choice: When, as here, the applicable State has forbidden the plaintiff to demand a specific sum, the defendant may fill the gap by alleging in its notice of removal that the claim satisfies the jurisdictional minimum. *See* 28 U.S.C. § 1446(c)(2)(A)(ii). If that allegation is challenged or questioned, the defendant must then satisfy the federal judge—by a preponderance of the evidence only—that the amount in controversy exceeds the jurisdictional threshold. *See id.* at § 1446(c)(2)(B). *See also Dart Cherokee Basin Operating Co., LLC v. Owens*, 135 S. Ct. 547, 553–54 (2014).

149. **Answer (A) is wrong:** As Answer (B) explains, the U.S. Government can be defaulted but, as Answer (D) explains, although default judgments can be entered against the U.S. Government, a special process governs such proceedings that makes them unlike those encountered by other defendants.

Answer (B) is wrong: The U.S. Government can be defaulted. *See Alameda v. Secretary of Health, Educ., & Welfare*, 622 F.2d 1044, 1048 (1st Cir. 1980). However, as explained in Answer (D), a judgment upon that default can only be entered if the requisite prior showing is first made.

Answer (C) is wrong: As explained in Answer (D), though disfavored, a default judgment can be entered against the U.S. Government, provided the requisite showing by claimant is made.

Answer (D) is the best choice: Judgments entered against the U.S. Government are borne by taxpayers; consequently, default judgments against the federal government are disfavored. *See Harvey v. U.S.*, 685 F.3d 939, 946 (10th Cir. 2012). But such default judgments are not foreclosed entirely. By evidence satisfactory to the presiding judge, if the claimant carries the burden of establishing a claim or right-to-relief against the U.S. Government, a default judgment can be entered. *See* Rule 55(d); *Campbell v. U.S.*, 375 Fed. Appx. 254, 261 (3d Cir. 2010).

150. **Answer (A) is the best choice:** Normally, a court will view all evidence in the light most favorable to the nonmoving party and will deny a motion for judgment as a matter of law when there is conflicting evidence on both sides of an issue. *See Gallway v. U.S.*, 319 U.S. 372, 404–05 (1943). However, a court will not deny a motion for judgment as a matter of law simply because the nonmoving party offers testimony contradicting proven physical facts. *See O'Connor v. Pennsylvania R. Co.*, 308 F.2d 911, 915 (2d Cir. 1962). Thus, if the court concluded that the United States Weather Bureau data conclusively demonstrated that the ice did not come from a previous snowstorm, it would not allow the pedestrian to create a factual dispute simply by contradicting that evidence with the pedestrian's testimony.

Answer (B) is wrong: It is generally true that a court will not make credibility determinations in the context of a motion for judgment as a matter of law. *See Reeves v. Sanderson Plumbing Prods., Inc.*, 530 U.S. 133, 150 (2000). As explained in Answer (A), however, the court may disregard witness testimony that is contradicted by physical facts that are conclusively established by documentary or non-testamentary evidence.

Answer (C) is wrong: As explained in Answer (A), a court will, under appropriate circumstances, deem physical facts so conclusively established by documentary or *non-testamentary* evidence that the court will not credit contradictory *testimony*. That rule is far from absolute, however, and there is no fixed rule that all documents are elevated above all testimony. To the contrary, as explained in Answer (A), in general the court will decline to weigh and compare conflicting testimony in the context of a motion for judgment as a matter of law, and instead will deny the motion when presented with conflicting testimony, unless the non-testamentary evidence establishing the disputed fact is so conclusive as to render conflicting testimony not credible.

Answer (D) is wrong: As explained in Answer (A), if the court deems evidence of a physical fact sufficiently established, it will not view contradictory testimony as creating a genuine issue of fact precluding judgment as a matter of law.

151. **Answer (A) is wrong:** The Federal Rules of Civil Procedure do not explicitly approve email service of original process. However, the Rules permit service on corporations, partnerships, and associations in any manner permitted by the law of the State where the service is made. *See* Rule 4(h)(1)(A). Consequently, if State law would permit service by email, so, too, would the federal court there.

Answer (B) is wrong: To satisfy the U.S. Constitution's Due Process Clause, service of process must indeed be reasonably calculated, under all the circumstances, to afford notice and an opportunity to be heard. *See Mullane v. Cent. Hanover Bank & Trust Co.*, 339 U.S. 306, 314 (1950). However, service here was not valid because "all" the circumstances that must be considered now include the failed email transmission notice, as explained in Answer (C) below.

Answer (C) is the best choice: A party serving original process may well satisfy the constitutional standard by *selecting* a means for service that appears to be, under the then-known circumstances, reasonably calculated to impart notice and permit an opportunity to be heard. However, if the serving party comes to learn that the service has failed to achieve its twin goals, a failure to undertake a further effort at service may violate due process if other, reasonable steps were available to deliver notice. *See Jones v. Flowers*, 547 U.S. 220, 229–39 (2006). Here, the attorney received actual notification that the original email failed and was invited to "try again later." The attorney also had the postal mailing address for Publishing House. Electing to neither re-transmit the email nor send the papers by postal mail likely violated the Constitution's Due Process Clause.

Answer (D) is wrong: For the reasons explained in Answer (A), email service may well be proper procedurally, if it is authorized by applicable State law. However, for the reasons explained in Answer (C), the attorney's failure here to take either of two other, reasonable steps to deliver notice to Publishing House likely violated constitutional due process.

152. **Answer (A) is wrong:** As noted in Answer (C), the deadline for taking an appeal in most civil cases is 30 days after entry of the judgment or order appealed from. The appeal time does not begin to run simply upon the return of a jury verdict. *See generally Hamilton v. Leavy*, 204 F. App'x 125, 126 (3d Cir. 2006).

Answer (B) is wrong: As explained in Answer (A), the appeal period runs from entry of the judgment on the docket, and not from the date it is issued by the court. *See Lemps v. Holder*, 636 F.3d 365, 367 (7th Cir. 2011).

Answer (C) is the best choice: Litigants intending to appeal from a federal civil judgment must file their Notice of Appeal within 30 days after entry of the judgment or order appealed from. *See* Fed. R. App. P. 4(a)(1)(A). "Entry" is defined as the date the judgment is entered in the civil docket (provided that judgment satisfies the requirement, if applicable, of being set out on a separate document). *See* Fed. R. App. P. 4(a)(7)(A). Consequently, the date court personnel type the judgment onto the docket is indeed the appeal-time triggering event.

Answer (D) is wrong: As explained in Answer (A), the appeal period runs from entry of the judgment on the docket, and not from the date it is received by the litigants. *See Nguyen v. Southwest Leasing & Rental Inc.*, 282 F.3d 1061, 1066 (9th Cir. 2002).

153. **Answer (A) is wrong:** Rule 11 of the Federal Rules of Civil Procedure authorizes the court to impose non-monetary sanctions designed to deter future misconduct, and continuing legal education fits within this framework. *See, e.g., Bergeron v. Northwest Publications Inc.,* 165 F.R.D. 518, 522 (D. Minn. 1996).

Answer (B) is the best choice: Because the purpose of Rule 11 sanctions is deterrence, Rule 11(c)(5)(A) explicitly prohibits sanctions against a represented party for violations of the Rule 11 certification relating to the legal support for the positions taken in submissions to the court. In other words, the lawyer is the one who is trained to evaluate the law and who is responsible for making sure the client's positions have appropriate legal support, so sanctioning the lawyer would deter future violations but sanctioning the party would not.

Answer (C) is wrong: Rule 11 also authorizes the court to impose monetary sanctions, and, as explained in Answer (B), such sanctions are appropriately imposed on the lawyer for violations of the certification regarding legal support for the party's positions. Rule 11(c)(5)(A).

Answer (D) is wrong: Rule 11 authorizes the court to impose non-monetary sanctions designed to deter future misconduct, and dismissal of complaint lacking legal support fits within this framework. *See Carman v. Treat,* 7 F.3d 1379, 1382 (8th Cir. 1993).

154. **Answer (A) is wrong:** As explained in Answer (C), the time limitation for bringing a motion for relief from a final judgment based on newly discovered evidence is one year, not two years. *See* Rule 60(c)(1).

Answer (B) is wrong: As explained in Answer (C), although one of the conditions for a motion for relief from a final judgment based on newly discovered evidence is that the moving party could not have discovered the evidence in time to move for a new trial, that is not the condition that dooms the construction worker's motion. Rather, the motion is untimely under Rule 60(c)(1), which sets a one-year time limit after entry of judgment for bringing a Rule 60(b)(2) motion.

Answer (C) is the best choice: Rule 60(b)(2) authorizes a party to seek relief from a final judgment based on "newly discovered evidence that, with reasonable diligence, could not have been discovered in time to move for a new trial under Rule 59(b)." However, Rule 60(c)(1) sets an outer time limit of one year after entry of judgment to bring a motion under Rule 60(b)(2). Because the construction worker did not file his Rule 60(b)(2) motion until 23 months after entry of judgment, his motion was untimely and the court should deny it on that basis.

Answer (D) is wrong: As explained in Answer (C), Rule 60(b)(2) authorizes a party to seek relief from a final judgment based on newly discovered evidence if the party files the motion within one year of the entry of final judgment and the party could not have discovered the evidence in time to move for a new trial. The Rule does not require that the failure to discover the evidence have been caused by an opposing party. *See* Rule 60(b)(2).

155. **Answer (A) is wrong:** Uncontested motions cannot be granted automatically for that reason. A party moving for dismissal bears the burden of proof, and the court must be persuaded—even in the absence of a response from the adversary—that the argument made in the motion entitles the movant to the dismissal it seeks. *See Servicios Azucareros de Venezuela, C.A. v. John Deere Thibodeaux, Inc.*, 702 F.3d 794, 806 (5th Cir. 2012).

    Answer (B) is the best choice: As explained in Answer (A), unless the court is satisfied that the position pressed on the motion entitles the movant to relief, the motion will be denied.

    Answer (C) is wrong: As explained in Answer (A), Harbor Worker's claim is not unripe simply because Employer asserts that it is unripe. The court has an independent duty—regardless of whether Harbor Worker's lawyer opposed the motion—to confirm that the motion warrants a dismissal.

    Answer (D) is wrong: A pre-answer motion to dismiss is a proper vehicle for testing whether the complaint asserts a legal theory that is not cognizable as a matter of law. *See Zixiang Li v. Kerry*, 710 F.3d 995, 999 (9th Cir. 2013). Rule 12(b)(6) expressly authorizes dismissals when the complaint fails to state a claim upon which relief can be granted.

156. **Answer (A) is wrong:** A responding party may file a "general denial" (that is, a simple statement advising that each and every allegation in the complaint is denied). *See* Rule 8(b)(3). Such general denials, though permitted, are infrequently used since the responding party—constrained by the ethics in the pleading mandate of Rule 11—must be able to honestly deny every single statement in the complaint. *See* 5 CHARLES ALAN WRIGHT & ARTHUR R. MILLER, FEDERAL PRACTICE & PROCEDURE § 1265, at 548 (2004).

    Answer (B) is the best choice: An allegation that is partly false and partly true may not be denied in its entirety. Instead, the pleader must admit that portion of the allegation that is true and then deny the rest. *See* Rule 8(b)(4).

    Answer (C) is wrong: A pleader who lacks knowledge or information that is sufficient to allow a belief as to the truth or falsity of an allegation may state that, and such a statement is considered to have the effect of a denial. *See* Rule 8(b)(5).

    Answer (D) is wrong: Parties raising defenses and objections listed in Rule 12(b) are authorized to assert them by a motion seeking immediate resolution by the court. *See* Rule 12(b). Such motions *must* be filed prior to the filing of an answer. *See* Rule 12(b). When properly filed, such motions postpone the time for the filing of an answer until 14 days after the court the rules on those motions. *See* Rule 12(a)(4).

157. **Answer (A) is the best choice:** Venue is proper over a non-resident of the United States "in any judicial district." *See* 28 U.S.C. § 1391(c)(3). Construing a predecessor to this statute, the U.S. Supreme Court explained that the law codifies the longstanding federal view that lawsuits against aliens "are wholly outside the operation of all the federal venue laws." *Brunette Mach. Works, Ltd. v. Kockum Indus., Inc.*, 406 U.S. 706, 714 (1972). Thus, because Molecular Biologist is subject to venue in any and every federal judicial district, he will lose his motion. This, of course, means only that Molecular Biologist has no venue objection; it does not address whether personal jurisdiction (something he did not challenge) was proper.

Answer (B) is wrong: The general federal venue statute permits venue where a substantial part of the events or omissions giving rise to the claim occurred. *See* 28 U.S.C. § 1391(b)(2). As Answer (A) explained, however, venue over alien defendants is treated differently.

Answer (C) is wrong: The general federal venue statute also permits venue where any defendant resides (so long as all defendants, in a multi-defendant lawsuit, reside in the same State). *See* 28 U.S.C. § 1391(b)(1). As Answer (A) explained, this provision does not limit the venue over alien defendants.

Answer (D) is wrong: A forum selection clause selecting a certain venue is likely to be enforced, absent a party bearing the "heavy burden" of proving it unenforceable. *See M/S Bremen v. Zapata Off-Shore Co.,* 407 U.S. 1, 17 (1972). But such a clause would not be needed here because, as explained in Answer (A), venue over an alien defendant is proper in any judicial district.

158. **Answer (A) is wrong:** The Rules authorize a court to alter or amend its judgment, a request often labeled in practice as a motion for "reconsideration." *See* Rule 59(e). This power exists to allow trial judges to clean up their own mistakes in the immediate post-judgment period. *See White v. New Hampshire Dep't of Employment Sec.*, 455 U.S. 445, 450 (1982). But a court generally will not use this authority to alter or amend a judgment on the basis of an issue to which the moving party had not earlier objected. *See Vasapolli v. Rostoff*, 39 F.3d 27, 36 (1st Cir. 1994) ("Unlike the Emperor Nero, litigants cannot fiddle as Rome burns. A party who sits in silence, withholds potentially relevant information, allows his opponent to configure the summary judgment record, and acquiesces in a particular choice of law does so at his peril.").

Answer (B) is the best choice: Courts may invoke their authority to alter to amend a judgment on the basis of newly discovered evidence, provided that evidence would likely change the outcome of the case, could not have been discovered earlier through proper diligence, and is not just cumulative or impeaching in nature. *Cf. Infusion Res., Inc. v. Minimed, Inc.*, 351 F.3d 688, 696–97 (5th Cir. 2003). Each of those elements seems present in this case.

Answer (C) is wrong: Courts generally will not invoke their authority to alter or amend a judgment on the basis of a legal argument that could have (and should have) been raised before entry of judgment. *See Markel Am. Ins. Co. v. Diaz-Santiago*, 674 F.3d 21, 32–33 (1st Cir. 2012) (noting that these alterations and amendments "are aimed at *re*consideration, not initial consideration," and refusing the defendant's "attempt to ante up and play a new hand when he is long past being a day late and well over a dollar short.").

Answer (D) is wrong: Courts ordinarily will not invoke their authority to alter or amend a judgment on the basis of a litigant's evolving view of the case, especially where that view is intended to reposition the case after the defeat of an original litigating position. *See Cochran v. Quest Software, Inc.*, 328 F.3d 1, 11 (1st Cir. 2003) ("Litigation is not a game of hopscotch. . . . Litigants normally must frame the issues in a case before the trial court rules. After that point, a litigant should not be allowed to switch from theory to theory like a bee in search of honey.").

159. **Answer (A) is wrong:** A plaintiff may join in a single federal action multiple defendants so long as: (i) the action asserts a right to relief against them jointly, severally, or in the alternative, (ii) which arises from the same transaction, occurrence, or series of transactions or occurrences, (iii) provided the action raises some question of law or fact common to all defendants. *See* Rule 20(a)(2). Although the transactional relatedness required of this Rule can sometimes be difficult to discern, it remains true that "[u]nrelated claims against different defendants belong in different suits." *See George v. Smith*, 507 F.3d 605, 607 (7th Cir. 2007). Merely showing that two defendants violated the same law in the same way will not alone satisfy the Rule 20(a)(2) test for transactional relatedness. *See AF Holdings, LLC v. Does 1-1058*, 752 F.3d 990, 998 (D.C. Cir. 2014). Here, the physical impediments in Food Store and Pet Store were designed by separate tenants, are structurally and legally unrelated to one another, and the decisions not to adjust them were made by each tenant. These facts do not demonstrate the requisite relatedness to permit the three-defendant joinder Customer proposes. *See Rush v. Sport Chalet, Inc.*, 779 F.3d 973, 975 (9th Cir. 2015).

Answer (B) is wrong: As explained in Answer (A), Food Store and Pet Store are separate tenants with different physical impediments that, the facts confirm, each store designed. The requisite transactional relatedness for permissive party joinder of both Food Store and Pet Store is absent.

Answer (C) is the best choice: Physical impediments that deny access to persons with disabilities are the responsibility of both the tenant who maintains them and the landlord who leases to that tenant, thereby supplying the transactional relatedness that Rule 20(a)(2) requires. *See Rush v. Sport Chalet, Inc.*, 779 F.3d 973, 974–75 (9th Cir. 2015). Accordingly, it is likely that Customer can jointly sue both the tenant (Food Store) and its landlord (Shopping Mall) for the allegedly unlawful physical impediment in Food Store, and/or jointly sue both the tenant (Pet Store) and its landlord (Shopping Mall) for the allegedly unlawful physical impediment in Pet Store.

Answer (D) is wrong: The goal of Rule 20 permissive party joinder is "to promote trial convenience and expedite the final determination of disputes, thereby preventing multiple lawsuits." *Mosley v. Gen. Motors Corp.*, 497 F.2d 1330, 1332 (8th Cir. 1974). When available, this type of joinder is obviously encouraged. As explained in Answer (C) above, there are some efficiencies Customer can obtain with Rule 20—by joining Shopping Mall in her lawsuit against Food Store and/or by joining Shopping Mall in her lawsuit against Pet Store. She is not required to file three separate lawsuits.

160. **Answer (A) is wrong:** Although the plain error standard sometimes allows an appellate court to review an issue that was not preserved by an objection or motion at the trial court level, it is an extraordinary measure not frequently used in civil cases. *See Walker v. Groot*, 867 F.3d 799, 802 (7th Cir. 2017). Here, there are no facts in the problem suggesting this extraordinary standard would apply.

Answer (B) is wrong: The clearly erroneous standard does apply to the trial judge's findings of fact. *See* Rule 52(a)(6). However, the applicability of this standard does not turn on whether there was an objection at trial. Furthermore, as explained in Answer (D), unless the contract was ambiguous, its interpretation is a matter of law reviewed *de novo*.

Answer (C) is wrong: Trial courts do have considerable discretion over many aspects of pretrial and trial proceedings, and those discretionary rulings are reviewed for abuse of discretion. *See Josendis v. Wall to Wall Residence Repairs, Inc.*, 662 F.3d 1292, 1306 (11th Cir. 2011). For example, most discovery rulings are discretionary and will only be reversed for abuse of discretion. *Id.* However, the court's findings of fact and conclusions of law are reviewed under the clearly erroneous and *de novo* standards, respectively. *See* Rule 52(a)(6).

Answer (D) is the best choice: In general, the court's findings of fact are reviewed under the "clearly erroneous" standard and its conclusions of law are reviewed *de novo*. *See* Rule 52(a)(6). The interpretation of contract language that is unambiguous is generally considered to be a matter of law, not fact, and therefore would be reviewed *de novo*. *BKCAP, LLC v. CAPTEC Franchise Tr. 2000-1*, 572 F.3d 353, 358 (7th Cir. 2009).

161. **Answer (A) is wrong:** In drafting an injunction order, a federal court must state the order's terms "specifically" and must "describe in reasonable detail . . . the act or acts restrained." *See* Rule 65(d)(1). Upon reading the order, an ordinary person should be clear what exactly is being forbidden. *See Scott v. Schedler*, 826 F.3d 207, 211 (5th Cir. 2016). Because the order here fails to supply any of that detail, it is likely to be vacated.

Answer (B) is wrong: Federal courts must also "state the reasons why" an injunction is being issued. *See* Rule 65(d)(1). The order here fails to provide any semblance of explanation and, for that reason, is vulnerable to being vacated.

Answer (C) is wrong: As explained in Answer (A), federal judges are required to be specific in their injunction orders. This requirement is not an idle, technical chore, but an obligation designed to avoid confusion by those whom the court intends to bind. *See Schmidt v. Lessard*, 414 U.S. 473, 476 (1974). The order here fails that standard.

Answer (D) is the best choice: Federal injunction orders can bind only those "who receive actual notice of it by personal service or otherwise." *See* Rule 65(d)(2). Where, as here, the enjoined party acquires actual notice of the order, a defect in service is insufficient to defeat the order's effect. *See Ex parte Lennon*, 166 U.S. 548, 554 (1897) ("To render a person amenable to an injunction, it is neither necessary that he should have been a party to the suit in which the injunction was issued, nor to have been actually served with a copy of it, so long as he appears to have had actual notice.").

162. **Answer (A) is wrong:** Federal litigants are permitted to specify that only certain, particular issues be tried by a jury. *See* Rule 38(c). Here, Zookeeper's only mention of a jury trial is, by its terms, limited to the question of the defendant's "negligence in installing the fence." Accordingly, that is the only issue that would be triable to a jury in Zookeeper's case. *See Lutz v. Glendale Union High Sch.*, 403 F.3d 1061, 1065 (9th Cir. 2005) ("A party seeking a jury trial thus has a choice: either list specific issues for the jury to consider, or make a general demand, which will be deemed to cover all issues triable to a jury. As the word 'otherwise' indicates, though, a jury demand will be deemed to cover all issues only if it doesn't specify particular issues.").

Answer (B) is the best choice: As explained in Answer (A), Zookeeper will receive a jury trial on the issue of the fence manufacturer's alleged negligence in installing the fence, and on that issue alone. *See Lutz v. Glendale Union High Sch.*, 403 F.3d 1061, 1065 (9th Cir. 2005) (noting court's obligation to remain "mindful that the purpose of a jury demand is to inform the court and opposing counsel that certain issues will be tried to a jury," and because plaintiff's complaint "asked for a jury on some issues but not others, a careful reader would not reasonably conclude that [plaintiff] wanted a jury on all issues presented in the complaint").

Answer (C) is wrong: As explained in Answers (A) and (B), guided by how Zookeeper's complaint was drafted, the court would find that Zookeeper is entitled only to a jury trial on the narrow issue of the fence manufacturer's alleged negligence in installing the fence. All other issues, including the amount of any damages, will be resolved by the court in a bench trial.

Answer (D) is wrong: Although Zookeeper's complaint request may seem odd, Rule 38(c) entitles litigants to request a jury trial for some but not all of the issues in dispute. (And no particular form or styling of the demand is required by Rule 38.) Zookeeper did so here, and Rule 38 compels that this request be honored. The one issue for which Zookeeper requested a jury trial—the question of the fence manufacturer's negligence in installing the fence—will be resolved by the jury.

163. **Answer (A) is wrong:** New trials may be awarded in federal court only for reasons that had been contemporaneously called to the court's attention during the trial. *See United States v. Walton*, 909 F.2d 915, 924 (6th Cir. 1990). If Spectator's attorney had failed to object when the image was offered by Arena, the right to contest its admission post-trial would be lost.

Answer (B) is the best choice: Post-verdict motions for judgment as a matter of law (JMOL) may not be made without having first made a pre-verdict motion for judgment on the same grounds. No such prerequisite exists for new trial motions, however. *See Pediatrix Screening, Inc. v. TeleChem Int'l, Inc.*, 602 F.3d 541, 546 (3d Cir. 2010) ("Unlike Rule 50, the text of Rule 59 does not require any pre-verdict motions."). Consequently, failure to make such a pre-verdict motion would not be good cause to deny Spectator's attorney's motion.

Answer (C) is wrong: Motions for new trial must be filed within 28 days of entry of the contested judgment. *See* Rule 59(b). Failure to do so would make the motion untimely.

Answer (D) is wrong: An error in admitting evidence is no basis for granting a new trial if the error was harmless (that is, it did "not affect any party's substantive rights"). *See* Rule 61. Wrongfully admitting evidence that is cumulative of other properly admitted evidence is usually harmless error. *See Jensen v. Solvay Chems., Inc.*, 721 F.3d 1180, 1184 (10th Cir. 2013).

164. **Answer (A) is wrong:** The federal time computation procedures generally exclude the triggering day and only begin counting the following day. *See* Rule 6(a)(1)(A). However, as explained in Answer (D), those procedures do not apply here.

Answer (B) is wrong: Prior to the 2009 Amendments to the Rules, intervening Saturdays, Sundays, and legal holidays were excluded in computing short time periods (those spanning less than 11 days). That approach was abrogated, however, by the 2009 Amendments.

Answer (C) is wrong: The federal time computation procedures ordinarily extend deadlines that would otherwise expire on a Saturday, Sunday, or legal holiday. *See* Rule 6(a)(1)(C) & 6(a)(2)(C). As explained in Answer (D), however, those procedures do not apply here.

Answer (D) is the best choice: The Rules establish procedures for computing time periods set in hours, in days, or in longer units. *See* Rule 6(a). Those procedures govern only when there is a time period to compute (*e.g.,* when a party must perform an act "within 14 days" of a certain event or court order). Those procedures "do not apply when a fixed time to act is set." *See* Rule 6(a) advisory committee note (2009) (adopting approach established by *Violette v. P.A. Days, Inc.,* 427 F.3d 1015, 1018 (6th Cir. 2005)). Because the court set a specific delivery deadline (a "date-certain") for the manuscript of September 1, the procedures used in computing time periods would have no bearing.

165. **Answer (A) is the best choice:** 28 U.S.C. § 1391(b)(1) authorizes venue based on the defendants' residences. It requires that all defendants be residents of the same State, then authorizes residence in any district where any of the defendants resides. Although corporations and partnerships are treated differently for purposes of citizenship in the diversity jurisdiction analysis, they are treated the same for purposes of residence and venue. 28 U.S.C. § 1391(c)(2) provides that an entity with the capacity to sue or be sued, "whether or not incorporated," shall be deemed to reside in any district where it would be subject to personal jurisdiction. Thus, unlike the citizenship analysis, the residence of a partnership is not based on the citizenship (or residence) of its partners, but instead is based on whether the partnership is subject to personal jurisdiction in the forum. Thus, Answer (A) properly conditions venue on Pesticide LP's personal jurisdiction status.

Answer (B) is wrong: While the convenience of the parties and witnesses and the interest of justice can be factors in the transfer of venue analysis under 28 U.S.C. §§ 1404 and 1406, those statutes only authorize transfer to a district where the case could have been brought originally, meaning, in part, one where venue is proper (absent consent by all parties). These concepts do not enter into the analysis of venue under 28 U.S.C. § 1391.

Answer (C) is wrong: Residence-based venue under 28 U.S.C. § 1391(b)(1) turns on the residence of the defendants—the plaintiff's residence does not factor into the federal venue analysis.

Answer (D) is wrong: As explained in Answer (A), the residences of the partners in a partnership do not determine the residence of the partnership for venue purposes.

166. **Answer (A) is wrong:** The general rule in federal court is that interim rulings that do not terminate a lawsuit in its entirety remain interlocutory and not subject to an immediate appeal. Instead, they must typically await the court's final judgment as to all parties. *See Sears, Roebuck & Co. v. Mackey*, 351 U.S. 427, 433–34 (1956). However, as explained in Answer (C), an exception to the general rule could be applicable here.

   Answer (B) is wrong: Although it is true, as Answer (C) confirms, that a district court must agree to permit Camper's immediate appeal, that permission, alone, would not be sufficient. Instead, both the district court and the court of appeals must agree to permit the appeal.

   Answer (C) is the best choice: A ruling that fully and finally resolves all claims against one of multiple defendants can be immediately appealed, provided the district court finds that there is "no just reason to delay" that appeal. *See* Rule 54(b). But the district court's determination is not binding on the court of appeals, which must independently confirm that the prerequisites for an immediate appeal are present. *See HSBC Bank USA, N.A. v. Townsend*, 793 F.3d 771, 778 (7th Cir. 2015). So, both courts must agree to the interlocutory appeal.

   Answer (D) is wrong: As explained in Answers (A) and (C), while the general rule in federal court is to permit appeals only from the final orders that terminate a lawsuit in its entirety, an exception is permitted in multi-party cases where the claims against one party are resolved completely (and, although not implicated by this fact pattern, in multi-claim cases where at least one claim is resolved completely).

167. **Answer (A) is wrong:** A motion for a new trial under Rule 59 must be filed within 28 days after entry of the judgment. *See* Rule 59(b). But a new trial is inappropriate for this situation, where it appears that the judgment contains a simple clerical error for which Rule 60(a) provides a remedy, as discussed in Answer (B).

   Answer (B) is the best choice: Rule 60(a) provides for relief from a judgment in the event of a clerical mistake, and that seems to be the best fit here. Such motions may be granted "whenever [a clerical error] is found in a judgment," *see* Rule 60(a); and, thus, is not bounded by a restrictive, fixed time period.

   Answer (C) is wrong: Rule 4(a)(1)(A) of the Federal Rules of Appellate Procedure requires that a party file a notice of appeal within 30 days of the entry of the judgment or order under appeal. Appeal periods are generally considered mandatory and jurisdictional. *See Bowles v. Russell*, 551 U.S. 205, 214 (2007). There are a few narrow circumstances where this period might be extended, such as when a party has filed certain post-trial motions, but the problem does not suggest any of these circumstances. Thus, an appeal would likely be deemed untimely. In any event, an appeal is unnecessary here, as Answer (B) explains.

   Answer (D) is wrong: As Answer (B) explains, Appliance Store may file a Rule 60 motion even though 61 days have elapsed since the entry of judgment.

168. **Answer (A) is the best choice:** The "most significant relationship" test for conflicts of laws is the one adopted by the Second Restatement and, for multi-State defamation lawsuits, prefers the law of the State where the allegedly defamed person was domiciled at the time of the publication, provided the publication had occurred in that State. *See* RESTATEMENT (SECOND) OF CONFLICT OF LAWS § 150(1) (1971). Accordingly, the federal court is most likely to apply the defamation laws of Wisconsin, the State of Dancer's domicile. *See McKee v. Cosby*, 874 F.3d 54, 59 (1st Cir. 2017).

   Answer (B) and (C) are wrong: As explained in Answer (A), application of the "most significant relationship" test ordinarily prefers the law of the State of the allegedly defamed person's domicile. So, both the State of Celebrity's domicile (California) and the State of the publisher (New York) are wrong.

   Answer (D) is wrong: To decide which State's substantive law to apply to a State-law claim, federal courts will generally follow the conflicts of law rules of the State in which they sit. *See Klaxon Co. v. Stentor Elec. Mfg. Co.*, 313 U.S. 487, 496 (1941). Accordingly, the federal court sitting in Massachusetts will indeed apply that State's law, but only its *conflicts* law; the *substantive defamation law* to be applied will be that of Wisconsin, as explained in Answer (A).

169. **Answer (A) is wrong:** The Federal Rules of Civil Procedure authorize service of process on a corporation by following the service rules of the State where the federal court sits. *See* Rule 4(e)(1) & 4(h)(1). Owner followed those State procedures here. However, meeting the requirements of Rule 4 does not necessarily also mean that Owner has satisfied the additional requirements for effective service imposed by the U.S. Constitution's Due Process Clause. Those two requirements often impose separate obligations. *See Williams v. GEICO Corp.*, 792 F. Supp. 2d 58, 65–66 (D.D.C. 2011). As explained in Answer (B), Owner's original service effort does not satisfy constitutional due process.

   Answer (B) is the best choice: Constitutional due process requires service of process in a manner that is "reasonably calculated, under all the circumstances, to apprise interested parties of the pendency of the action and afford them an opportunity to present their objections." *Mullane v. Cent. Hanover Bank & Tr. Co.*, 339 U.S. 306, 314 (1950). This requires that the method chosen for service "must be such as one desirous of actually informing the absentee might reasonably adopt to accomplish it." *Id.* at 315. The Supreme Court has ruled that this service standard is not satisfied when a sender knows that an attempted mail delivery failed and has a reasonable opportunity to accomplish actual service through other means, but fails to do so. *See Jones v. Flowers*, 547 U.S. 220, 229–39 (2006). Here, Owner knows that her original attempt at service has failed, and by merely consulting the defendant's Internet website, can rectify the error and accomplish actual service. To satisfy constitutional due process under these circumstances, Owner must re-serve using the updated address. Because this is a constitutional obligation, it applies regardless of whether the lawsuit is pending in federal court or State court.

   Answers (C) and (D) are wrong: As Answer (A) explained, Owner's original service effort met the service requirements imposed by the Federal Rules and State X's procedures. It did not, however, comport with constitutional due process, as Answer (B) demonstrated.

170. **Answers (A) and (B) are wrong:** 28 U.S.C. § 1292(b) authorizes the district courts to issue orders stating that issues are appropriate for interlocutory review when, "there is substantial ground for difference of opinion and . . . an immediate appeal from the order may materially advance the ultimate termination of the litigation." The party seeking interlocutory appeal must then apply to the court of appeals within ten days, and the court of appeals then has discretion to accept the interlocutory appeal. *Id.* Thus, interlocutory review under 28 U.S.C. § 1292(b) requires that both the district court and the court of appeals exercise their discretion to allow the appeal. As explained in Answer (C), 28 U.S.C. § 1292(a) allows Chemical Company to appeal immediately without depending on the discretion of two courts.

Answer (C) is the best choice: Ordinarily a party may only appeal final orders that resolve all the issues in the case, or may seek leave to take an interlocutory appeal under 28 U.S.C. § 1292(b) (as discussed in Answers (A) and (B)). However, 28 U.S.C. § 1292(a)(1) creates a right to an immediate appeal of rulings granting, denying, dissolving, continuing, or modifying a preliminary injunction. Thus, Chemical Company has a right to appeal the district court's preliminary injunction order.

Answer (D) is wrong: Some orders are only susceptible to appellate review by disobeying the order, then appealing any contempt sanctions. *See Hickman v. Taylor,* 329 U.S. 495, 500 (1947). As explained in Answer (C), however, rulings granting, denying, dissolving, continuing, or modifying a preliminary injunction are immediately appealable without resort to defying a court order and incurring contempt sanctions.

171. **Answer (A) is wrong:** Although Rule 12(d) allows a court to treat a Rule 12(b) motion as a motion for summary judgment, that is not the "only" way the court could consider the pleading, as explained in Answer (B). Be sensitive to absolute words like "only" in answers—they may convert an answer that sounds correct into one that is wrong.

Answer (B) is the best choice: When ruling on a Rule 12(b) motion, a court may take judicial notice of pleadings filed in other matters, even if not attached to or described in the complaint. *See Auto-Owners Ins. Co. v. Morris,* 191 F. Supp. 3d 1302, 1304 (N.D. Ala. 2016).

Answer (C) is wrong: As explained in Answer (B), while the general rule for some Rule 12(b) motions is that the parties and court are confined to consideration of the matters in the complaint, an exception exists for matters of which a court may take judicial notice.

Answer (D) is wrong: The court may take judicial notice of a pleading from another court proceeding, regardless of whether the parties consent. *See EduMoz, LLC v. Republic of Mozambique,* 968 F. Supp. 2d 1041, 1049 (C.D. Cal. 2013) (taking judicial notice over certain documents over one party's objection).

172. **Answer (A) is the best choice:** Rule 23(a)(2) establishes a prerequisite for a class action that "there are questions of law or fact common to the class." This prerequisite is sometimes referred to as "commonality." (In fact, in most commercial classes, the common questions must actually "predominate" over individual ones. *See* Rule 23(b)(3).) Thus, the court should not certify the class if Consumer's claim shares no questions of fact or law with the other members of the class.

Answer (B) is wrong: Rather than *defeating* class treatment, the presence of small claims actually *validates* using the class action device. One purpose of a class action is to authorize claims to be brought collectively where the claims are too small to be pursued individually. *See, e.g., Smilow v. Sw. Bell Mobile Sys., Inc.,* 323 F.3d 32, 41 (1st Cir. 2003).

Answer (C) is wrong: While merits issues are not strictly off-limits at the class certification stage, the court may only consider them "to the extent—but only to the extent—that they are relevant to determining whether the Rule 23 prerequisites for class certification are satisfied." *See Amgen Inc. v. Connecticut Ret. Plans & Tr. Funds,* 568 U.S. 455, 466 (2013). Thus, likelihood of success on the merits is not a prerequisite for class certification.

Answer (D) is wrong: The wording of this Answer is actually the opposite of what the class action rules require. Rule 23(a)(3) establishes as a prerequisite for a class action that "the claims or defenses of the representative parties are typical of the claims or defenses of the class." This prerequisite is sometimes referred to as "typicality." Thus, if the court found that the class representative had unique claims, atypical from the class he or she proposed to represent, it would not certify the class.

173. **Answers (A) and (B) are wrong:** As explained in Answer (D), if the defendants are potentially jointly liable to the plaintiff, the entire amount in controversy can be applied to each defendant. Furthermore, a defendant cannot avoid diversity jurisdiction by arguing that the ultimate recovery is likely to be below $75,000.01. Rather, the court will disregard the amount of damages requested in good faith in the complaint only if it is legally certain that the plaintiff will not recover in excess of $75,000. *See Chase Manhattan Bank, N.A. v. Am. Nat. Bank & Tr. Co. of Chicago,* 93 F.3d 1064, 1070 (2d Cir. 1996).

Answer (C) is wrong: The amount in controversy rules, including the aggregation rules, do not turn on whether there are common questions of law or fact.

Answer (D) is the best choice: The question here is one of aggregation—if Employee is successful against both defendants, he is unlikely to recover more than $75,000 from either, and certainly cannot recover more than $75,000 from both, as he is only seeking $80,000. However, the courts have recognized an exception to the general rule of non-aggregation in multi-party cases: a plaintiff may aggregate claims against multiple defendants if the defendants would be jointly liable to the plaintiff. *See Jewell v. Grain Dealers Mut. Ins. Co.,* 290 F.2d 11, 13 (5th Cir. 1961). Accordingly, if the judge concludes that the applicable substantive law provides for joint liability, the claims would satisfy the amount in controversy requirement for diversity jurisdiction and the judge will deny the motion to dismiss.

174. **Answer (A) is wrong:** A determination that a jury's verdict is against the weight of the evidence could offer a basis for granting a new trial, but will not justify the entry of a judgment as a matter of law (JMOL). *See Ortiz v. Jordan*, 562 U.S. 180, 189 n.6 (2011). The standard for a JMOL is different and much more demanding. JMOLs may be granted only if "a reasonable jury would not have a legally sufficient evidentiary basis to find for the [non-moving party]." *See* Rule 50(a)(1). *See also Lavender v. Kurn,* 327 U.S. 645, 653 (1946) (approving such judgments "[o]nly when there is a complete absence of probative facts to support the conclusion reached"). Parsing through the evidence, deciding which evidence to credit and which to disbelieve, is the province of the jury. *See Reeves v. Sanderson Plumbing Prod., Inc.*, 530 U.S. 133, 150 (2000).

Answer (B) is wrong: As explained in Answer (A), the correct standard for assessing whether to grant a JMOL asks whether a reasonable jury had a sufficient evidentiary basis to return the verdict they did. Nonetheless, as explained in Answer (C), the motion here was improperly made and could not be granted.

Answer (C) is the best choice: In federal court, litigants are permitted to make post-verdict JMOL motions only if they had previously made a JMOL motion before the jury was sent out to deliberate. *See* Rule 50(b). *See also Mosley v. Wilson*, 102 F.3d 85, 90 (3d Cir. 1996) ("A motion for judgment as a matter of law rendered after trial must be made on grounds that were previously asserted in a motion for directed verdict prior to submission of the case to the jury."). This is why post-verdict JMOL motions are called "renewed" motions. Here, Athlete's counsel had made no pre-verdict JMOL motion; consequently, there could be no "renewed" JMOL motion post-trial. This motion will have to be denied.

Answer (D) is wrong: The time period for filing a proper post-verdict JMOL motion is 28 days from judgment, not 10 days after the verdict. *See* Rule 50(b). In any event, as explained in Answer (C), the JMOL motion filed here was improper.

175. **Answer (A) is wrong:** Formerly, only the same litigants who were parties to a first lawsuit could invoke issue preclusion against one another in a later lawsuit. This "mutuality rule" was discarded by the U.S. Supreme Court in favor of a more flexible, discretionary inquiry into fairness. *See Parklane Hosiery Co. v. Shore*, 439 U.S. 322, 331 (1979). Thus, the mere fact that NextGuest was not a party to Guest's lawsuit against Amusement Park would not, by itself, foreclose her use of issue preclusion.

Answer (B) is wrong: Issue preclusion does not foreclose an entire lawsuit (that's claim preclusion); instead, it forecloses the relitigation of a particular *issue* resolved in that first lawsuit. Necessarily, the issue seeking to be precluded must be identical to the issue resolved the first time. But the context need not be identical. *See Spence v. TRW, Inc.*, 92 F.3d 380, 382 (6th Cir. 1996) (judicial finding from earlier defamation lawsuit that credit report statement was not untrue precluded the ability to contest the truthfulness of that same statement in a later federal Fair Credit Reporting Act lawsuit). Here, the issue of the negligent failure to maintain the lap-bar in row 7, seat 2 was decided against Amusement Park in Guest's lawsuit (it had to have been, otherwise he would not have won). That identical issue is raised by NextGuest's lawsuit.

Answer (C) is the best choice: As introduced in Answer (A), the Supreme Court has embraced a more flexible, fact-intensive inquiry for the use of issue preclusion by someone who was not a party to the original lawsuit. In previewing this discretion, the Court used the very sort of example this fact pattern implicates: offensive use of issue preclusion by a non-identical party "may be unfair to a defendant" if, in the first lawsuit, the defendant was "sued for small or nominal damages" which "he may have little incentive to defend vigorously, particularly if future suits are not foreseeable." *Parklane Hosiery Co. v. Shore*, 439 U.S. 322, 330 (1979). The $103.72 liability in Guest's first lawsuit, along with NextGuest's apparent fitness after leaving the SuperCoaster, suggests that this sort of discretion would be prudent here.

Answer (D) is wrong: Issue preclusion also requires that the resolution of the issue in the first lawsuit be necessary (or "essential") to that judgment. *See Rios v. Davis*, 373 S.W.2d 386, 388 (Tex. Civ. App. 1963). If the court's decision on the contested issue was not needed for the result or was otherwise not essential to that earlier case's outcome, it cannot act to preclude a revisiting of that issue in a later lawsuit. Here, that analysis is simple. Guest would not—could not—have won his lawsuit unless the factfinder actually decided that Amusement Part had negligently failed to properly maintain the lap-bar in row 7, seat 2. The requisite "essentiality" of the earlier judgment is clearly present.

176. **Answer (A) is wrong:** The Rules permit Sculptor to join Electric Corp. if the requirements for permissive joinder are satisfied. *See* Rule 20(a)(2). But complying with the Rules does not also answer the separate question of personal jurisdiction. *See* Rule 82. Instead, personal and subject-matter jurisdiction must both be proper for this joinder to proceed. Here, the facts confirm that Electric Corp. lacks contacts with Rhode Island to support personal jurisdiction, so the court would lack authority to proceed.

Answer (B) is the best choice: The Rules permit Stove Corp. to join Electric Corp. as a third-party defendant if the requirements for impleader are satisfied (and they seem to be on these facts). *See* Rule 14(a)(1). Although Electric Corp. lacks the requisite contacts with Rhode Island to support personal jurisdiction there, the company is located 70 miles from the courthouse—which places it within the 100-mile "bulge" region. A third-party defendant (that is, an impleaded party) located outside the forum State but within 100 miles of the courthouse is amenable to that court's personal jurisdiction. *See* Rule 4(k)(1)(B). Consequently, if Stove Corp.'s joinder of Electric Corp. is proper under Rule 14, the 100-mile "bulge" rule will supply personal jurisdiction.

Answer (C) is wrong: A party who agrees to waive service of process is not deemed to have consented to personal jurisdiction. Instead, any objections the waiving party might have to personal jurisdiction are expressly preserved. *See* Rule 4(d)(5).

Answer (D) is wrong: As explained in Answer (B), the Rhode Island federal court may exercise personal jurisdiction if Electric Corp. was joined properly through impleader.

177. **Answer (A) is wrong:** Rule 11 establishes the certification/safe harbor/sanctions process for signatures on pleadings, briefs, and many other court documents, but not for signatures on discovery documents. *See* Rule 11(d) (noting that Rule 11 "does not apply to disclosures and discovery requests, responses, objections, and motions" under the federal discovery Rules). As Answer (B) explains, Rule 26(g) applies instead of Rule 11 for signatures of discovery documents.

Answer (B) is the best choice: Rule 26(g) imposes a certification/sanctions procedure for signatures on discovery documents. *See* Rule 26(g)(1)(B)(i) (signature certifies that discovery response is "consistent with these rules"). If Counsel signed the discovery responses in violation of the Rule 26(g) certifications, Rule 26(g) authorizes all of the sanctions listed in Rule 37(b). *See Laukus v. Rio Brands, Inc.*, 292 F.R.D. 485, 506 (N.D. Ohio 2013).

Answer (C) is wrong: Rule 37(d) provides for sanctions when a party has failed altogether to respond to written discovery. Here, the issue is whether Flag Designer responded fully and properly in good faith, not a total failure to respond. Thus, Rule 37(d) does not apply.

Answer (D) is wrong: The duty to supplement is tied in part to whether the information has otherwise been disclosed in discovery. *See* Rule 26(e)(1)(A). For example, if a party finds a document after the Rule 26(a)(1) disclosure has occurred, it may have an obligation to supplement that disclosure. However, if the party has already provided the document during some other aspect of discovery, it likely does not also have to provide it a second time in a supplemental disclosure. At the same time, a violation of Rule 26(g) is not necessarily cured by subsequent disclosure.

178. **Answer (A) is the best choice:** Absent a motion to expedite discovery or an early motion for a protective order (neither of which is a listed option), the first step in the discovery process is typically the parties' Rule 26(f) discovery planning conference, followed by the parties' preparation and submission of their Rule 26(f) discovery plan to the court, in which Software Company could raise its concern about access to the computer code. Absent a court ruling, no discovery responses are due earlier than 30 days following the Rule 26(f) discovery planning conference. As explained in the following Answers, each of those options would likely occur after the Rule 26(f) report.

Answer (B) is wrong: Rule 26(f)(1) requires the parties to conduct their discovery conference at least 21 days prior to the court's initial Rule 16 conference (or, if the court is not going to conduct an initial conference, then at least 21 days before its initial scheduling order is due). Rule 26(f)(2) then requires the parties to submit their discovery plan within 14 days, Thus, at the latest, the discovery plan is due 7 days before the initial Rule 16 conference. Consequently, the Rule 26(f) report of the parties' discovery plan presents an earlier opportunity to raise a discovery issue, as Answer (A) demonstrates.

Answer (C) is wrong: Rule 34(b)(2)(A) authorizes parties to serve production requests before the parties have conducted their discovery planning conference, in contrast to virtually all other discovery (which normally may not be served until after the discovery planning conference). However, the purpose of this early service of production requests is designed to uncover potential discovery disputes so that they may be addressed in the discovery conference, in the discovery plan, and at the Rule 16 conference with the court. Responses are not due until 30 days after the parties' discovery conference. *See* Rule 34(b)(2)(A). Thus, early production requests present an opportunity to raise the issue with Competitor, but not with the court.

Answer (D) is wrong: Rule 37(e) controls spoliation sanctions for failure to preserve Electronically Stored Information, or ESI. Unless it was only preserved on paper, the computer source code would qualify as ESI, but Software Company's concern about preservation of the source code, without more, would not support a motion for sanctions. One of the prerequisites of a Rule 37(e) motion is loss of the ESI, and the problem does not contain any facts suggesting that the source code has already been lost.

179. **Answer (A) is the best choice:** While the Due Process Clause generally entitles people to an opportunity to be heard before they are deprived of liberty or property, the nature of the "hearing" depends on the particular issue before the court. Rule 78 explicitly provides that courts may rule on motions based on the briefs, without conducting oral hearings. *See also Brown-Bey v. United States,* 720 F.2d 467, 470 (7th Cir. 1983) (summary judgment may be granted without an oral hearing). Thus, the court afforded Downloaders appropriate due process when it adjudicated the motion for summary judgment based on the parties' briefs and evidentiary submissions.

Answer (B) is wrong: Under some circumstances, such as at the ultimate trial, the Due Process Clause does require an evidentiary hearing, so Answer (B)'s blanket statement goes too far. Rather, as explained in Answer (A), Rule 78 and case law authorize a district court to rule on motions without conducting an oral hearing.

Answer (C) is wrong: As explained in Answer (A), the due process right to an opportunity to be heard does not always guarantee an oral hearing; Rule 78 and case law authorize courts to rule on motions based on the parties' briefs, without an oral argument or hearing.

Answer (D) is wrong: Although under some circumstances, such as at the ultimate trial, the Due Process Clause may require an evidentiary hearing, as explained in Answer (A), Rule 78 and case law authorize courts to rule on motions based on the parties' briefs, without an oral argument or hearing.

180. **Answer (A) is wrong:** Although the parties are free to enter into a settlement agreement (and typically would), that private agreement does not, on its own, terminate the litigation. Rather, as explained in Answer (C), the normal way to end a lawsuit following settlement is through a voluntary dismissal under Rule 41.

Answer (B) is wrong: Rule 12(b) provides for dismissal of a complaint, but the list of grounds for dismissal in subsections (1) through (7) do not include voluntary dismissal for settlement. Rather, as explained in Answer (C), Rule 41 is the preferred mechanism for such dismissals.

Answer (C) is the best choice: Rule 41(a)(1)(A)(ii) provides for voluntary dismissal by a plaintiff upon stipulation of all parties. This is the provision commonly used to terminate litigation following settlement. *See, e.g., McCall-Bey v. Franzen*, 777 F.2d 1178, 1184 (7th Cir. 1985).

Answer (D) is wrong: Motions for summary judgment under Rule 56 turn on whether there is a genuine dispute of material fact, and are not designed to accomplish voluntary dismissal for settlement. Rather, as explained in Answer (C), Rule 41 is the preferred mechanism for such dismissals.

181. **Answer (A) is wrong:** The constitutional right to an opportunity to be heard can be satisfied by the opportunity to submit written briefs, and does not require oral argument before the court rules on a motion. *See* Rule 78; *Killer Joe Nevada, LLC v. Does 1-20*, 807 F.3d 908, 913 (8th Cir. 2015).

Answer (B) is wrong: As explained in Answer (C), Rule 52(a) does not require findings of fact and conclusions of law for matters decided on motion for summary judgment.

Answer (C) is the best choice: Rule 52(a) requires findings of fact and conclusions of law in an action tried on the facts. It does not impose that obligation on matters decided on motion for summary judgment. *See* Rule 52(a)(3); *Barry v. Moran*, 661 F.3d 696, 702, n.9 (1st Cir. 2011).

Answer (D) is wrong: The obligation to prepare findings of fact and conclusions of law is mandatory under Rule 52(a), and is not dependent on a request by one of the parties. But, as explained in Answer (C), Rule 52(a) does not require findings of fact and conclusions of law for matters decided on motion for summary judgment.

182. **Answer (A) is the best choice:** If a judgment is potentially based on two independent grounds, each of which would be sufficient to support the result, neither is entitled to issue preclusion. *See Ritter v. Mount St. Mary's College*, 814 F.2d 986, 993–94 (4th Cir.1987). Here, the jury rendered a general verdict, which means it did not specify its reasoning for ruling against Programmer. The jury could have ruled in favor of Tech Company either because Programmer was not an employee or because it didn't discriminate against Programmer. Because both reasons would have supported the jury's decision, the court cannot tell which the jury used to support its verdict. Thus, neither finding is entitled to issue preclusion because the court cannot confirm that the issue for which preclusion is sought was actually and necessarily litigated to conclusion in the first lawsuit.

Answer (B) is wrong: Offensive issue preclusion refers to the use of issue preclusion to establish a claim, not to defeat a claim. *See Parklane Hosiery Co. v. Shore*, 439 U.S. 322, 326 (1979). Offensive issue preclusion is not implicated on these facts. Here, Tech Company seeks to use issue preclusion to defeat Programmer's claim, and thus is seeking to use defensive issue preclusion.

Answer (C) is wrong: A party is not automatically subject to issue preclusion simply by deciding not to appeal an issue. Rather, the party seeking issue preclusion must still establish the elements of the doctrine.

Answer (D) is wrong: As explained in Answer (A), Tech Company cannot establish the requirement for issue preclusion that the issue have been actually and necessarily litigated.

183. **Answer (A) is wrong:** A jury trial in federal court, once properly demanded, may only be withdrawn if all parties (or their attorneys) file a written stipulation consenting to a bench trial or otherwise stipulate their consent on the record in open court. *See* Rules 38(d) & 39(a)(1). Thus, the litigant who demanded the jury trial may not unilaterally withdraw that demand.

Answer (B) is wrong: The trial judge is afforded no discretion to convene or not convene a jury trial; when a proper demand has been made, "[t]he trial on all issues so demanded must be by jury" unless it is later withdrawn by consent of all parties or it is later discovered that no federal right to a jury trial exists. *See* Rule 39(a).

Answer (C) is wrong: Scientist's lawsuit involved three parties: the plaintiff (herself), the defendant (Lab Shop), and a third-party defendant (Glass Corp.). All parties must agree before a jury demand may be withdrawn. *See Solis v. Cty. of Los Angeles*, 514 F.3d 946, 955 (9th Cir. 2008). Thus, Lab Shop's stipulation of consent would be immaterial—unless it was accompanied by Glass Corp.'s consent (which the facts here do not suggest).

Answer (D) is the best choice: For the reasons explained in Answers (A), (B), and (C), no effective withdrawal of the jury demand occurred in this litigation. Consequently, the federal judge "must" convene a jury trial.

184. **Answer (A) is the best choice:** The Rules permit a disappointed litigant to simultaneously seek a judgment as a matter of law and—either jointly or in the alternative—a new trial, and to do so in the same, single post-trial motion. *See* Rule 50(b). That option makes great strategic sense where, as here, the moving party believes a JMOL ought to be granted but, still acknowledging the risk that it might not, can offer up to the court a strong new trial argument in the alternative.

     Answer (B) is wrong: The time for filing post-trial motions is fixed, and that deadline can be extended only in rare cases. That deadline (applicable to both JMOL motions and new trial motions) is 28 days after entry of the judgment. *See* Rules 50(b) & 59(b). Consequently, a litigant generally may not file one post-trial motion, wait to see how the court rules, and then, if disappointed, file a second post-trial motion. The second motion would very likely be already time-barred.

     Answer (C) is wrong: As explained in Answer (A), the Rules grant litigants the right to a simultaneous post-trial motion filing. No permission from the court is needed.

     Answer (D) is wrong: As explained in Answer (A), the Rules permit the simultaneous filing of a JMOL motion and a motion for a new trial.

185. **Answer (A) is the best choice:** Diversity of jurisdiction requires complete diversity of "citizenship." For diversity jurisdiction purposes, an individual is deemed a citizen of the State where the individual is domiciled, which is not necessarily the same as where the citizen is a "resident." *See Mas v. Perry*, 489 F.2d 1396, 1399 (5th Cir. 1974). A partnership is a citizen of every State where its partners are citizens. *See Carden v. Arkoma Assocs.*, 494 U.S. 185, 195 (1990). Thus, by alleging only the residence of the parties, Client failed to include enough information to assess diversity of citizenship.

     Answer (B) is wrong: A complaint is generally required to assert sufficient facts to support its claims, but is not required to articulate the legal theories or support accurately. *See generally Johnson v. City of Shelby*, 135 S. Ct. 346, 346 (2014).

     Answer (C) is wrong: Complaints are required to include sufficient *allegations*, but are not required to plead the *evidence* supporting those allegations. *See In re Beef Indus. Antitrust Litig.*, 600 F.2d 1148, 1169 (5th Cir. 1979).

     Answer (D) is wrong: As explained in Answer (A), the complaint does not include enough factual detail to determine the parties' citizenship, and thus to determine if there is complete diversity of jurisdiction.

186. **Answer (A) is wrong:** A federal court hearing a State law claim under diversity or supplemental jurisdiction applies State substantive law, not federal common law. *See* 28 U.S.C. § 1652. *See also Erie R. Co. v. Tompkins,* 304 U.S. 64, 78 (1938).

Answer (B) is wrong: As explained in Answer (C), federal courts sitting in diversity apply the law selected by the choice-of-law provisions of the forum State; they do not have discretion to select a different law from that dictated by the applicable choice-of-law provisions.

Answer (C) is wrong: As explained in Answer (D), following transfer under 28 U.S.C. § 1404, the court applies the substantive law selected by the choice-of-law provisions of the transferor State, not the transferee State.

Answer (D) is the best choice: Normally, a federal court hearing a State law claim under diversity applies the State substantive law selected by the forum State's choice-of-law provisions. *See Sarver v. Chartier,* 813 F.3d 891, 897 (9th Cir. 2016). However, when a case is transferred under 28 U.S.C. § 1404—when venue was proper in the original court, and the transfer is merely for convenience—the choice-of-law provisions travel with the case, and the transferee court applies the substantive law dictated by the choice-of-law principles of the transferor court. *Id.* Because Taxi, Inc. was incorporated in Delaware, it is subject to general personal jurisdiction in Delaware, and thus is a resident of Delaware for venue purposes. As Taxi Inc. is the only defendant, venue was proper in Delaware under 28 U.S.C. § 1391(b)(1). Following transfer, therefore, the California court will apply the substantive law selected by Delaware's choice-of-law provisions.

187. **Answer (A) is wrong:** Although the citizenship of the parties is generally measured at the time the complaint is filed, complete diversity of citizenship is destroyed by the subsequent addition of a non-diverse additional party required to be joined under Rule 19. *See Cobb v. Delta Exports, Inc.*, 186 F.3d 675, 677 (5th Cir. 1999).

Answer (B) is wrong: As explained in Answer (A), the addition of a non-diverse party required to be joined under Rule 19 would destroy diversity jurisdiction. That proposition, while true, does not dictate whether the court should grant or deny the motion to dismiss; it simply confirms that the court cannot order Philanthropist to join Art Collector to the case. *See Delgado-Caraballo v. Hosp. Pavia Hato Rey, Inc.*, 889 F.3d 30, 36-38 (1st Cir. 2018). As explained in Answer (C), the court does have discretion in this situation, but that discretion does not include the option to proceed without subject-matter jurisdiction.

Answer (C) is the best choice: Rule 19(b) controls the court's options when a party, who is required to be joined under a Rule 19(a) analysis, nonetheless cannot be joined (for reasons such as jurisdiction or venue). It provides the court with discretion to either dismiss the action altogether or to allow it to proceed without the required party. *See Teamsters Local Union No. 171 v. Keal Driveaway Co.*, 173 F.3d 915, 918 (4th Cir. 1999). Thus, if the court determines that it can adequately protect Art Collector's interests (such as through a carefully crafted judgment), the court may proceed without Art Collector.

Answer (D) is wrong: As a starting point, a plaintiff is not acting improperly by choosing to file in federal court and, to do so, leaving out a defendant who would destroy federal subject-matter jurisdiction. *See, e.g., St. Paul Mercury Indem. Co. v. Red Cab Co.*, 303 U.S. 283, 294 (1938). This type of "forum shopping" is thus permissible. Additionally, the plaintiff's preference for one court over another is not a factor in the analysis under Rule 19(a) as to whether the missing party is required—rather, Rule 19(a) focuses on whether the rights of the missing party and the existing parties can adequately be protected. Likewise, the plaintiff's preference for the selected forum is not a factor in the analysis under Rule 19(b) as to whether to dismiss or proceed without the missing required party, in the event it is not feasible to join the missing required party. Again, the test under Rule 19(b) is oriented towards prejudice to the existing and missing parties if the court proceeds without the missing party.

188. **Answer (A) is the best choice:** Rule 48 normally requires a jury of at least 6 and not more than 12 jurors. However, parties may stipulate to a jury of less than 6 jurors. *See Meyers v. Wal-Mart Stores, E., Inc.*, 77 F. Supp. 2d 826, 828 (E.D. Mich. 1999), aff'd, 257 F.3d 625 (6th Cir. 2001). So, if the parties had stipulated to a jury of less than 6 members, the court could properly enter judgment based on the 5-juror verdict.

Answer (B) is wrong: Rule 47(b) and the interpretive case law do not permit a party to exercise *peremptory strikes* on the basis of race or gender. *See Edmonson v. Leesville Concrete Co., Inc.*, 500 U.S. 614 (1991). But, the parties do not have a right to a jury of any particular composition. *See Taylor v. Louisiana*, 419 U.S. 522, 538 (1975).

Answer (C) is wrong: The court has broad discretion when deciding whether to excuse a juror. *See In re Wright Med. Tech. Inc., Conserve Hip Implant Prod. Liab. Litig.*, 178 F. Supp. 3d 1321, 1344 (N.D. Ga. 2016). Thus, the court's excusing of the jurors without the parties' consent was not necessarily improper. Answer (C) does not address the more difficult issue—the consequence of the number of jurors dropping below 6.

Answer (D) is wrong: As explained in Answer (A), a jury of fewer than 6 members is allowable with the parties' stipulation.

189. **Answer (A) is wrong:** Claim preclusion, anchored in principles of finality and fairness, bars a party who has already litigated a claim from litigating it anew in a different tribunal. In its typical formulation, claim preclusion requires proof of three elements: the parties to the two lawsuits are identical (or in privity); the claims in the two lawsuits are identical; and the first lawsuit ended in a valid, final judgment on the merits. *See Lenox MacLaren Surgical Corp. v. Medtronic, Inc.*, 847 F.3d 1221, 1239 (10th Cir. 2017). Here, the first two elements of claim preclusion are absent. The parties to the two lawsuits are different, and the claims are different—one is a claim of personal injury suffered by Skier 1 and the other is a claim of personal injury suffered by Skier 2. That the *factual causes* for the two claims is the same is not dispositive.

Answer (B) is wrong: Defining when two lawsuits involve the "same claim" for preclusion purposes can sometimes prove difficult. Varying tests are applied by different jurisdictions. Alabama, for example, tests whether the claims in the two lawsuits derive from a "single wrongful act." *See Equity Res. Mgmt., Inc. v. Vinson*, 723 So. 2d 634, 638 (Ala. 1998). California asks whether the two claims are based on the same invasion of the party's "primary rights" (or whether multiple rights were invaded). *See Manufactured Home Cmtys. Inc. v. City of San Jose*, 420 F.3d 1022, 1031 (9th Cir. 2005). South Carolina applies a "same transaction or occurrence" test which considers several factors holistically, including "single wrongful act" and "primary rights." *See Judy v. Judy*, 712 S.E.2d 408, 414 (2011). In any event, as explained in Answer (A), regardless of the way "same claim" is defined, these two lawsuits will fail at least the party-identity element.

Answer (C) is wrong: The plaintiffs in these two cases are surely not identical. But that does not necessarily foreclose issue preclusion. At one time, the courts did require party-identity for issue preclusion to apply, an approach known as the "mutuality rule." Because issue preclusion does not automatically foreclose a claim (but, rather, only a sub-issue within that claim), the courts came to find that the inflexibility of the mutuality rule was ill-suited to issue preclusion. In issue preclusion contexts, the mutuality rule has now been largely discarded in favor of a more pliable, discretionary inquiry into whether applying preclusion would be fair. *See Parklane Hosiery Co. v. Shore*, 439 U.S. 322, 331 (1979).

Answer (D) is the best answer: One element that is generally required for issue preclusion to apply is that the resolution of the contested issue in the first lawsuit must have been necessary (or "essential") to that first judgment. *See Rios v. Davis*, 373 S.W.2d 386, 388 (Tex. Civ. App. 1963). If the court's decision on the contested issue was not needed for the result or was otherwise not essential to that earlier case's outcome, it cannot be used to preclude a revisiting of that issue in a later lawsuit. Here, this element of "essentiality" is readily satisfied. Skier 1 won his lawsuit against the resort. The only way he could have won is if the jury decided that resort was negligent in leaving the powercord on the ski slope. The resort will likely be precluded from relitigating that issue in Skier 2's lawsuit.

190. **Answer (A) is wrong:** Motions to strike are disfavored by the federal courts because they often delay the progress of litigation without much in the way of corresponding benefit. *See Bureerong v. Uvawas*, 922 F. Supp. 1450, 1478 (C.D. Cal. 1996). Although the Rules permit the court to strike allegations that are "scandalous," *see* Rule 12(f), courts exercise this authority with great restraint. Allegations will not be stricken merely because a litigant finds them harsh, discourteous, or offensive. *See In re Gitto Glob. Corp.*, 422 F.3d 1, 12 (1st Cir. 2005) ("it is not enough that the matter offends the sensibilities of the objecting party if the challenged allegations describe acts or events that are relevant to the action"). Instead, courts will ordinarily strike allegations only if they are entirely irrelevant to the pleader's claims and would prejudice the moving party if they remain unstricken. *See Sun Microsystems, Inc. v. Versata Enters., Inc.*, 630 F. Supp. 2d 395, 402 (D. Del. 2009). Consequently, the fact that Private School considers the allegations discourteous and offensive will not, alone, justify a motion to strike.

Answer (B) is wrong: The approach applied in assessing Rule 12(b) motions to dismiss is generally the same approach used in testing Rule 12(f) motions to strike. The court will accept all of the pleader's well-pleaded facts as true, draw all reasonable inferences in the pleader's favor, and resolve all facts in favor of denying the motion to strike. *See State of New York v. United Parcel Serv., Inc.*, 160 F. Supp. 3d 629, 637 (S.D.N.Y. 2016). Accordingly, a court's disbelief as to how well a jury will weigh the pleader's allegations will not warrant striking them.

Answer (C) is the best choice: As explained in Answer (A), the burden lies with the moving party to show that the allegations are truly "scandalous," irrelevant to the pleader's claims, and prejudicial. Allegations are considered "scandalous" if they "cast a cruelly derogatory light on a party." *See In re 2TheMart.com, Inc. Sec. Litig.*, 114 F. Supp. 2d 955, 965 (C.D. Cal. 2000). Here, Private School is likely to carry these heavy burdens. The incendiary terms Teacher has included in his complaint "add[ ] nothing to the material allegations" in the complaint, were probably added "only for their inflammatory effect," and are likely "highly prejudicial" to Private School. *Cf. Bureerong v. Uvawas*, 922 F. Supp. 1450, 1479 (C.D. Cal. 1996).

Answer (D) is wrong: That a defendant can disprove scandalous allegations later at trial offers little remedy for the prejudice they may inflict now. Consequently, Rule 12(f) expressly authorizes the striking of "scandalous" allegations, provided the constraints explained in Answers (A), (B), and (C) are honored.

191. **Answer (A) is the best choice:** Supplemental jurisdiction permits a party who has invoked a federal court's original subject-matter jurisdiction over a federal claim to join into that lawsuit a State law claim (over which no original subject-matter jurisdiction exists), provided that State law claim is "so related" to the federal claim that, together, they form part of the same "case or controversy." *See* 28 U.S.C. § 1367(a). If, however, the court later dismisses the federal claim, it is also entitled to decline to exercise supplemental jurisdiction over the added State law claim. *See id.* at § 1367(c)(3). If that happens, the State law claim could be at risk: its limitations period might have expired during the time it was pending in federal court. To avoid the risk of time-bar, Congress directed that the applicable statute of limitations for the State law claim is deemed "tolled" during the time that claim was pending in federal court *and* for 30 days after it is dismissed from federal court (unless State law provided an even longer tolling period). *See id.* at § 1367(d). The U.S. Supreme Court has interpreted this tolling language as suspending (like a paused-clock) the applicable State statute of limitations on the day the federal case is filed and for an additional 30 days following the federal dismissal, after which the paused-clock is un-paused and begins running again. *See Artis v. D.C.*, 138 S. Ct. 594, 603–04 (2018). Here, Professor filed his lawsuit with 30 days remaining on his State law claim statute of limitations. The running of that limitations period was paused during the 60 days the case was pending in federal court. Once his case was dismissed, he had what was left on his remaining State law statute of limitations (30 days) plus the additional 30 days provided by Congress, for a total of 60 days to re-file in State court.

Answer (B) is wrong: As Answer (A) explained, Professor must re-file in State court within 60 days from his dismissal. Waiting 120 days after dismissal would be too long.

Answer (C) is wrong: As in Answer (A), the deadline for Professor to re-file in State court is 60 days, not 30 days.

Answer (D) is wrong: As explained in Answer (A), Congress's supplemental jurisdiction protected Professor's State law claim from becoming time-barred while it was pending in federal court.

192. **Answer (A) is wrong:** As Answer (C) explains, Racket Company's claim for specific performance is an equitable claim, so Squashplayer does not have the right to a jury trial for that claim.

Answer (B) is wrong: Answer (B) has the claims reversed as to which entitles the parties to a jury trial, as Answer (C) explains.

Answer (C) is the best choice: Rule 38(a) preserves the right to a jury trial that is embodied in the Seventh Amendment to the Constitution. The Seventh Amendment "preserves" the right to jury trials for suits "at common law." In general, claims that were, at the time of the ratification of the Seventh Amendment in 1791, tried in courts of law— typically claims seeking money damages like tort or breach of contract claims—were suits at common law entitling the parties to a jury trial. *See Chauffeurs, Teamsters & Helpers, Local No. 391 v. Terry*, 494 U.S. 558, 564 (1990). In contrast, suits seeking equitable remedies, like injunctions or specific performance, were tried in courts of equity, and did not entitle the parties to a jury. *Id.* Here, Racket Company's claim for lost profits is a claim at law, for which Squashplayer has a right to a jury trial, and the company's claim for specific performance is equitable, for which Squashplayer does not have a right to a jury trial. Rule 38(b) requires parties to make serve their jury trial demand for an issue within 14 days of service of the last pleading directed to the issue. Thus, Squashplayer made a timely jury trial demand and has the right to a jury trial on the lost profits claim.

Answer (D) is wrong: As Answer (C) explains, Racket Company's claim for lost profits is a claim at law and Squashplayer made a timely jury trial demand, so Squashplayer has the right to a jury trial for that claim.

193. **Answer (A) is wrong:** Rule 36(b) authorizes withdrawal or amendment of an admission upon motion, if doing so would promote the presentation of the merits of the action and the withdrawal or amendment would not prejudice the *requesting* party. Here, the answer refers to prejudice to the *responding* party as a prerequisite. Although the court might consider prejudice to the responding party in its overall analysis, it is not a prerequisite under Rule 36(b).

Answer (B) is wrong: As explained in Answer (A), Rule 36(b) does authorize withdrawal or amendment of an admission. However, the responding party's good faith mistake is not sufficient to warrant withdrawal or amendment—the court must also find that the propounding party would not be prejudiced. *See In re Durability Inc.*, 212 F.3d 551, 556 (10th Cir. 2000) ("The court's focus must be on the effect upon the litigation and prejudice to the resisting party rather than [ ] on the moving party's excuses for an erroneous admission.").

Answer (C) is the best choice: Rule 36(b) provides that a matter admitted is "conclusively established." Generally, that means that the responding party may not contradict the admitted matter at trial. *See Sec'y U.S. Dep't of Labor v. Kwasny*, 853 F.3d 87, 91 (3d Cir. 2017). While it is possible that the court would grant a motion by Purchaser to withdraw or amend its admission, Answer (C) is the only answer that is consistent with the standards under Rule 36(b).

Answer (D) is wrong: Matters admitted under Rule 36 are conclusively established by operation of Rule 36(b), without the need for a motion for sanctions under Rule 37.

194. **Answers (A) and (B) are wrong:** As explained in Answer (C), residence-based venue requires all defendants to reside in the same State, and then is proper in any district in which any of the defendants resides. Accordingly, residence-based venue is either proper or improper for all the defendants—it cannot be proper for one defendant and improper for another.

Answer (C) is the best choice: 28 U.S.C. § 1391(b)(1) authorizes venue based on the defendants' residence. It requires that all defendants be residents of the same State, then authorizes residence in any district where, within that State, any of the defendants resides. 28 U.S.C. § 1391(c)(1) provides that an individual is a resident of the district where the individual is domiciled. Here, Gardner is domiciled in, and therefore, for venue purposes, is a resident of, the Eastern District of Missouri. 28 U.S.C. § 1391(c)(2) provides that a corporation is a resident of each district where it is subject to personal jurisdiction. Lawnmower, Inc. has its principal place of business in the Eastern District of Missouri, and therefore is both subject to general personal jurisdiction and a resident of the Eastern District of Missouri. *See Daimler AG v. Bauman*, 571 U.S. 117, 137 (2014). Accordingly, all defendants are residents of Missouri (satisfying the first requirement), and at least one defendant is a resident of the Eastern District of Missouri, so venue is proper there.

Answer (D) is wrong: As explained in Answer (C), venue is proper in the Eastern District of Missouri.

195. **Answer (A) is wrong:** The U.S. Supreme Court in *Brady v. Maryland,* 373 U.S. 83 (1963), announced that it is a violation of constitutional due process to fail to provide the accused with certain information. That principle, however, applies in criminal cases, not in civil ones. *See Perez v. Wallis*, 77 F. Supp. 3d 730, 746–47 (N.D. Ill. 2014).

Answer (B) is the best choice: A party who has responded to an interrogatory (or, for that matter, a production request or admission request) is under a continuing duty to supplement its responses in a timely manner if that party comes to learn that any of its earlier responses was incomplete or incorrect in any material respect, unless the additional information has otherwise been made known to the other side. *See* Rule 26(e)(1)(A). As the language of this Rule makes clear, this duty is imposed automatically; no nudging by the other side or additional discovery request is needed to trigger it. Here, Government purportedly uncovered 650 additional acts of racketeering eight months earlier, yet failed to supplement its earlier interrogatory answer as Rule 26(e) required. Accordingly, the motion should be granted. *See United States v. Philip Morris USA, Inc.*, 219 F.R.D. 198, 200–01 (D.D.C. 2004).

Answer (C) is wrong: The fact that Government's earlier interrogatory response was truthful, accurate, and complete when made is immaterial. The federal discovery supplementation duty is specifically intended to encompass later-acquired knowledge. *See West v. Bell Helicopter Textron, Inc.*, 803 F.3d 56, 71 (1st Cir. 2015). Government breached that duty here, as Answer (B) explained.

Answer (D) is wrong: As Answer (B) explained, the duty to supplement federal discovery responses is an automatic and continuing one. No new discovery request from Manufacturer was needed to trigger it.

196. **Answer (A) is wrong:** Litigants in federal court are not limited in using interrogatories only to pursue information they "may use" in proving their cases. Although the "may use" standard governs certain initial disclosure obligations a federal litigant may have, *see* Rule 26(a)(1)(A)(i)–(ii), that constraint does not apply to the Rule governing interrogatories. *Cf.* Rule 33.

Answer (B) is wrong: The Rules set a default limit of 25 interrogatories (including subparts) for federal practice, though this limit can be altered by written stipulation among the parties or court order. *See* Rule 33(a)(1). However, as explained in Answer (D), Driver would only be able to serve interrogatories on Happy's Bar & Grill if it was a named party.

Answer (C) is wrong: Like all discovery requests, interrogatories may only seek information that is unprivileged, relevant, and proportional to the needs of the case. *See* Rule 26(b)(1). Nevertheless, as explained in Answer (D), Driver would only be able to serve interrogatories on Happy's Bar & Grill if it was a named party.

Answer (D) is the best choice: Some of the federal discovery tools may be used with non-parties (provided those tools are implemented with a subpoena). *See, e.g.,* Rules 30 & 34. Interrogatories, however, are not among those tools. Instead, interrogatories may only be used in federal court to pursue information from actual parties to the lawsuit. *See Univ. of Texas at Austin v. Vratil,* 96 F.3d 1337, 1340 (10th Cir. 1996). Here, Happy's Bar & Grill (a non-party) might well be an important source of information for Driver, but the information Happy's Bar & Grill knows must be pursued with other discovery tools unless it is added to the lawsuit as a party.

197. **Answer (A) is wrong:** Courts do have substantial inherent authority over cases on their dockets, and discretion to impose a variety of sanctions including dismissal. *See Alabama Aircraft Indus., Inc. v. Boeing Co.,* 319 F.R.D. 730, 739 (N.D. Ala. 2017). However, that authority is typically reserved for situations where the Rules do not already provide a mechanism for addressing the parties' conduct. *See Chambers v. NASCO, Inc.,* 501 U.S. 32, 50 (1991) (courts should ordinarily rely on the Rules for sanctioning authority, but may impose sanctions under their inherent authority when the Rules are "not up to the task."). As explained in Answer (D), Rule 41(b) provides a procedure for addressing Surfer's failure to comply with Rule 26(f) and the court's scheduling order, and Internet Corporation should file its motion under that Rule.

Answer (B) is wrong: Rule 12(b) authorizes motions to dismiss for many grounds in subsections (1)–(7). However, failure to comply with the Rules or a court order is not covered by any of the provisions in Rule 12. As explained in Answer (D), Rule 41(b) is the proper procedure for addressing Surfer's failure to comply with Rule 26(f) and the court's scheduling order.

Answer (C) is wrong: Rule 37 is the Rule containing sanctions for discovery violations and Rule 37(b)(2)(A)(v) does authorize dismissal as a sanction. However, failure to participate in the Rule 26(f) process, while a discovery-related transgression, is not covered by any of the provisions in Rule 37. As explained in Answer (D), Rule 41(b) is the proper procedure for addressing Surfer's failure to comply with Rule 26(f) and the court's scheduling order.

Answer (D) is the best choice: Rule 41(b) provides for involuntary dismissal when a plaintiff either fails to prosecute an action or fails to comply with the Federal Rules of Civil Procedure or a court order. Here, Surfer has failed to comply with: 1) the obligations under Rule 26(f) to conduct a discovery conference and prepare a discovery plan; and 2) the court's order to appear for a Rule 16 conference. While the court might give Surfer another chance given his *pro se* status, Rule 41(b) is the proper procedure for addressing Surfer's conduct.

198. **Answer (A) is wrong:** Although federal law sets a minimum age for a person to *serve* process on someone else (namely: at least 18 years old, Rule 4(c)(2)), there is no fixed minimum age for a *recipient* on whom process is served.

Answer (B) is wrong: Service of process on an individual may be accomplished by leaving the service papers at that person's "dwelling house or usual place of abode with someone of suitable age and discretion who resides there." *See* Rule 4(e)(2)(B). There is no additional requirement, however, that the recipient have any familial relationship to the person being served.

Answer (C) is the best choice: Service at an individual's dwelling house or usual place of abode is only effective if the recipient of the service papers is a person "of suitable age and discretion" who actually "resides there." *See* Rule 4(e)(2)(B). Consequently, if Alice did not reside at New Author's home at 123 Maple Street, service on her would fail this requirement.

Answer (D) is wrong: Federal law also does not impose any express requirement that service at an individual's dwelling house or usual place of abode is dependent on whether the individual is physically present (or physically absent) from the home at the moment service occurs.

199. **Answer (A) is wrong:** Rule 11(b)(2) provides that, by signing a brief, the signer is certifying that the legal contentions are warranted under existing law or by a nonfrivolous argument for extending, modifying, or reversing existing law. This duty applies to pro se litigants as well as attorneys and represented parties, and is an *objective* standard. *Bus. Guides, Inc. v. Chromatic Commc'ns Enterprises, Inc.*, 498 U.S. 533, 534–45 (1991). Thus, Prisoner's *subjective* good faith belief that the law was incorrectly decided would not satisfy the Rule 11 certification requirement unless it also qualified as an objective, nonfrivolous argument for extending, modifying, or reversing existing law.

Answer (B) is wrong: As explained in Answer (C), compliance with Rule 11(c)(2)'s twenty-one-day safe harbor is a prerequisite for sanctions pursuant to a party's motion.

Answer (C) is the best choice: Rule 11(c)(2) provides that, before a party may file a motion for sanctions under Rule 11, the party must first *serve* the motion on the opposing party and request that the opposing party withdraw or modify the offending paper. The moving party may only *file* the motion if 21 days pass and the opposing party has not withdrawn or corrected the challenged paper.

Answer (D) is wrong: Rule 11(c)(3) provides the procedures for a court to issue Rule 11 sanctions *sua sponte*, and requires the court to order the party to be sanctioned to show cause why the conduct did not violate Rule 11(b). Rule 11(c)(2), addressing motions for sanctions, does not contemplate a show cause demonstration. Thus, the "show cause" requirement pertains to sanctions issued *sua sponte*, not sanctions issued pursuant to a motion.

200. **Answer (A) is the best choice:** By Rule, a plaintiff asserting a claim against an opponent may join in that lawsuit "as many claims as it has" against that same opponent, and may do so regardless of whether those claims are related to one another. *See* Rule 18. Consequently, the Rules permit Wedding Planner to join the October overcharge claim into her April overcharge lawsuit. But Wedding Planner must also have subject-matter jurisdiction over the joined claim; the fact that the Rules permit the joinder does not ensure that jurisdiction is proper. *See* Rule 82. Here, original subject-matter jurisdiction exists. Because Wedding Planner (a single plaintiff) is suing only City Yacht Club (a single defendant), the two claims can be aggregated together for diversity purposes. *See Snyder v. Harris*, 394 U.S. 332, 335 (1969). Provided the as-aggregated claims exceed the jurisdictional minimum and the parties are completely diverse (and, here, both requirements are met), original subject-matter jurisdiction exists under 28 U.S.C. § 1332. Accordingly, there would be no need for supplemental jurisdiction on these facts.

Answer (B) is wrong: As explained in Answer (A), original subject-matter jurisdiction is not absent here and, thus, supplemental jurisdiction is not relevant.

Answer (C) is wrong: When original subject-matter jurisdiction is absent, Congress has permitted the court to exercise "supplemental" jurisdiction over a claim that is so related to a qualifying federal claim that, together, they form part of the same case or controversy. *See* 28 U.S.C. § 1367(a). Whether Wedding Planner's two claims satisfy this "relatedness" requirement sufficiently to supply supplemental jurisdiction is, however, irrelevant. Supplemental jurisdiction is not needed here because original, diversity jurisdiction exists, as explained in Answer (A).

Answer (D) is wrong: Supplemental jurisdiction is not always available to a plaintiff seeking to join a claim that would otherwise fall outside the authority of the federal courts. For example, Congress has foreclosed a plaintiff, in a diversity case, from resorting to the supplemental jurisdiction statute to assert an otherwise jurisdictionally-improper claim against a party joined into the lawsuit by Rules 14, 19, 20, and 24. *See* 28 U.S.C. § 1367(b). But Rule 18 claim joinder is not among the categories that Congress foreclosed, nor is that inquiry even relevant here. As explained in Answer (A), no supplemental jurisdiction is needed on these facts. Although Wedding Planner's October overcharge claim fails to meet the Section 1332 amount-in-controversy minimum of $75,000.01, when aggregated with the earlier April overcharge claim, the two claims together easily pass that threshold.

PART 4
Questions Listed by Question Number

Q #	NCBE Group	NCBE Master Category	NCBE Sub-Category	Tested Knowledge Area
1	3(D)	Pretrial Procedures	Joinder	Counterclaims: Compulsory and Permissive
2	7(B)	Appealability & Review	Final Judgment Rule	Jurisdictional Nature of Appeal Period
3	1(A)	Jurisdiction & Venue	Federal SMJ	Federal Question: Well-Pleaded Complaint Rule
4	1(B)	Jurisdiction & Venue	Personal Jurisdiction	"Tag" (Transient) Jurisdiction
5	3(E)	Pretrial Procedures	Discovery, Disclosures, Sanctions	Types: Physical and Mental Examinations
6	5(A)	Motions	Pretrial Motions	Voluntary Dismissals: Procedures
7	7(C)	Appealability & Review	Scope of Review	Constitutional Right of Appeal
8	5(A)	Motions	Pretrial Motions	Pre-Answer Motions: Lack of Subject-Matter Jurisdiction
9	6(D)	Verdicts & Judgments	Claim and Issue Preclusion	Claim Preclusion: Generally
10	1(A)	Jurisdiction & Venue	Federal SMJ	Diversity: Amount in Controversy
11	2(B)	Law Applied by Federal Courts	Federal Common Law	General versus Specific Federal Common Law
12	4(B)	Jury Trials	Selection and Composition of Juries	Peremptory and For-Cause Strikes
13	3(F)	Pretrial Procedures	Adjudication Without Trial	Voluntary Dismissals: Procedures
14	1(C)	Jurisdiction & Venue	Service & Notice	Serving at Defendant's Abode
15	5(A)	Motions	Pretrial Motions	Summary Judgment Motions: Inferences
16	3(G)	Pretrial Procedures	Pretrial Conferences and Orders	Rule 16 Orders: Post-Order Amendments
17	7(C)	Appealability & Review	Scope of Review	Supersedeas

Q #	NCBE Group	NCBE Master Category	NCBE Sub-Category	Tested Knowledge Area
18	3(E)	Pretrial Procedures	Discovery, Disclosures, Sanctions	Disclosures and Discovery of Experts
19	1(C)	Jurisdiction & Venue	Service & Notice	Waiver of Service
20	4(C)	Jury Trials	Jury Instructions	Failure to Object to Instructions
21	3(B)	Pretrial Procedures	Pleadings, Amendments, Supplements	Amendments: Variance and Conforming Amendments
22	1(B)	Jurisdiction & Venue	Personal Jurisdiction	In Rem Jurisdiction
23	3(D)	Pretrial Procedures	Joinder	Interpleader: Statutory and Rule Bases
24	4(B)	Jury Trials	Selection and Composition of Juries	Fair Cross-Section Requirement
25	4(A)	Jury Trials	Right to Jury Trial	Jury Demand: Removal Cases
26	1(B)	Jurisdiction & Venue	Personal Jurisdiction	Specific Jurisdiction: Motions to Dismiss
27	2(A)	Law Applied by Federal Courts	State Law in Federal Courts	*Erie:* State Procedures, Federal Procedures
28	5(A)	Motions	Pretrial Motions	Summary Judgment Motions: Ruling Independent of Motion
29	4(A)	Jury Trials	Right to Jury Trial	Jury Demand: Timing
30	1(C)	Jurisdiction & Venue	Service & Notice	Summons and Complaint Served Together
31	3(D)	Pretrial Procedures	Joinder	Class Actions: Prerequisites
32	5(B)	Motions	JMOL Motions	Timing
33	1(B)	Jurisdiction & Venue	Personal Jurisdiction	Long-Arm Statutes
34	6(D)	Verdicts & Judgments	Claim and Issue Preclusion	Claim Preclusion: Privity
35	3(C)	Pretrial Procedures	Rule 11	General Rule Operation
36	3(B)	Pretrial Procedures	Pleadings, Amendments, Supplements	Pleading in the Alternative
37	2(A)	Law Applied by Federal Courts	State Law in Federal Courts	*Erie:* Vertical Choice of Law
38	3(D)	Pretrial Procedures	Joinder	Counterclaims: Subject-Matter Jurisdiction

Q #	NCBE Group	NCBE Master Category	NCBE Sub-Category	Tested Knowledge Area
39	5(A)	Motions	Pretrial Motions	Summary Judgment Motions: Support for Motions/Responses
40	6(D)	Verdicts & Judgments	Claim and Issue Preclusion	Issue Preclusion: Offensive Issue Preclusion
41	5(A)	Motions	Pretrial Motions	Judgment on the Pleadings Motions: Procedures
42	3(D)	Pretrial Procedures	Joinder	Impleader: Third-Party Complaints Generally
43	5(A)	Motions	Pretrial Motions	Pre-Answer Motions: Service of Process— Dismissal/Quashing
44	1(D)	Jurisdiction & Venue	Venue, FNC, Transfer	Forum Non Conveniens
45	2(B)	Law Applied by Federal Courts	Federal Common Law	*Erie:* Federal Statues on Treble Damages
46	1(B)	Jurisdiction & Venue	Personal Jurisdiction	National-Contacts Jurisdiction: Rule 4(k)(2) Requirements
47	3(E)	Pretrial Procedures	Discovery, Disclosures, Sanctions	Failure to Disclose
48	5(A)	Motions	Pretrial Motions	Pre-Answer Motions: Attaching Documents and SJ Conversion
49	2(A)	Law Applied by Federal Courts	State Law in Federal Courts	*Erie:* State Procedures, Federal Practices
50	7(A)	Appealability & Review	Interlocutory Review	Review of Interlocutory Orders Generally
51	3(B)	Pretrial Procedures	Pleadings, Amendments, Supplements	Answers: Proper Content
52	5(A)	Motions	Pretrial Motions	Summary Judgment Motions: Discovery Postponement
53	1(D)	Jurisdiction & Venue	Venue, FNC, Transfer	Venue Based on Residence
54	4(A)	Jury Trials	Right to Jury Trial	Right to a Jury: Seventh Amendment in State Courts
55	3(B)	Pretrial Procedures	Pleadings, Amendments, Supplements	The *Twombly* Standard
56	1(B)	Jurisdiction & Venue	Personal Jurisdiction	General Jurisdiction

Q #	NCBE Group	NCBE Master Category	NCBE Sub-Category	Tested Knowledge Area
57	2(A)	Law Applied by Federal Courts	State Law in Federal Courts	*Erie:* "Predicting" Content of State Law
58	5(A)	Motions	Pretrial Motions	Summary Judgment Motions: Affidavits
59	1(B)/ (C)	Jurisdiction & Venue	Personal Jurisdiction/ Service & Notice	Personal Jurisdiction/Service on Nonresident Motorists
60	4(A)	Jury Trials	Right to Jury Trial	Ordering of Jury/Nonjury Issues
61	1(D)	Jurisdiction & Venue	Venue, FNC, Transfer	Improper Venue
62	5(A)	Motions	Pretrial Motions	Pre-Answer Motions: Failure to State Claim Procedures
63	3(B)	Pretrial Procedures	Pleadings, Amendments, Supplements	Answers: Timing
64	5(C)	Motions	Post-Trial Motions	New Trials: Grounds
65	3(E)	Pretrial Procedures	Discovery, Disclosures, Sanctions	Types: Depositions—Use at Trial
66	6(C)	Verdicts & Judgments	Judicial Findings and Conclusions	Procedures
67	5(A)	Motions	Pretrial Motions	Pre-Answer Motions: Failure to State Claim and "Built-In" Defenses
68	1(A)	Jurisdiction & Venue	Federal SMJ	Diversity: Principal Place of Business
69	3(E)	Pretrial Procedures	Discovery, Disclosures, Sanctions	Types: Electronically Stored Information (ESI)
70	1(C)	Jurisdiction & Venue	Service & Notice	Serving Individuals: Manner of Service
71	3(D)	Pretrial Procedures	Joinder	Impleader: Upsloping and Downsloping Rule 14 Claims
72	1(A)	Jurisdiction & Venue	Federal SMJ	Diversity: Aggregation of Claims
73	3(A)	Pretrial Procedures	Preliminary Injunctions & TROs	Preliminary Injunctions: Criteria
74	5(A)	Motions	Pretrial Motions	Pre-Answer Motions: Attaching Documents Generally
75	5(C)	Motions	Post-Trial Motions	Relief from Judgment: Grounds Generally

Q #	NCBE Group	NCBE Master Category	NCBE Sub-Category	Tested Knowledge Area
76	7(A)	Appealability & Review	Interlocutory Review	Review of Privilege Determinations
77	5(A)	Motions	Pretrial Motions	Voluntary Dismissals: Two-Dismissal Rule
78	7(B)	Appealability & Review	Final Judgment Rule	Definition of Final Judgments
79	1(A)	Jurisdiction & Venue	Federal SMJ	Federal Question: Centrality Test
80	5(A)	Motions	Pretrial Motions	Summary Judgment Motions: Summary Judgment Record
81	5(A)	Motions	Pretrial Motions	Pre-Answer Motions: Failure to State Claim Standards
82	1(A)	Jurisdiction & Venue	Federal SMJ	Removal: Joining by All Defendants
83	1(D)	Jurisdiction & Venue	Venue, FNC, Transfer	Transfer of Venue
84	3(D)	Pretrial Procedures	Joinder	Intervention
85	4(B)	Jury Trials	Selection and Composition of Juries	*Batson* and Discriminatory Strikes
86	5(A)	Motions	Pretrial Motions	Summary Judgment Motions: Declaring Undisputed Facts
87	3(C)	Pretrial Procedures	Rule 11	Allowable Sanctions
88	2(A)	Law Applied by Federal Courts	State Law in Federal Courts	*Erie:* *Hanna* Inquiry versus Classic *Erie* Inquiry
89	1(A)	Jurisdiction & Venue	Federal SMJ	Consent to Jurisdiction
90	6(B)	Verdicts & Judgments	Jury Verdict Types/Challenges	Jury Verdicts: Composition
91	5(B)	Motions	JMOL Motions	Standards
92	7(C)	Appealability & Review	Scope of Review	Time for Taking Appeals
93	5(A)	Motions	Pretrial Motions	Summary Judgment Motions: Blatant Contradictions
94	1(B)	Jurisdiction & Venue	Personal Jurisdiction	Specific Jurisdiction: Purposeful Customer Targeting
95	1(A)	Jurisdiction & Venue	Federal SMJ	Supplemental Jurisdiction: Joined Parties
96	3(D)	Pretrial Procedures	Joinder	Required Parties
97	6(D)	Verdicts & Judgments	Claim and Issue Preclusion	Issue Preclusion: Decision on the Merits

Q #	NCBE Group	NCBE Master Category	NCBE Sub-Category	Tested Knowledge Area
98	3(D)	Pretrial Procedures	Joinder	Class Actions: Class Action Fairness Act
99	7(C)	Appealability & Review	Scope of Review	Reviewing Findings of Fact/ Conclusions of Law
100	3(E)	Pretrial Procedures	Discovery, Disclosures, Sanctions	Discovery Sanctions
101	6(A)	Verdicts & Judgments	Defaults & Involuntary Dismissals	Entry of Default Judgment
102	7(B)	Appealability & Review	Final Judgment Rule	Appeal of Interlocutory Orders After Final Order
103	4(A)	Jury Trials	Right to Jury Trial	Jury Demand: Waiver
104	3(E)	Pretrial Procedures	Discovery, Disclosures, Sanctions	Scope: Proportionality
105	1(C)	Jurisdiction & Venue	Service & Notice	Constitutionally Minimum Service
106	3(B)	Pretrial Procedures	Pleadings, Amendments, Supplements	Amendments: Relation Back Doctrine
107	2(B)	Law Applied by Federal Courts	Federal Common Law	*Erie:* Horizontal Choice of Law
108	1(B)	Jurisdiction & Venue	Personal Jurisdiction	Territorial Limits of Federal Personal Jurisdiction
109	6(B)	Verdicts & Judgments	Jury Verdict Types/Challenges	Jury Verdicts: Inconsistencies
110	3(A)	Pretrial Procedures	Preliminary Injunctions & TROs	Temporary Restraining Orders: Elements
111	5(C)	Motions	Post-Trial Motions	New Trials: Timing
112	1(A)	Jurisdiction & Venue	Federal SMJ	Diversity: Post-Filing Events
113	2(A)	Law Applied by Federal Courts	State Law in Federal Courts	*Erie:* Harmonizing in Non-Clash Cases
114	5(C)	Motions	Post-Trial Motions	Relief from Judgment: Fraud
115	5(A)	Motions	Pretrial Motions	Pre-Trial Motions: Waiver of Defenses
116	1(B)	Jurisdiction & Venue	Personal Jurisdiction	Specific Jurisdiction: "Effects" Test
117	4(A)	Jury Trials	Right to Jury Trial	Right to a Jury: Newly Enacted Statutory Claims

Q #	NCBE Group	NCBE Master Category	NCBE Sub-Category	Tested Knowledge Area
118	5(A)	Motions	Pretrial Motions	Pre-Answer Motions: Personal Jurisdiction Procedures
119	6(A)	Verdicts & Judgments	Defaults & Involuntary Dismissals	Entry of Default
120	1(A)	Jurisdiction & Venue	Federal SMJ	Removal: Removal by Forum State Resident
121	7(C)	Appealability & Review	Scope of Review	Reviewing Jury Verdicts
122	2(A)	Law Applied by Federal Courts	State Law in Federal Courts	*Erie:* State Statutes on Lost Profits
123	6(A)	Verdicts & Judgments	Defaults & Involuntary Dismissals	Setting Aside Default Judgments
124	5(A)	Motions	Pretrial Motions	Involuntary Dismissals
125	6(B)	Verdicts & Judgments	Jury Verdict Types/Challenges	Advisory Juries
126	5(B)	Motions	JMOL Motions	Application of Standards
127	4(C)	Jury Trials	Jury Instructions	Plain Error
128	1(A)	Jurisdiction & Venue	Federal SMJ	Removal: Venue After Removal
129	5(A)	Motions	Pretrial Motions	Summary Judgment Motions: Standards
130	1(B)	Jurisdiction & Venue	Personal Jurisdiction	Specific Jurisdiction: Stream of Commence & Purposeful Availment
131	2(A)	Law Applied by Federal Courts	State Law in Federal Courts	*Erie:* "Predicting" Content Mistakes
132	4(C)	Jury Trials	Jury Instructions	Standard for Testing Error
133	1(D)	Jurisdiction & Venue	Venue, FNC, Transfer	Venue Based on Section 1391(b)(3)
134	5(A)	Motions	Pretrial Motions	Pre-Answer Motions: Service of Process—Timeliness
135	3(G)	Pretrial Procedures	Pretrial Conferences and Orders	Scheduling Orders: Contents
136	2(A)	Law Applied by Federal Courts	State Law in Federal Courts	*Erie:* Supplemental Jurisdiction
137	7(A)	Appealability & Review	Interlocutory Review	Discretionary Interlocutory Appeals
138	5(A)	Motions	Pretrial Motions	Pre-Answer Motions: Motions for More Definite Statement

Q #	NCBE Group	NCBE Master Category	NCBE Sub-Category	Tested Knowledge Area
139	4(A)	Jury Trials	Right to Jury Trial	Right to a Jury: Restitution Claims
140	3(B)	Pretrial Procedures	Pleadings, Amendments, Supplements	Amendments: General Standards
141	3(B)	Pretrial Procedures	Pleadings, Amendments, Supplements	Supplemental Pleadings
142	6(C)	Verdicts & Judgments	Judicial Findings and Conclusions	Level of Detail
143	1(D)	Jurisdiction & Venue	Venue, FNC, Transfer	Convenience Transfers by Consent
144	2(A)	Law Applied by Federal Courts	State Law in Federal Courts	Choice-of-Law: Following Transfers
145	7(B)	Appealability & Review	Final Judgment Rule	Premature Appeals
146	1(C)	Jurisdiction & Venue	Service & Notice	Serving at Defendant's Place of Business
147	3(F)	Pretrial Procedures	Adjudication Without Trial	Voluntary Dismissals: Two-Dismissal Rule
148	1(A)	Jurisdiction & Venue	Federal SMJ	Removal: Missing Amount in Controversy
149	6(A)	Verdicts & Judgments	Defaults & Involuntary Dismissals	Defaults Against the Federal Government
150	5(B)	Motions	JMOL Motions	Testimony Contrary to Physical Facts
151	1(C)	Jurisdiction & Venue	Service & Notice	Knowingly Failed Service
152	7(B)	Appealability & Review	Final Judgment Rule	Appeal Time and Entry of Judgment
153	3(C)	Pretrial Procedures	Rule 11	Purpose of Sanctions
154	5(C)	Motions	Post-Trial Motions	Relief from Judgment: Newly Discovered Evidence
155	5(A)	Motions	Pretrial Motions	Pre-Answer Motions: Burden of Proof
156	3(B)	Pretrial Procedures	Pleadings, Amendments, Supplements	Answers: Defensive Pleading Options
157	1(D)	Jurisdiction & Venue	Venue, FNC, Transfer	Venue Over Aliens
158	5(C)	Motions	Post-Trial Motions	Motions for Reconsideration
159	3(D)	Pretrial Procedures	Joinder	Permissive Parties

Q #	NCBE Group	NCBE Master Category	NCBE Sub-Category	Tested Knowledge Area
160	7(C)	Appealability & Review	Scope of Review	Reviewing Findings of Fact/ Conclusions of Law
161	3(A)	Pretrial Procedures	Preliminary Injunctions & TROs	Contents of Injunction Orders
162	4(A)	Jury Trials	Right to Jury Trial	Partial Jury Trials
163	5(C)	Motions	Post-Trial Motions	New Trials: Procedures
164	3(B)	Pretrial Procedures	Pleadings, Amendments, Supplements	Computing Time
165	1(D)	Jurisdiction & Venue	Venue, FNC, Transfer	Venue Based on Residence
166	7(A)	Appealability & Review	Interlocutory Review	Review in Multiple Parties Cases
167	5(C)	Motions	Post-Trial Motions	Relief from Judgment: Clerical Errors
168	2(A)	Law Applied by Federal Courts	State Law in Federal Courts	Conflicts-of-Law: Most Significant Relationship
169	1(C)	Jurisdiction & Venue	Service & Notice	Constitutional Requirements
170	7(A)	Appealability & Review	Interlocutory Review	Review of Interlocutory Orders Generally
171	5(A)	Motions	Pretrial Motions	Pre-Answer Motions: Judicial Notice
172	3(D)	Pretrial Procedures	Joinder	Class Actions: Class Certification
173	1(A)	Jurisdiction & Venue	Federal SMJ	Diversity: Aggregation of Joint Claims
174	5(B)	Motions	JMOL Motions	Renewed Motion Prerequisite
175	6(D)	Verdicts & Judgments	Claim and Issue Preclusion	Issue Preclusion: Discretion with Offensive Issue Preclusion
176	1(B)	Jurisdiction & Venue	Personal Jurisdiction	100-Mile Bulge Rule
177	3(E)	Pretrial Procedures	Discovery, Disclosures, Sanctions	Signing Discovery
178	3(G)	Pretrial Procedures	Pretrial Conferences and Orders	Discovery Planning
179	1(C)	Jurisdiction & Venue	Service & Notice	Opportunity to be Heard
180	5(A)	Motions	Pretrial Motions	Voluntary Dismissals: Settlement
181	6(C)	Verdicts & Judgments	Judicial Findings and Conclusions	Summary Judgment Rulings

Q #	NCBE Group	NCBE Master Category	NCBE Sub-Category	Tested Knowledge Area
182	6(D)	Verdicts & Judgments	Claim and Issue Preclusion	Issue Preclusion: Prior Independent Grounds
183	4(A)	Jury Trials	Right to Jury Trial	Jury Demand: Withdrawal of Demand
184	5(B)	Motions	JMOL Motions	New Trial in the Alternative
185	1(A)	Jurisdiction & Venue	Federal SMJ	Diversity: Residence of Parties
186	2(A)	Law Applied by Federal Courts	State Law in Federal Courts	Choice-of-Law: Following Venue Transfer
187	5(A)	Motions	Pretrial Motions	Pre-Answer Motions: Required Parties Dismissal
188	4(B)	Jury Trials	Selection and Composition of Juries	Fewer than Six Jurors
189	6(D)	Verdicts & Judgments	Claim and Issue Preclusion	Distinguishing Preclusion Types
190	5(A)	Motions	Pretrial Motions	Pre-Answer Motions: Motions to Strike
191	1(A)	Jurisdiction & Venue	Federal SMJ	Supplemental Jurisdiction: Tolling of SOLs
192	4(A)	Jury Trials	Right to Jury Trial	Right to a Jury: Legal/Equitable Claims
193	3(E)	Pretrial Procedures	Discovery, Disclosures, Sanctions	Types: Admissions—Effect/Withdrawal
194	1(D)	Jurisdiction & Venue	Venue, FNC, Transfer	Venue Based on Residence
195	3(E)	Pretrial Procedures	Discovery, Disclosures, Sanctions	Duty to Supplement
196	3(E)	Pretrial Procedures	Discovery, Disclosures, Sanctions	Types: Interrogatories
197	3(F)	Pretrial Procedures	Adjudication Without Trial	Involuntary Dismissals: Failure to Comply with Rules
198	1(C)	Jurisdiction & Venue	Service & Notice	Serving Individuals: Manner of Service
199	3(C)	Pretrial Procedures	Rule 11	Procedures
200	3(D)	Pretrial Procedures	Joinder	Claim Joinder

PART 5

Questions Listed by Category and Knowledge Area

Q #	NCBE Group	NCBE Master Category	NCBE Sub-Category	Tested Knowledge Area
89	1(A)	Jurisdiction & Venue	Federal SMJ	Consent to Jurisdiction
72	1(A)	Jurisdiction & Venue	Federal SMJ	Diversity: Aggregation of Claims
173	1(A)	Jurisdiction & Venue	Federal SMJ	Diversity: Aggregation of Joint Claims
10	1(A)	Jurisdiction & Venue	Federal SMJ	Diversity: Amount in Controversy
112	1(A)	Jurisdiction & Venue	Federal SMJ	Diversity: Post-Filing Events
68	1(A)	Jurisdiction & Venue	Federal SMJ	Diversity: Principal Place of Business
185	1(A)	Jurisdiction & Venue	Federal SMJ	Diversity: Residence of Parties
79	1(A)	Jurisdiction & Venue	Federal SMJ	Federal Question: Centrality Test
3	1(A)	Jurisdiction & Venue	Federal SMJ	Federal Question: Well-Pleaded Complaint Rule
82	1(A)	Jurisdiction & Venue	Federal SMJ	Removal: Joining by All Defendants
148	1(A)	Jurisdiction & Venue	Federal SMJ	Removal: Missing Amount in Controversy
120	1(A)	Jurisdiction & Venue	Federal SMJ	Removal: Removal by Forum State Resident
128	1(A)	Jurisdiction & Venue	Federal SMJ	Removal: Venue After Removal
95	1(A)	Jurisdiction & Venue	Federal SMJ	Supplemental Jurisdiction: Joined Parties
191	1(A)	Jurisdiction & Venue	Federal SMJ	Supplemental Jurisdiction: Tolling of SOLs
176	1(B)	Jurisdiction & Venue	Personal Jurisdiction	100-Mile Bulge Rule
56	1(B)	Jurisdiction & Venue	Personal Jurisdiction	General Jurisdiction

Q #	NCBE Group	NCBE Master Category	NCBE Sub-Category	Tested Knowledge Area
22	1(B)	Jurisdiction & Venue	Personal Jurisdiction	In Rem Jurisdiction
33	1(B)	Jurisdiction & Venue	Personal Jurisdiction	Long-Arm Statutes
46	1(B)	Jurisdiction & Venue	Personal Jurisdiction	National-Contacts Jurisdiction: Rule 4(k)(2) Requirements
116	1(B)	Jurisdiction & Venue	Personal Jurisdiction	Specific Jurisdiction: "Effects" Test
26	1(B)	Jurisdiction & Venue	Personal Jurisdiction	Specific Jurisdiction: Motions to Dismiss
94	1(B)	Jurisdiction & Venue	Personal Jurisdiction	Specific Jurisdiction: Purposeful Customer Targeting
130	1(B)	Jurisdiction & Venue	Personal Jurisdiction	Specific Jurisdiction: Stream of Commence & Purposeful Availment
4	1(B)	Jurisdiction & Venue	Personal Jurisdiction	"Tag" (Transient) Jurisdiction
108	1(B)	Jurisdiction & Venue	Personal Jurisdiction	Territorial Limits of Federal Personal Jurisdiction
59	1(B)/ (C)	Jurisdiction & Venue	Personal Jurisdiction/ Service & Notice	Personal Jurisdiction/Service on Nonresident Motorists
169	1(C)	Jurisdiction & Venue	Service & Notice	Constitutional Requirements
105	1(C)	Jurisdiction & Venue	Service & Notice	Constitutionally Minimum Service
151	1(C)	Jurisdiction & Venue	Service & Notice	Knowingly Failed Service
179	1(C)	Jurisdiction & Venue	Service & Notice	Opportunity to be Heard
14	1(C)	Jurisdiction & Venue	Service & Notice	Serving at Defendant's Abode
146	1(C)	Jurisdiction & Venue	Service & Notice	Serving at Defendant's Place of Business
70	1(C)	Jurisdiction & Venue	Service & Notice	Serving Individuals: Manner of Service
198	1(C)	Jurisdiction & Venue	Service & Notice	Serving Individuals: Manner of Service
30	1(C)	Jurisdiction & Venue	Service & Notice	Summons and Complaint Served Together
19	1(C)	Jurisdiction & Venue	Service & Notice	Waiver of Service
143	1(D)	Jurisdiction & Venue	Venue, FNC, Transfer	Convenience Transfers by Consent

Q #	NCBE Group	NCBE Master Category	NCBE Sub-Category	Tested Knowledge Area
44	1(D)	Jurisdiction & Venue	Venue, FNC, Transfer	Forum Non Conveniens
61	1(D)	Jurisdiction & Venue	Venue, FNC, Transfer	Improper Venue
83	1(D)	Jurisdiction & Venue	Venue, FNC, Transfer	Transfer of Venue
53	1(D)	Jurisdiction & Venue	Venue, FNC, Transfer	Venue Based on Residence
194	1(D)	Jurisdiction & Venue	Venue, FNC, Transfer	Venue Based on Residence
165	1(D)	Jurisdiction & Venue	Venue, FNC, Transfer	Venue Based on Residence
133	1(D)	Jurisdiction & Venue	Venue, FNC, Transfer	Venue Based on Section 1391(b)(3)
157	1(D)	Jurisdiction & Venue	Venue, FNC, Transfer	Venue Over Aliens
144	2(A)	Law Applied by Federal Courts	State Law in Federal Courts	Choice-of-Law: Following Transfers
186	2(A)	Law Applied by Federal Courts	State Law in Federal Courts	Choice-of-Law: Following Venue Transfer
168	2(A)	Law Applied by Federal Courts	State Law in Federal Courts	Conflicts-of-Law: Most Significant Relationship
131	2(A)	Law Applied by Federal Courts	State Law in Federal Courts	*Erie:* "Predicting" Content Mistakes
57	2(A)	Law Applied by Federal Courts	State Law in Federal Courts	*Erie:* "Predicting" Content of State Law
88	2(A)	Law Applied by Federal Courts	State Law in Federal Courts	*Erie:* *Hanna* Inquiry versus Classic *Erie* Inquiry
113	2(A)	Law Applied by Federal Courts	State Law in Federal Courts	*Erie:* Harmonizing in Non-Clash Cases
49	2(A)	Law Applied by Federal Courts	State Law in Federal Courts	*Erie:* State Procedures, Federal Practices
27	2(A)	Law Applied by Federal Courts	State Law in Federal Courts	*Erie:* State Procedures, Federal Procedures
122	2(A)	Law Applied by Federal Courts	State Law in Federal Courts	*Erie:* State Statutes on Lost Profits
136	2(A)	Law Applied by Federal Courts	State Law in Federal Courts	*Erie:* Supplemental Jurisdiction
37	2(A)	Law Applied by Federal Courts	State Law in Federal Courts	*Erie:* Vertical Choice of Law

Q #	NCBE Group	NCBE Master Category	NCBE Sub-Category	Tested Knowledge Area
45	2(B)	Law Applied by Federal Courts	Federal Common Law	*Erie:* Federal Statues on Treble Damages
107	2(B)	Law Applied by Federal Courts	Federal Common Law	*Erie:* Horizontal Choice of Law
11	2(B)	Law Applied by Federal Courts	Federal Common Law	General versus Specific Federal Common Law
161	3(A)	Pretrial Procedures	Preliminary Injunctions & TROs	Contents of Injunction Orders
73	3(A)	Pretrial Procedures	Preliminary Injunctions & TROs	Preliminary Injunctions: Criteria
110	3(A)	Pretrial Procedures	Preliminary Injunctions & TROs	Temporary Restraining Orders: Elements
140	3(B)	Pretrial Procedures	Pleadings, Amendments, Supplements	Amendments: General Standards
106	3(B)	Pretrial Procedures	Pleadings, Amendments, Supplements	Amendments: Relation Back Doctrine
21	3(B)	Pretrial Procedures	Pleadings, Amendments, Supplements	Amendments: Variance and Conforming Amendments
156	3(B)	Pretrial Procedures	Pleadings, Amendments, Supplements	Answers: Defensive Pleading Options
51	3(B)	Pretrial Procedures	Pleadings, Amendments, Supplements	Answers: Proper Content
63	3(B)	Pretrial Procedures	Pleadings, Amendments, Supplements	Answers: Timing
164	3(B)	Pretrial Procedures	Pleadings, Amendments, Supplements	Computing Time
36	3(B)	Pretrial Procedures	Pleadings, Amendments, Supplements	Pleading in the Alternative
141	3(B)	Pretrial Procedures	Pleadings, Amendments, Supplements	Supplemental Pleadings
55	3(B)	Pretrial Procedures	Pleadings, Amendments, Supplements	The *Twombly* Standard
87	3(C)	Pretrial Procedures	Rule 11	Allowable Sanctions

Q #	NCBE Group	NCBE Master Category	NCBE Sub-Category	Tested Knowledge Area
35	3(C)	Pretrial Procedures	Rule 11	General Rule Operation
199	3(C)	Pretrial Procedures	Rule 11	Procedures
153	3(C)	Pretrial Procedures	Rule 11	Purpose of Sanctions
200	3(D)	Pretrial Procedures	Joinder	Claim Joinder
31	3(D)	Pretrial Procedures	Joinder	Class Actions: Prerequisites
98	3(D)	Pretrial Procedures	Joinder	Class Actions: Class Action Fairness Act
172	3(D)	Pretrial Procedures	Joinder	Class Actions: Class Certification
1	3(D)	Pretrial Procedures	Joinder	Counterclaims: Compulsory and Permissive
38	3(D)	Pretrial Procedures	Joinder	Counterclaims: Subject-Matter Jurisdiction
42	3(D)	Pretrial Procedures	Joinder	Impleader: Third-Party Complaints Generally
71	3(D)	Pretrial Procedures	Joinder	Impleader: Upsloping and Downsloping Rule 14 Claims
23	3(D)	Pretrial Procedures	Joinder	Interpleader: Statutory and Rule Bases
84	3(D)	Pretrial Procedures	Joinder	Intervention
159	3(D)	Pretrial Procedures	Joinder	Permissive Parties
96	3(D)	Pretrial Procedures	Joinder	Required Parties
18	3(E)	Pretrial Procedures	Discovery, Disclosures, Sanctions	Disclosures and Discovery of Experts
100	3(E)	Pretrial Procedures	Discovery, Disclosures, Sanctions	Discovery Sanctions
195	3(E)	Pretrial Procedures	Discovery, Disclosures, Sanctions	Duty to Supplement
47	3(E)	Pretrial Procedures	Discovery, Disclosures, Sanctions	Failure to Disclose
104	3(E)	Pretrial Procedures	Discovery, Disclosures, Sanctions	Scope: Proportionality
177	3(E)	Pretrial Procedures	Discovery, Disclosures, Sanctions	Signing Discovery
193	3(E)	Pretrial Procedures	Discovery, Disclosures, Sanctions	Types: Admissions—Effect/Withdrawal
65	3(E)	Pretrial Procedures	Discovery, Disclosures, Sanctions	Types: Depositions—Use at Trial

Q #	NCBE Group	NCBE Master Category	NCBE Sub-Category	Tested Knowledge Area
69	3(E)	Pretrial Procedures	Discovery, Disclosures, Sanctions	Types: Electronically Stored Information (ESI)
196	3(E)	Pretrial Procedures	Discovery, Disclosures, Sanctions	Types: Interrogatories
5	3(E)	Pretrial Procedures	Discovery, Disclosures, Sanctions	Types: Physical and Mental Examinations
197	3(F)	Pretrial Procedures	Adjudication Without Trial	Involuntary Dismissals: Failure to Comply with Rules
147	3(F)	Pretrial Procedures	Adjudication Without Trial	Voluntary Dismissals: Two-Dismissal Rule
13	3(F)	Pretrial Procedures	Adjudication Without Trial	Voluntary Dismissals: Procedures
178	3(G)	Pretrial Procedures	Pretrial Conferences and Orders	Discovery Planning
16	3(G)	Pretrial Procedures	Pretrial Conferences and Orders	Rule 16 Orders: Post-Order Amendments
135	3(G)	Pretrial Procedures	Pretrial Conferences and Orders	Scheduling Orders: Contents
25	4(A)	Jury Trials	Right to Jury Trial	Jury Demand: Removal Cases
29	4(A)	Jury Trials	Right to Jury Trial	Jury Demand: Timing
103	4(A)	Jury Trials	Right to Jury Trial	Jury Demand: Waiver
183	4(A)	Jury Trials	Right to Jury Trial	Jury Demand: Withdrawal of Demand
192	4(A)	Jury Trials	Right to Jury Trial	Right to a Jury: Legal/Equitable Claims
117	4(A)	Jury Trials	Right to Jury Trial	Right to a Jury: Newly Enacted Statutory Claims
139	4(A)	Jury Trials	Right to Jury Trial	Right to a Jury: Restitution Claims
54	4(A)	Jury Trials	Right to Jury Trial	Right to a Jury: Seventh Amendment in State Courts
60	4(A)	Jury Trials	Right to Jury Trial	Ordering of Jury/Nonjury Issues
162	4(A)	Jury Trials	Right to Jury Trial	Partial Jury Trials
85	4(B)	Jury Trials	Selection and Composition of Juries	*Batson* and Discriminatory Strikes
24	4(B)	Jury Trials	Selection and Composition of Juries	Fair Cross-Section Requirement

Q #	NCBE Group	NCBE Master Category	NCBE Sub-Category	Tested Knowledge Area
188	4(B)	Jury Trials	Selection and Composition of Juries	Fewer than Six Jurors
12	4(B)	Jury Trials	Selection and Composition of Juries	Peremptory and For-Cause Strikes
20	4(C)	Jury Trials	Jury Instructions	Failure to Object to Instructions
127	4(C)	Jury Trials	Jury Instructions	Plain Error
132	4(C)	Jury Trials	Jury Instructions	Standard for Testing Error
124	5(A)	Motions	Pretrial Motions	Involuntary Dismissals
41	5(A)	Motions	Pretrial Motions	Judgment on the Pleadings Motions: Procedures
48	5(A)	Motions	Pretrial Motions	Pre-Answer Motions: Attaching Documents and SJ Conversion
74	5(A)	Motions	Pretrial Motions	Pre-Answer Motions: Attaching Documents Generally
155	5(A)	Motions	Pretrial Motions	Pre-Answer Motions: Burden of Proof
67	5(A)	Motions	Pretrial Motions	Pre-Answer Motions: Failure to State Claim and "Built-In" Defenses
81	5(A)	Motions	Pretrial Motions	Pre-Answer Motions: Failure to State Claim Standards
62	5(A)	Motions	Pretrial Motions	Pre-Answer Motions: Failure to State Claim Procedures
171	5(A)	Motions	Pretrial Motions	Pre-Answer Motions: Judicial Notice
8	5(A)	Motions	Pretrial Motions	Pre-Answer Motions: Lack of Subject-Matter Jurisdiction
138	5(A)	Motions	Pretrial Motions	Pre-Answer Motions: Motions for More Definite Statement
190	5(A)	Motions	Pretrial Motions	Pre-Answer Motions: Motions to Strike
118	5(A)	Motions	Pretrial Motions	Pre-Answer Motions: Personal Jurisdiction Procedures
187	5(A)	Motions	Pretrial Motions	Pre-Answer Motions: Required Parties Dismissal
43	5(A)	Motions	Pretrial Motions	Pre-Answer Motions: Service of Process— Dismissal/Quashing

Q #	NCBE Group	NCBE Master Category	NCBE Sub-Category	Tested Knowledge Area
134	5(A)	Motions	Pretrial Motions	Pre-Answer Motions: Service of Process—Timeliness
115	5(A)	Motions	Pretrial Motions	Pre-Trial Motions: Waiver of Defenses
58	5(A)	Motions	Pretrial Motions	Summary Judgment Motions: Affidavits
93	5(A)	Motions	Pretrial Motions	Summary Judgment Motions: Blatant Contradictions
86	5(A)	Motions	Pretrial Motions	Summary Judgment Motions: Declaring Undisputed Facts
52	5(A)	Motions	Pretrial Motions	Summary Judgment Motions: Discovery Postponement
15	5(A)	Motions	Pretrial Motions	Summary Judgment Motions: Inferences
28	5(A)	Motions	Pretrial Motions	Summary Judgment Motions: Ruling Independent of Motion
129	5(A)	Motions	Pretrial Motions	Summary Judgment Motions: Standards
80	5(A)	Motions	Pretrial Motions	Summary Judgment Motions: Summary Judgment Record
39	5(A)	Motions	Pretrial Motions	Summary Judgment Motions: Support for Motions/Responses
77	5(A)	Motions	Pretrial Motions	Voluntary Dismissals: Two-Dismissal Rule
6	5(A)	Motions	Pretrial Motions	Voluntary Dismissals: Procedures
180	5(A)	Motions	Pretrial Motions	Voluntary Dismissals: Settlement
126	5(B)	Motions	JMOL Motions	Application of Standards
184	5(B)	Motions	JMOL Motions	New Trial in the Alternative
174	5(B)	Motions	JMOL Motions	Renewed Motion Prerequisite
91	5(B)	Motions	JMOL Motions	Standards
150	5(B)	Motions	JMOL Motions	Testimony Contrary to Physical Facts
32	5(B)	Motions	JMOL Motions	Timing
158	5(C)	Motions	Post-Trial Motions	Motions for Reconsideration
64	5(C)	Motions	Post-Trial Motions	New Trials: Grounds
163	5(C)	Motions	Post-Trial Motions	New Trials: Procedures

Q #	NCBE Group	NCBE Master Category	NCBE Sub-Category	Tested Knowledge Area
111	5(C)	Motions	Post-Trial Motions	New Trials: Timing
167	5(C)	Motions	Post-Trial Motions	Relief from Judgment: Clerical Errors
114	5(C)	Motions	Post-Trial Motions	Relief from Judgment: Fraud
75	5(C)	Motions	Post-Trial Motions	Relief from Judgment: Grounds Generally
154	5(C)	Motions	Post-Trial Motions	Relief from Judgment: Newly Discovered Evidence
149	6(A)	Verdicts & Judgments	Defaults & Involuntary Dismissals	Defaults Against the Federal Government
119	6(A)	Verdicts & Judgments	Defaults & Involuntary Dismissals	Entry of Default
101	6(A)	Verdicts & Judgments	Defaults & Involuntary Dismissals	Entry of Default Judgment
123	6(A)	Verdicts & Judgments	Defaults & Involuntary Dismissals	Setting Aside Default Judgments
125	6(B)	Verdicts & Judgments	Jury Verdict Types/Challenges	Advisory Juries
90	6(B)	Verdicts & Judgments	Jury Verdict Types/Challenges	Jury Verdicts: Composition
109	6(B)	Verdicts & Judgments	Jury Verdict Types/Challenges	Jury Verdicts: Inconsistencies
142	6(C)	Verdicts & Judgments	Judicial Findings and Conclusions	Level of Detail
181	6(C)	Verdicts & Judgments	Judicial Findings and Conclusions	Summary Judgment Rulings
66	6(C)	Verdicts & Judgments	Judicial Findings and Conclusions	Procedures
9	6(D)	Verdicts & Judgments	Claim and Issue Preclusion	Claim Preclusion: Generally
34	6(D)	Verdicts & Judgments	Claim and Issue Preclusion	Claim Preclusion: Privity
189	6(D)	Verdicts & Judgments	Claim and Issue Preclusion	Distinguishing Preclusion Types
175	6(D)	Verdicts & Judgments	Claim and Issue Preclusion	Issue Preclusion: Discretion with Offensive Issue Preclusion
97	6(D)	Verdicts & Judgments	Claim and Issue Preclusion	Issue Preclusion: Decision on the Merits
40	6(D)	Verdicts & Judgments	Claim and Issue Preclusion	Issue Preclusion: Offensive Issue Preclusion

Q #	NCBE Group	NCBE Master Category	NCBE Sub-Category	Tested Knowledge Area
182	6(D)	Verdicts & Judgments	Claim and Issue Preclusion	Issue Preclusion: Prior Independent Grounds
137	7(A)	Appealability & Review	Interlocutory Review	Discretionary Interlocutory Appeals
166	7(A)	Appealability & Review	Interlocutory Review	Review in Multiple Parties Cases
170	7(A)	Appealability & Review	Interlocutory Review	Review of Interlocutory Orders Generally
50	7(A)	Appealability & Review	Interlocutory Review	Review of Interlocutory Orders Generally
76	7(A)	Appealability & Review	Interlocutory Review	Review of Privilege Determinations
102	7(B)	Appealability & Review	Final Judgment Rule	Appeal of Interlocutory Orders After Final Order
152	7(B)	Appealability & Review	Final Judgment Rule	Appeal Time and Entry of Judgment
78	7(B)	Appealability & Review	Final Judgment Rule	Definition of Final Judgments
2	7(B)	Appealability & Review	Final Judgment Rule	Jurisdictional Nature of Appeal Period
145	7(B)	Appealability & Review	Final Judgment Rule	Premature Appeals
7	7(C)	Appealability & Review	Scope of Review	Constitutional Right of Appeal
160	7(C)	Appealability & Review	Scope of Review	Reviewing Findings of Fact/ Conclusions of Law
99	7(C)	Appealability & Review	Scope of Review	Reviewing Findings of Fact/ Conclusions of Law
121	7(C)	Appealability & Review	Scope of Review	Reviewing Jury Verdicts
17	7(C)	Appealability & Review	Scope of Review	Supersedeas
92	7(C)	Appealability & Review	Scope of Review	Time for Taking Appeals